PROSPECTS FOR ECONOMIC GROWTH IN THE UNITED STATES

Although economic growth has historically been an engine of prosperity in the United States, recent trends have generated uncertainty regarding the prospects for sustaining such growth. Economists disagree about the relative importance of many factors affecting future growth, including rapid technological advances, immigration, the growth of the financial sector, problems with the educational system, increasing income inequality, an aging population, and large fiscal imbalances that have not been addressed by the political system. This collection of chapters, authored by many of today's leading economists, addresses the prospects for economic growth in the United States over the next few decades. During a time of great economic uncertainty, this book engages with both sides in the debate over economic growth, focusing on policy options that increase the prospects for vigorous economic growth in the future.

John W. Diamond is the Director of the Center for Public Finance and the Edward A. and Hermena Hancock Kelly Fellow in Public Finance at Rice University's Baker Institute.

George R. Zodrow is the Allyn R. and Gladys M. Cline Professor of Economics and Economics Department Chair at Rice University, and a Faculty Scholar at the Center for Public Finance at Rice University's Baker Institute.

Prospects for Economic Growth in the United States

Edited by

JOHN W. DIAMOND

Rice University

GEORGE R. ZODROW

Rice University

CAMBRIDGE
UNIVERSITY PRESS

University Printing House, Cambridge CB2 8BS, United Kingdom

One Liberty Plaza, 20th Floor, New York, NY 10006, USA

477 Williamstown Road, Port Melbourne, VIC 3207, Australia

314–321, 3rd Floor, Plot 3, Splendor Forum, Jasola District Centre, New Delhi – 110025, India

79 Anson Road, #06–04/06, Singapore 079906

Cambridge University Press is part of the University of Cambridge.

It furthers the University's mission by disseminating knowledge in the pursuit of education, learning, and research at the highest international levels of excellence.

www.cambridge.org
Information on this title: www.cambridge.org/9781108479684
DOI: 10.1017/9781108856089

© Cambridge University Press 2021

First published 2021

A catalogue record for this publication is available from the British Library.

Library of Congress Cataloging-in-Publication Data
Names: Diamond, John W., editor. | Zodrow, George R., editor.
Title: Prospects for economic growth in the United States / edited by John W. Diamond, Rice University, Houston, George R. Zodrow, Rice University, Houston.
Description: New York, NY : Cambridge University Press, 2021. | Includes index.
Identifiers: LCCN 2021024994 (print) | LCCN 2021024995 (ebook) | ISBN 9781108479684 (hardback) | ISBN 9781108856089 (ebook)
Subjects: LCSH: Economic development – United States. | United States – Economic conditions – 21st century. | United States – Economic policy – 21st century. | United States – Social policy – 21st century. | Fiscal policy – United States. | Income distribution – United States. | BISAC: BUSINESS & ECONOMICS / Economics / Macroeconomics | BUSINESS & ECONOMICS / Economics / Macroeconomics
Classification: LCC HC106.84 .P76 2021(print) | LCC HC106.84 (ebook) | DDC 338.973–dc23
LC record available at https://lccn.loc.gov/2021024994
LC ebook record available at https://lccn.loc.gov/2021024995

ISBN 978-1-108-47968-4 Hardback
ISBN 978-1-108-79050-5 Paperback

To Martin Feldstein, whose pathbreaking contributions and profound insights into the theory and practice of public finance established the standard for the profession and inspired a generation of scholars

Contents

Figures

Tables

Notes on Contributors

Robert J. Barro is Paul M. Warburg Professor of Economics at Harvard University, a visiting scholar at the American Enterprise Institute, and a research associate of the National Bureau of Economic Research. He has a PhD in economics from Harvard University and a BS in physics from Caltech. Barro is coeditor of Harvard's *Quarterly Journal of Economics* and was previously president of the Western Economic Association, vice president of the American Economic Association, a viewpoint columnist for *Business Week*, and a contributing editor of *The Wall Street Journal*. Noteworthy research includes empirical determinants of economic growth, economic effects of public debt and budget deficits, and the economics of religion. Current research focuses on the impact of rare disasters on asset markets and macroeconomic activity, with recent applications to environmental protection, quantities of safe assets, and pricing of stock options. Books include *The Wealth of Religions: The Political Economy of Believing and Belonging* (with Rachel M. McCleary; Princeton University Press, 2019); *Economic Growth* (with Xavier Sala-i-Martin; 2nd ed., MIT Press, 2004); *Education Matters: Global Schooling Gains from the 19th to the 21st Century* (with Jong-Wha Lee; Oxford University Press, 2015); *Macroeconomics: A Modern Approach* (Cengage Learning, 1980); *Nothing Is Sacred: Economic Ideas for the New Millennium* (MIT Press, 2003); *Determinants of Economic Growth: A Cross-Country Empirical Study* (MIT Press, 1997); and *Getting It Right: Markets and Choices in a Free Society* (MIT Press, 1996).

George J. Borjas is the Robert W. Scrivner Professor of Economics and Social Policy at the Harvard Kennedy School. He was awarded the IZA Prize in Labor Economics in 2011. Borjas is a research associate at the National Bureau of Economic Research and a research fellow at IZA. He has authored several books, including *Immigration Economics* (Harvard University Press, 2014), *Heaven's Door: Immigration Policy and the American Economy* (Princeton University Press, 1999), the widely used textbook *Labor Economics* (7th ed., McGraw-Hill, 2016), and his latest, *We Wanted Workers: Unraveling the Immigration Narrative* (W. W. Norton, 2016). He has also published over 150 articles in books and scholarly journals, and has citations in *Who's Who in the World* and *Who's Who in America*. Borjas was elected a fellow of the Econometric Society in 1998 and a fellow of the Society of Labor Economists in 2004. In 2016, Politico ranked Borjas seventeenth in its list of the fifty "thinkers, doers and visionaries transforming American politics … For telling it like it really is on immigration." He received his PhD in economics from Columbia University in 1975.

Timothy Bresnahan is Landau Professor of Technology and the Economy, Emeritus, Stanford University. His research focuses on industrial organization, applied econometrics, and the economics of technology. His current research focuses on competition and returns to innovation in technology industries, application of information and communications technology in the economy, economic organization for high social return to technical progress, and the economic history of mass market computing. Bresnahan has served as director of undergraduate studies, vice chair, and chair in the economics department; head of the Employment and Economic Growth Center in SIEPR; and chief economist of the Antitrust Division of the US Department of Justice. He is a fellow of both the Econometric Society and the American Academy of Arts and Sciences, and a 2017 laureate of the BBVA Foundation Frontiers of Knowledge Award.

Flávio Cunha is Professor of Economics at Rice University. He studies human capital formation and its link to long-run economic growth, inequality, and poverty. In his research, Cunha develops economic theory and statistical methods to study human capital formation from birth to adulthood. In partnership with the World Bank and the State of Ceara in Brazil, he developed, implemented, and evaluated a new home visitation program targeted to low-income families living in isolated rural areas in Brazil. In research funded by the National Institute of Health, he has shown that well-developed parenting programs foster human capital formation by improving the quality of the environment children have in their early years. He is a founding faculty affiliate of the Texas Policy Lab –

a new initiative of the Rice University School of Social Sciences – which provides scientific expertise in designing, implementing, and evaluating public policies conducted by state or local government agencies.

John W. Diamond is the Edward A. and Hermena Hancock Kelly Fellow in Public Finance and director of the Center for Public Finance at Rice University's Baker Institute, an adjunct professor of economics at Rice University, and CEO of Tax Policy Advisers, LLC. His research interests are federal tax and expenditure policy, state and local public finance, and the construction and simulation of computable general equilibrium models. His current research focuses on economic effects of corporate tax reform, economic and distributional effects of fundamental tax reform, taxation and housing values, public sector pensions, and various other tax and expenditure policy issues. Diamond is coeditor of *Pathways to Fiscal Reform in the United States* (with George R. Zodrow; MIT Press, 2015) and *Fundamental Tax Reform: Issues, Choices and Implications* (with George R. Zodrow; MIT Press, 2008). He has testified before the US House Ways and Means Committee, the US House Budget Committee, the Senate Finance Committee, the Joint Economic Committee, and other federal and state committees on issues related to tax policy and the US economy. He served as forum editor for the *National Tax Journal* (2009–17) and on the staff of the Joint Committee on Taxation, US Congress (2000–4). He has also served as a consultant for the World Bank on the efficacy of structural adjustment programs. He received his PhD in economics from Rice University in 2000.

Martin Feldstein passed away on June 11, 2019. He was the George F. Baker Professor of Economics at Harvard University and President Emeritus of the National Bureau of Economic Research. From 1977 to 1982 and from 1984 to 2008, he served as president and CEO of the NBER, a private, nonprofit research organization that has specialized for more than eighty years in producing nonpartisan studies of the American economy. From 1982 through 1984, Feldstein was chairman of the Council of Economic Advisers and President Reagan's chief economic adviser. He served as president of the American Economic Association in 2004. In 2006, President Bush appointed him a member of his Foreign Intelligence Advisory Board, and in 2009, President Obama appointed him a member of his Economic Recovery Advisory Board. Feldstein was a member of the American Philosophical Society, a corresponding fellow of the British Academy, a fellow of the Econometric Society, and a fellow of the National Association of Business Economics. He was a trustee of the Council on Foreign Relations and a member of the Trilateral Commission, the Group of 30, the American Academy of Arts and Sciences, and the Council of Academic Advisors of the American Enterprise Institute. Feldstein received honorary doctorates from several universities and was an honorary fellow of Nuffield College, Oxford. In 1977, he received the John Bates Clark Medal of the American Economic Association, a prize awarded every two years to the economist under the age of forty who is judged to have made the greatest contribution to economic science. He was the author of more than 300 research articles on economics. Feldstein was a director of several public corporations and an economic adviser to several businesses and government organizations in the United States and abroad. He was a regular contributor to *The Wall Street Journal* and other publications. Feldstein was a graduate of Harvard College and Oxford University.

Glenn Hubbard is dean emeritus of Columbia Business School. A Columbia faculty member since 1988, he is also the Russell L. Carson Professor of Finance and Economics. Hubbard received his BA and BS degrees summa cum laude from the University of Central Florida. He also holds AM and PhD degrees in economics from Harvard University. In addition to writing more than 100 scholarly articles in economics and finance, Hubbard is the author of three popular textbooks, as well as co-author of *The Aid Trap: Hard Truths About Ending Poverty* (with William Duggan; Columbia Business School Publishing, 2009); *Balance: The Economics of Great Powers from Ancient Rome to Modern America* (with Tim Kane; Simon and Schuster, 2013); and *Healthy, Wealthy, and Wise: Five Steps to a Better Health Care System* (with John F. Cogan and Daniel P. Kessler; 2nd ed., Hoover Institution Press, 2011). His commentaries appear on television and radio. In government, Hubbard served as deputy assistant secretary for tax policy at the US Treasury Department from 1991 to 1993. From February 2001 until March 2003, he was chairman of the US Council of Economic Advisers (CEA) under President George W. Bush. While serving as CEA chairman, he also chaired the economic policy committee of the OECD. In the corporate sector, he is a director of ADP, BlackRock Fixed-Income Funds, and MetLife. Hubbard is co-chair of the Committee on Capital Markets Regulation; he is a past chair of the Economic Club of New York and a past co-chair of the Study Group on Corporate Boards.

Ross Levine is the Willis H. Booth Chair in Banking and Finance at the Haas School of Business, University of California, Berkeley. He is also a research associate at the National Bureau of Economic Research and a member of the Council on Foreign Relations. He completed his undergraduate studies at Cornell University in 1982 and received his PhD in economics from UCLA in 1987. Before moving to academia, he worked at the Board of Governors of the Federal Reserve System and the World Bank, where he conducted and managed research and operational programs. His work focuses on how financial sector policies and the operation of financial systems shape economic growth, entrepreneurship, and economic prosperity. Two of his co-written books, *Rethinking Bank Regulation: Till Angels Govern* (with James R. Barth and Gerard Caprio Jr.; Cambridge University Press, 2006) and *Guardians of Finance: Making Regulators Work for Us* (with James R. Barth and Gerard Caprio Jr.; MIT Press, 2012), stress that regulatory policies often stymie competition and encourage excessive risk-taking, with deleterious effects on living standards.

Stephen J. Turnovsky received his PhD from Harvard University in 1968 and currently holds the Van Voorhis Professorship of Economics at the University of Washington. He was previously a member of the faculties of the University of Pennsylvania, the University of Toronto, the Australian National University, and the University of Illinois at Urbana-Champaign, where he was IBE Distinguished Professor of Economics. In 2005, he received a Doctorat honoris causa from the University of Aix-Marseille, France, and in 2009, he was awarded an honorary Doctor of Literature from Victoria University of Wellington, New Zealand. He was elected fellow of the Econometric Society in 1981 and was president of the Society of Economic Dynamics and Control from 1982 to 1984 and of the Society for Computational Economics from 2004 to 2006. He was co-chair of the Program Committee of the Eighth World Congress of the Econometric Society in 2000. He served on several editorial boards including the *Journal of Economic Dynamics and Control* (editor, 1981–7, 1995–2001; advisory editor (2002–), the *Journal of Money, Credit, and Banking* (1977–2010), the *Journal of Public Economic Theory* (2000–), *Macroeconomic Dynamics* (2001–), the *Journal of Human Capital* (2006–), the *International Economic Review* (1972–93), the *Journal of Public Economics* (1982–7), and the *Journal of International Economics* (1995–8). His main area of research is in the general area of macroeconomic dynamics and growth. Within this area, his interests are quite far-ranging, with particular focus on fiscal policy issues and optimal policy, extending to both closed and open economies.

George R. Zodrow is Allyn R. and Gladys M. Cline Professor of Economics and Faculty Scholar at the Center for Public Finance, Baker Institute for Public Policy, at Rice University. He is also an international research fellow at the Centre on Business Taxation at Oxford University. Zodrow is the recipient of the 2009 Steven D. Gold Award, presented by the National Tax Association to recognize significant contributions to state and local fiscal policy and a capacity to cross the boundaries between academic research and public policy-making. Zodrow's research interests are tax reform in the United States and in developing countries, state and local public finance, and computable general equilibrium models of the effects of tax reforms. His articles have appeared in numerous scholarly publications and collective volumes on taxation, and he is the author or editor of several books on the topic. Zodrow recently served for ten years as editor of the *National Tax Journal* and has also been an editor of the "Policy Watch" section of *International Tax and Public Finance*. He was a visiting economist at the US Treasury Office of Tax Analysis in 1984–5 during the preparation of Treasury I, the precursor to the Tax Reform Act of 1986, and has been involved in tax reform projects in numerous countries.

Foreword

James A. Baker III

President Ronald Reagan understood the importance of economic growth in creating prosperity and a higher standard of living for successive generations. At the time he took office in 1981, however, the prospects for economic growth in the United States were uncertain. The country faced a number of critical challenges, including rapid inflation, high unemployment, stagnant income growth, and increasing trade conflicts, not to mention military threats from abroad. As President Reagan's White House Chief of Staff in the early 1980s and his Secretary of the Treasury starting in 1985, I was deeply involved in the administration's efforts to enact sweeping economic reforms, including major reform of individual and corporate income tax policy, market deregulation, and working with the monetary authorities to create sound monetary policies to contain inflation. As is well known, Reagan's policies resulted in one of the longest uninterrupted non-inflationary economic expansions in American history.

Today, the level of uncertainty and the challenges facing the US economy are similar. But the nature of the problems we face are very different. In particular, the challenges that confront us today include rapid technological change, slow economic growth, an aging and slowly growing population, unsustainable fiscal policies, increasing inequality, and low interest rates that leave little room for effective monetary policy. Given the considerable level of uncertainty facing the US economy, it is essential to enact sound economic policies that allow economic growth to continue to provide prosperity to future generations.

This volume lays out in detail the economic issues that are fundamental to understanding how to maintain vigorous economic growth of the US economy. The various chapters discuss a range of subjects – including issues related to demographics, social insurance programs, technological progress, human capital accumulation, immigration, income inequality, the importance of financial institutions, and fiscal policy – that are critical inputs in determining the future level of economic growth in the United States. The contributors to the volume represent a "who's who" of renowned economists in the United States.

Baker Institute fellows John Diamond and George Zodrow deserve great credit for organizing both this volume and the conference at which these chapters were originally presented as papers. I am delighted that they dedicated this book to the memory of Martin Feldstein. Marty had a huge impact on public policy and his profound insights and wise council will be sorely missed. Their conference, which was entitled "Prospects for Economic Growth in the United States," was one of a series of events celebrating the twenty-fifth anniversary of Rice University's Baker Institute for Public Policy. Their understanding and exploration of the country's complex economic challenges play a critical role in keeping our nation the strong one that President Reagan desired, promoted, and achieved.

Preface

Robust economic growth has long been the engine of prosperity in the United States, and has resulted in a sustained increase in living standards that has made the US economy the envy of much of the modern world. Prospects for future economic growth in the United States, however, are uncertain. For example, some researchers argue that technological advances, especially in the area of artificial intelligence, are likely to result in rapid automation-related increases in future growth – indeed, to the point that serious shortages in labor demand may result. In marked contrast, other observers believe that recent economic, demographic, and political trends, including an educational system that is ineffective in many dimensions, increasing income inequality, an aging population coupled with a lower labor force participation rate, and the absence of the political will to address large-scale fiscal imbalances, have created pervasive headwinds that will seriously limit future US economic growth.

This volume brings together a distinguished group of world-renowned economists to explore the challenges of maintaining vigorous economic growth in the United States, including issues related to demographics, social insurance programs, technological progress, human capital accumulation, immigration, income inequality, financial institutions, and fiscal policy. The volume consists of a set of chapters that were presented as papers at a conference on "Prospects for Economic Growth in the United States," which was one of a series of events celebrating the twenty-fifth anniversary of Rice University's Baker Institute for Public Policy. The conference was sponsored by the Baker Institute's Center for Public Finance and held at Rice on December 6–7, 2018.

Given the timing of the conference and the subsequent paper revisions, the chapters in this volume were essentially complete before the onset of the COVID-19 pandemic. As a result, none of the papers discuss the implications of the pandemic for the prospects for economic growth in the United States. Although this is clearly a subject that could be adequately treated only with a second book, we offer several brief observations as follows.

There is no question that the short run implications of the pandemic have been dire with large declines in output and employment. For example, in July 2020, the Congressional Budget Office (CBO)[1] estimated that over the period 2020–2030 annual real GDP will on average be 3.4 percent lower than it projected in January 2020, and that the unemployment rate will average 6.1 percent relative to an earlier prediction of 4.2 percent. We note that the accuracy of these economic projections will naturally depend on the course of pandemic – especially the extent to which the development of vaccines and more effective treatments is successful, and the extent to which the prospects for the success of efforts to continue reopening the economy are enhanced by effective procedures to ensure the wearing of masks, the maintenance of social distancing, widespread cleaning and disinfecting, and effective protocols for testing and health monitoring, contact tracing, and quarantining of those infected with or exposed to COVID-19.

From a medium run and longer run perspective, it is clear that the pandemic has the potential to accentuate all four of the "pervasive head-winds that will seriously limit future U.S. economic growth" noted above. First, from an educational standpoint, the learning lost due to school shutdowns and difficulties with remote learning will have a negative impact on the affected students. For example, Hanushek and Woessmann (2020)[2] estimate students in grades in 1–12 might suffer a decline of 3 percent in their lifetime incomes and annual GDP might be an average of 1.5 percent lower for the rest of the century as a result of the pandemic. They note that these effects can be ameliorated only with more effective instruction going forward, perhaps with more individualized instruction and if new and effective pedagogical techniques learned by coping with the pandemic, especially in the areas of remote teaching and technological innovation in teaching, are successfully implemented.

Second, the pandemic is likely to increase income inequality. Hanushek and Woessmann stress that educational losses will be concentrated among

---

[1] Congressional Budget Office, July 2020, "An Update to the Budget Outlook: 2020–2030," Congressional Budget Office, Washington, DC.

[2] Hanushek, Eric A., and Ludger Woessmann, 2020, "The Economic Impacts of Learning Losses," OECD, Paris.

disadvantaged students. More generally, numerous commentators have described the likelihood of a "K-shaped" recovery under which the poor bear a disproportionate share of the burden of the costs of the pandemic due to the collapse of the labor market, especially for relatively low paying jobs that cannot be done remotely, and reductions in pandemic relief packages, while higher income individuals are largely insulated from the effects of the pandemic, especially to the extent that the recovery in the nation's financial assets continues.

Third, declines in the labor force participation rate may be accelerated as individuals, especially those in the later stages of their life cycles, lose their jobs and have difficulty finding re-employment even as the pandemic subsides, especially in light of the increase in unemployment predicted by CBO. In addition, from a longer run perspective, Spence (2020)[3] notes that the pandemic has accelerated trends toward the increasing economic importance of relatively low labor-intensity firms with high levels of intangible assets per employee, partly due to increased adoption of digital technologies during the pandemic and partly because economic difficulties have been concentrated among relatively labor-intensive business sectors.

Finally, although the massive fiscal and monetary responses of governments in the United States and around the world are appropriate in light of the economic threat posed by the worldwide spread of COVID-19, there is no question that the fiscal situation of the United States has deteriorated as a result of the pandemic. For example, in September 2020, the CBO (2020)[4] projected a federal budget deficit of $3.3 trillion in 2020, more than three times the 2019 deficit, and that privately held federal debt will increase to a historical record of 109 percent of GDP by 2030, relative to its January 2020 projection of a debt of 98 percent of GDP. However, we should note that historically low interest rates – and the prospect that they may continue for an extended period of time, especially if Federal Reserve policy continues to be accommodating, global savings continue to be large relative to investment needs (the "savings glut"), and debt issued by the U.S. Treasury continues to be perceived to be an international investment safe haven – are of course one reason that high levels of debt may have less of an impact on future economic growth rates than they otherwise might.

---

[3] Spence, Michael, 2020, "Winners and Losers of the Pandemic Economy," Project Syndicate, Prague.

[4] Congressional Budget Office, September 2020, "An Update to the Budget Outlook: 2020–2030," Congressional Budget Office, Washington, DC; Congressional Budget Office, January 2020, "The Budget and Economic Outlook: 2020–2030," Congressional Budget Office, Washington, DC.

Despite concerns about such increases in these four headwinds facing future economic growth, we close on a more optimistic note. The effects of the pandemic on the four headwinds are largely medium term rather than long term factors. Indeed, it may be true, as suggested by former Federal Reserve Board Chair Ben Bernanke, that – as long as public health efforts to contain the pandemic are successful – the effect of the coronavirus pandemic on the economy will be akin to an extended "major snowstorm" that will have relatively little impact on long run growth. Moreover, the acceleration of trends toward increasing digitization noted above may have a positive effect on growth, along the lines suggested by those who are optimistic about the long run growth effects of ongoing advances in technology and artificial intelligence. Finally, some of the trends forced by the COVID-19 pandemic may have positive effects on long run productivity and thus long run growth, including increased use of telemedicine and greater business flexibility in allowing remote work when effective and the resulting reduction in congestion. Given all of these uncertainties, the net effect of the pandemic on long run growth is far from clear.

Acknowledgments

This volume and the conference that preceded it would not have been possible without the financial support of the Charles Koch Foundation. We are very thankful to Jonathan Reck of the Charles Koch Foundation for supporting our efforts to obtain funding and for continually encouraging us to produce unbiased research that brings about a healthy national debate on important issues of our time. We would also like to thank Baker Institute Founding Director Edward Djerejian for his enthusiastic support of the conference and this volume, our colleagues at the Baker Institute's Center for Public Finance, Jorge Barro, Joyce Beebe, and Thomas Hogan for their wise counsel on numerous issues in developing the idea and planning for this conference, Anne Dayton and Laura Livingston for excellent administrative assistance, and the Baker Institute staff, especially Regina Dennis, Lianne Hart, Laura Hotze, Jason Lyons, Giovanna Marciano, Andrew Murillo, Shawn O'Neill, Daniel Padilla, Christine Pfeffer, Ben Stevenson, Macy Stewart, and Kevin Young, for their assistance throughout the project. Finally, we would like to thank Anna Kucera, Allison Price, and Varun Cidambi, whose cheerful yet painstaking editorial assistance was essential to the preparation of this volume.

PART I

OVERVIEW

1

Introduction

John W. Diamond and George R. Zodrow

1.1 Prospects for Growth

Robust economic growth has long been the engine of prosperity in the United States, and has resulted in a sustained increase in living standards that has made the US economy the envy of much of the modern world. The prospects for future economic growth in the United States, however, are uncertain. For example, some researchers argue that technological advances, especially in the area of artificial intelligence, are likely to result in automation-related rapid increases in future growth – indeed, to the point that serious shortages in labor demand may result. In marked contrast, other observers believe that recent economic, demographic, and political trends, including an educational system that is ineffective in many dimensions, increasing income inequality, an aging population coupled with a lower labor force participation rate, and the absence of the political will to address large-scale fiscal imbalances, have created pervasive headwinds that will seriously limit future US economic growth.

This volume brings together a distinguished group of world-renowned economists to explore the challenges of maintaining vigorous economic growth in the United States, including issues related to demographics, social insurance programs, technological progress, human capital accumulation, immigration, income inequality, financial institutions, and fiscal policy. The volume consists of a set of chapters that were presented as papers at a conference on "Prospects for Economic Growth in the United States," which was one of a series of events celebrating the twenty-fifth anniversary of Rice University's Baker Institute for Public Policy. The conference was sponsored by the Baker Institute's Center for Public Finance and held at Rice on December 6–7, 2018.

1.2 A Broad Perspective on the Future of Economic Growth

The volume begins with a broad perspective on the future of economic growth in the United States by Martin Feldstein, who passed away on June 11, 2019.[1] Feldstein first notes that in recent years the growth rate in the United States has exceeded the growth rates in other industrial countries. He identifies ten key structural characteristics of the US economy that have contributed to this superior economic performance.

Feldstein then argues that the official data on real GDP understate actual economic growth, as they mismeasure changes in the quality of existing goods and services or the contribution to GDP attributable to new products and services. In particular, he notes that cost-based methods of measuring improvements in the quality of existing goods and services do not capture the many cost-reducing ways in which producers improve their products. In addition, he argues that current measurement techniques understate both the value of new goods and services and their declines in cost over time. Feldstein stresses that this understatement of economic growth is of considerable significance, as it contributes to the pessimism about the effectiveness and desirability of the economic and political system in the United States that has had far-reaching political implications in recent years. Moreover, this effect is augmented by calculations of the time path of real incomes that ignore compensation in the form of fringe benefits, including health insurance, and government transfers, both of which have grown in relative importance in recent years.

Feldstein then turns to the effects of current fiscal policy on the prospects for growth, arguing that projected increases in deficits and in the national debt, especially when calculated taking into account changes from current law that seem likely to be enacted (e.g., elimination of some of the tax cut phaseouts scheduled under the Tax Cuts and Jobs Act (TCJA) passed in 2017), are likely to slow future economic growth. In particular, he argues that higher deficits will absorb an ever-increasing share of national savings, reducing funds available for business investment and research and development, which may also be negatively affected by higher interest rates attributable to higher levels of debt. Moreover, he notes that expectations of higher future tax rates to reduce future deficits and the national debt also discourage current investment.

Feldstein considers two potential solutions to the fiscal problems that he concludes are diminishing prospects for future growth. First, he argues that

---

[1] We thank James Poterba for his assistance in making the final revisions to Professor Feldstein's paper.

raising revenues is part of the solution but should be done in such a way as to minimize the negative effects of taxation on economic growth. For example, he stresses that reducing tax expenditures (e.g., items such as the deduction for home mortgage interest and the exclusion for employer-provided health insurance) would both raise revenue and reduce costly distortions attributable to the tax preferences for these consumer expenditures. Similarly, he notes that a carbon tax (discussed by Diamond and Zodrow in Chapter 8 of this volume) would both raise revenue and reduce carbon emissions by aligning the private and social cost of emissions.

Second, Feldstein notes that much of the fiscal problem in the United States is attributable to rising deficits in the Social Security, Medicare, and Medicaid programs. He focuses on Social Security reform, which he notes can be designed to increase future economic growth both by reducing fiscal deficits and by encouraging individuals to save for their own retirement. For example, he supports a gradual increase in the retirement age from sixty-seven to seventy, following the Social Security program changes enacted in 1983. Feldstein concludes by discussing a more comprehensive reform proposal that he designed with Andrew Samwick (1988); under this plan, Social Security benefits would be supplemented with returns from Personal Retirement Accounts that would be funded by a mixture of private and government contributions (including 1.5 percent from individual earnings and 1.5 percent from current payroll taxes) and invested in a mixture of stocks and bonds.

The next two chapters of the volume examine two key aspects of how labor markets affect economic growth – the accumulation of human capital and immigration.

1.3 Human Capital and Economic Growth

In Chapter 3, Flávio Cunha of Rice University examines how the development of human capital affects economic growth. He begins by making three critical observations. The first is that labor productivity in the United States has declined in recent years, from an average rate of growth of 2.75 percent from 1948 to 1981 to slightly less than 2 percent from 1982 to 2016. The second is that income inequality has been increasing over the same period; for example, using one measure of average weekly earnings, earnings at the ninetieth percentile of the wage distribution increased by 30 percent from 1948 to 2016, while the fiftieth percentile experienced no growth over the same time period and the tenth percentile declined by 12 percent. The third is that human capital accumulation in the United

States has declined relative to other Organisation for Economic Co-operation and Development (OECD) countries over the same time period. For example, in 2014, the share of the population with a tertiary education in the United States was fourth among OECD nations for individuals aged fifty-five to sixty-four, but only twelfth for individuals between twenty-five and thirty-four years of age, as the United States ranks next to last in the growth rate of this population share over the time period.

Cunha argues that both lower productivity growth and greater income inequality can be at least partially attributed to the decline in human capital accumulation in the United States. A larger stock of human capital facilitates technology adoption and technological progress, which, in turn, promotes growth in labor productivity. Using the examples of the biotechnology and semiconductor industries, Cunha stresses that this is especially important for economic growth since technological advances are largely nonrival and thus can be widely utilized (rather than just by the developer of the technological advance). Moreover, a smaller supply of skilled labor leads to a higher skill wage premium, which exacerbates income inequality. Policies that would increase human capital formation in the United States would thus help address issues of both declining productivity growth and accelerating income inequality.

Cunha begins his discussion of possible policy interventions by noting that the downward trend in human capital accumulation has occurred despite steadily increasing access to college, especially for low-income students. The key reasons that increasing enrollments have not led to large increases in human capital among disadvantaged students are that (1) their graduation rates are relatively low, primarily because such students are not well prepared for college, and (2) high-ability, low-income students tend not to apply to the selective institutions that would have the most dramatic positive impact on their accumulation of human capital.

Cunha notes briefly that the latter problem might be addressed by providing low-income students with more information about the accessibility and affordability of highly selective institutions. However, he focuses on how to improve college readiness for low-income students to increase the likelihood that they will complete their post-secondary education. He notes that empirical research has established that both cognitive skills and socioemotional skills are critical to increasing the likelihood that a student graduates from college. However, it is very difficult to increase these skills among disadvantaged children because empirical research also indicates that they start to lag behind in the development of both cognitive and socioemotional skills (as well as health) early in childhood, that these deficits increase during early school years, and that, in relative terms, these shortfalls have been increasing in recent years. Cunha convincingly documents that these cognitive and socioemotional deficits are attributable to inequality in the investments in the human capital of children, in terms of both the quantity and the quality of interaction time between parents and children as well as inequality in the expenditures that facilitate a child's human capital formation.

Cunha concludes by summarizing experimental evidence on interventions designed to increase investments in the human capital of disadvantaged children. For example, numerous programs have focused on providing early childhood education and estimating both the short-run effects on skills and investments in human capital, as well as the long-run impacts on outcomes relating to labor market performance, educational attainment, and participation in criminal activities. Other programs attempt to improve the human capital accumulation of children by educating parents through home visitations; one example is the Nurse-Family Partnership, which provides disadvantaged first-time mothers with instructional home visits that begin during pregnancy and continue until the child turns two years old. Other programs target the formation of noncognitive skills in school-age children, in some cases coupled with parental interventions. Cunha describes in detail both the programs and the extent to which they are successful (e.g., programs that focus on improving cognitive skills typically improve such skills in the short run but the effect often dissipates over time), as well as the characteristics of the programs that were not successful. He concludes that policies that will be successful in increasing the human capital accumulation of disadvantaged children must start early by changing their home environments as well as by engaging parents to improve the quality of their interactions with their children. In addition, Cunha emphasizes that the empirical evidence strongly suggests that efforts that are successful, especially in the long run, are primarily driven by programs that improve noncognitive skills, an area that deserves more focus in the future.

1.4 Immigration and Economic Growth

George Borjas of Harvard University provides a theoretical and empirical analysis of how increased immigration would affect economic growth in the United States. He begins by noting that the fact that 16.6 percent of workers in the US labor market in 2016 were foreign-born naturally implies that immigrants are responsible for a sizable fraction of US GDP, and that an increase in immigration would naturally lead to a corresponding increase in GDP. It is far less clear, however, that such an immigrant supply shock would necessarily increase per capita income or provide net gains to natives; the latter topic is the focus of his analysis.

Borjas begins by examining various theoretical aspects of the effects of an increase in immigration on overall and per capita growth. He shows that within the context of the canonical Solow growth model, a one-time increase in immigration increases output but has no effect on per capita income, as the economy returns to its original steady state after a transition period. In contrast, a permanent increase in the rate of immigration is effectively an increase in the growth rate of the labor force. Borjas shows that although such an increase in immigration increases the level of output, it results in a decline in per capita income, as a higher rate of labor supply growth implies a lower equilibrium effective capital–labor ratio in both the short and long runs. Moreover, he argues that this theoretical prediction is borne out by the empirical analyses that have examined this issue, which show that the "correlation between immigration and per capita income is, at best, zero" (Chapter 4, p. 84). Another way of thinking about the effects of immigration is whether there is an "immigration surplus" – an increase in the wealth of the "native" population – and Borjas shows that, in his model, the immigration surplus is modest in the short run and zero in the long run.

Borjas then investigates the implications of various extensions of the standard Solow growth model, focusing on whether such extensions can result in a significantly positive immigration surplus. The first extension adds two types of labor to the model – low-skill and high-skill – and assumes that the influx of immigrants is predominantly either low-skill or high-skill. He notes that the short-run immigration surplus might double if immigrants were all high-skill, although this effect would be significantly attenuated in the long run. However, he shows that a potentially much larger and more permanent immigration surplus may arise when high-skill immigrants have positive human capital externalities on native productivity, since immigration in this case results in a permanent increase in the demand for native labor.

Borjas also examines the effects of immigration on income distribution. He begins by examining several studies of the "Mariel boatlift," which occurred in April 1980 when Fidel Castro allowed free immigration from Cuba and approximately 125,000 Cubans moved to the United States, increasing Miami's labor force by approximately 8 percent. Borjas argues that the results obtained in the literature examining the effects of this influx of immigrants on wages vary widely, depending primarily on the sample studied and because natives may respond to a reduction in local wages by moving elsewhere. An alternative approach designed to avoid the second problem uses national "skill cells" to examine the effects on the wages of specific skill groups of an increase in the number of immigrants in those groups. Borjas observes that this literature, however, has also been relatively inconclusive thus far, as has the empirical literature on whether immigration generates human capital externalities.

Borjas also discusses several additional results from the empirical literature on immigration: (1) more recent cohorts of immigrants have lower earnings potential at the time of entry and do not exhibit earnings growth as fast as earlier cohorts, (2) high-skill immigrant groups experience faster wage growth, indicating a higher contribution to aggregate output, and (3) the long run aggregate fiscal impact of immigrants tends to be positive only if immigrants do not affect the cost of public goods and if one assumes continuation of current policies (rather than Congressional Budget Office (CBO) projections of the likely path of such policies), but the long-run impact of high- (low-) skill immigrants is always positive (negative).

Borjas concludes that if the goal of immigration policy is to help the United States achieve a high rate of economic growth, it should adopt a policy favoring immigration of high-skill individuals. He readily acknowledges, however, that it is not clear that immigration policy should be set primarily to promote economic growth.

The next two chapters of the volume examine the interplay between technology and economic growth.

1.5 Technology and the Future of Economic Growth

In Chapter 5, Glenn Hubbard of Columbia University examines the role that ongoing and future technological advances are likely to play in determining future economic growth in the United States. He casts the issue as a debate between two groups of researchers. The first is the "techno-optimists," such as Andrew McAfee and Erik Brynjolfsson, whose 2017 book *Machine, Platform, Crowd* emphasizes recent and future productivity and growth enhancing developments in artificial intelligence and robotics. These researchers believe that the United States is about to enter a new era of technology-induced increases in productivity that will lead to faster economic growth – while nevertheless recognizing that there may be a long time period between technological advance and broad productivity gains. The second group is the "techno-pessimists," such as Robert Gordon, whose 2016 book *The Rise and Fall of American Growth* argues that the country faces strong economic headwinds – due to weaknesses in the educational system, increasing income inequality, an aging population coupled with a lower labor force participation rate, and large-scale fiscal imbalances. Moreover, Gordon believes that these headwinds are unlikely to be offset by the relatively modest productivity gains attributable to the current wave of technological advances, which in his view are not as transformative as earlier revolutionary general purpose technologies, such as the steam engine, electricity, the internal combustion engine, improved manufacturing processes, new materials, and advances in communications and media, chemicals, and computers. Gordon concludes that the net result will be significantly diminished economic growth in future years. Other observers, such as Lawrence Summers (2015) and Tyler Cohen (2011), have similarly concluded that the United States is not likely to experience a dramatic revival of productivity growth and instead may enter a new period of "secular stagnation."

Hubbard stresses that these diametrically opposed views can be reconciled to at least some extent by the fact that there are typically long lags between the introduction of a new technology and its productivity impact, especially since the latter often involves complementary innovations and organizational change in addition to the time required to accumulate the stock of new technology. He also notes that the recent slowdown in productivity growth often stressed by the techno-pessimist camp is not historically unprecedented and, like previous episodes of slow growth, may be reversed. Moreover, he stresses that the recent productivity growth slowdown can at least partly be attributable to economic policies that have reduced investment in new capital equipment and software. Such policies can be – and he argues to some extent recently have been – reversed with lower tax rates on capital income and regulatory reform. More generally, Hubbard argues that microeconomic policies that would promote productivity and economic growth would center on improvements in infrastructure broadly defined, development and dissemination of better management practices including more rapid diffusion of productivity gains from technological advances, and reduced barriers to competition with a focus on policies that would enhance the ability of technologically disruptive younger firms to compete effectively against established firms.

Although he stresses microeconomic policies that would improve productivity and economic growth, Hubbard also notes that economic policies can reduce the impact of the macroeconomic headwinds highlighted by Gordon. In particular, he argues that policies for improving skills and rewarding work are critical for dealing with both income inequality and educational issues; these might include an expanded Earned Income Tax Credit or alternative wage subsidies as well as a federal block grant to community colleges to support college completion and skill enhancement. With respect to the nation's fiscal problems, Hubbard agrees that the United States faces difficult choices in choosing spending levels on social insurance, defense, and domestic goods and will have to consider tax increases that will be detrimental to future growth.

1.6 Artificial Intelligence Technologies and Economic Growth

In Chapter 6, Timothy Bresnahan of Stanford University examines in detail the commercial application of artificial intelligence technologies (AITs), explaining how they have changed the ways in which businesses operate and their current and potential impact on economic growth. His main conclusion is that the notion of "labor task substitution," or using AITs to perform tasks previously performed by humans, plays no role in the highly valuable systems that rely on AITs. Instead, the substitution of information and communications technologies (ICTs) and AITs has occurred at the production system level, primarily in the form of ICT capital deepening in industries that are already relatively capital-intensive and engaging in targeted rather than mass media advertising. In addition, Bresnahan argues that although AITs may contribute to growth, that growth is likely to come primarily from capital deepening, yielding improvements in AITs and their applications that will lead to growth-enhancing scale economies in certain firms, industries and functions, rather than from broadening the range of applications of AITs to a wider range of industries and functions.

Bresnahan begins by detailing the use of AITs in one of their most valuable roles – matching specific buyers and sellers, including generating product recommendations at Amazon, targeted advertising at Google and Facebook, and providing movies and television show suggestions at Netflix, which he describes as a marketing revolution. He notes that, in general, applying machine learning to earlier matching algorithms was facilitated by two factors. The first is widespread use of system modularization as a management technique, which limits the number of changes that must be made in other parts of the system when AITs are adopted and increases scalability (the ease with which a production system can be increased without changes to its basic architecture and thus at relatively low marginal cost). The second is a "low stakes loss function" – that is, the costs associated with AIT mistakes are often relatively low (e.g., a sales recommendation that is not accepted by the consumer). He emphasizes, however, that this is by no means always the case, with a prime example being the posting of content such as hate speech on Facebook that some viewers perceive as highly inappropriate while it is actively promoted by others – a case where Facebook now relies heavily on "people power" rather than AITs.

Bresnahan stresses that these examples make clear that task-level substitution or replacing labor with AITs in the performance of a specific task plays no role in these applications of AITs. Instead, it is system-level substitution – for example, the substitution of the Amazon supply chain for bricks-and-mortar stores – that has led to the substitution of capital and human-capital-intensive labor for less-skilled labor in the ICT era.

Bresnahan also discusses AIT applications in user interface (UI), including voice-based personal assistants (such as Alexa, Siri, Cortana, and Google Assistant, which use the AIT referred to as natural language processing), as well as smartphones and tablets. All of these AITs have greatly increased access to a wide range of technological applications but again do not reflect task-level substitution of AIT capital for labor.

Bresnahan closes by discussing how new AITs might increase business productivity more generally and lead to more economic growth. He notes that, thus far, there is relatively little application of AITs outside the uses by the Internet giants already discussed, and that some systems are only now moving from the laboratory to "real world" applications. These include marketing applications that enhance the "consumer experience," such as chatbots, the use of digital assistants at work to perform basic tasks and to advise employees and facilitate the use of software packages, the use of AITs and big data to improve decision support systems, and new projects such as driverless vehicles. Other applications include advances in performing standard business tasks, such as production scheduling, inventory management, shipment scheduling, and related systems, as well as applications in specific industries, such as asset trading models in finance, and credit card fraud detection systems. AITs are also playing a role in drug discovery and development, computer and network security and many other security systems, and photo and voice recognition systems.

More generally, and consistent with Hubbard's analysis in this volume, Bresnahan emphasizes that the leap from developing an AIT and applying it successfully in a commercial setting typically requires both recombination of new and existing technologies and the invention of complementary technologies and thus takes decades. Thus far, applications of AITs have been concentrated in marketing, customer service, and their interactions. These applications have generally taken the form of supporting very rapid technical advance by complementing existing capital, that is, capital deepening. Bresnahan notes that more "broadening" applications of AITs have been limited due to high-stakes transactions in certain industries (e.g., health care, government services, and professional services) and to a lack of modularity and other organizational features of businesses that have led to slow increases in productivity attributable to the application of AITs. He concludes by noting that there has been a steady increase in the relative success of the leading firms in a large number of industries, and that these firms seem to have been especially successful in applying AITs in their industries – which may be a harbinger of the future of wider successful application of AITs.

The next two chapters in the volume use simulation analysis to examine the effects of fiscal policy on growth, focusing on the TCJA enacted in 2017 and the macroeconomic and distributional effects of enacting a carbon tax.

1.7 Taxes and Economic Growth

The effects of taxes on economic growth are a contentious topic. In Chapter 7, Robert Barro of Harvard University examines the macroeconomic effects of the recently enacted TCJA, which, among many other things, lowered the corporate tax rate to 21 percent, moved to a territorial system for the taxation of foreign-source income coupled with new anti-avoidance provisions, introduced a 20 percent deduction for certain pass-through businesses, allowed expensing of business purchases of equipment, reduced individual tax rates, expanded the standard deduction, and reduced the deductibility of home mortgage interest and state and local taxes.

Barro draws on a recent paper with Jason Furman (Barro and Furman, 2018) that simulated the effects of the TCJA under the assumption that all provisions in effect in 2018 will be permanent (some of these provisions, such as expensing, are currently scheduled to be phased out, but many observers expect that some of them will be made permanent). Barro begins by describing the multistep process Barro and Furman (2018) used in modeling the effects of the business taxation elements of the reform. First, they calculated the effects of the various business provisions on the user costs of five types of capital (equipment, structures, residential rental property, research and development (R&D) intellectual property, and other intellectual property) for both C-corporations subject to the corporate income tax and pass-through entities such as S-corporations, partnerships, and sole proprietorships. The changes in user costs were then applied to a standard neoclassical framework to estimate the long-run effects of reform on capital–labor ratios, output per worker, and the real wage rate. Finally, they estimated the short run effects of the reform by using empirically estimated rates of convergence from the empirical growth literature. For the individual-level elements of the TCJA, Barro and Furman (2018) estimated the reductions in effective tax rates due to the reform and used empirical results from existing reduced-form time-series regression models to estimate their effects on growth.

Barro and Furman (2018) estimate that the average user cost of capital fell by 8 percent for C-corporations and by 5 percent for pass-through entities, which led to a long-run increase in the capital–labor ratio of 13 percent in the corporate sector and 8 percent in the pass-through sector. They estimate that the overall effect of the business tax components of the reform is a long-run increase in output per worker of 3 percent, which translates into an increase in per capita GDP of 0.2 percentage points per year for the first ten years after enactment. They also estimate that the individual components of the TCJA reduced the labor-income-weighted average marginal income tax rate by 2.3 percentage points, which raised per capita real GDP by 0.9 percentage points per year for the first two years after enactment but had no growth effects thereafter. Barro notes that combining these estimates implies that the TCJA will raise the GDP growth rate by 1.1 percentage points per year for 2018–19 and by 0.2 percentage points per year for 2020–8. Thus, the main short-run growth response is attributable to changes in the individual income tax, and the main long-run response is due to changes in business taxation.

Barro also updates the revenue estimates provided in Barro and Furman (2018) to reflect these growth estimates. His calculations suggest that the revenue generated by additional economic growth is roughly equal to existing estimates of the revenue loss due to TCJA. He concludes that "a net revenue contribution of the reform of approximately zero is plausible" (Chapter 7, p. 181).

Finally, Barro discusses some ongoing research estimating the extent to which the TCJA will encourage pass-through entities to switch to C-corporation status, and various implications of such a change. He estimates that taking this factor into account increases the long-run gain in per capita real GDP attributable to the TCJA from 3 percent to 4 percent.

1.8 Carbon Taxes and Economic Growth

Although the recently enacted TCJA did not include any environmental tax provisions, numerous discussions of tax policy options in the United States have considered the possibility of implementing a carbon tax. Indeed, Feldstein in Chapter 2 of this volume discussed implementation of a carbon tax as a means of reducing carbon emissions and thus addressing the climate change issues. However, many observers have raised concerns about the potential negative effects of a carbon tax on output and economic growth and on income distribution. In Chapter 8 of this volume, these two concerns are addressed by John Diamond and George Zodrow of Rice University.

Diamond and Zodrow begin with a brief discussion of the direct economic effects of climate change – a topic that is ignored in many computable general equilibrium (CGE) simulation analyses of the effects of a carbon tax (including their own). They note that a recent comprehensive analysis of carbon taxes by Goulder and Hafstead (2018) estimates that the ratio of total climate benefits to the total welfare costs associated with the carbon tax varies from 1.69 to 5.10 depending on how the revenues are used, and that the health benefits of the reductions in pollution associated with reduced carbon emissions, primarily reduced carbon monoxide, nitrous oxides, sulfur dioxide, volatile organic compounds, ammonia, and particulate matter, are even larger, with benefit–cost ratios that vary from 2.90 to 6.58. Although these estimates are subject to considerable uncertainty, the Goulder and Hafstead (2018) simulation results suggest that the climate and health benefits associated with reductions in carbon emissions are significant. Moreover, these benefits are of sufficient magnitude that they are likely to offset any welfare costs of implementing a carbon tax at a level equal to current consensus estimates of the social cost of carbon (SCC) estimated in models that ignore these climate and health benefits.

After providing a selective review of the literature on the macroeconomic and distributional effects of carbon taxes, Diamond and Zodrow turn to their simulation results, which use the closed economy version of the Diamond-Zodrow (DZ) model, a dynamic, overlapping generations CGE model of the US economy that focuses on the macroeconomic, distributional (across fifty-five generations with twelve income groups in each generation), and transitional effects of tax reforms (Zodrow and Diamond, 2013). Because their model includes only four production/consumer sectors, they import into their model the carbon tax–induced price changes for nineteen different consumer goods calculated by Larsen, Mohan, Marsters, and Herndon (2018), which they used in an earlier project (Diamond and Zodrow, 2018). When translated into changes in the four consumer prices in the DZ model, the carbon tax not only generates revenue but also offsets consumer price distortions due to the existing tax system, which implies that the macroeconomic effects of a carbon tax are more positive than they otherwise might be if the model included all existing price distortions.

The results of the Diamond-Zodrow simulations can be summarized as follows. First, any negative effects on the level of future GDP are moderate for the carbon tax modeled (which begins at roughly $50 per metric ton of CO_2 and increases in real terms at 2 percent per year for thirty years), with changes in GDP fifty years after enactment that range from −0.4 percent to 1.4 percent, which imply negligible effects on the rate of economic growth. Consistent with other studies, Diamond and Zodrow find: (1) the least favorable results are obtained when carbon tax revenues are used to finance per-household rebates, since such rebates do not have the advantage of reducing other distortionary taxes; (2) more favorable results are obtained when carbon tax revenues are used to finance either payroll tax cuts or wage tax cuts, thus reducing disincentives to work under the current tax structure, with the larger effects occurring with the wage tax since it is concentrated on workers in the middle- and upper-income groups who are relatively productive; (3) the most favorable macroeconomic results are obtained when carbon tax revenues are used to lower personal income taxes on dividends and capital gains as the taxation of capital income, including both corporate and individual-level taxes, is relatively more distortionary than the taxation of labor income (this result obtains even though some of the carbon tax revenues in this case are used to finance per-household rebates and the overall level of taxation of capital income was reduced with the implementation of a 21 percent corporate income tax rate and other changes under the TCJA passed in 2017); and (4) relatively modest effects with increases in investment coupled with declines in labor supply and output, falling in between those for per-household rebates and payroll tax cuts, are obtained when carbon tax revenues are used to reduce the national debt for ten years and then used to finance per-household rebates.

Second, Diamond and Zodrow show that any regressive effects of a carbon tax reform due to tax-induced increases in the prices of goods consumed disproportionately by the poor can readily be offset with the appropriate revenue-recycling policy. In particular, their simulations show that the net impact of policies that use carbon tax revenues to finance uniform per-household rebates, either entirely or as part of a plan that includes policies that are favorable to capital formation, such as the elimination of personal taxes on dividends and capital gains or reductions in the national debt, can be highly progressive.

The last two chapters in the volume address two critical special issues – the effects of the financial system on economic growth and the relationship between income inequality and growth.

1.9 The Financial System and Economic Growth

Economic growth cannot occur without a well-functioning banking system and countries with well-functioning banking systems tend to have faster long-run growth. However, as discussed by Ross Levine of the University of California at Berkeley in Chapter 9, some observers, especially after the financial crisis of 2008, wonder whether banking systems often function poorly, hindering economic growth and curtailing economic opportunities, especially for new ventures. Levine addresses these questions in a wide-ranging discussion of the links between banking and economic prosperity.

Levine begins by detailing the ways in which an effective banking system promotes economic growth. First, he describes empirical evidence that demonstrates that countries with better-functioning banking systems grow faster. Well-functioning banks spur growth by improving the allocation of resources (rather than by increasing savings), especially by loaning funds to productive entrepreneurs, and in some cases providing management expertise to ensure that those resources are used effectively. In contrast, banking systems that direct funds to cronies or exclusively to well-established wealthy clients hinder growth since the funds are not allocated efficiently.

Moreover, the gains of a well-functioning banking system are not limited to improvements in economic efficiency. An effective banking system helps to improve the distribution of income by loaning funds to the most promising entrepreneurs, thereby expanding economic opportunities for lower-income individuals, thus reducing income inequality. This effect is reinforced as new companies increase market competition, especially in the labor market, thus increasing wages and lowering unemployment often for lower-income individuals. Levine shows that this contention is also supported by empirical evidence, including evidence across states in the United States, which indicates that countries (or states) with better-functioning banking systems experience larger reductions in income inequality, and in particular increase the incomes of the extremely poor.

Levine also notes that banks must innovate constantly if they are to continue to be successful in an ever-changing environment. Financial innovation is not always beneficial, as shown by the proliferation of complex instruments that led to the financial crisis of 2008. Nevertheless, Levine notes that because production becomes more specialized and technology becomes more complex over time, it is essential to growth that financial firms innovate to cope with this ever-increasing complexity. He provides numerous historical examples of this phenomenon, including (1) the creation of specialized financiers who provided the funds and management expertise to facilitate the expansion of the railroad system in the 1800s, (2) the critical role of venture capitalists in providing funds and management expertise during the information technology revolution, and (3) the role of large pharmaceutical companies in assisting banks and venture capital firms in financing new projects during the biotechnology revolution of the twenty-first century.

Levine concludes that "a well-functioning financial system is vital for fostering economic growth and expanding economic opportunities, especially for those at the lower end of the distribution of income" (Chapter 9, p. 260). Although financial systems and financial innovation are not always socially productive, as demonstrated by the recent financial crisis, "sustained improvements in living standards are much less likely when financial systems function poorly" (Chapter 9, p. 260). Moreover, Levine argues that the importance of a well-functioning banking system implies that financial regulation and the policies that govern the operation of the financial sector are a critical component in generating economic growth.

1.10 Income and Wealth Inequality and Economic Growth

The volume concludes (apart from a final overview chapter by the editors) with Chapter 10 by Stephen Turnovsky of the University of Washington, which examines the relationship between income and wealth inequality and economic growth. Turnovsky begins by noting that the empirical evidence on the relationship between inequality and economic growth is rather mixed, which he argues is unsurprising given that aggregate measures, such as GDP and its growth rate, and the distribution of income across individual agents reflect endogenous outcomes of a large and complex economic system, with many forces with diverse effects on such measures changing over time and varying across economies. Accordingly, he suggests that the growth–inequality relationship can best be understood as a joint equilibrium outcome of a consistently specified general equilibrium growth model.

Turnovsky's chapter focuses on one such approach – the "representative consumer theory of distribution" (RCTD) – which combines homogeneous preferences and individual heterogeneity (with respect to items such as initial endowments of assets), coupled with complete markets in a general equilibrium growth framework that has a simple solvable recursive structure. His primary objective in the chapter is to present a systematic approach to the RCTD, and to highlight the insights that it offers into the growth–inequality relationship in a range of applications.

Turnovsky begins by incorporating the RCTD with different individuals with different initial endowments of capital in a basic Ramsey growth model and derives the solutions for endogenous labor supply and the evolution of capital ownership and thus relative wealth, and then examines the properties of the model. For example, one critical result is that in an expanding economy (an increasing capital stock), wealth inequality will decrease during transition, and the long-run distribution of wealth will be more equal than the initial distribution, which, in turn, tends to reduce income inequality.

Turnovsky also examines the effects of various shocks in the model, such as an increase in labor productivity. Although the standard approach is to assume that such shocks occur instantaneously, he argues that most productivity increases occur over time as economies gradually adopt new technologies. When the productivity shock takes place gradually, he shows that the time path of the productivity increase affects not only the transitional time paths of wealth and income inequality but also their long-run equilibrium values. This path-dependence implies that the effects of policies such as foreign aid or tax reform on wealth and income inequality depend on whether the policies are implemented immediately or phased in over time.

Fiscal policy can also be incorporated into the model. For example, Turnovsky shows that an increase in government expenditures on a pure public good financed with a reduction in transfers reduces long-run wealth inequality but has a theoretically ambiguous effect on income inequality. He also investigates the effects of an increase in government expenditures financed with various distortionary flat-rate and progressive taxes, which are quite complex and depend on a wide variety of factors.

Although most of Turnovsky's results focus on heterogeneity in initial asset ownership in the RCTD, he also considers the case of heterogeneity in skill levels. A critical result in this model is that individuals may change relative wealth and income positions. For example, individuals with above-average capital but below-average skills may, over time, end up with below-average wealth, as they tend to accumulate capital more slowly, both because they are initially wealthy and consume more leisure and because their relatively low skill level implies relatively low wage income and saving.

Turnovsky also examines the effects of adding human capital and public investment to the model. In particular, in the case of human capital, he focuses on the effects of the skill premium and how it responds to the skill-biased technological change and the capital-skill complementarity that have attracted recent attention.

Turnovsky concludes by arguing that the various modifications and extensions of the RCTD illustrate its versatility in addressing the complex relationships between wealth and income inequality and economic growth. He closes by suggesting some additional ways in which it might be extended to provide additional insight into these complex relationships, in all cases using a consistently specified general equilibrium growth approach to modeling the many factors that affect inequality and growth.

As discussed in our concluding Chapter 11, the chapters in this volume provide wide-ranging insights into the prospects for future growth in the United States. We hope that our readers find the volume both informative and thought-provoking, and a useful guide as they observe our nation's ongoing attempts to continue its impressive record of fostering economic growth.

References

Barro, Robert J., and Jason Furman, 2018. "Macroeconomic Effects of the 2017 Tax Reform." *Brookings Papers on Economic Activity* 49 (1) Spring, 257–345.

Cohen, Tyler, 2011. *The Great Stagnation: How America Ate All the Low-Hanging Fruit of Modern History, Got Sick, and Will (Eventually) Feel Better*. Penguin Group, New York, NY.

Diamond, John W., and George R. Zodrow, 2018. "The Effects of Carbon Tax Policies on the US Economy and the Welfare of Households." Report. Columbia SIPA Center on Global Energy Policy, New York, NY, https://energypolicy.columbia.edu/research/report/effects-carbon-tax-policies-us-economy-and-welfare-households.

Feldstein, Martin and Andrew Samwick, 1998. "The Transition Path in Privatizing Social Security." In Martin Feldstein (ed.), *Privatizing Social Security*, 215–64. University of Chicago Press, Chicago, IL.

Gordon, Robert, 2016. *The Rise and Fall of American Growth: The U.S. Standard of Living Since the Civil War.* Princeton University Press, Princeton, NJ and Oxford, UK.

Goulder, Lawrence H., and Marc Hafstead, 2018. *Confronting the Climate Challenge: U.S. Policy Options.* Columbia University Press, New York, NY.

Larsen, John, Shashank Mohan, Peter Marsters, and Whitney Herndon, 2018. "Energy and Environmental Implications of a Carbon Tax in the United States." Columbia SIPA Center on Global Energy Policy, New York, NY.

McAfee, Andrew, and Erik Brynjolfsson, 2017. *Machine, Platform, Crowd: Harnessing Our Digital Future.* W.W. Norton, New York, NY.

Summers, Lawrence H., 2015. "Have We Entered an Age of Secular Stagnation?" *IMF Economic Review* 63 (1), 277–80.

Zodrow, George R., and John W. Diamond, 2013. "Dynamic Overlapping Generations Computable General Equilibrium Models and the Analysis of Tax Policy." In Peter B. Dixon and Dale W. Jorgenson (eds.), *Handbook of Computable General Equilibrium Modeling, Volume 1,* 743–813. Elsevier, Amsterdam, Netherlands.

The Future of Economic Growth in the United States

Martin Feldstein

In recent decades, the US economy has grown more rapidly than most other major industrial countries. Looking ahead, though, the rate of US growth seems likely to slow.

In this chapter, which draws on Feldstein (2005, 2015, 2017a, 2017b, 2018), I examine several aspects of economic growth in the United States. I begin in Section 2.1 by showing the extent to which the US growth rate has exceeded the growth rates in other industrial countries. I then discuss several important structural reasons why this has been true.

Moreover, I believe that the official measure of the rate of economic growth understates the true rise in real income for two reasons. First, the basic measure of money income ignores fringe benefits and the impact of taxes and transfers. Second, the official measure of real output growth fails to capture the contribution of quality change and of new products. Section 2.2 discusses these mismeasurement problems.

The primary reason why the pace of US growth as officially measured is likely to decline in the next few years is the growth of the fiscal deficit and the national debt. Section 2.3 explains why the growth of deficits and debt will reduce the rise of real gross domestic product (GDP). It also explains why deficits and debt will grow rapidly unless there is significant legislative reform.

Section 2.4 discusses how revenue could be raised without taxing households and businesses in ways that discourage output. It focuses on reducing tax expenditures and introducing a carbon tax.

Since the rising cost of Social Security benefits is a major part of the increase in deficits and debt, Section 2.5 discusses the reason for that cost increase and what could be done to slow it in the future.

The chapter concludes in Section 2.6 with a brief summary.

2.1 Why Has the United States Grown So Rapidly?

The growth of real GDP in the United States in 2018 at nearly 3 percent outpaced the growth rates in Germany, France, the United Kingdom, and Japan.[1] More significantly, the cumulative growth over many years puts the real level of GDP per capita in the United States ahead of the levels in other major OECD (Organisation for Economic Co-operation and Development) countries. In 2017, real GDP per capita in the United States was $58,000. In contrast, per capita real GDP was only $49,000 in Germany, $41,000 in France, $43,000 in the United Kingdom, and just $37,000 in Italy.

The following ten major structural features of the US economy contribute to this superior growth performance:

An entrepreneurial culture. Individuals in the United States demonstrate a desire to start businesses and to grow them. There is less penalty in the United States for failing and starting again.

A financial system that supports entrepreneurship. The United States has a more developed system of equity finance than the countries of Europe, including angel investors who are willing to finance startups and a very active venture capital market that helps finance those firms as they grow. The United States also has a large decentralized banking system with more than 7,000 small banks that provide loans to entrepreneurs (Greenspan, 1997).

World-class research universities. Universities provide much of the basic research that drives high-tech entrepreneurship. Faculty members and doctoral students often spend time with nearby startups, and the culture of the universities and the businesses encourages this activity. Top research universities attract the best students from around the world, many of whom end up staying in the United States.

Efficient labor markets. US labor markets link workers and jobs, unimpeded by labor unions, state-owned industries, or excessively restrictive labor regulations. Approximately 7 percent of the private sector US labor force is unionized, and there are virtually no state-owned enterprises.[2] While the United States does regulate working conditions and hiring, the rules are much less onerous than in Europe. As a result, workers have a better chance of finding the right job, firms

[1] International Monetary Fund, 2020, World Economic Outlook Database, www.imf.org /external/pubs/ft/weo/2020/01/weodata/index.aspx.
[2] Bureau of Labor Statistics, "Economic News Release," www.bls.gov/news.release/union2 .t03.htm, table 3: "Union affiliation of employed wage and salary workers by occupation and industry, 2018–2019 annual averages."

find it easier to innovate, and new firms find it easier to get started and grow.

A population that is growing, including from immigration, and geographically mobile within the United States. America's growing population means a younger and therefore more trainable and flexible workforce. Although there are restrictions on immigration to the United States, there are also special rules to provide access to the US economy and a path to citizenship based on individual talent and industrial sponsorship. A separate "green card lottery" system provides a way for eager people to come to the United States. The country's ability to attract qualified immigrants has been an important factor in its prosperity.

A culture and a tax system that encourage hard work and long hours. The average employee works 1,800 hours per year, substantially more than the 1,500 hours worked in France and the 1,400 hours worked in Germany – although not as much as the 2,200 hours in Hong Kong, Singapore, and South Korea (Roxburgh et al., 2010). In general, working longer hours means producing more and therefore means higher real incomes.

An independent supply of energy. Natural gas hydraulic fracturing or fracking has, in particular, provided US businesses with plentiful and relatively inexpensive energy.

A favorable regulatory environment. Although US regulations are far from perfect, they are less burdensome on businesses than the regulations imposed by European countries and the European Union.

A smaller government than in other industrial countries. According to the OECD, outlays of the US governments at the federal, state, and local levels totaled 38 percent of GDP while the corresponding figure was 44 percent in Germany, 51 percent in Italy, and 57 percent in France.[3] The higher level of government spending in other countries implies not only a higher share of income taken in taxes but also higher transfer payments that reduce incentives to work.

A decentralized system in which states and local governments compete. Competition among states and communities encourages entrepreneurship and work. States also compete for businesses and for individual residents with their legal rules and tax regimes. Some states have no income taxes and have labor laws that limit unionization. The United States is perhaps unique among major high-income nations in its degree of political decentralization.

---

[3] OECD Data, "General Government Spending, Total, % of GDP, 2015," https://data .oecd.org/gga/general-government-spending.htm.

2.2 How the Official Data Understate Real Income Growth

The official data report that real GDP grew at an average rate of 2.3 percent a year for the past twenty years, implying that the per capita real GDP grew at just 1.4 percent a year during those twenty years.[4]

I believe that the official data substantially understate the real growth of output and incomes. This is not only important to economists; it also reduces the public's faith in our economic and political system, and it creates pessimism that contributes to populist political attitudes that foster opposition to trade.

2.2.1 Mismeasurement Issues

The government's method of calculating real growth results in serious underestimation of that growth for the following reason.[5] The government surveys a large number of firms and collects data on the market value of their sales of goods and services (US Bureau of Economic Analysis, 2015). The total of these sales is the *nominal* value of GDP. Government statisticians must then convert that change in nominal GDP into a change in the price level and a change in real output, with the latter reflecting the real value of output to consumers and to other final users. In doing so, they face two very difficult problems: reflecting the changing quality of existing products and services, and measuring the value created by new products and services. In my view, the official estimates of real output created in this way contain virtually no useful information.

Consider first how the government statisticians deal with quality change.[6] Their method tells us about the increase in inputs rather than the value of output. The most common method for dealing with quality

---

[4] Economic Report of the President, "Percent Changes in Real Gross Domestic Product, 1965–2014," https://obamawhitehouse.archives.gov/sites/default/files/docs/cea_2015_erp_complete.pdf, table B-1.

[5] Landefeld, Seskin, and Fraumeni (2008) provide a very useful description of how nominal GDP and related measures are estimated from a variety of primary sources. Boskin (2000) shows that these estimates are subject to substantial revisions, with nearly all revisions from 1959 to 1998 in the upward direction and some quite large.

[6] More than fifty years ago, the Stigler Commission (Stigler, 1961) wrote: "If a poll were taken of economists and statisticians, in all probability they would designate (and by a wide margin) the failure of price indexes to take full account of quality changes as the most important defect of these indexes." There is a vast literature that comments on the effect of product innovation on the difficulty of measuring real output, reaching back to Sidgwick (1883), Marshall (1887), Kuznets (1934), Kuznets, Epstein, and Jenks (1941), and including, among others, Griliches (1992), the Boskin Commission (1996), Nordhaus (1997), Hausman (1996, 1999, 2003), and Gordon (2016). The NBER Conference on Research in Income and Wealth has focused attention on this issue for more than eighty years; see Hulten (2015).

change is what the government calls the "resource cost method," which indicates that the method primarily estimates the cost of production rather than the value to consumers and other end-users.

The Bureau of Labor Statistics (BLS) follows more than 5,000 product categories. For each, it asks the manufacturer: "Has the product changed since the time of the last survey?" If the answer is "no," then any change in the price of the product is correctly regarded as inflation and there is no quality change. But if the manufacturer says "yes, the current model is different from the previous one," the BLS asks about the "marginal cost of the new input requirements that are directly tied to the change in product quality."

If and only if there is a reported increase in the *cost* of making the product does the BLS conclude that there is a quality improvement. This is a narrow and incorrect way to measure quality improvement. In reality, of course, producers improve products in ways that don't cost more and may cost less. Indeed, that is the essence of technical progress.

But the "resource cost method" focuses on the cost of inputs rather than on the true value of the output. That is why the government doesn't measure the "output" change; it measures only the volume of inputs. I have described this for products, but the same approach is generally applied to services. This is true for health care, where there have been enormous improvements in the quality of care over the years but where the official statistics imply that productivity has been declining for many years!

Let me be clear: I recognize that the problem of measuring quality change is a very difficult one, so I am not being critical of the efforts of government statisticians. My point is that these estimates are mislabeled and misinterpreted. When it comes to quality change of existing products, what is called "quality change" is really the growth of real inputs. The result is probably a major underestimate of the growth of real GDP that comes from quality improvements.[7]

The other major source of underestimation of real GDP growth is the failure to capture the benefits of new goods and services. The current procedure works as follows: First, a new product or service is developed and sold to the public, and its market sales enter into nominal GDP. Second, the nominal value of GDP is converted to real GDP using price indexes that do not reflect the new

---

[7] See Fernald (2014), Syverson (2016), and Byrne, Fernald, and Reinsdorf (2016) for a discussion of the recent productivity slowdown. They provide convincing analysis that the recent slowdown cannot be explained by the fact that services provided by Google and a few other companies are omitted from GDP because they are not sold at market prices but are provided without charge and supported by the advertising revenue.

product at all. The process therefore never takes into account the value created by the new product per se.

Consider, for example, the introduction of statins, the pharmaceutical product that lowers cholesterol and reduces deaths from heart attacks and strokes. Within a few years of being introduced, statin drugs had become the bestselling pharmaceutical products in history. When the patents on statins expired and the prices of those products fell, the BLS concluded that, since statins could be bought at a lower price, real incomes had increased. But nothing in this process reflected the improvements to health and longevity and the reduced costs to hospitals that resulted from the introduction of statins.

The major contribution that statins made to public health was never reflected in real output and real incomes. The National Center for Health Statistics (2011) finds that between 2000 and 2007, the percentage of men over age sixty-five taking a statin doubled to 50 percent. High cholesterol levels fell to half of what they had been and death rates from heart disease among those over age sixty-five fell by one-third. But none of this remarkable contribution to the public's well-being was reflected in real GDP.

To summarize this discussion of the mismeasurement of the growth of real GDP, official methods do not capture the contribution of new products and understate the contribution of improvements in quality because they measure the increase in the cost of inputs rather than the value of outputs. To the extent that the official method of converting nominal GDP to real GDP understates the rise in real GDP, it also overstates the implicit rate of inflation.

2.2.2 From GDP to Personal Incomes

The official census data report that median real household incomes rose by less than 10 percent between 1984 and 2013, which translates to an annual rate of growth of less than 0.4 percent a year (Weicher, 2016). A study by the Congressional Budget Office (CBO) (2014) that examined the middle quintile of households in the thirty-two years from 1979 to 2011 confirmed that the real cash earnings of these households rose by about the same annual rate as median household incomes.

But these middle-class households receive near-cash benefits from employers and the government, including health insurance and food stamps. Moreover, the federal tax share paid by these middle-class households also fell during those years from 19 percent to 11.5 percent.

Taking these omissions into account, the CBO calculated the real incomes of these middle quintile households to have increased by 45 percent over the same thirty-two years, which is more than three times the size of the gain reported using census data. And – as described in Section 2.2.1 – that estimate is based on the overstated GDP price index that is implicit in the calculation of real GDP, which further understates the gain in real incomes to middle-class households in recent years.

2.3 Budget Deficits and Future Growth

2.3.1 Rising Deficits and Debt

Although real GDP and personal incomes have grown rapidly in the recent past, the future will see a lower rate of growth. In the next few years, the economy may slip into a recession after nearly a decade of strong growth. But looking past that potential recession to the rest of the decade and beyond, we are likely to see lower growth because of the rapid rise in the fiscal deficit and the national debt.

Before the economic downturn that began in 2007, the federal debt was generally less than 40 percent of GDP. By 2017, the debt as a share of GDP had nearly doubled to about 75 percent. And looking ahead to the year 2028, the CBO (2018) projects that the debt will be 96 percent of GDP. Annual fiscal deficits are also projected to increase. The deficit was 3.5 percent in 2017 and is projected by the CBO (2018) to rise to 5.1 percent in 2028.

These official projected deficit and debt levels are based on the CBO convention of making forecasts based on current law. The CBO does not use its judgment to guess what will happen that is not in current law. For example, the 2017 tax legislation reduced personal tax rates substantially, but those reductions are scheduled to expire in 2025 (Joint Committee on Taxation, 2018b). If Congress votes to maintain the lower tax rates after 2025, deficits will be substantially higher.

Congress recently voted to increase defense spending slightly to 3.1 percent of GDP in 2018 and to raise the level of nondefense discretionary spending to 3.3 percent in 2018. But current law specifies that defense spending will decline to 2.6 percent of GDP in 2028 and that nondefense discretionary spending will also decrease to 2.8 percent of GDP in 2028 (CBO, 2018). The history of defense outlays in the past and the challenges facing the US military around the world suggest that defense spending will rise more rapidly than current law implies. For example, defense outlays in

1970 were 8.1 percent of GDP and in 1980 were 4.4 percent of GDP.[8] If Congress votes to raise defense outlays, Democrats are likely to insist on an equal increase in nondefense discretionary outlays.

An increase in defense and nondefense discretionary spending and a continuation of the current tax rates after 2025 would cause the deficit in 2028 to rise substantially from the currently projected 5.1 percent. In the long-run equilibrium, the debt to GDP ratio is equal to the ratio of the annual deficit to the rate of nominal GDP growth. If the future deficit rises from 5.1 percent to 7 percent and the growth rate of nominal GDP is 4 percent, the implied equilibrium debt to GDP ratio would be 7/4 = 175 percent. Of course, if that were the future debt ratio, the interest rate on the federal debt would rise, causing the deficit and the debt to be even higher.

Even without these future changes in tax rules and budget outlays, the equilibrium debt to GDP ratio will exceed 100 percent. Combining the CBO (2018) estimate of the 2028 deficit of 5.1 percent of GDP with a plausible nominal GDP growth rate of 4 percent would imply an equilibrium debt to GDP ratio of more than 125 percent. That would be enough to cause a higher interest rate on government debt, which would further raise the deficit and the debt.

2.3.2 The Impact of the Rising Deficit and Debt on Future Economic Growth

A larger annual budget deficit and an increasing debt to GDP ratio can slow the growth of real GDP through several channels. The key mechanism is a reduction in investment in plant and equipment and in research and development.

The most direct impact of deficits and the debt on investment is in absorbing funds that would otherwise be invested in plant and equipment or used by firms to finance research and development. Since the combination of household saving and corporate retained earnings is only about 8 percent of GDP, a fiscal deficit that is approaching 5 percent of GDP or higher will absorb more than half of national savings. After offsetting the funds needed for investment in residential construction, there is little left for business investment.

---

[8] Office of Management and Budget Data, "National Defense Outlays for Major Public Direct Physical Capital Investment 1940–2020," www.whitehouse.gov/wp-content/up loads/2019/03/hist-fy2020.pdf, table 9.4.

Business investment is also discouraged by higher real interest rates. Large-scale government borrowing to finance the budget deficit causes real interest rates to rise. The higher interest rates then discourage borrowing by businesses to finance business investment.

Even when the annual deficit isn't large, the cumulative effect of past deficits produces a large national debt. Households and other portfolio investors require higher interest rates to hold the larger quantity of government debt. And those higher interest rates raise the cost of capital to firms and reduce business investment.

Higher interest rates also depress equity prices and thereby raise the cost of equity capital. Business investment responds to the higher cost of equity capital by reducing business investment.

Increases in budget deficits and debt also cause business decision-makers to fear that taxes will have to be raised in future years to service the future debt or to reduce those deficits. This expectation of higher future taxes also discourages current investment.

2.3.3 The Sources of Rising Deficits and Debt

The adverse effect on economic growth of larger deficits makes it important to understand the sources of the larger deficits. The annual deficit is projected by the CBO (2018) to rise from 4.0 percent of GDP in 2018 to 5.1 percent in 2028. Why will that happen?

Much attention has been focused on the tax legislation enacted in 2017 (Joint Committee on Taxation, 2018a). The legislation was designed subject to a mandatory limit on the resulting debt increase over ten years of $1.5 trillion. The corporate tax changes added $500 billion to the ten-year debt forecast and the changes in the personal income tax added the other $1 trillion. The CBO (2018) estimates that the tax legislation raised the national debt in 2028 from 91 percent of GDP to 96 percent of GDP, reflecting the fact that the $1.5 trillion would be 5 percent of the 2028 GDP of $30 trillion.

More generally, the CBO (2018) forecasts that total annual tax revenue will rise from 16.6 percent of GDP in 2018 to 18.5 percent in 2028. Thus, the annual revenue as a percentage of GDP will increase by 1.9 percent of GDP over the decade despite the permanent corporate tax cut.

What else has been driving the deficits and debt during the coming ten years? As noted in Section 2.3.1, it is not discretionary spending on defense or nondefense programs. Defense outlays as a percentage of GDP are forecast to decline from 3.1 percent of GDP in 2018 to 2.6 percent of GDP in 2028. Similarly, nondefense discretionary programs are forecast to decline from

3.3 percent of GDP in 2018 to 2.8 percent in 2028 (CBO, 2018). Thus, each is projected to decline by 0.5 percent of GDP, implying that total discretionary spending will fall by 1 percent of GDP during the coming decade.

Interest payments on the national debt are projected to rise from 1.4 percent of GDP in 2018 to 2.4 percent of GDP in 2028. This reflects the combination of the larger national debt and the higher interest rate that the government will pay on that debt. The extra 1 percent of GDP that the government will pay in interest on the national debt just balances the reduced outlays on discretionary spending.

All of the net increase in the 2028 deficit comes from the increased outlays on Social Security and the major health programs, Medicare and Medicaid. The CBO (2018) projects that outlays for Social Security will rise from 4.9 percent of GDP in 2018 to 6.0 percent in 2028, a rise of 1.1 percent of GDP. During the same time period, outlays for Medicare and Medicaid will rise from 5.4 percent of GDP to 7.3 percent of GDP.

The higher cost of the Social Security program reflects the aging of the population and the higher percentage of the population choosing to retire at younger ages. The higher cost of the Medicare and Medicaid programs also reflects the aging of the population as more people are becoming eligible for Medicare and Medicaid and choosing to be covered by those programs. But the rising cost of the health programs also reflects the changing health of the older population and the increasing cost of medical care.

Looking further ahead, the healthcare programs are the major source of rising outlays. The CBO (2018) estimates that, with no change in program rules, the outlays for the health programs will rise in the twenty years after 2028 from 6.8 percent of GDP to 9.2 percent of GDP. In those same years, the outlays for the Social Security program will increase only from 6.0 percent of GDP to 6.3 percent of GDP.

It is clear that slowing the growth of the deficit requires changing the Social Security and healthcare program rules. Dealing with the healthcare programs involves a much more complicated set of changes than slowing the growth of Social Security. Section 2.5 discusses how policy changes could slow the growth of Social Security, but, before then, I turn to how revenue might be raised without causing the adverse effects on growth that would result from higher tax rates on individuals and businesses.

2.4 Raising Revenues

Raising tax rates on households and businesses would reduce budget deficits but would also directly hurt economic growth. It is possible, however, to raise revenue without the disincentive effects of raising tax rates. There are two ways to achieve this: limiting tax expenditures and taxing the sources of carbon emissions.

2.4.1 Limiting Tax Expenditures

Tax expenditures are features of the tax code that substitute for direct government spending. For example, because the government wants to encourage home ownership, it allows individuals to deduct mortgage interest payments when calculating taxable income. Similarly, to encourage the purchase of health insurance, the tax rules exclude employer payments for health insurance from taxable income. The revenue loss from such deductions, exclusions, and credits was $1.6 trillion in 2014 (Feldstein, 2015).

Limiting tax expenditures would not only raise revenue but would also reduce the efficiency losses that result from distorting expenditure decisions. Eliminating deductions would also simplify tax filing by causing taxpayers to shift from itemizing deductions to using the standard deduction.

The 2017 tax legislation took a step in this direction by limiting the deductibility of state and local taxes. Walczak (2017) estimates that this change will raise $100 billion a year and induce a large number of taxpayers to shift from itemizing to using the standard deduction.

2.4.2 Taxing Bads

Taxing output and income discourages desirable activities and hurts economic growth. But taxing bad activities is desirable because it discourages those activities. The leading candidate for this is the taxation of carbon emissions that create climate change problems.

The most practical and efficient way to do this is to tax the production of coal, oil, and gas. Producers would pass these taxes on in the form of higher prices. The users of these products – businesses and households – would respond to the higher prices by reducing their use of these products. For example, a higher tax on oil would lead to a higher price of gasoline, causing users to drive less and to prefer smaller cars.

The separate tax rates on oil, coal, and natural gas could be set so that each of them had the same effect on the production of carbon dioxide. Gale, Brown, and Saltiel (2013) calculate that setting the rates equivalent to $40 per metric ton of CO_2 would produce revenue of about 1 percent of GDP.

2.5 Slowing the Growth of Social Security

Slowing the growth of Social Security will contribute to faster growth of real GDP in two ways. First, it will increase national savings by reducing future budget deficits and the need for higher taxes in the future. Second, lower future Social Security benefits will encourage working-age individuals to increase their own saving for retirement.

The politically simplest way to slow the growth of Social Security benefits would be to repeat the kind of change that was enacted in 1983 (DeWitt, 2010). At that time, the White House and Congress agreed on a bipartisan basis to raise the age for full benefits from sixty-five to sixty-seven. To protect those individuals who were near retirement age, the legislation provided for a delay before the increase would begin and, more importantly, for a very gradual rate of increase. After the initial delay, the age for full benefits was scheduled to rise at a rate of just one month per year. The two-year increase in the age for full benefits would therefore take more than twenty-five years.

The great advantage of this combination of delay and gradual rise is that it was enacted on a bipartisan basis and never experienced any political opposition as it was gradually phased in. Although later polls showed that the public opposed plans to raise the age for full benefits, no member of Congress ever introduced legislation to repeal the original delay in the age for full benefits.

When fully phased in, the two-year delay in benefit availability had a substantial effect on the cost of the Social Security program. An individual of age sixty-five in 1983 had a life expectancy of about eighteen years.[9] Since benefits are now actuarially adjusted to age sixty-seven regardless of the individual's actual age of retirement, raising the age for full benefits by two years reduced the expected number of years of benefits from eighteen to sixteen, a reduction of about 11 percent. Since Social Security benefits are now about 5 percent of GDP and are expected to rise to 6.3 percent, the 11 percent reduction amounts to about 0.6 percent of GDP (Congressional Budget Office, 2016).

Raising the retirement age from sixty-five to sixty-seven also had a positive effect on the private savings rate. Since individuals typically retire before the age of full benefits, it is likely that raising the age for full benefits would cause most individuals to leave their actual retirement age

---

[9] CDC (Kenneth D. Kochanek, Sherry L. Murphy, and Jiaquan Xu), 2015. "Deaths: Final Data for 2011." *National Vital Statistics Reports* 63 (3), 27 July, p. 31, table 8: "Life expectancy at birth, by race, Hispanic origin, race for non-Hispanic population, and sex: United States, 1940, 1950, 1960, 1970 and 1975–2011," www.cdc.gov/nchs/data/nvsr/nvsr63/nvsr63_03.pdf.

unchanged or increased only slightly. As a result, their annual benefits would be reduced by the corresponding actuarial reduction. These individuals would then have an incentive to increase their lifetime saving rates to maintain their consumption in retirement.

Since 1983 – when the legislation to delay the age for full benefits was enacted – life expectancy for individuals at age sixty-seven has increased by about three years.[10] It seems reasonable therefore to raise the full benefit retirement age by another three years, from sixty-seven to seventy; this would reduce the number of expected benefit years from about seventeen years to fourteen years, a reduction of about 18 percent. The 18 percent reduction in benefits would reduce benefits by about 1 percent of GDP.

Although these are large savings in the Social Security program, they do not fix its most important problem. The rules that govern the Social Security program provide that its payroll taxes are all deposited into the Social Security Trust Fund. The Trust Fund is not a true investment fund that invests in stocks and bonds; it is essentially an accounting system that keeps track of the funds deposited and the benefits paid out. The Trust Fund receives interest from the government on the accumulated net difference between past taxes and past benefits. It also receives the personal income tax revenue that the government collects from upper-income retirees.

The key fact about the Trust Fund is that all Social Security benefits must be paid out of it. Thus, aggregate annual benefits now exceed aggregate payroll taxes. The other sources of income of the Trust Fund have slowed the rate at which the Trust Fund balance is declining, yet the Social Security actuaries now estimate that the Trust Fund will be exhausted in 2034, just over a decade from now. Slowing the growth of benefits by raising the retirement age would delay the time of exhaustion but would not prevent the Trust Fund from eventually reaching zero.

It isn't clear what will happen then since, under current law, benefits can be paid only when there is a positive balance in the Trust Fund. Social Security payroll taxes will, of course, continue to be collected in the future and the 12.4 percent payroll tax revenue that will be deposited in that year in the Trust Fund will be enough to pay about two-thirds of the benefits that are projected for that year. It would be possible but unlikely to cut the benefits by one-third so that they could be financed by the available revenue.

An alternative option would be to raise the payroll tax rate. If the age of full retirement is not adjusted, it would take an increase of the payroll tax from 12.4 percent to about 19 percent to meet the cost of the benefits

[10] Ibid.

projected under current law in 2034. Yet a further option would be to supplement the funds going into the Trust Fund with transfers from general revenue. It would take a transfer equal to about 5 percent of GDP to maintain the benefits. Total tax collections are less than 20 percent of GDP and personal income taxes are less than 10 percent of GDP, therefore the increase in taxes to maintain benefits would be equal to 50 percent of personal income taxes or 25 percent of total taxes (CBO, 2018).

I have proposed an alternative approach to the Social Security financing problem in research with Andrew Samwick (Feldstein and Samwick, 1998). The basic idea is a mixed system that continues the current pay-as-you-go system with a 12.4 percent payroll tax but supplements the pay-as-you-go benefits with investment-based annuities. In our research, we showed that the pay-as-you-go benefits could be gradually reduced while the investment-based benefits grow. The combination would yield benefits as large as the benefits projected under current law.

The Feldstein-Samwick option would work as follows:

(1) Each individual would continue to have a pay-as-you-go Social Security account to which the employee and the employer would continue to contribute 12.4 percent of covered earnings.

(2) In addition, each individual would have a Personal Retirement Account that would be invested in a mixture of stocks and bonds. We assumed that the portfolio would be 60 percent in a broad stock index like the Standard and Poor's 500 or the Russell 3000. The bonds would be high-quality investment bonds. Historic experience shows that such a mixture would generate a real return of 5.5 percent a year.

(3) The individuals would be required to deposit 1.5 percent of their payroll earnings each year into their Personal Retirement Account.

(4) The government would transfer 1.5 percent of payroll earnings to the Personal Retirement Account. That is essentially equivalent to reducing the 12.4 percent pay-as-you-go tax by 1.5 percent.[11]

(5) The Trust Fund would therefore grow more slowly than it would under current law.

(6) The pay-as-you-go benefits would also be calibrated to grow more slowly than under current law so that the Trust Fund would not be exhausted.

[11] Some of the current 12.4 percent pay-as-you-go tax is used to finance the disability program. We would continue to use part of the pay-as-you-go-tax for the disability program.

(7) Individuals would receive the reduced pay-as-you-go benefits and an annuity financed by their Personal Retirement Account.

Our research showed that it would be possible to slow the pay-as-you-go benefits in a way that met two criteria: (i) the Trust Fund would never be exhausted, and (ii) the combination of the pay-as-you-go benefits and the Personal Retirement Account annuity would equal or exceed the pay-as-you-go benefits scheduled under current law.

The mixed system would contribute to long-run growth in three ways: (1) by increasing the personal savings rate due to the extra 1.5 percent that individuals would contribute to their Personal Retirement Account; (2) by earning a return on Personal Retirement Accounts; and (3) by eliminating the need for a sharp increase in future tax rates.

2.6 Summary

This chapter began by explaining why the United States has experienced higher real GDP growth rates than other industrial countries. Section 2.2 then discussed the ways in which the government methods of measuring real GDP growth have led to an understatement of the true rate of increase in real output and real incomes. Section 2.3 dealt with the ways in which future increases in budget deficits and the national debt will slow the growth of real GDP. Section 2.4 showed that deficits can be reduced by tax changes that do not discourage favorable economic activities. Finally, Section 2.5 discussed how changes in the Social Security program – the largest program in the government budget – could increase savings and avoid the need for large future taxes.

References

Boskin Commission, comprising Michael J. Boskin, Ellen R. Dulberger, Zvi Griliches, Robert J. Gordon, and Dale Jorgensen, 1996. "Toward a More Accurate Measure of the Cost of Living." Final report to the Senate Finance Committee for the Advisory Commission to Study the Consumer Price Index. US Senate, Finance Committee, Washington, DC.

Boskin, Michael J., 2000. "Economic Measurement: Progress and Challenges." *American Economic Review* 90 (2), 247–52.

Byrne, David M., John G. Fernald, and Marshall B. Reinsdorf, 2016. "Does the United States Have a Productivity Slowdown or a Measurement Problem?" *Brookings Papers on Economic Activity* 47 (1), 109–57.

CDC (Kenneth D. Kochanek, Sherry L. Murphy, and Jiaquan Xu), 2015. "Deaths: Final Data for 2011." *National Vital Statistics Reports* 63 (3), 27 July, p. 31, table 8: "Life

Expectancy at Birth, by Race, Hispanic Origin, Race for Non-Hispanic Population, and Sex: United States, 1940, 1950, 1960, 1970 and 1975–2011," www.cdc.gov/nchs/data/nvsr/nvsr63/nvsr63_03.pdf.

Congressional Budget Office (CBO), 2014. *The Distribution of Household Income and Federal Taxes, 2011*. Congressional Budget Office, Washington, DC.

Congressional Budget Office (CBO), 2016. *Spending for Social Security and Major Health Care Programs in the Long-Term Budget Outlook*. Congressional Budget Office, Washington, DC.

Congressional Budget Office (CBO), 2018. *The Budget and Economic Outlook: 2018 to 2028*. Congressional Budget Office, Washington, DC.

DeWitt, Larry, 2010. "The Future Financial Status of the Social Security Program." *Social Security Bulletin* 70 (3), 1–2.

Feldstein, Martin, 2005. "Rethinking Social Insurance." NBER Working Paper No. 11250. National Bureau of Economic Research, Cambridge, MA.

Feldstein, Martin, 2015. "Raising Revenue by Limiting Tax Expenditures." *Tax Policy and the Economy* 29 (1), 1–11.

Feldstein, Martin, 2017a. "Underestimating the Real Growth of GDP, Personal Incomes, and Productivity." NBER Working Paper No. 23306. National Bureau of Economic Research, Cambridge, MA.

Feldstein, Martin, 2017b. "Why Is Growth Better in the United States than in Other Industrial Countries?" NBER Working Paper No. 23221. National Bureau of Economic Research, Cambridge, MA.

Feldstein, Martin, 2018. "The Future of Economic Growth in the United States." Hoover Institution Economics Working Paper No. 18122. Hoover Institution, Stanford, CA.

Feldstein, Martin and Andrew Samwick, 1998. "The Transition Path in Privatizing Social Security." In Martin Feldstein (ed.), *Privatizing Social Security*, 215–64. University of Chicago Press, Chicago, IL.

Fernald, John G., 2014. "Productivity and Potential Output Before, During and After the Great Recession." NBER Working Paper No. 20248. National Bureau of Economic Research, Cambridge, MA.

Gale, William, Samuel Brown, and Fernando Saltiel, 2013. "Carbon Taxes as Part of the Fiscal Solution." Report. Brookings Institution, Washington, DC.

Gordon, Robert J., 2016. *The Rise and Fall of American Growth: The US Standard of Living Since the Civil War*. Princeton University Press, Princeton, NJ.

Greenspan, Alan, 1997. "Financial Reform and the Importance of a Decentralized Banking Structure: Remarks at the Annual Convention of the Independent Bankers Association of America," March 22, Phoenix, Arizona.

Griliches, Zvi (ed.), 1992. *Output Measurement in the Service Sectors. National Bureau of Economic Research Studies in Income and Wealth*. University of Chicago Press, Chicago, IL.

Hausman, Jerry A, 1996. "Valuation of New Goods under Perfect and Imperfect Competition." In Timothy Bresnahan and Robert J. Gordon (eds.), *The Economics of New Goods*, 207–48. University of Chicago Press, Chicago, IL.

Hausman, Jerry A, 1999. "Cellular Telephone, New Products, and the CPI." *Journal of Business and Economic Statistics* 17 (2), 188–94.

Hausman, Jerry A, 2003. "Sources of Bias and Solutions to Bias in the Consumer Price Index." *Journal of Economic Perspectives* 17 (1), 23–44.

Hulten, Charles R, 2015. "Measuring the Economy of the 21st Century." NBER Reporter (4), 1–7. National Bureau of Economic Research, Cambridge, MA.

Joint Committee on Taxation, 2018a. *General Explanation of Public Law No. 115–97 (JCS-1-18)*. Joint Committee on Taxation, Washington, DC.

Joint Committee on Taxation, 2018b. *List of Expiring Federal Tax Provisions 2016–2027 (JCX-1-18)*. Joint Committee on Taxation, Washington, DC.

Kuznets, Simon, 1934, *National Income, 1929–1932*. National Bureau of Economic Research, New York, NY.

Kuznets, Simon, Lillian Epstein, and Elizabeth Jenks, 1941. *National Income and Its Composition, 1919–1938, Volume I*. National Bureau of Economic Research, New York, NY.

Landefeld, J. Steven, Eugene P. Seskin, and Barbara L. Fraumeni, 2008. "Taking the Pulse of the Economy: Measuring GDP." *Journal of Economic Perspectives* 22 (2), 193–216.

Marshall, Alfred, 1887. "Remedies for Fluctuations of General Prices." In A. C. Pigou (ed.), *Memorials of Alfred Marshall*. MacMillan and Co., London, UK.

National Center for Health Statistics, 2011. *Health, United States, 2010: With Special Feature on Death and Dying*. National Center for Health Statistics, Washington, DC.

Nordhaus, William D, 1997. "Traditional Productivity Estimates Are Asleep at the (Technological) Switch." *Economic Journal* 107 (444), 1548–59.

Roxburgh, Charles, Jan Mischke, Baudouin Regout, Davide Archetti, Alexandre Chau, Paolo D'Aprile, Akshat Harbola, Harald Proff, Dirk Schmautzer, Manuela Thomys, and Andreas Weber, 2010. "Beyond Austerity: A Path to Economic Growth and Renewal in Europe." Report. McKinsey Global Institute, New York, NY.

Sidgwick, Henry, 1883. *The Principles of Political Economy*. MacMillan and Co., London, UK.

Stigler, George (ed.), 1961. "The Price Statistics of the Federal Government." Report to the Office of Statistical Standards, Bureau of the Budget. National Bureau of Economic Research, New York, NY.

Syverson, Chad, 2016. "Challenges to Mismeasurement Explanations for the U.S. Productivity Slowdown." Working Paper No. 21974. National Bureau of Economic Research, Cambridge, MA.

US Bureau of Economic Analysis, 2015. "Updated Summary of NIPA Methodologies." *Survey of Current Business* 95 (11), 1–20.

Walczak, Jared, 2017. "The State and Local Tax Deduction: A Primer." Fiscal Fact No. 545. Tax Foundation, Washington, DC.

Weicher, John C., 2016. *The Distribution of Wealth in America, 1983–2013*. Hudson Institute, Washington, DC.

PART II

LABOR AND ECONOMIC GROWTH

Human Capital and Long-Run Economic Growth

Flávio Cunha

3.1 Introduction

Recent research on labor productivity and labor income inequality has captured the attention of academia and policy-makers alike. Gordon (2016) provides a compelling argument that the growth rate of innovation in the US economy has been decreasing over time. Figure 3.1 illustrates this fact and shows the yearly growth rate of labor productivity from 1948 to 2016. The geometric average growth rate for the entire period is approximately 2.35 percent per year, which means that the level of labor productivity at the end of 2016 was almost five times greater than that at the beginning of 1948. Figure 3.1 highlights the disturbing fact that there is a downward trend in the growth rate of productivity over this period. To quantify the relevance of this reduction in growth rates, I divide the entire period into two segments – the first from 1948 to 1981 and the second from 1982 to 2016 – and then compute the average growth rate within each segment. This partition shows that the growth rate declined from about 2.75 percent per year in the first period to a little less than 2 percent per year in the second period. If the growth rate in the second segment had been as large as in the first, then the level of productivity at the end of 2016 would have been six and a half times that found at the beginning of 1948.

Piketty (2014) documents an increase in economic inequality. Figure 3.2 depicts the time series of the share of national income that is allocated to the top 10 percent of income earners, from 1948 to 2014. Between 1948 and 1981, the share decreases from a little below 39 percent to less than 35 percent. From 1981 to 2014, the share increases to 47 percent.[1] While the

---

[1] These data are available through the World Inequality Database (WID) at https://wid .world/. These estimates are based on pre-tax income, so they do not include government transfers. Similarly, measures of labor income do not include fringe benefits, including

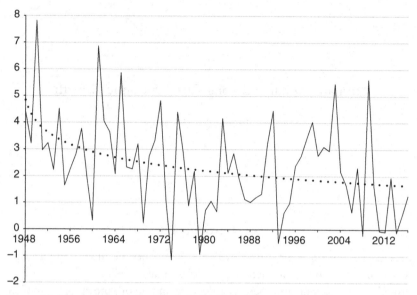

Figure 3.1 Labor productivity growth in the United States, 1948–2016
Source: Bureau of Labor Statistics, www.bls.gov/bls/productivity.htm.

literature on inequality focuses on the share of the income of the top 1 percent, I focus on the top 10 percent. In spite of this difference, the story is the same: there is a robust increase in income inequality. However, the focus on the top 10 percent makes it clear that the increase in inequality is not only due to the increase in the returns to physical capital, because there are many workers in the group of the top 10 percent of income earners. In fact, as I show in Section 3.3, the increase in inequality presented in Figure 3.2 is partially attributable to an increase in the returns to education. For example, Valletta (2017) shows that the college premium increased from approximately 23 percent in 1979 to around 45 percent in 2015 and that the premium for a graduate degree rose from roughly 30 percent to nearly 70 percent over the same period.

The downward trend in labor productivity and the upward trend in income inequality are themselves correlated with trends in human capital

healthcare insurance premiums, which have been increasing over time. However, accord- ing to the Bureau of Labor Statistics (2019), there is inequality in access to benefits: the higher the wage rate, the higher the fraction of workers who receive benefits (e.g., retirement, healthcare insurance, life insurance, and paid vacation). As a result, the inequality in weekly earnings represents a lower bound on inequality once we include fringe benefits.

Figure 3.2 Top 10 percent national income shares in the United States, 1948–2014
Source: World Inequality Database, https://wid.world/data/.

formation. Since the 1980s, the US economy has lagged behind its Organisation for Economic Co-operation and Development (OECD) peers in terms of the growth rate of the share of the population with a tertiary education. This includes not only the students who obtain a four-year college degree but also those individuals who acquire a certificate from a technical program (e.g., an associate's degree in welding or nursing). Figure 3.3 compares the share of workers between fifty-five and sixty-four years old with a tertiary education certificate in 2014 with the share of workers who were twenty-five to thirty-four years old with a tertiary education certificate in the same year. When we focus on the older cohort, the United States was the country with the fourth highest share of workers with a tertiary education, surpassed only by the Russian Federation, Canada, and Israel. However, this is no longer true for the younger cohort because an additional eight countries (Australia, Ireland, Japan, Luxembourg, New Zealand, Norway, South Korea, and United Kingdom) have higher shares. Figure 3.3 ranks countries from right to left in order of the growth in the share of workers with a tertiary education. South Korea occupies the first position in the ranking because its share increased from about 14 percent in the older cohort to nearly 66 percent in the younger. The United States is next to last

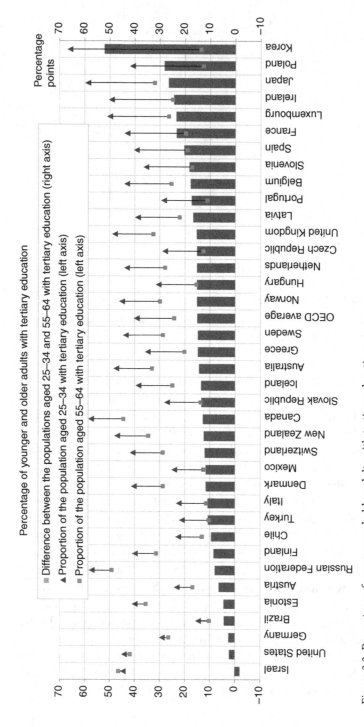

Figure 3.3 Percentage of younger and older adults with tertiary education
Source: "Education at a Glance 2016," Organisation for Economic Co-operation and Development, http://download.ei-ie.org/Docs/WebDepot/ EaG2016_EN.pdf.

because it showed no gain whatsoever. According to the Survey of Adult Skills (OECD, 2016) conducted by the OECD, the picture is very similar when we order countries according to literacy proficiency, with virtually little to no gain across cohorts for the United States. In contrast, in many OECD countries, young workers have not only surpassed the literacy proficiency of the older workers in their own country but also surpassed the literacy rates of both young and old US workers.

To see how these trends in human capital formation can simultaneously explain decelerating productivity and accelerating inequality, I start from the model constructed by Nelson and Phelps (1966), who propose that human capital facilitates technology adoption. Their analysis suggests that the cost of adopting new technologies increases as skilled labor becomes more expensive. The lower the rate of return to research and development (R&D), the smaller the amount of investment in R&D and, consequentially, the lower the growth rate of technical progress. If the growth rate of labor productivity is proportional to the growth rate of technical progress (Romer 1990), then a reduction in the growth rate of the supply of skilled labor drives a decrease in the growth rate of labor productivity.

Katz and Murphy (1992) have shown that the dynamics of the wage premium are determined by the dynamics of the growth rate of the demand for and supply of skilled labor (relative to the demand for and supply of unskilled labor). To illustrate this argument, suppose that the growth rate of the demand for skilled labor were constant over time. If there were a reduction in the growth rate of the relative supply of skilled labor, then there would be an increase in the wage premium, and this increase would be larger the lower the elasticity of substitution between skilled and unskilled labor.[2] Therefore, a model in which skilled labor is not only a direct input in the production of final goods (Katz and Murphy, 1992) but also an input in technology adoption (Nelson and Phelps, 1966) could simultaneously generate a downward trend in the growth rate of labor productivity and an upward trend in income inequality as a product of the lower growth rate of the relative supply of skilled labor. Section 3.2 elaborates on this

---

[2] The assumption that the growth rate of the relative demand for skilled labor remains constant is not internally consistent because if skilled labor influences the costs of technology adoption, then the growth rate of the supply of skilled labor should also influence the growth rate of the demand for skilled labor. However, the qualitative analysis is still correct if the direct reduction in the growth rate of the relative supply of skilled labor is greater than (in absolute value) its indirect effect in the reduction in the growth rate of relative demand.

issue more deeply by presenting the canonical model of endogenous growth; it uses two case studies to highlight the role that human capital plays in determining long-run economic growth.

The combination of the Nelson-Phelps and Katz-Murphy models suggests that a reversal of the trends in human capital formation could help reverse the trends in labor productivity and inequality. Therefore, it is important to review the empirical literature on human capital formation and to identify potential bottlenecks that prevent an increase in the growth rate of skilled labor. Section 3.3 starts by considering the data on post-secondary enrollment and attainment. I review evidence that shows that unconditional attainment rates have grown at a slower pace even though enrollment rates have grown much faster. The divergence between enrollment and attainment rates seems to be explained by the fact that the marginal enrollee is not college ready. Therefore, it does not seem to be feasible to increase college attainment simply by increasing access to college.

Section 3.3 also discusses literature that decomposes college readiness in terms of cognitive and noncognitive skills, demonstrating that socioeconomic inequality in college readiness starts to emerge early on in the lives of children. I finish Section 3.3 by showing that inequality in skills is associated with inequality in investments, and I further summarize literature that documents that the inequality in skills that make up college readiness as well as inequality in investments into those skills have been growing over time.

Section 3.4 summarizes the literature on human capital formation based on experimental data. These data have a dual role. First, I show that the experimental manipulation of investments in the human capital of children and adolescents leads to higher levels of cognitive and noncognitive skills. Second, the experiments I consider are by themselves interesting because they can be feasibly adopted as policy interventions. A common message across all of the successful interventions that I summarize in Section 3.4 is that they are broad in their objectives: they form both cognitive and noncognitive skills. This finding suggests that it is important for policy-makers and researchers in the economics of education to abandon their narrow focus on cognitive skills and standardized tests and to embrace the importance of other dimensions of human capital. Additionally, the focus of research and policy should not be cast by decisions about early versus late, but, rather, which dimensions of human capital should be targets of intervention in different stages of the life cycle.

3.2 Human Capital and Long-Run Economic Growth

Heckman and Masterov (2007) provide a thorough summary of the literature that shows how increases in human capital not only lead to higher labor force productivity but also reduce the probability of involvement in criminal activities and increase labor force participation (and thus reduce welfare dependency). I will postpone discussion about the research on costs and benefits of specific strategies to invest in human capital to Section 3.4. In this section, I focus instead on a different channel that links human capital to economic prosperity: innovation. I will do so by considering two different case studies: the birth of the biotechnology industry and the formation of industrial clusters such as the semiconductor industry in Silicon Valley since the late 1950s. The discussion of these cases is illustrative of the role that human capital plays in partially determining long-run economic growth; it is also especially relevant for Houston, given the large investment in the expansion of the Texas Medical Center and the formation of the Innovation District in Midtown Houston.

3.2.1 Theory

The theoretical framework that links human capital to long-run economic growth is made clear in the model of endogenous growth proposed by Romer (1990). In Romer's model, long-run economic growth is the result of technological innovation that allows humans to produce a larger amount of output using the same (or sometimes even smaller) amounts of resources. Romer (1990) rescues Arrow's (1962) discovery that technology and ideas are different economic goods because they are nonrival: my use of an idea does not preclude anyone else in the world from using the same idea. In particular, if I have a great idea for an innovative product, someone else can then build on the idea and launch an innovative product in the same or in a completely different field. For example, the invention of the smartphone created opportunities for independent developers to produce innovative new apps. In Romer's model, the production of new ideas uses ideas produced in previous periods as well as human capital, and both of these inputs may generate large knowledge spillovers. In Section 3.2.2, I first discuss two case studies and then present literature that uses patents to document the importance of knowledge spillovers. The lesson that comes from the case studies as well as the research that uses patent data is that the geographic distribution of human capital – which is the embodiment of knowledge – generates geographic concentration of economic activity.

The re-introduction by Romer (1990) of the insight that ideas and technology are nonrival changed a critical foundational element of the economic models used to study economic growth. Traditional models (e.g., Solow (1956)) linked output to the use of physical capital and labor, both of which are rival goods because a firm cannot employ a machine or a worker employed by its competitor at exactly the same time. In these traditional models, the production function exhibits constant returns to scale, meaning that output should double when firms double the use of physical capital and labor. Romer (1990) remarked that the production of goods uses not only rival but also nonrival inputs embedded in technology. This is an important insight because two competing firms can simultaneously use the same technology even though they cannot use the same workers or the same machines. The consequence for the aggregate economy is that aggregate output would more than double if we also doubled not only physical capital and labor but also the productivity of existing technology.

3.2.2 Two Case Studies: The Biotech and Semiconductor Industries

3.2.2.1 The Biotechnology Industry

As described in Evens and Kaitin (2015), the birth of the biotech industry is deeply associated with the path-breaking work by Stanley Cohen and Herbert Boyer who established the technique to combine different sequences of DNA – thereby resulting in a new genetic combination – and to copy this new combination in a very low-cost way.[3] The invention of this technique, in turn, has made it possible to advance medicine by allowing the mass production of insulin and human growth hormone, as well as vaccines for hepatitis B, herpes, and malaria. It has also proved useful in solving crime through DNA fingerprinting. Finally, recombinant DNA has transformed agriculture by allowing scientists to create crops that are resistant to insects and herbicides, thus increasing productivity and improving the quality of food. In the health area alone, in approximately four decades, the biotech industry has seen the birth of about four thousand companies that have developed innovative technologies leading to new products, obtained approval for novel human therapeutics covering

---

[3] The term biotechnology refers to the use of living systems or molecular engineering to create and manufacture biologic therapies and products. In the healthcare industry alone, major product categories include large-molecule proteins; peptides; monoclonal antibodies; cell, tissue, and genetic therapies; liposomes; polymers; and molecularly engineered vaccines.

hundreds of indications, and reached global sales close to $200 billion (Giovannetti and Jaggi, 2014; Truelove, 2013; Lawrence and Lahteenmaki, 2014; Walsh, 2014). The emergence of the biotech industry illustrates the concept of nonrivalry in the Romer model: the development of the technique to recombine and copy DNA unleashed a chain reaction of applications of new ideas, leading to new goods and services that have greatly increased life expectancy and improved the quality of life.

The biotech industry illustrates that the agglomeration of economic activity in a highly innovative sector reflects the agglomeration of sector-specific human capital. The geographical distribution of major firms in the biotech sector reflects the geographic distribution of star researchers in the biotech sector (Zucker, Darby, and Brewer, 1998). In spite of the fact that ideas are nonrival, scientific innovations require knowledge (i.e., human capital) to be able to put these ideas into practice. As proposed in Jacobs (1961), there is an important difference between information and knowledge (both of which are nonrival) in terms of transmission. One can easily codify and disseminate information (such as the price of a share of Johnson & Johnson stock) via public media channels such as newspapers, radio, TV, or even through informal channels such as social media or word-of-mouth. On the other hand, knowledge, especially tacit knowledge (such as how to conduct a polymerase chain reaction, an important step in recombining and copying DNA), is a lot vaguer and thus much harder to codify. In this case, as explained by von Hipple (1994), tacit knowledge is best disseminated through face-to-face interaction and frequent and repeated contact. As noted by Audretsch and Feldman (2004), this distinction between information and tacit knowledge explains why it is possible to have localized knowledge spillovers in modern times. The abundant resources in telecommunications make the cost of disseminating information invariant with respect to distance (it is just as easy for someone in New York and someone in Tokyo to know the price of a stock being traded at any time on the New York Stock Exchange). However, the costs of transmitting tacit knowledge rise steeply with distance, in spite of dramatic improvements in communications technology.

In the context of the biotech industry, the technique for recombinant DNA is tacit knowledge, not information. As explained by Zucker et al. (1998), the returns to this knowledge were far more productive when embodied in a scientist with the genius and vision to continually innovate and define the research frontier and apply the new research techniques in the most promising areas. Furthermore, even if star scientists understand how to apply the technique to create a new product, they will not be able to accomplish much unless they are able to find employees who know how to conduct polymerase chain reactions in order to recombine and copy DNA sequences in ways that are desired. Therefore, existing human capital may be a bottleneck not only for the creation of new products but also for the adoption of the new technology required for the mass production of these new products. If the growth rate of the supply of human capital slows, not only will the speed of innovation eventually start to decrease but also the economy will not be able to produce enough workers to transform codified knowledge into new products.

3.2.2.2 The Semiconductor Industry

The case of the semiconductor industry shows the importance of human capital in innovation and agglomeration even more clearly. As described in Klepper (2010), in the late 1940s, Bell Labs created the transistor – a new "semiconductor" device that could control and amplify electric signals. Bell Labs disseminated its know-how and licensed its transistor patents to other firms because of antitrust pressure. William Shockley, one of the physicists involved in the invention of the transistor, decided to leave Bell Labs and start his own transistor company in California, close to where he had grown up. A major problem of choosing California was that, at that point in time, California did not have a large supply of employees who could readily start working in Shockley's firm. According to Lojek (2007), Shockley was able to solve the employee problem by placing ads in academic journals and traveling across the United States to meet graduate students with knowledge in the area of semiconductors. This focused search yielded eight promising researchers and engineers who formed the core of his new firm – but who quit after one year because they could not work with Shockley. In 1957, the group of eight engineers received not only funding but also a portfolio of customers from Sherman Fairchild, creating Fairchild Semiconductor in Palo Alto (Lécuyer, 2006). After finding key clients such as IBM and the military, the group continued to innovate in the area of integrated circuitry and their success, in turn, inspired some of their employees to leave Fairchild Semiconductor and start their own businesses. This was the start of the spinning-off process that led to the agglomeration of the semiconductor industry in Silicon Valley (Klepper, 2010).

The force behind spinning off and agglomeration relates to the process of intraregion, interfirm mobility of highly qualified workers. Almeida and Kogut (1999) investigate the relationship between the mobility of major patent holders and the localization of technological knowledge through analysis of patent citations of important semiconductor innovations. They find that knowledge localization is specific to only certain regions (particularly Silicon Valley) and that the degree of localization varies across regions. By analyzing data on the interfirm mobility of patent holders, they show empirically that the interfirm mobility of engineers influences the local transfer of knowledge. The main conclusion of their paper is that highly qualified workers in the semiconductor industry in Silicon Valley move from one firm to another and carry knowledge acquired in previous firms to develop new products in new spin-off firms. Again, ideas are nonrival, but it is necessary to have human capital to build on these ideas and continue to invent and innovate.

While a thorough evaluation of policies regulating patents is outside the scope of this chapter, it is important to remark that such policies can have nontrivial effects on growth because they alter the incentives for firms to invest in innovation and change the returns to the acquisition of skills. The research into the economic history of patents suggests that there is little, if any, impact of patents on the level of innovation even though patents may shift the direction of technological change (for a review, see Moser, 2016). This body of evidence confirms theoretical research on the negative impacts of patents on growth (e.g., Boldrin and Levine, 2013). Thus, the theoretical and empirical research on the impact of patents on innovation suggests limiting the scope and the length of time according to which inventions are protected under patent rights.

The research on patents reveals that many inventions are not patented. In particular, the easier it is for firms to maintain trade secrets, the less likely it is that firms will patent their inventions. Noncompete agreements are an example of a mechanism for firms to keep trade secrets. While this approach may favor innovation by the firm, Marx, Strumsky, and Fleming (2009) present evidence that noncompete agreements reduce worker mobility and, thus, may negatively influence innovation at the economy-wide level.

3.3 Investments and Skills

Having clarified the dual role that human capital plays in the production of new ideas and the development of new services and products using these ideas, I now turn to an analysis of the growth rate of the supply of human capital.

3.3.1 Post-Secondary Enrollment and Attainment Rates in the United States

The analysis by Goldin and Katz (2008) describes trends in college enrollment and college graduation rates – typical measures of the supply of skills – as well as the evolution of the demand for skills. In the aggregate, college enrollment increased at high rates for the cohorts born between the 1920s and the 1960s and increased at lower rates for the more recent cohorts. In contrast, college graduation rates – conditional on enrolling – have been more or less stable over time. As a result, unconditional college graduation rates have been growing at lower rates in recent years.

Goldin and Katz (2008) do not find any break in the growth rate of the demand for skills for the US economy. As a result, their study provides compelling evidence that the increase in income inequality is partially driven by the increase in the returns to skills that is the product of steady growth rates for the demand for skills combined with diminishing growth rates for the supply of skills.

The evidence I describe next suggests that, for the contemporary US economy, the most immediate goals of any human capital policy designed to increase the growth rate of the supply of skills should be to promote college readiness among children who grow up in low-income households and to improve the matches between college-ready, low-income students and colleges.

The evidence suggests that, in the US economy, most of the noncollege enrollees or graduates come from low-income households. Bailey and Dynarski (2011) compare the college enrollment rates of two cohorts of children. The first cohort was born in the early 1960s and the second cohort was born approximately twenty years later. Bailey and Dynarski (2011) show that college attendance rates for the high-income children increased from 58 percent in the first cohort to 80 percent in the second cohort. An analysis by Belley and Lochner (2007) demonstrates that the increase in college attendance among high-income children occurred at all levels of ability, but it was disproportionately high for children in the lower quartiles of the Armed Forces Qualification Test (AFQT). According to Hoxby and Avery (2013), low-ability, high-income children apply to a range of institutions and enroll in colleges or universities with better graduation rates than those of least-selective institutions, such as community colleges.

In contrast, Bailey and Dynarski (2011) show that college enrollment rates for children born in low-income families rose from 19 percent in the first cohort to 29 percent in the second. Belley and Lochner (2007) find that this increase in enrollment rates is driven by the increase in enrollment of high-ability, low-income children. Hoxby and Avery (2013) empirically demonstrated that college-ready, low-income students do not usually apply to selective institutions. For these children, selective institutions would be a better match because they have both a curriculum that is more appropriate and a financial-aid package that is more generous. Instead of applying to selective institutions, many of the high-achieving, low-income students apply to the least-selective institutions, which have dismal graduation rates. The findings about mismatch suggest that a low-hanging fruit is to encourage high-ability, low-income students to apply to selective institutions. In order to design a policy, we need to understand why college-ready, low-income students are not applying to more selective colleges. One explanation may be a lack of information combined with a segmentation of the market for higher education in the United States. According to Hoxby (2009), the fiercer competition for a seat in selective universities has made these selective institutions even more selective and, as a result, their typical SAT scores have increased over time. For example, for the most selective institutions, the typical entrant's SAT score went from the ninetieth percentile in the 1960s to the ninety-seventh percentile in the 2000s. The opposite end of this market consists of institutions that are nonselective. For nonselective institutions, the increase in college enrollment has not translated into an increase in mean SAT scores – quite the contrary. In other words, college-ready, low-income children attend institutions in which the quality of peer students has continuously deteriorated over time. It is possible that because of the fact that the competition for a seat in selective institutions has become fiercer and fiercer, college-ready, low-income students have formed beliefs that they would have no chance of being accepted by selective institutions or that, even if they were accepted, they would not be able to afford such an education. Hoxby and Turner (2013) show that it is possible to change the enrollment behavior of college-ready, low-income students by providing information about the application process and the costs, net of financial aid, that these students would have to bear if they attended a selective institution. The findings of their study suggest a feasible, low-cost policy that increases college graduation rates by improving the matching between students and institutions.

Unfortunately, it is unlikely that improvements in the process of matching students to colleges will be sufficient to substantially change the growth rate of the supply of skills because a large percentage of low-income children do not even enroll in college (Bailey and Dynarski, 2011).

Therefore, to increase college graduation rates in the United States over the next decades, it will be necessary not only to increase access but also to raise the share of children growing up in low-income households that are college ready. These findings suggest increasing investments in human capital prior to college-going years.

Indeed, as shown by Cunha and Heckman (2007), college readiness is partially a product of a series of investments that start at birth and continue through infancy and adolescence. In what follows, we discuss the set of skills that is associated with college readiness. Later, we present programs that can successfully attack the formation of these skills at different stages of the life cycle. The findings from a large body of research suggest that, if we address human capital formation constraints at certain critical periods in individuals' lives, we will be successful in increasing the college enrollment and graduation rates of low-income children. This accomplishment, in turn, will lead to higher growth and lower inequality in outcomes.

3.3.2 College Readiness: Cognitive and Noncognitive Skills

College readiness is a function of the cognitive and socioemotional skills that students possess at the time they start attending college. This function is clearly shown in the work of Heckman, Stixrud, and Urzua (2006), which draws from the National Longitudinal Survey of Youth (NLSY). According to the authors, when holding constant socioemotional skills at mean value, the probability of graduating from college doubles as one moves from the third to the seventh decile of cognitive skills. The same magnitude is found when moving an individual from the third to the seventh decile in socioemotional skills while holding constant cognitive skills at mean value. The probability of graduating from college nearly triples when both skills move from the third to the seventh decile simultaneously. Cunha, Heckman, and Navarro (2005) show that the higher the stocks of skills at enrollment, the more enjoyable the experience of attending college, the higher the probability of graduating from college, and the higher the rewards after graduating from college.

Inequality in the skills that determine college readiness starts to emerge in early childhood. Cunha, Heckman, Lochner, and Masterov (2006) describe the evolution of stocks of skills from age five to age fourteen. To do so, the authors use the longitudinal data from the Children of the NLSY/ 79 (CNLSY/79) to conduct their analysis. The CNLSY/79 sample consists of all children born to the women who are members of the NLSY/79, which implies that the sample is representative of children whose mothers were born between 1957 and 1964. The CNLSY is a valuable resource because the study assesses several dimensions of child development biannually, from early childhood to adolescence. The authors take advantage of these data and estimate each child's stocks of cognitive skills, at each wave of the study, by the child's performance in standardized math tests. The authors normalize the scores at each age to have mean zero and variance one. Additionally, the authors calculate permanent income[4] for all families, estimate the four quartiles of the distribution of permanent income, allocate each of the families to one of the four mutually exclusive groups of permanent income, and calculate mean scores within permanent income groups. Their analysis shows that at age fourteen, the difference in cognitive skills between the children in the top and bottom quartiles of permanent income is above one standard deviation. The inequality at age five is approximately 80 percent of a standard deviation. This finding suggests that inequality in skills is already present and relevant by the time children start elementary school. Although schools certainly contribute to widening the gap, it is necessary to understand why the gap is already so large by the time children start school.

It is notoriously difficult to measure skills when children are very young. However, one ingenious way of doing it is by keeping track of a child's language development, for example by making periodic lists of the words spoken by the child. Hart and Risley (1995) assigned a research assistant to record the language environment of every child in their study for one hour a month, every month, from the time that the children were nine months old to the month they turned thirty-six months old. The research assistants transcribed the tape and counted the number of words spoken to the child by adults in the household, the number of words spoken by the child, and the number of conversation turns between adults and the child. The results were striking: it was not until age thirty-six months that the low-income children had attained the vocabulary level of the high-income children when the latter were twenty-four months old, even though they all started with the same level of language development at birth. In other words, by the time the children were three years old, the low-income children had already experienced a one full year delay in one important dimension of human capital. The work by Marchman and Fernald (2008) and Fernald, Marchman, and Weisleder (2013) shows that children who have delays in language development at a young age are unable to follow and contribute to complex conversations at later ages.

---

[4] Cunha et al. (2006) define permanent income as the average annual family income in all years between the year the child is born and the year the child turns eighteen.

The emergence of socioeconomic gaps is not restricted to cognitive or language skills. Unfortunately, similar gaps start to appear for socioemotional skills and health. Cunha et al. (2006) reproduce the same analysis for measures of socioemotional skills (including antisocial behavior, which predicts participation in crime) and find the same parallel trends with respect to permanent income. Case, Lubotsky, and Paxson (2002) analyze health and income data from the National Health Interview Survey and the Panel Study of Income Dynamics. Both datasets demonstrate that most of the socioeconomic inequality in maternal-reported health is already present by the time children are three years old.

Thus, the evidence is clear. Individuals who are college ready are more likely to graduate from college. College readiness is a combination of cognitive and noncognitive skills. Families and schools invest time and resources into forming these skills from when children are at an early age, and the formation process continues through adolescence. In Section 3.3.3, I show that inequality in the evolution of skills is mirrored in the inequality in investments in the human capital of children. Therefore, to increase college readiness in the United States, it will be necessary to close the socioeconomic gaps in investments in human capital during childhood and adolescence.

3.3.3 Inequality in Investments in the Human Capital of Children

Investments in the human capital of children (and adolescents) take many forms. At early ages, it is possible to measure the quality and quantity of interactions between adults and children as well as the amount of financial resources that adults spend on children. Regardless of the measure of investments considered in the different analyses that I report in this section, the conclusion is clear: socioeconomic inequality in investments is large regardless of the way that investment is measured.

Guryan, Hurst, and Kearney (2008) use the American Time Use Survey to measure the socioeconomic gaps in the quantity of interactions between parents and children. Among nonworking mothers, a mother with sixteen years of education spends 54 percent and 71 percent more time with her children in educational and recreational activities, respectively, than do mothers who are high-school dropouts. Among working mothers, these differences are 41 percent and 117 percent, respectively.[5] Interestingly, the

---

[5] These large differences persist even after accounting for differences in the characteristics of the mother and of the family.

college-educated mothers (whether they are working or not) spend more time with their children and less time in leisure. For example, among nonworking mothers, the college-educated mothers have eight fewer hours per week of their own leisure time than the high-school-dropout mothers. Working mothers with a college degree choose to spend four fewer hours of their week on their own leisure activities than their working high-school-dropout counterparts.

The difference matters not only in the amount of time spent with the child but also in how that time is used. In a fascinating study, Kalil, Ryan, and Corey (2012) look at detailed descriptions of parent–child activity and the child's age. They find that the time gap is larger specifically in the activities that are appropriate for the child's age. For example, when the child is about one year old, the largest gap in time relates to time playing with the child (e.g., peek-a-boo). When the child is about three years old, the largest gap in time relates to time devoted to educational activities that are important to promoting the child's school readiness (teaching colors, numbers, shapes, etc.). Finally, when the child is an adolescent, the socio-economic gap in time attains its maximal difference in time spent on "management" (e.g., making sure that the child has done homework). The fact that college-educated parents can better suit interaction to the child's age may be an important determinant of the emergence of the early gaps in development I described in Section 3.3.2.

It is also possible to measure the difference in investments during early childhood by looking at the quality of the language interaction between parents and children (Hart and Risley, 1995). One straightforward way to measure the quality of the language environment is to count the number of words that adult individuals speak to or around the child. In their study, Hart and Risley (1995) estimated that the children from low socioeconomic backgrounds were exposed to approximately 750 words per hour from the time they were nine months old to the day they turned thirty-six months old. Children in high-socioeconomic-status families heard approximately 1,500 words per hour when they were nine months old. Furthermore, the number of words tended to increase over time for these children and reached approximately 2,250 words per hour. In other words, the gaps in the language environment, which are large by age nine months, increase as children age.

The human capital formation of children also requires expenditures on goods and services such as housing, clothing, food, health care, child care, transportation, and other miscellaneous expenditures. There is a positive correlation between family income and expenditures on investment goods and the child's human capital. According to the United States Department of Agriculture (Lino et al., 2015), families in the bottom third of the distribution of family income (i.e., families whose income was below $59,200 in 2015) spent a little under $10,000 per year on their children. In contrast, families with incomes in the top third of the distribution (i.e., with income above $107,000) spent around $20,000 on investment goods for their children's human capital.

3.3.4 Socioeconomic Gaps in Skills Are Increasing

Unfortunately, socioeconomic inequality in skills has been increasing over time. Reardon (2013) finds that the achievement gap between children from high- and low-income families is roughly 30 to 40 percent larger among children born in 2001 than among those born twenty-five years earlier. In fact, the achievement gap between low- and high-income families is now twice as large as the achievement gap between black and white children.[6] The gap has grown partly because of an increase in the association between family income and children's academic achievement for families above the median income level. A given difference in family incomes now corresponds to a 30 to 60 percent larger difference in achievement than it did for children born in the 1970s. Ramey and Ramey (2010) argue that the increase in competition for a seat at selective institutions is the driving force behind the rising trend in the association between family income and academic achievement.

It is possible to analyze the trends in health by focusing on one simple, yet important, statistic: the share of children who are obese. Putnam (2016) shows that in the early 1970s, the socioeconomic gap in child obesity was nearly nonexistent: only around 5 percent of all children were obese, and there was no difference according to the child's family background. By 2010, over 20 percent of the children whose parents had at most a high-school diploma were obese while there was no change for the children whose parents had at least a bachelor's degree. Putnam (2016) also presents evidence suggesting that gaps in socioemotional skills, as measured by trust, have also been increasing over time.

3.3.5 Socioeconomic Gaps in Investments Are Increasing

There is also evidence that the inequality in measures of investments in the human capital of children and adolescents has been increasing over time.

---

[6] This fact is the result of an achievement gap that has been increasing across income groups but decreasing across racial groups.

Kornrich and Furstenberg (2013) analyze data from the Consumer Expenditure Survey (CEX) from the 1970s to the late 2000s. They show that parental expenditures on investment goods per child have increased from $2,832 to $6,573 for the parents in the top decile in the distribution of income. In contrast, for the parents in the bottom decile of income, investments have increased from $607 to $750. In other words, in the early 1970s, parents in the top income decile invested approximately five times more than their counterparts in the bottom decile. By the end of the last decade, the ratio went up to almost nine. Most of the increase in inequality in investments is driven by the increase in inequality in income. However, there is an important countervailing force at work: low-income parents greatly raised the share of their income that they devoted to investment in their children. In fact, while the propensity to invest (out of current income) rose from 4.1 percent to 5.6 percent for the parents in the top decile, it more than doubled from 7.9 percent to 16.3 percent for the parents in the bottom decile. If it were not for this fact, a simple Oaxaca-Blinder decomposition suggests that the ratio of investments of high-income parents to that of low-income parents would have been over 10:1 by the late 2000s.

Altintas (2016) combines data from the American Time Use Survey to study how time spent with children has changed for both mothers and fathers from 1975–6 to 2008–13. In 1975–6, the typical high-school mother spent approximately eight minutes a day on developmental activities with her child. In contrast, the typical college mother spent around six minutes a day. By 2008–13, average times spent on developmental activities with the child are thirty-three and sixty minutes for the high-school and college mothers, respectively.[7] In other words, the gap in time jumped from nonexistent to approximately half an hour per day. Combining gaps for fathers and mothers and transforming the unit of account from hours per day to hours per year, children whose parents both have a college degree (as do the majority of the families in the top decile of the family income) have around 300 more hours per year of parent–child interaction that influences child development.

---

[7] The averages hide the fact that many high-school and college mothers report spending no time on developmental activities with their children. In 1975–6, 38 percent of the mothers (regardless of the mother's educational attainment) reported not spending any time at all with their children. In 2008–13, the fraction of high-school-dropout mothers who reported spending no time with their children rose to 42 percent. For college mothers, this fraction decreased to 22 percent.

3.4 Experimental Manipulation of Investments and Their Impact on Skills

Section 3.3 summarized literature that is correlational: families that invest more in their children are also families whose children develop more skills. In this section, I show that the relation is causal by reporting evidence based on experimental data. My discussion focuses on early childhood education, parenting programs, and interventions that focus on improving socioemotional skills in adolescent years.

3.4.1 Early Childhood Education

This section discusses early childhood education projects that were executed in the 1960s (the Perry Preschool Program), the 1970s and 1980s (the Carolina Abecedarian), and the 1990s (the Infant Health Development Program (IHDP)). I choose to focus on these cases because they have data that permit researchers to estimate short-term impacts on measures of skills and investments as well as long-term impacts on outcomes relating to labor market performance, educational attainment, and crime participation.

The programmatic characteristics of the Perry Preschool Program, the Abecedarian, and the IHDP are discussed in depth by Schweinhart (2005), Ramey, Sparling, and Ramey (2012), and Brooks-Gunn, Gross, Kraemer, Spiker, and Shapiro (1992), respectively. The three programs used curricula that have as common features the promotion of play-based, child-directed forms of learning and an emphasis on the development of language, cognitive, and socioemotional skills. The programs recruited educated staff and maintained relatively low student–teacher ratios. These commonalities are important because large-scale programs such as Head Start are built around the same principles as these small-scale interventions.

The three programs differed in terms of the intensity of services. The Perry Preschool Program served three- and four-year-old children three hours per day, and the parents were visited once a week. In contrast, the Carolina Abecedarian served children as young as one month old until they reached age five years, for eight hours per day, while the IHDP served children from birth until age three for up to nine hours per day and fifty weeks per year. The Perry and Abecedarian programs targeted children born in disadvantaged families. IHDP, in contrast, targeted low-birth-weight children regardless of the family's economic circumstance. The IHDP targeting and its larger sample size allowed researchers to investigate the impact of early childhood intervention on children across the entire spectrum of socioeconomic backgrounds.

A major advantage of these programs is that participants were followed until ages forty and thirty-four in the Perry Preschool and Carolina Abecedarian programs, respectively. So far, IHDP participants have been followed until age eighteen. The disadvantage of these studies is that the sample sizes are small (123 in the Perry, 111 in the Carolina Abecedarian, but 985 in IHDP) and there was imperfect adherence to the randomization protocol. The programs had low attrition rates at data collection rounds. However, not all outcomes are observed for all participants at all data collection points, so item nonresponse is an issue that affects the evaluation of these programs.

The analyses of these programs are enriched by the fact that participants are assessed in a large number of human capital dimensions – cognitive skills, socioemotional skills, and health – as well as numerous adult outcomes relating to earnings, labor force participation, interactions with the criminal justice system, and even marriage and family formation. However, the fact that the econometrician has numerous outcomes to measure the impact of an intervention may increase the chances of rejecting null hypotheses – finding that the treatment does not have an impact on an outcome – erroneously.[8] Arguably, the chance of rejecting a null finding becomes more serious the larger the number of outcomes and the smaller the sample size. Many studies that report impacts of early childhood programs do not account for this multiple testing problem; nor do they take account of compromised randomization, small sample size, and item nonresponse. The exceptions are Heckman, Moon, Pinto, Savelyev, and Yavitz (2010) in their analysis of the Perry Preschool data, García, Heckman, Leaf, and Prados (2017) in their analyses of the Abecedarian data, and Elango, García, Heckman, and Hojman (2015) in their joint analyses of the Perry, Abecedarian, and IHDP data. In what follows, I report the findings by Elango et al. (2015) because they also examine the combination and outcomes that are common across the three programs. By focusing the analysis on a common set of outcomes, it becomes possible to separate robust findings (i.e., outcomes that are impacted in at least two

---

[8] To see why, suppose the econometrician runs the regressions and tests the hypotheses separately for each of the twenty outcomes. If the econometrician fixes the significance level at 5 percent, then the probability of observing at least one significant result out of twenty just due to chance is approximately 64 percent.

out of the three programs) from fragile findings (i.e., outcomes that are impacted in at most one of the programs).

Elango et al. (2015) show that the three programs have a large impact on IQ measured at the end of the intervention (age five for the Perry and Abecedarian programs and age three for the IHDP). However, in all of the programs, the early gains in cognitive skills fade as children age. By the time children are eight years old, the gains in IQ have become very small and statistically insignificant. In spite of this fact, Elango et al. (2015) report a large impact from the Perry and Abecedarian programs on adult outcomes (which are not measured in the IHDP). The impacts of the program differ by gender. For example, both programs increased educational attainment and reduced arrests for females (but not males). In contrast, both programs increased the probability of employment for males, but no effects were detected for females for this variable.[9]

The fact that the Perry and Abecedarian programs had no long-term impact on IQ but had long-term impact on important adult outcomes is reconciled by Heckman, Pinto, and Savelyev (2013) and Conti, Heckman, Moon, and Pinto (2012) by conducting mediation analyses. These authors show that the Perry and Abecedarian programs improved adult measures of noncognitive skills relating to academic motivation, which explains 40 percent of the rise in academic motivation. Both programs also reduced externalizing behavior, which, in turn, explains up to 40 percent of the effect of the program on arrests and up to 20 percent of the impact on unemployment. Their findings are important not only because they confirm that both the link between investments and skills and the relationship between skills and adult outcomes are partially causal but also because they point out that human capital formation programs that aim to have long-term impacts should address the production of skills that are not necessarily captured by standardized tests that measure IQ or cognitive skills.

Both the Perry and Abecedarian programs have influenced the organization of the Head Start Program. According to the data from the Head Start Impact Study (HSIS), 30 percent of the Head Start centers adopted the HighScope curriculum used by the Perry Preschool Program. When combined, the Early Head Start Program and the Head Start Program are similar to the Abecedarian, which not only offers full day care from birth to age five but also offers components that include medical and nutritional services (Puma et al., 2010).

---

[9] The Perry Program reduced arrests for males. The analysis by Elango et al. (2015) reports large point estimates for the Abecedarian Program, but they are not statistically significant.

Unfortunately, it is difficult to evaluate the Head Start Program for a number of reasons. First, the population and the type of program vary according to centers (Puma et al., 2010). Second, the HSIS stopped following up on children when they turned nine years old, and the impact of the Head Start Program on adult outcomes can only be assessed using observational data. Third, there are no reliable measures of noncognitive skills. Fourth, there is contamination of the control group. Not all Head Start centers participated in the HSIS. Therefore, a child that was assigned to the control group was denied enrollment in the centers that participated in the study, but the child was not necessarily denied enrollment in another Head Start center that did not participate in the study or in some other childcare center with similar quality. According to figures reported by HSIS, 15 percent of the children in the control group enrolled in a Head Start center not participating in HSIS and an additional 40 percent of the children in the control group used other forms of center-based care.[10]

Therefore, impacts of the Head Start Program must be interpreted with caution. The analysis by Puma et al. (2010) finds that the Head Start Program, as in the Perry and the Abecedarian, has a large impact on cognitive skills by the time children exit the program, but the difference between children assigned to control and treatment groups disappears by age nine.[11] The analysis of long-term impacts by Carneiro and Ginja (2014) finds that Head Start positively impacted physical and mental health – as measured by obesity and depression scales – as well as crime participation.

The summary of the literature is that early education programs targeted at disadvantaged children generate short- and long-term impacts.[12] This finding suggests that policy-makers should pay close attention to the common characteristics of the programs that work. In particular, it is important to recognize that these programs were built around curricula that emphasized the formation of both cognitive and socioemotional skills and health. Furthermore, skills beget skills, so the higher the level of school

---

[10] Unfortunately, there is no measure of the quality of the centers other than the Head Start centers that were part of the evaluation study.

[11] Feller, Grindal, Miratrix, and Page (2016) and Kline and Walters (2016) find that cognitive skills no longer converge when they account for contamination of the control group.

[12] Because IHDP did not use as a targeting mechanism the family's socioeconomic status, it is possible to investigate the impact of early education programs on children from different family backgrounds. The analysis by Duncan and Sojourner (2013) finds that IHDP had no impact on child development, at any age, for children from high-income families but had a large impact on children from low-income families.

readiness of children, the higher the productivity of schools and teachers (Cunha and Heckman, 2007).

3.4.2 Parenting Interventions

Other interventions during early childhood aim to improve the well-being and skills of children by directly educating parents through home visitation (Currie and Rossin-Slater, 2015). In the United States, home visitation programs currently serve approximately 300,000 families per year. Unfortunately, most of the home visitation programs do not have long-term follow-up, and many programs have not been subjected to high-quality evaluation. Two important exceptions are the Nurse-Family Partnership (NFP) (Olds, 2006) and the Jamaica Nutritional Supplementation and Cognitive Stimulation Program (Grantham-McGregor, Powell, Walker, and Himes, 1991).

The NFP provides disadvantaged first-time mothers with home visits that start during the second trimester of the pregnancy and continue until the child turns two years old. The home visits are executed by registered nurses who follow a detailed curriculum of activities specific to the different stages of pregnancy and child development. The NFP conducted three randomized-controlled trials before it began to be implemented on a large scale. The program currently operates in forty-three states and has served, since 1996, approximately 200,000 families.

Heckman, Holland, Makino, Pinto, and Rosales-Rueda (2017) provide a comprehensive analysis of the impacts of the NFP program. The authors account for the specific details of the randomization procedure, describe the large number of outcomes that are measured, and uncover the channels that generate the treatment effects.[13] Heckman et al. (2017) use data from birth until the year in which the child turns twelve years old and find that the NFP increased birth weight for boys but not girls. By the end of visits (when the child turned two years old), the NFP led to an improvement in parenting attitudes and a better home environment. Interestingly, the authors also find that the NFP produced better socioemotional skills for mothers (lower levels of anxiety and higher levels of self-control). The higher level of maternal investments and the improvement in maternal

---

[13] Heckman et al. (2017) rely on the data from the Memphis randomized controlled trial because the research team in Memphis not only collected very detailed data on many aspects of child development but also interviewed and assessed mothers and children frequently.

skills translated into school readiness by age six: both boys and girls had higher scores in tests of cognitive skills. Girls in the treatment group also scored higher in assessments of socioemotional skills. The program had no impact on children by the time they were twelve years old except for the fact that boys in the NFP program had higher scores on tests of cognitive skills than boys in the control group. Long-term impacts on cognition were not found in the early childhood programs described in this section.

The Jamaica Program provided psychosocial stimulation and nutritional supplementation to stunted children in Jamaica (Grantham-McGregor et al., 1991). At enrollment, parents were randomly assigned to one of four treatment groups: control, only nutritional supplementation, only cognitive stimulation, and both cognitive and nutritional supplementation. Families in all four groups received weekly visits by community health workers. The visits to families in the control group were used to obtain information about illnesses. The families in the intervention groups with nutritional supplementation received one kilogram of milk-based formula per week. The parents in the cognitive stimulation groups were trained to interact and play with their children to foster their cognitive development. The cognitive stimulation intervention used a structured curriculum that was appropriate to the child's age. During the one-hour weekly visit, the community health worker demonstrated play techniques and involved the mother in a play session with the child.

The Jamaica Nutritional Supplementation and Cognitive Stimulation Program followed children at ages seven, eleven, seventeen, and twenty-two. The first three follow-up data collections were marked by high attrition rates because of emigration. This issue was properly addressed for the age twenty-two follow-up because the authors were able to locate and interview the emigrant participants. Walker, Chang, Vera-Hernández, and Grantham-McGregor (2011) show that the nutritional supplementation by itself (i.e., without cognitive stimulation) did not have long-term impacts on any aspects of human development. In contrast, the children born into families assigned to cognitive stimulation (with or without the nutritional supplementation) had higher scores on tests that measure cognitive skills, in assessments of math and reading skills, and in scales of socioemotional skills. Furthermore, their analysis uncovers positive effects on educational attainment and negative effects on delinquency and violent behavior. The analysis by Gertler et al. (2014) shows that the Jamaica Program found that children who received cognitive stimulation (with or without nutrition) had earnings 42 percent higher at age twenty-two.

Gertler et al. (2014) study the mechanisms that explain treatment effects. They show that the parents in the cognitive stimulation groups provided their children with higher-level maternal investment during the intervention period. This explains why their children had higher levels of cognitive and psychosocial development at the end of the program. Furthermore, treated children were more likely to migrate to the United States or to the United Kingdom. Gertler et al. (2014) argue that higher levels of school readiness and access to higher-quality schools and better labor markets in the United States or the United Kingdom explain the gains observed at age twenty-two.

The analyses of NFP and the Jamaica Program show that home visitation programs can positively impact the investments in children that, in turn, positively impact the children's development of cognitive and psychosocial skills. The data from NFP suggest that the increase in investments could be due to an improvement in maternal socioemotional skills or the child's health at birth. However, this explanation seems unlikely when we consider the fact that the Jamaica Program did not address maternal health and had no impact on health at birth because it started after birth. An alternative explanation is that parenting education programs such as the NFP and the Jamaica Program provide important information to the mother that, in turn, affects her perception about the importance of investments in the child's development. In other words, high-quality home visitation programs raised maternal expectations about the returns to investments in their children.

To see this, consider a simple model proposed by Cunha, Elo, and Culhane (2013). Let h_0 and h_1 denote the child's human capital before and after the intervention, respectively. Let x_1 denote maternal investments and assume that the production function of human capital is

$$\ln h_1 = \gamma_0 + \gamma_1 \ln h_0 + \gamma_2 \ln x + \gamma_3 \ln h_0 \ln x. \tag{1}$$

Let Ω denote the maternal information set. Let $\mu_j = E(\gamma_j|\Omega)$. Assume that mothers cannot borrow or save; thus, $c + px = y$, where c, y, and p denote consumption, income, and investment price, respectively. Assume that maternal preferences are described by the utility function

$$U(c, h_1) = \ln c + \alpha \ln h_1, \quad \alpha > 0. \tag{2}$$

Suppose that the problem of the mother is to maximize expected utility subject to her information set, budget constraints, and preferences, as well as the production function of human capital. In this simple version of the model, optimal maternal investments are determined by

$$x = \frac{\alpha\mu_2 + \alpha\mu_3 \ln h_0}{1 + \alpha\mu_2 + \alpha\mu_3 \ln h_0} \frac{y}{p}. \tag{3}$$

The policy function states that maternal investments will be higher the higher are the maternal expectations μ_2 and μ_3. Note that these parameters are generally heterogeneous across mothers since different mothers may have different expectations about the importance of investments. Indeed, Cunha et al. (2013) survey low-income mothers and find that not only are maternal expectations heterogeneous but they are also too low, given existing knowledge about the parameters γ_2 and γ_3 of the production function of human capital. Their findings offer a consistent explanation of why early investments in disadvantaged families are low and why successful home visitation programs may impact investments and, consequently, child development.

One should not conclude that the successes of the NFP and the Jamaica Program are a guarantee that all home visitation programs will also produce the same types of impact. Unfortunately, there are large home visitation programs that do not produce any measurable gains in child development, parenting attitudes, or home environments. For example, the Early Head Start Home Visitation Program achieved modest impacts on parenting behavior, with effect sizes in the range of 0.10 to 0.22 (Love et al., 2005). In 1989, the US Department of Education launched the Even Start Program. This program was conceived under the philosophy that at-risk families need comprehensive services and, as a result, the intervention included not only early childhood education and parenting education but also adult literacy training and joint parent–child activities (St. Pierre, Ricciuti, and Rimdzius, 2005). Unfortunately, the program had no impact on cognitive or socio-emotional development of children, no change in parental investments, and no gains in adult literacy (Ricciuti, St. Pierre, Lee, Parsad, and Rimdzius, 2004). A possible explanation for the lack of success is that the program did not affect parental expectations. The data are not rich enough to provide direct evidence that supports this conclusion. However, the evidence on lack of parental engagement is consistent with this inference. The review of home visitation programs by Gomby, Larson, Lewit, and Behrman (1993) and the evaluation of the Parent as Teachers Program by (Wagner and Clayton, 1999) reveal an attrition rate of 35 percent to 50 percent. In Early Head Start, approximately one-third of the families drop out before they complete half of the program, and only 40 percent of the parents actually graduate (Roggman, Cook, Peterson, and Raikes, 2008). Therefore, it seems reasonable to conclude that if parents are not engaged in the program, then the intervention will not affect their beliefs.

Low expectations about the impact of early investments on child development may also lead parents not to participate in a home visitation program. If the parent does not believe that the home environment and the parenting attitude impact child development, why bother enrolling and attending parenting classes? This issue is important because the literature on home visitation programs reports disappointing data on the frequency with which a family rejects an offer to participate in a home visitation randomized-controlled trial. For example, the NFP reports a rejection rate of nearly 37 percent. Similarly, Child FIRST is a promising parenting education program that aims to decrease the incidence of emotional and behavioral disturbance, developmental and learning problems, and abuse and neglect among high-risk young children and families. The evaluation by Lowell, Carter, Godoy, Paulicin, and Briggs-Gowan (2011) indicates a rejection rate of nearly 45 percent. Unfortunately, because families who reject participation are not included in the evaluation study, it is impossible to know whether the rejection rates are higher for low-expectation families.

3.4.3 Socioemotional Interventions for School-Aged Children

Recent interventions that targeted the formation of noncognitive skills in adolescence have reported successes in outcomes relating to educational attainment, labor market performance, and low participation in crime. These successes have certainly rekindled interest in programs that target skills formed during adolescence.[14] Unfortunately, because they are recent,

---

[14] Two recent programs are particularly promising. The first is the Becoming a Man (B.A. M.) Program that combines mentorship for the development of noncognitive skills and academic tutoring for improvement of academic outcomes. The B.A.M. Program takes place during the ninth and tenth grades and lasts for three-quarters of an academic year. The mentorship curriculum consists of a one-hour weekly cognitive behavioral training implemented in groups to maintain low costs. The tutors conduct daily hour-long sessions focused on the development of math skills. According to the analysis by Cook et al. (2014), the program increased math scores by half a standard deviation in math achievement tests and increased math GPA by 40 percent of a standard deviation. The program also caused a reduction of absences by ten days. The second program is the Pathways to Education Program. Pathways is also an adolescent intervention that operates in housing projects in Toronto. Similar to B.A.M., it combines mentoring and tutoring. In the Pathways program, the mentor works directly with students and parents. Furthermore, when the students are in the ninth and tenth grades, they attend group

it is impossible to assess their long-term impacts. However, it is possible to draw inferences about long-term impacts by summarizing the findings of research that have analyzed similar interventions since the 1980s. The current subsection summarizes the common features of these interventions as well as their impacts on adult outcomes.

3.4.3.1 The Seattle Social Development Project

The Seattle Social Development Project (SSDP) targeted public elementary schools in high-crime areas of Seattle. The goal of the intervention was to foster the children's noncognitive skills formation and to improve their socialization experience within schools, families, and peers. The intervention team pursued these goals by providing training not only to school-aged children but also to their parents. The parental intervention aimed to increase the quality of family management, to reduce family conflict, and to involve parents in their children's problem behaviors. By engaging directly with the children, the intervention aimed to reduce academic failure, to diminish exposure to negative peer influences, to discourage antisocial behavior, and to deem as unacceptable favorable attitudes toward behavior problems.

The researchers divided the schools into one of three groups. The first group was the full-intervention group, consisting of those who received at least one semester of intervention in grades one through four and at least one semester of intervention in grades five and six, with an average of 4.13 years of intervention exposure. The second group was the late-intervention group, consisting of those who received the intervention during grades five and six only, with an average of 1.65 years of exposure. The third group was the control group, which received no intervention.

The teachers in intervention schools received five days of in-service training to promote proactive classroom management, interactive teaching, and cooperative learning (Slavin, 1978). Teachers serving children in the full-intervention group also received instruction on the use of a training curriculum that emphasized the development of interpersonal, cognitive, and problem-solving skills. This curriculum sought to develop

mentorship sessions every two weeks. According to Oreopoulos, Brown, and Lavecchia (2017), Pathways increased secondary school completion and post-secondary enrollment by about 15 percentage points. Although the authors report improvements in achievement test scores, there are no measures of noncognitive skills, so it is impossible to estimate the contributions that are due to the different types of skill.

children's social skills for involvement in cooperative learning groups and other social activities without resorting to aggression or other problem behaviors (Shure and Spivack, 1982).

The intervention offered parents training classes that were appropriate to the developmental level of the children. When children were in the first and second grades, the project staff trained full-intervention parents in child behavior management skills. When children were in the third and fourth grades, the project staff coached full-intervention parents to strengthen their skills for supporting their children's academic development. Finally, when their children were in the fifth and sixth grades, project staff helped full- and late-intervention parents learn how to enhance family bonding and strengthen parents' skills to reduce their children's risks for drug use (Haggerty, Kosterman, Catalano, and Hawkins, 1999).

When in grade six, students in the full- or late-intervention groups received training from project staff in skills to recognize and resist social influences to engage in problem behaviors and to generate and suggest positive alternatives in order to stay out of trouble while still keeping friends (Park et al., 2000; Mason et al., 2007).

The evaluation study by Hawkins, Kosterman, Catalano, Hill, and Abbott (2005) found that the program improved the adult outcomes of the full-intervention students. At age twenty-one, full-intervention students were functioning better as young adults: they had completed more education, were more likely to be constructively engaged in school or work, were less likely to have changed jobs in the past year, and had more responsibility at work. Full-intervention students were more likely to have positive emotional regulation (less depression, suicide ideation, and social phobia) and were less likely to have comorbid substance use and mental health disorders. Also, compared to control participants, fewer participants from the full-intervention group were involved in a wide variety of crimes, including property crimes, violent crimes, and fraud. In the long run, the program did not produce a statistically significant effect on achievement test scores, but it generated improvements in non-cognitive skills and in important adult outcomes.

3.4.3.2 The Montreal Longitudinal Experimental Study

The Montreal Longitudinal Experimental Study (MLES) provides further evidence that noncognitive skills can be shaped during elementary school for disruptive kindergarten boys from low socioeconomic environments. MLES lasted two years: boys started their participation when they were seven years old and finished by the time they were nine. The program was designed to foster the development of social-emotional skills. The development of the socioemotional skills was executed during nineteen sessions in which professional staff interacted with children. Similar to the SSDP, the MLES also had a parental intervention aimed to help parents reinforce the skills developed in the sessions.

Algan, Beasley, Vitaro, and Tremblay (2014) evaluate the intervention by the method of random assignment and find that the program improved a range of adult outcomes. During adolescence, the program increased measures of noncognitive skills and grades. MLES increased full-time employment or school enrollment at ages seventeen to twenty-six by 11 percentage points and increased secondary school graduation at ages twenty-three to twenty-four by 19 percentage points. It reduced the probability of having a criminal record by ages twenty-three to twenty-four by 1 percentage point. An important advantage of the MLES evaluation study is that the authors measured impulse control, aggression control, and trust. The study found that school-related outcomes were mediated by improvements in impulse control and trust. In contrast, crime-related outcomes were explained largely by improvements in aggression control.

3.5 Conclusion

Economic growth is an important tool for lifting individuals out of poverty. Economic theory links long-run economic growth to a nation's human capital. Additionally, inequality in human capital is an important factor in determining inequality in socioeconomic outcomes. The research summarized in this chapter suggests that the reduction in the growth rate of the supply of skilled labor observed in the last thirty years partially and simultaneously explains the reduction in productivity growth and the increase in inequality during the same period. Therefore, to increase productivity growth and to reduce inequality, it is important to foster the formation of skilled labor. This will require increasing the number of disadvantaged children who are college ready. The challenge is that college readiness is a process that starts at birth and continues during childhood and adolescence. College readiness is composed of different types of skill, both cognitive and noncognitive, that are shaped in different stages of an individual's life cycle. Socioeconomic inequality in the skills that constitute college readiness starts to emerge early on, continues to increase over the individual's life cycle, and is partially driven by the inequality in investments that families and schools make into the formation of these skills. To complicate matters, inequality in investments itself has increased over time, and, in response, there is an increase in inequality of skills.

The literature summarized in this chapter suggests that policies need to start early by changing the environment that disadvantaged children experience at home and in any other place where they receive care. Improvement in this environment can be done either by changing the quality of the care environment directly or by engaging parents so that they improve the quality of the interactions that they have with their children. More importantly, the research summarized in this chapter shows that long-term impacts are mostly driven by programs that can affect the formation of the noncognitive skills that are usually not measured by standardized tests that measure performance in language or math. If the noncognitive skills are malleable over longer periods of time, then the findings summarized in the literature provide yet another reason to abandon the extremely narrow focus on the role played by cognitive skills in economic inequality and labor productivity.

References

Algan, Yann, Elizabeth Beasley, Frank Vitaro, and Richard E. Tremblay, 2014. "The Impact of Non-cognitive Skills Training on Academic and Non-academic Trajectories: From Childhood to Early Adulthood." Working Paper. SciencesPo, Paris, France.

Almeida, Paul, and Bruce Kogut, 1999. "Localization of Knowledge and the Mobility of Engineers in Regional Networks." *Management Science* 45 (7), 905–17.

Altintas, Evrim, 2016. "The Widening Education Gap in Developmental Child Care Activities in the United States, 1965–2013." *Journal of Marriage and Family* 78 (1), 26–42.

Arrow, Kenneth J., 1962. "Economic Welfare and the Allocation of Resources for Inventions." In Richard R. Nelson (ed.), *The Rate and Direction of Inventive Activity: Economic and Social Factors*, 609–26. Princeton University Press, Princeton, NJ.

Audretsch, David, and Maryann P. Feldman, 2004. "Knowledge Spillovers and the Geography of Innovation." In J. Vernon Henderson and Jacques Thisse (eds.), *Handbook of Regional and Urban Economics*, 2713–39. Elsevier, Amsterdam, Netherlands.

Bailey, Martha J., and Susan M. Dynarski, 2011. "Inequality in Postsecondary Education." In Greg J. Duncan and Richard J. Murnane (eds.), *Whither Opportunity? Rising Inequality, Schools, and Children's Life Chances*, 117–32. Russell Sage, New York, NY.

Belley, Philippe, and Lance Lochner, 2007. "The Changing Role of Family Income and Ability in Determining Educational Achievement." *Journal of Human Capital* 1 (1), 37–89.

Boldrin, Michele, and David K. Levine, 2013, "The Case Against Patents." *Journal of Economic Perspectives* 27 (1), 3–22.

Brooks-Gunn, Jeanne, Ruth T. Gross, Helena C. Kraemer, Donna Spiker, and Sam Shapiro, 1992. "Enhancing the Cognitive Outcomes of Low Birth Weight, Premature Infants: For Whom Is the Intervention Most Effective?" *Pediatrics* 89 (6, Part 2), 1209–15.

Bureau of Labor Statistics, 2019. "Employer Costs for Employee Compensation." News Release USDL-19-1649, www.bls.gov/news.release/pdf/ecec.pdf.

Carneiro, Pedro, and Rita Ginja, 2014. "Long-Term Impacts of Compensatory Preschool on Health and Behavior: Evidence from Head Start." *American Economic Journal: Economic Policy* 6 (4), 135–73.

Case, Anne, Darren Lubotsky, and Christina Paxson, 2002. "Economic Status and Health in Childhood: The Origins of the Gradient." *American Economic Review* 92 (5), 1308–34.

Conti, Gabriella, James J. Heckman, Seong Moon, and Rodrigo Pinto, 2012. "The Long-Term Health Effects of Early Childhood Interventions." Working Paper. University of Chicago, Chicago, IL.

Cook, Philip J., Kenneth Dodge, George Farkas, Roland G. Fryer Jr., Jonathan Guryan, Jens Ludwig, Susan Mayer, Harold Pollack, and Laurence Steinberg, 2014. "The (Surprising) Efficacy of Academic and Behavioral Intervention with Disadvantaged Youth: Results from a Randomized Experiment in Chicago." NBER Working Paper No. 19862. National Bureau of Economic Research, Cambridge, MA.

Cunha, Flávio, Irma Elo, and Jennifer Culhane, 2013. "Eliciting Maternal Expectations about the Technology of Cognitive Skill Formation." NBER Working Paper No. 19144. National Bureau of Economic Research, Cambridge, MA.

Cunha, Flávio, and James J. Heckman, 2007. "The Technology of Skill Formation." *American Economic Review* 97 (2), 31–47.

Cunha, Flávio, James J. Heckman, Lance Lochner, and Dimitriy V. Masterov, 2006. "Interpreting the Evidence on Life Cycle Skill Formation." In Eric Hanushek and Finis Welch (eds.), *Handbook of the Economics of Education*, 697–812. Elsevier, Amsterdam, Netherlands.

Cunha, Flávio, James J. Heckman, and Salvador Navarro, 2005. "Separating Uncertainty from Heterogeneity in Life Cycle Earnings." *Oxford Economic Papers* 57 (2), 191–261.

Currie, Janet, and Maya Rossin-Slater, 2015. "Early-Life Origins of Life-Cycle Well-Being: Research and Policy Implications." *Journal of Policy Analysis and Management* 34 (1), 208–42.

Duncan, Greg J., and Aaron J. Sojourner, 2013. "Can Intensive Early Childhood Intervention Programs Eliminate Income-Based Cognitive and Achievement Gaps?" *Journal of Human Resources* 48 (4), 945–68.

Elango, Sneha, Jorge Luis García, James J. Heckman, and Andrés Hojman, 2015. "Early Childhood Education." NBER Working Paper No. 21766. National Bureau of Economic Research, Cambridge, MA.

Evens, Ronald, and Kenneth Kaitin, 2015. "The Evolution of Biotechnology and Its Impact on Health Care." *Health Affairs* 34 (2), 210–19.

Feller, Avi, Todd Grindal, Luke Miratrix, and Lindsay C. Page, 2016. "Compared to What? Variation in the Impacts of Early Childhood Education by Alternative Care Type." *The Annals of Applied Statistics* 10 (3), 1245–85.

Fernald, Anne, Virginia A. Marchman, and Adriana Weisleder, 2013. "SES Differences in Language Processing Skill and Vocabulary Are Evident at 18 Months." *Developmental Science* 16 (2), 234–48.

García, Jorge Luis, James J. Heckman, Duncan Ermini Leaf, and María José Prados, 2017. "Quantifying the Life-Cycle Benefits of a Prototypical Early Childhood Program." NBER Working Paper No. 10811. National Bureau of Economic Research, Cambridge, MA.

Gertler, Paul, James Heckman, Rodrigo Pinto, Arianna Zanolini, Christel Vermeersch, Susan Walker, Susan M. Chang, and Sally Grantham-McGregor, 2014. "Labor Market Returns to an Early Childhood Stimulation Intervention in Jamaica." *Science* 344 (6187), 998–1001.

Giovannetti, Glen T., and Gautam Jaggi, 2014. "Biotechnology Industry Report 2013: Beyond Borders; Matters of Evidence." Ernst and Young, London, UK.

Goldin, Claudia, and Lawrence F. Katz, 2008. *The Race between Education and Technology.* Harvard University Press, Cambridge, MA.

Gomby, Deanna S., Carol S. Larson, Eugene M. Lewit, and Richard E. Behrman, 1993. "Home Visiting: Analysis and Recommendations." *The Future of Children* 3 (3), 6–22.

Gordon, Robert J., 2016. *The Rise and Fall of American Growth: The U.S. Standard of Living Since the Civil War.* Princeton University Press, Princeton, NJ.

Grantham-McGregor, Sally M., Christine A. Powell, Susan P. Walker, and John H. Himes, 1991. "Nutritional Supplementation, Psychosocial Stimulation, and Mental Development of Stunted Children: The Jamaican Study." *The Lancet* 338 (8758), 1–5.

Guryan, Jonathan, Erik Hurst, and Melissa Kearney, 2008. "Parental Education and Parental Time with Children." *Journal of Economic Perspectives* 22 (3), 23–46.

Haggerty, Kevin, Rick Kosterman, Richard F. Catalano, and J. David Hawkins, 1999. *Preparing for the Drug Free Years.* Office of Justice Programs, Washington, DC.

Hart, Betty, and Todd R. Risley, 1995. *Meaningful Differences in the Everyday Experience of Young American Children.* Paul H. Brookes Publishing, Baltimore, MD.

Hawkins, J. David, Rick Kosterman, Richard F. Catalano, Karl G. Hill, and Robert D. Abbott, 2005. "Promoting Positive Adult Functioning through Social Development Intervention in Childhood: Long-Term Effects from the Seattle Social Development Project." *Archives of Pediatrics and Adolescent Medicine* 159 (1), 25–31.

Heckman, James J., Margaret L. Holland, Kevin K. Makino, Rodrigo Pinto, and Maria Rosales-Rueda, 2017. "An Analysis of the Memphis Nurse-Family Partnership Program." NBER Working Paper No. 23610. National Bureau of Economic Analysis, Cambridge, MA.

Heckman, James J., and Dimitriy V. Masterov, 2007. "The Productivity Argument for Investing in Young Children." *Review of Agricultural Economics* 29 (3), 446–93.

Heckman, James J., Seong H. Moon, Rodrigo Pinto, Peter Savelyev, and Adam Yavitz, 2010. "Analyzing Social Experiments as Implemented: A Reexamination of the Evidence from the HighScope Perry Preschool Program." *Quantitative Economics* 1 (1), 1–46.

Heckman, James J., Rodrigo Pinto, and Peter Savelyev, 2013. "Understanding the Mechanisms through Which an Influential Early Childhood Program Boosted Adult Outcomes." *American Economic Review* 103 (6), 2052–86.

Heckman, James J., Jora Stixrud, and Sergio Urzua, 2006. "The Effects of Cognitive and Noncognitive Abilities on Labor Market Outcomes and Social Behavior." *Journal of Labor Economics* 24 (3), 411–82.

Hoxby, Caroline M., 2009. "The Changing Selectivity of American Colleges." *Journal of Economic Perspectives* 23 (4), 95–118.

Hoxby, Caroline, and Christopher Avery, 2013. "The Missing 'One-Offs': The Hidden Supply of High-Achieving, Low-Income Students." *Brookings Papers on Economic Activity* 2013 (1), 1–65.

Hoxby, Caroline, and Sarah Turner, 2013. "Expanding College Opportunities for High-Achieving, Low-Income Students." Working Paper. Stanford University, Stanford, CA.

Jacobs, Jane, 1961. *The Economy of Cities*. Random House, New York, NY.

Kalil, Ariel, Rebecca Ryan, and Michael Corey, 2012. "Diverging Destinies: Maternal Education and the Developmental Gradient in Time with Children." *Demography* 49 (4), 1361–83.

Katz, Lawrence F., and Kevin M. Murphy, 1992. "Changes in Relative Wages, 1963–1987: Supply and Demand Factors." *Quarterly Journal of Economics* 107 (1), 35–78.

Klepper, Steven, 2010. "The Origin and Growth of Industry Clusters: The Making of Silicon Valley and Detroit." *Journal of Urban Economics* 67 (1), 15–32.

Kline, Patrick, and Christopher Walters, 2016. "Evaluating Public Programs with Close Substitutes: The Case of Head Start." *Quarterly Journal of Economics* 131 (4), 1795–1848.

Kornrich, Sabino, and Frank Furstenberg, 2013. "Investing in Children: Changes in Parental Spending on Children, 1972–2007." *Demography* 50 (1), 1–23.

Lawrence, Stacy, and Riku Lahteenmaki, 2014. "Public Biotech 2013: The Numbers." *Nature Biotechnology* 32 (7), 626–32.

Lécuyer, Christopher, 2006. *Making Silicon Valley: Innovation and the Growth of High Tech, 1930–1970*. MIT Press, Cambridge, MA.

Lino, Mark, Kevin Kuczynski, Nestor Rodriguez, and TusaRebecca Schap, 2017. "Expenditures on Children by Families, 2015." Miscellaneous Publication No. 1528-2015. U.S. Department of Agriculture, Center for Nutrition Policy and Promotion, Washington, DC.

Lojek, Bo, 2007. *History of Semiconductor Engineering*. Springer, New York, NY.

Love, John M., Ellen Eliason Kisker, Christine Ross, Helen Raikes, Jill Constantine, Kimberly Boller, Jeanne Brooks-Gunn, Rachel Chazan-Cohen, Louisa Banks Tarullo, and Christy Brady-Smith, 2005. "The Effectiveness of Early Head Start for Three-Year-Old Children and Their Parents: Lessons for Policy and Programs." *Developmental Psychology* 41 (6), 885–901.

Lowell, Darcy I., Alice S. Carter, Leandra Godoy, Belinda Paulicin, and Margaret J. Briggs-Gowan, 2011. "A Randomized Controlled Trial of Child FIRST: A Comprehensive Home-Based Intervention Translating Research into Early Childhood Practice." *Child Development* 82 (1), 193–208.

Marchman, Virginia A., and Anne Fernald, 2008. "Speed of Word Recognition and Vocabulary Knowledge in Infancy Predict Cognitive and Language Outcomes in Later Childhood." *Developmental Science* 11 (3), F9–16.

Marx, Matt, Deborah Strumsky, and Lee Fleming, 2009. "Mobility, Skills, and the Michigan Non-compete Experiment." *Management Science* 55 (6), 875–89.

Mason, W. Alex, Rick Kosterman, J. David Hawkins, Kevin P. Haggerty, Richard L. Spoth, and Cleve Redmond, 2007. "Influence of a Family-Focused Substance Use Preventive Intervention on Growth in Adolescent Depressive Symptoms." *Journal of Research on Adolescence* 17 (3), 541–64.

Moser, Petra, 2016. "Patents and Innovation in Economic History." *Annual Review of Economics* 8 (1), 241–58.

Nelson, Richard R., and Edmund S. Phelps, 1966. "Investment in Humans, Technological Diffusion, and Economic Growth." *American Economic Review* 56 (1/2), 69–75.

OECD, 2016. *The Survey of Adult Skills: Reader's Companion*, 2nd edition, OECD Skills Studies. OECD Publishing, Paris, https://doi.org/10.1787/9789264258075-en.

Olds, David L., 2006. "The Nurse-Family Partnership: An Evidence-Based Preventive Intervention." *Infant Mental Health Journal* 27 (1), 5–25.

Oreopoulos, Philip, Robert S. Brown, and Adam M. Lavecchia, 2017. "Pathways to Education: An Integrated Approach to Helping At-Risk High School Students." *Journal of Political Economy* 125 (4), 947–84.

Park, Jisuk, Rick Kosterman, J. David Hawkins, Kevin P. Haggerty, Terry E. Duncan, Susan C. Duncan, and Richard Spoth, 2000. "Effects of the 'Preparing for the Drug-Free Years' Curriculum on Growth in Alcohol Use and Risk for Alcohol Use in Early Adolescence." *Prevention Science* 1 (3), 125–38.

Piketty, Thomas, 2014. *Capital in the Twenty-First Century*. Harvard University Press, Cambridge, MA.

Puma, Michael, Stephen Bell, Ronna Cook, Camilla Heid, Gary Shapiro, Pam Broene, Frank Jenkins, Philip Fletcher, Liz Quinn, and Janet Friedman, 2010. *Head Start Impact Study: Final Report*. U.S. Department of Health and Human Services, Washington, DC.

Putnam, Robert D., 2016. *Our Kids: The American Dream in Crisis*. Simon and Schuster, New York, NY.

Ramey, Garey, and Valerie A. Ramey, 2010. "The Rug Rat Race." *Brookings Papers on Economic Activity* 41 (1), 129–99.

Ramey, Craig T., Joseph Sparling, and Sharon L. Ramey, 2012. *Abecedarian: The Ideas, the Approach, and the Findings*. Sociometrics Corporation, Palo Alto, CA.

Reardon, Sean F., 2013. "The Widening Income Achievement Gap." *Educational Leadership* 70 (8), 10–16.

Ricciuti, Anne E., Robert G. St. Pierre, Wang Lee, Amanda Parsad, and Tracy Rimdzius, 2004. *Third National Even Start Evaluation: Follow-Up Findings from the Experimental Design Study*. National Center for Education Evaluation and Regional Assistance, Washington, DC.

Roggman, Lori A., Gina A. Cook, Carla A. Peterson, and Helen H. Raikes, 2008. "Who Drops Out of Early Head Start Home Visiting Programs?" *Early Education and Development* 19 (4), 574–99.

Romer, Paul M., 1990. "Endogenous Technological Change." *Journal of Political Economy* 98 (5), S71–102.

Schweinhart, Lawrence J., 2005. *Lifetime Effects: The High/Scope Perry Preschool Study through Age 40*. High/Scope Press, Ypsilanti, MI.

Shure, Myrna B., and George Spivack, 1982. "Interpersonal Problem-Solving in Young Children: A Cognitive Approach to Prevention." *American Journal of Community Psychology* 10 (3), 341–56.

Slavin, Robert E., 1978. *Using Student Team Learning*. The Johns Hopkins Team Learning Project. Johns Hopkins University Press, Baltimore, MD.

Solow, Robert M., 1956. "A Contribution to the Theory of Economic Growth." *Quarterly Journal of Economics* 70 (1), 65–94.

St. Pierre, Robert G., Anne E. Ricciuti, and Tracy A. Rimdzius, 2005. "Effects of a Family Literacy Program on Low-Literate Children and Their Parents: Findings from an Evaluation of the Even Start Family Literacy Program." *Developmental Psychology* 41 (6), 953–70.

Truelove, Christiane, 2013. "27th Annual Report: Top 50 Pharma Companies." *MedAdNews* 32 (10), 10–11.

Valletta, Robert G., 2017. "Recent Flattening in the Higher Education Wage Premium: Polarization, Skill Downgrading, or Both?" In Charles R. Hulten and Valerie A. Ramey (eds.), *Education, Skills, and Technical Change: Implications for Future US GDP Growth*, 313–56. University of Chicago Press, Chicago, IL.

Von Hippel, Eric, 1994. "'Sticky Information' and the Locus of Problem Solving: Implications for Innovation." *Management Science* 40 (4), 429–39.

Wagner, Mary M., and Serena L. Clayton, 1999. "The Parents as Teachers Program: Results from Two Demonstrations." *The Future of Children* 9 (1), 91–115.

Walker, Susan P., Susan M. Chang, Marcos Vera-Hernández, and Sally Grantham-McGregor, 2011. "Early Childhood Stimulation Benefits Adult Competence and Reduces Violent Behavior." *Pediatrics* 127 (5), 849–957.

Walsh, Gary, 2014. "Biopharmaceutical Benchmarks 2014." *Nature Biotechnology* 32 (10), 992–1000.

Zucker, Lynne, Michael Darby, and Marilynn B. Brewer, 1998. "Intellectual Human Capital and the Birth of US Biotechnology Enterprises." *American Economic Review* 88 (1), 290–306.

Immigration and Economic Growth

George J. Borjas

From 1990 to 2014, U.S. economic growth would have been 15 percentage points lower without the benefit of migration.
–Citi GPS (2018)

There's a way for President Trump to boost the economy by four percent, but he probably won't like it . . . For every one percent increase in U.S. population made of immigrants, GDP rises 1.15 percent. So a simple way to get to Trump's 4 percent GDP bump? Take in about eight million net immigrants per year.
–ProPublica (2017)

4.1 Introduction

There has been a worldwide surge in international migration in recent decades. In the US context, the immigrant share of the population almost tripled from a historic low of 4.7 percent in 1970 to 13.7 percent by 2017.

It is sometimes claimed that the immigration surge has been a key contributor to economic growth, and that an even larger number of immigrants would increase our national wealth even more – although these claims tend to appear in reports produced by think tanks, policy advocates, and business associations. In fact, few academic studies document a direct link between immigration and growth. And the evidence on the outcomes that the studies do examine (such as the impact on wages, employment, and government receipts and expenditures) is far too mixed and unsettled to justify blanket statements that immigration accounts for a substantial part of economic growth – or, conversely, that it does not contribute to economic growth at all.

Despite the relative scarcity of credible research on the link between immigration and growth, there is *no* doubt that immigrants contribute significantly to aggregate output. In 2016, 16.6 percent of workers in the US labor market were foreign-born. The large immigrant presence in the workforce inevitably implies that foreign-born labor was directly responsible for a sizable fraction of GDP. And, by definition, the immigration surge must have led to a correspondingly large increase in GDP. It is far less clear, however, that the immigrant supply shock necessarily increased *per-capita* income.

This chapter presents a theoretical and empirical survey of what it is that we know about the link between immigration and economic growth. The canonical Solow growth model has striking implications about what happens as the economy adjusts to supply shocks. A one-time supply shock increases output *and* decreases per-capita income in the short run. As the economy adjusts, there will be relatively rapid "catch-up" growth. In the end, however, per-capita income ends up in *exactly* the same steady state that would have been observed had there been no immigration. In contrast, a permanent increase in the rate of growth of the workforce due to a persistent immigrant flow will lead to increased output but at a permanently lower per-capita income.

I use these insights to frame the discussion of what economics has to say about immigration and growth. The link obviously depends on many variables, including (1) the skills that immigrants bring to the country; (2) the rate at which immigrants become more productive (which is typically thought of as "economic assimilation"); (3) the impact of immigration on the employment opportunities of native workers; (4) the impact that immigrants have on total income accruing to the preexisting population (i.e., the "immigration surplus"); and (5) the fiscal impact of immigration, as measured by a comparison of the taxes that immigrants pay with the cost of the services that they receive. The net impact of immigration on economic growth will depend on the direction and magnitude of all of these effects.

Despite the uncertainty about the measurement of each of these effects, there is a consensus on one important point: Immigration has a more beneficial impact when the immigrant influx is composed of high-skill workers. In the end, there is little doubt about the type of immigration policy a country should pursue if it wishes to use immigration as a tool to spur growth: Admit high-skill immigrants (although the literature is totally silent on just how many high-skill immigrants should be admitted). There is, however, an important normative question that economics – and economists – cannot answer: Should spurring economic growth be the sole objective of immigration policy?

4.2 Immigration in the Solow Model

It is useful to fix ideas by illustrating the link between immigration and growth in the canonical Solow model (Barro and Sala-i-Martin, 1999). The model is summarized by

$$Y_t = (K_t)^{\alpha}(A_t L_t)^{1-\alpha}, \tag{1}$$

$$\dot{K}_t = sY_t - \delta K_t, \tag{2}$$

$$L_t = L_0 e^{gt}, \text{ and} \tag{3}$$

$$A_t = A_0 e^{\eta t}. \tag{4}$$

Thus, (1) reflects a linearly homogeneous Cobb-Douglas production function where Y_t denotes output at time t, K_t is the capital stock, and $A_t L_t$ is the number of efficiency units in the labor market, with A_t being the efficiency parameter and L_t the number of workers. Then, (2) gives the equation of motion for the capital stock, with constant savings rate s and depreciation rate δ. Finally, (3) and (4) specify that the number of workers grows at rate g and that the efficiency of a worker grows at rate η.

Let k_t denote the "effective" capital–labor ratio, $K_t/A_t L_t$. Income per efficiency unit (which is not observed) is

$$y_t = \frac{Y_t}{A_t L_t} = k_t^{\alpha}, \tag{5}$$

while the *observed* per capita income $\bar{y}_t$ is

$$\bar{y}_t = \frac{Y_t}{L_t} = A_t k_t^{\alpha}. \tag{6}$$

Finally, the wage and the rental rate of capital at time t are given by the marginal productivity conditions

$$w_t = (1-\alpha)A_t k_t^{\alpha}, \text{ and} \tag{7}$$

$$r_t = \alpha k_t^{\alpha-1}. \tag{8}$$

Equation (2) can be rewritten in terms of the effective capital–labor ratio as $\dot{k} = sy_t - (\delta + \eta + g)k_t$. This implies that the steady-state effective capital–labor ratio is

$$k^* = \left(\frac{s}{\delta + \eta + g}\right)^{\frac{1}{1-a}}. \tag{9}$$

Note that the rental rate of capital is constant in the steady state. If labor efficiency is increasing at rate $\eta > 0$, however, both the wage and per-capita income will also increase at rate η in the steady state.

Suppose the economy is in steady state, and immigration produces a *one-time* increase in the size of the workforce. Consider the special case where the size of the workforce was constant prior to the supply shock $(g = 0)$. A one-time influx of immigrants who are perfect substitutes for preexisting workers can then be modeled as a simple shift in L. The one-time supply shock produces an immediate drop in the effective capital–labor ratio (which, in turn, increases the rental rate of capital and reduces the wage). It follows that the immediate impacts on output and per-capita income are given by

$$\frac{\partial Y_t}{\partial L} = (1-a)\bar{y}_t > 0, \text{ and} \tag{10}$$

$$\frac{\partial \bar{y}_t}{\partial L} = \alpha A_t k_t^{\alpha-1} \left(\frac{\partial k_t}{\partial L}\right) < 0. \tag{11}$$

The one-time supply shock trivially increases GDP, as more workers produce more output. But the supply shock reduces per-capita income in the short run.

This short-run drop is attenuated as the economy adjusts to the larger workforce. The decline in the capital–labor ratio increases the rate of return to capital, inducing an increase in the capital stock. As (9) shows, however, the steady-state effective capital–labor ratio does *not* depend on the size of the workforce. As a result, the one-time supply shock does not change the steady-state level of per-capita income:

$$\frac{\partial \bar{y}^*}{\partial L} = 0. \tag{12}$$

Once the steady-state equilibrium is reestablished, the economy has a larger GDP, and per-capita income continues to grow at the same rate η.[1]

---

[1] The transitional dynamics after the one-time shock are interesting. Per capita income was growing at a constant rate of η prior to the shock. After the shock (and before the economy

The model can also be used to analyze the impact of a continuous supply shock, which can be modeled as an increase in g, the rate of growth in the size of the workforce. This persistent shock has long-term consequences. As (9) implies that it reduces the steady-state level of the effective capital–labor ratio, $\partial k^*/\partial g < 0$, it then follows that

$$\frac{\partial \bar{y}^*}{\partial g} = \alpha A_t k_t^{\alpha-1} \left(\frac{\partial k^*}{\partial g}\right) < 0. \tag{13}$$

In short, a persistent immigrant flow permanently reduces per-capita income. Because the saving rate is assumed to be constant, the increase in the rate of population growth reduces the steady-state effective capital–labor ratio and generates a drop in per-capita income.

An augmented version of the Solow model (Mankiw, Romer, and Weil, 1992; Dolado, Goria, and Ichino, 1994) can be used to derive the implications if immigrants also increase the country's human capital stock H. The linearly homogeneous production function in the augmented model is typically written as

$$Y_t = (K_t)^\alpha (H_t)^\beta (A_t L_t)^{1-\alpha-\beta}, \tag{14}$$

and the equations of motion for the physical and human capital stocks are

$$\dot{K}_t = s_K Y_t - \delta K_t \text{ and} \tag{15}$$

$$\dot{H}_t = s_H Y_t - \delta H_t + M_t\, \pi(H_t/L_t), \tag{16}$$

where s_K and s_H are the (constant) investment rates for physical and human capital, respectively; the depreciation rate δ is assumed to be the same for both types of capital; M_t is the net number of immigrants; and π measures the relative contribution of an immigrant to the human capital stock. The immigrant is as skilled as a preexisting worker if $\pi = 1$.

The change in the number of workers is $\dot{L}_t = gL_t + M_t$. Suppose that the number of immigrants increases at the same rate as the native population, so that the net migration rate $m = M_t/L_t$ is con-

---

is reequilibrated), the growth rate increases to $\eta + a\dot{k}/k$ where $\dot{k} > 0$. The growth spurt is short-lived; it reflects only that the shock immediately reduced per capita income and the economy is reverting to the original steady state.

stant. The workforce then grows at constant rate $(g + m)$, and the equations of motion for the effective capital–labor ratios are given by

$$\dot{k} = s_K y_t - [\delta + \eta + g + m] \, k_t \text{ and} \tag{17}$$

$$\dot{h} = s_H y_t - [\delta + \eta + g + (1-\pi)m] \, h_t. \tag{18}$$

The steady state is defined by $\dot{k} = 0$ and $\dot{h} = 0$. The effective capital–labor ratios in the steady state are

$$k^* = \left(\frac{s_K}{\delta + \eta + g + m} \right)^{\frac{1-\beta}{1-\alpha-\beta}} \left(\frac{s_H}{\delta + \eta + g + (1-\pi)m} \right)^{\frac{\beta}{1-\alpha-\beta}} \text{ and} \tag{19}$$

$$h^* = \left(\frac{s_K}{\delta + \eta + g + m} \right)^{\frac{\alpha}{1-\alpha-\beta}} \left(\frac{s_H}{\delta + \eta + g + (1-\pi)m} \right)^{\frac{1-\alpha}{1-\alpha-\beta}}. \tag{20}$$

The steady-state capital–labor ratios in (19) and (20) are constant. As a result, effective per-capita income (given by $y = k^\alpha h^\beta$) will also be constant. In contrast, actual per-capita income $\bar{y} = A k^\alpha h^\beta$ will still grow at a rate of η (as was the case in the simpler version of the Solow model).

Thus, (19) and (20) imply that immigration alters steady-state per-capita income

$$\frac{\partial \log(\bar{y}^*)}{\partial m} = -\frac{\alpha}{(1-\alpha-\beta)C} - \frac{\beta}{(1-\alpha-\beta)D}[1-\pi], \tag{21}$$

where $C = [\delta + \eta + g + m]$, and $D = [\delta + \eta + g + (1-\pi)m] > 0$. Per-capita income will certainly decline if $\pi \leq 1$ (a case relevant for the recent US context with high numbers of low-skill immigrants).[2] In fact, the diminishing marginal productivity of labor implies that per-capita income might fall even if immigrants are relatively more skilled (with π being slightly above 1). Equation (21) shows that immigration can spur long-term growth only if the influx is very skilled, with sufficiently high values of π.

An important lesson from this brief overview of the Solow model is that persistent immigration will often reduce per-capita income in the steady

---

[2] In 2017, for example, data from the American Community Survey indicated that 6.2 percent of prime-age native persons (aged twenty-five to sixty-four) lacked a high school diploma, while the respective statistic for foreign-born persons was 22.4 percent.

state, particularly when the immigrants are perfect substitutes or less skilled than the natives. Immigration may spur long-term growth only if the supply shock is composed of very highly skilled workers. In fact, such a supply shock could increase per-capita incomes by far more than the model suggests if the immigrants also produce human capital externalities that permanently increase the productivity of native workers.

4.3 Immigration and GDP: Evidence

Despite the contentious policy debate over immigration, only a handful of studies examine the empirical link between immigration and long-term growth.[3] Hence, it is useful to begin by illustrating the relationship between GDP and immigration trends in the United States.

Each decennial census since 1850 reports the number of foreign-born persons, allowing the calculation of net immigration in each decade. Define the net migration rate in the decade between years t and $t + 10$ as the net number of immigrants arriving in that decade divided by the population at time t. For expositional convenience, I multiply the net migration rate by 100 so that it gives the number of new immigrants per 100 persons. As Figure 4.1 shows, there have been periods of very high and of very low immigration. Between 1900 and 1910 and between 1990 and 2000, the net migration rate was about 4 new immigrants per 100 persons per decade. In contrast, the net migration rate was negative between 1930 and 1970.

The two panels of the figure also show the decadal rate of change in (real) GDP and in per-capita GDP. It is visually obvious that the simple correlation implied by the historical record does not suggest that there was more rapid economic growth during those periods of high immigration. In fact, the slope of a regression that relates the rate of change in GDP to the net migration rate is 0.008 (with a standard error of 0.014), while the respective coefficient in the per-capita growth regression is −0.010 (0.012).

Obviously, these weak correlations do not prove the absence of a causal link between immigration and growth. There are far too many other

---

[3] See Boubtane, Dumont, and Rault (2016), Dolado et al. (1994), and Kane and Rutledge (2018). Related work by Peri (2012) correlates immigration with total factor productivity (TFP), where TFP is a residual from a regression that links state-level GDP to the size of the workforce and measures of the capital stock. It is particularly difficult to interpret the correlation between TFP and immigration as much depends on the regression specification, and on what exactly is included and left out of the first-stage regression.

(a)

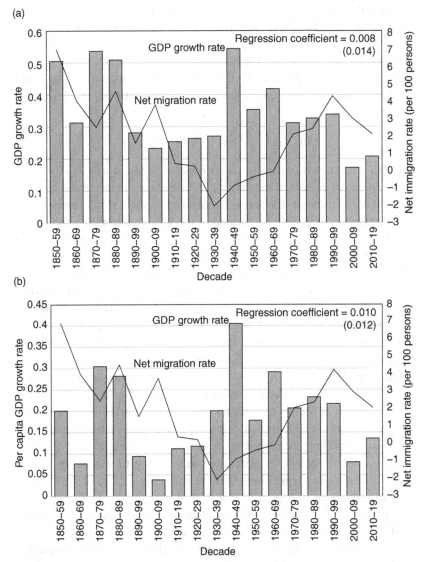

(b)

Figure 4.1 Immigration and economic growth in decadal data, 1850–2017
(a) GDP
(b) Per-capita GDP
Notes: The historical GDP series was obtained from MeasuringWorth.com and the net migration data were drawn from the decennial censuses. The data for 2010–20 are extrapolations from the changes observed between 2010 and 2017. The reported regression coefficient is the slope from an OLS regression of the decadal GDP growth rate on the net migration rate (with standard errors in parentheses).

factors that influence the evolution of economic output and Figure 4.1 does not control for any of these factors. It is possible, however, to examine the causal relationship by linking trends in state-level economic growth and immigration during the 1960–2017 period.

Specifically, I use the decadal census data to calculate the immigrant share in the workforce of each state r at time t and estimate the regression model[4]

$$\log(y_{rt}) = \theta_r + \theta_t + \beta p_{rt} + \gamma h_{rt} + \varepsilon, \tag{22}$$

where y_{rt} is a measure of the gross state product (GSP) in state r at time t; θ_r and θ_t represent vectors of state and year fixed effects, respectively; p_{rt} gives the ratio of the number of working immigrants to the size of the workforce in the state ($\times$ 100); and h_{rt} measures the human capital of the state's workforce (which I proxy by the log mean years of education and by the fraction of workers aged twenty-five and fifty-four).

The top panel of Table 4.1 reports the coefficients estimated by ordinary least squares. There is a positive (and significant) correlation between immigration and GSP across states and over time. An increase in the immigrant share of 1 percent is associated with a 3.2 percent increase in GSP. Note, however, that the coefficient becomes insignificant when the regression uses per-capita GSP as the dependent variable.

The regression model in (22) – which is exactly analogous to the panel regression typically estimated to measure the wage impact of immigration (Borjas, 2014) – suffers from potential endogeneity bias. Income-maximizing immigrants will likely settle in states that offer vibrant economic conditions, building in a positive correlation between y_{rt} and p_{rt}. The bottom panel of Table 4.1 reports the coefficients estimated from instrumental variable (IV) regressions that use the generic "shift-share" instrument to control for endogeneity (Card, 2001).

In particular, I used the 1960 census to observe the geographic settlement of immigrants who originated in a particular country. The key assumption of the shift-share instrument is that this initial geographic distribution influences the settlement of later waves of immigrants from that same country. Future immigrants will find it cheaper to settle in those

---

[4] Kane and Rutledge (2018) conduct a similar analysis for the 1980–2015 period. The panel used in Table 4.1 consists of seven cross-sections (1960, 1970, 1980, 1990, 2000, 2010, and 2017) and fifty states (the District of Columbia is excluded from the regressions). I also estimated the regressions using a first-difference specification. The results are qualitatively similar to those reported in Table 4.1.

Table 4.1 *Immigration and GSP across US states, 1960–2017*

	Log GSP		Log per-capita GSP	
Characteristics of workforce	(1)	(2)	(1)	(2)
A. OLS				
Immigrant share	0.032	0.031	−0.002	−0.000
	(0.008)	(0.008)	(0.005)	(0.003)
Log years of schooling		−0.702		1.358
		(0.745)		(0.302)
Percent prime age		−0.045		1.113
		(1.317)		(0.743)
B. IV				
Immigrant share	0.027	0.019	−0.012	−0.007
	(0.011)	(0.013)	(0.005)	(0.005)
Log years of schooling		−1.497		0.920
		(1.042)		(0.526)
Percent prime age		0.299		1.091
		(1.128)		(0.715)

Notes: Standard errors are reported in parentheses and clustered at the state level. All regressions include state and year fixed effects. The pre-2000 GSP data were obtained from usgovernment spending.com, and the post-1997 data from the Bureau of Economic Analysis. The immigrant share was calculated using data from the 1960–2000 decennial censuses and the 2010 and 2017 American Community Surveys. The mean schooling and prime-age variables were calculated in the sample of native workers. The IV regressions use the 1960 census to construct an instrument based on the geographic settlement of immigrants at that time (within each national origin group); see text for additional details. The OLS regressions have 350 observations, and the IV regressions have 300 observations.

parts of the country where ethnic networks facilitate the move. The shift-share instrument uses the 1960 geographic distribution to geographically allocate the immigrants from that country observed in a subsequent cross-section τ. The predicted number of immigrants living in state r at time τ is then obtained by adding up across countries of origin, and this prediction is used to calculate the predicted fraction of immigrants in the workforce. Note, however, that if the economic conditions that induced the 1960 immigrants to settle in particular states persist over time, the shift-share instrument does not solve the endogeneity problem (Jaeger, Ruist, and Stuhler, 2018).

The IV estimates of the "causal" link between immigration and GDP reported in Table 4.1 are again positive for the level of GSP but turn negative (and insignificant) when looking at per-capita GSP. A one point increase in the immigrant share is associated with a 1.9 percent increase in GSP, and with a 0.7 percent decrease in per-capita GDP.

The prudent inference from the exercises reported in this section seems to be that the correlation between immigration and per-capita income is, at best, zero. The data do not provide any support for the hypothesis that the two variables are strongly and positively correlated, either historically or across regions. It seems that a finding of strong positive effects will require much more data manipulation (and many more assumptions).

4.4 The Immigration Surplus

The negative short-run impact of immigration on wages and the positive impact on the return to capital imply that immigration has distributional consequences. They also raise the possibility that the gains to firms exceed the losses to workers, and there might be an immigration surplus, that is, a net increase in the wealth of the "native" population.

The simplest model of the immigration surplus assumes that immigrants and natives are perfect substitutes (Borjas, 1995). The workforce has N native and M immigrant workers, with $L = N + M$. The aggregate production function $Y = f(K, L)$ is linearly homogeneous. Suppose further that natives own the capital stock and that the supplies of both natives and immigrants are perfectly inelastic. The assumption of inelastic labor supply greatly simplifies the calculation because it implies that the change in well-being accruing to workers who are "encouraged" to leave the labor force when a supply shock lowers the wage can be ignored.

Each factor price equals the respective value of the marginal product in a competitive labor market. The rental rate of capital in the pre-immigration equilibrium is $r_0 = f_K(K, N)$, and the price of labor is $w_0 = f_L(K, N)$, where the output price is the numeraire. Linear homogeneity implies that the entire output is distributed to the owners of capital and to workers. In the pre-immigration regime, the national income accruing to natives, Y_N, is given by $Y_N = r_0 K + w_0 N$.

Figure 4.2 illustrates this initial equilibrium. The value of Y_N is given by the area under the marginal product of labor curve f_L, or trapezoid ABN0. In the short run, the capital stock is fixed. The entry of M immigrants shifts the supply curve and lowers the wage to w_1. The area in the trapezoid ACL0 gives national income in the post-immigration economy. Part of the increase in national income goes to immigrants (who earn $w_1 M$ dollar). The area in the triangle BCD gives the immigration surplus, the increase in income that accrues to natives.

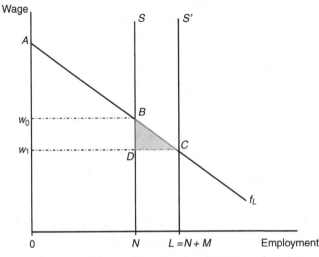

Figure 4.2 Immigration surplus

The immigration surplus, as a fraction of national income, approximately equals

$$\frac{\Delta Y_N}{Y} = -\frac{1}{2} s_L \varepsilon p^2, \qquad (23)$$

where s_L is labor's share of income ($s_L = wL/Y$), ε is the wage elasticity ($\varepsilon = d\log w/d\log L$), and p is the immigrant share of the workforce ($p = M/L$).

Equation (23) gives a simple formula for doing a "back-of-the-envelope" calculation (summarized in Table 4.2). The share of labor income hovered around 70 percent for some decades (although it has declined to roughly 60 percent in recent years) and the fraction of immigrants in the workforce is 16.6 percent. Suppose further that the linearly homogeneous production function is Cobb-Douglas. It is then easy to show that the absolute value of the wage elasticity ε equals capital's share of income, or about 0.3. The immigration surplus is then 0.29 percent of GDP. In 2017, GDP was $19.5 trillion, so the short-run immigration surplus is about $56 billion a year, a relatively small number in the context of a very large economy.

Figure 4.2 shows that immigration redistributes income from labor to capital. Native workers lose the area in the rectangle $w_0 B D w_1$ and this quantity plus the surplus accrues to employers. Table 4.2 also reports the implied dollar value of these losses and gains (see Borjas (1995) for the

Table 4.2 *Short-run immigration surplus*
($ billion), 2017

Immigration surplus	56.4
Loss to native workers	566.9
Gain to native firms	623.3
Total increase in GDP	2,322.3
Payments to immigrants	2,265.9

Source: Updated from Borjas, 1995. The calculation assumes that labor's share of income is 0.7 and that the immigrant share of the workforce is 16.6 percent. The value of GDP in 2017 was $19.5 trillion.

algebraic details). Native-born workers lose about 2.9 percent of GDP, while native-owned capital gains about 3.2 percent of GDP. The $19.5 trillion GDP implies that workers lose $567 billion while employers gain $623 billion. The small surplus of $56 billion masks a sizable redistribution from workers to the users of immigrant labor.

Note that the immigration surplus, which measures the dollar gains accruing to natives, is conceptually different from the total increase in GDP. As Table 4.2 also shows, a supply shock that increases the workforce by almost 17 percent generates a very sizable increase in GDP of over $2 trillion. Almost all of this increase, however, goes to the immigrants themselves as payments for their services. The calculation, therefore, suggests that immigrants are the main beneficiaries from immigration, as the $2 trillion they receive for their labor services in the United States is a far larger amount than they would have received had they never migrated.

Finally, the short-run surplus derived in Figure 4.2 assumed that capital was fixed. The rise in the returns to capital encourages capital inflows until the rental rate is again equalized across markets. The assumption of constant returns implies that the expansion in the capital stock reestablishes the pre-immigration capital–labor ratio. In the end, immigration does not alter the price of labor or the returns to capital and natives neither gain nor lose from immigration. In the long run, the immigration surplus must be zero.

4.4.1 Heterogeneous Labor

Figure 4.2 assumed that natives and immigrants are perfect substitutes. There may exist production complementarities between the two groups that can increase the gains from immigration. Suppose there are two types of worker, low-skill L_U and high-skill L_H. The linearly homogeneous production function is now $Y = f(K, L_U, L_H)$. Suppose further that the supply shock is not "balanced" across skill groups (i.e., immigrants are predominantly low-skill or high-skill). The long-term adjustment in the capital stock would *not* lead to a new equilibrium with the economy simply operating at a proportionately higher scale for all inputs.[5] The potential complementarities between immigrants and natives would help produce a larger immigration surplus.

Not surprisingly, capital-skill complementarity suggests that the short-run surplus might be larger if the immigrant flow was composed of high-skill workers. By assumption, natives own the capital stock and capital-skill complementarity implies that the returns to capital increase more when immigrants are high-skill. In fact, simulations of the model suggest that estimates of the short-run immigration surplus might double if the United States admitted only high-skill immigrants (Borjas, 2014). However, the long-run capital adjustments would attenuate the importance of capital-skill complementarity and greatly reduce the gains from high-skill supply shocks.

4.4.2 Human Capital Externalities

The calculation of the immigration surplus with a linearly homogeneous production function suggests that even a large supply shock of high-skill workers may not generate relatively large gains for the native population. Nevertheless, there is a widespread (and unshakeable) perception that some types of immigration, and particularly the immigration of high-skill workers, can be hugely beneficial. This perception relies on a crucial departure from the textbook model, the belief that high-skill immigrants generate human capital externalities. The sudden presence of high-skill immigrants exposes natives to new forms of knowledge, increases their human capital, and makes them more productive.

It is easy to illustrate how externalities change the immigration surplus. If high-skill immigrants have positive spillover effects on native productivity, an influx of immigrants produces an outward shift in the labor

---

[5] In the homogeneous labor case, an increase of x percent in the number of workers induces an x percent increase in the capital stock so that the long-run equilibrium has the economy operating at a larger scale with the same proportionate increase in capital, labor, and output. In the heterogeneous labor case with an unbalanced supply shock, the input ratios would be different in the pre- and post-shock equilibriums.

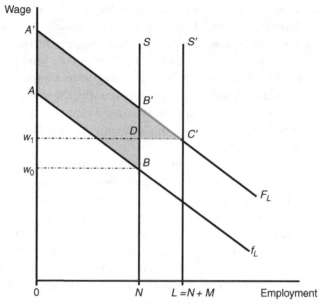

Figure 4.3 Immigration surplus and human capital externalities

demand curve because the value of the marginal product for every native worker rises. Immigration then not only shifts the supply curve but also shifts the demand curve to F_L in Figure 4.3. The change in income accruing to natives is then given by the sum of the triangle $B'C'D$ (or the traditional immigration surplus) *plus* the shaded area of the trapezoid $A'B'BA$, which measures the impact of immigration on the total product of native workers. It is obvious that if the externalities are sufficiently important, high-skill immigration could be an important driver of economic growth.

Figure 4.3 suggests a trivial back-of-the-envelope calculation that illustrates just how important these externalities can be. Suppose a high-skill supply shock raises the marginal product of every native worker by φ percent, so that the new demand curve $F_L = (1 + \varphi)f_L$. This formulation implies that the gains produced by the externalities equal φ percent of the original GDP. Table 4.2 suggests that the pre-immigration GDP, measured by trapezoid ABN0 in Figure 4.3, is about $17 trillion. If the externality increases marginal product by 1 percent, the gains produced by high-skill immigration would be about $170 billion. In short, the gains from human capital externalities can easily dwarf those measured by the traditional immigration surplus. Moreover, these large gains do not disappear in the long run, as the increased productivity of the native workforce is a permanent fixture of the labor market.

4.5 The Distributional Impact of Immigration

In the absence of human capital externalities, the canonical model of the labor market suggests that a one-time supply shock will depress the wage of competing workers in the short run, and that this negative effect is attenuated over time as the economy adjusts to the larger workforce. Despite the intuitive appeal of these insights, the literature that estimates the wage elasticity (*the* crucial parameter for calculating both the gains from immigration and the distributional impact) has instead produced a confusing labyrinth, with estimates that often depend on the methodological approach, the sample used, and the period examined.

Because immigrants cluster in a relatively small number of geographic areas, many studies exploit the geographic dispersion of immigrants to measure the wage effect. These studies compare native earnings in cities where the immigrant share of the workforce is large (e.g., Los Angeles) with earnings in cities where there are relatively few immigrants. A negative spatial correlation would then be interpreted as showing that the supply shock reduced the wage of substitutable natives.

The regression model is typically given by

$$\log(w_{rt}) = \beta p_{rt} + \gamma X_{rt} + \varepsilon, \tag{24}$$

where w_{rt} is the mean wage of native workers in city r at time t, and p_{rt} is the immigrant share. The vector X typically includes variables that also generate wage dispersion across cities and over time and are often proxied by city and year fixed effects.

It is well known that the OLS estimate of β does not measure the causal effect of immigration. Immigrants tend to settle in high-wage cities. The endogenous geographic distribution then generates a positive spurious correlation between immigration and native wages. As noted earlier, most studies use a shift-share instrument to address the problem. This instrument gives the predicted number of immigrants in a city at time t based on the geographic distribution of earlier waves. The shift-share instrument, however, is valid only if the economic conditions that motivated earlier waves to settle in particular cities are uncorrelated with the conditions in those cities today.

Some studies avoid the endogeneity problem by searching for natural experiments where large numbers of immigrants are randomly "dropped off" in a particular location at a particular time, with the Mariel boatlift being the classic context. On April 20, 1980, Fidel Castro declared that Cubans wishing to move to the United States could leave freely from the port of Mariel. By September 1980, about 125,000 Cubans had accepted the invitation, and Miami's labor force had unexpectedly grown by 8 percent.

Card (1990) concluded that the average wage in Miami was barely affected by the Mariel supply shock (relative to wage trends in comparable cities). Borjas (2017), however, noted that the refugees were predominantly low-skill. Nearly two-thirds of the *Marielitos* did not have a high-school diploma, increasing the number of high-school dropouts in Miami by nearly 20 percent. It would then make sense to look for the impact of the Mariel boatlift in Miami's low-skill labor market. Figure 4.4a shows the wage trends revealed by the March Current Population Surveys (CPS) in the sample of non-Hispanic men, aged twenty-five to fifty-nine, who did not have a high-school diploma. The relative wage of this group in Miami took a nosedive after 1980, and it took a decade for the wage to recover.

Several subsequent studies have argued that other definitions of the "low-skill" workforce and that adjusting for sampling issues in the CPS yield different results. Peri and Yasenov (2015), for instance, examine the wage trends in a low-skill sample given by non-Cuban workers, aged sixteen to sixty-one, who did not have a high-school diploma. As Figure 4.4b shows, the wage trends in this sample suggest that Mariel did not affect the low-skill wage.[6] The question then becomes: Which sample best captures conditions in Miami's "low-skill" labor market? As an example of the nuances involved, the addition of workers aged sixteen to eighteen to the low-skill sample implies that *high-school students* are classified as "high-school dropouts" because they do not yet have a high-school diploma and the CPS (at the time) did not provide information on whether a person was enrolled in school. The very large number of high-school students overwhelms the data and potentially contaminates the wage trend.[7]

---

[6] This is the sample used in the original draft of Peri and Yasenov (2015). Recent work by Clemens and Hunt (2019) notes an additional problem with the March CPS sample: the fraction of the low-skill workforce that is black jumped dramatically in 1979, potentially contaminating the wage trend. Borjas (2019), however, documents that much of the wage decline documented in Figure 4.4a actually occurred during a time when the fraction of black workers in the CPS sample was relatively constant.

[7] The reconciliation of the Mariel evidence will likely require data that examine aspects of the Miami labor market not measured by the CPS. Anastasopoulos, Borjas, Cook, and Lachanski (2018) examine trends in the number of job vacancies (as measured by the Conference Board Help-Wanted Index) and document a sizable post-Mariel decline in the relative number of help-wanted classifieds in the *Miami Herald*.

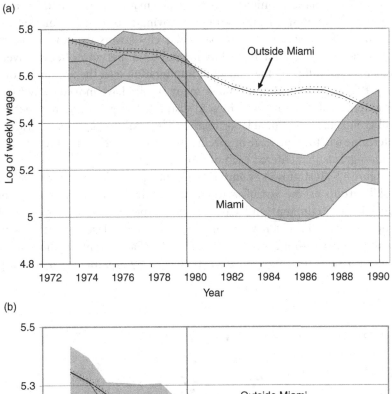

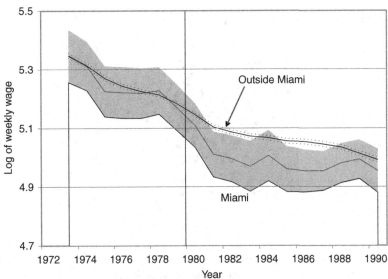

Figure 4.4 Mariel and the wage of high-school dropouts
(a) Non-Hispanic men aged twenty-five to fifty-nine
(b) Non-Cuban workers aged sixteen to sixty-one
Notes: Adapted from Borjas, 2017. The wage data represent a three-year moving average and the shaded area is the 95 percent confidence interval.

Spatial correlations might also be problematic because natives may respond to supply shocks migration by moving to other labor markets. If the entry of immigrants into a particular city lowers the wage, natives might move to places unaffected by immigration that now offer relatively higher wages, diffusing the impact of immigration over the national economy. Beginning with Borjas (2003), many studies have moved away from geographic comparisons and instead examined wage trends for specific skill groups in the national labor market. The "skill-cell approach" tries to determine whether the wage of specific skill groups is related to the number of immigrants that entered each of those groups.

Figure 4.5 illustrates a key empirical implication of this approach. Define a skill group as the set of workers with a particular combination of educational attainment and labor market experience (e.g., high-school dropouts with six to ten years of experience, or college graduates with twenty to twenty-four years of experience). Each point in the scatter diagram relates the wage growth experienced by a particular skill group

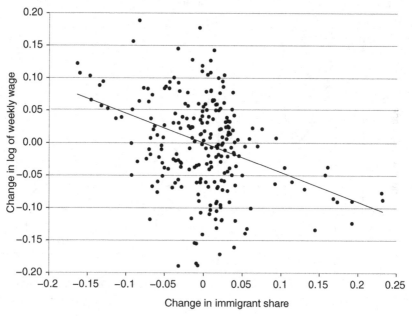

Figure 4.5 Scatter relating wages and immigrant share across skill groups and over time, 1960–2010
Source: Borjas, 2014, p. 95. Each point in the scatter diagram gives the decadal wage change and the decadal change in the immigrant share for native working men with a particular level of education and labor market experience.

of natives over a particular decade to the change in the percent of the group that is foreign-born (using decadal census data from 1960 through 2010). There is an obvious negative correlation between the two variables, and the regression line suggests that a 10 percent increase in the size of the skill group reduces the wage of that group by 3 to 4 percent.

As this brief overview of a huge literature suggests, there are methodological and sampling choices that often lead to *very* different conclusions. A recent National Academy of Sciences (NAS) report on the economic impact of immigration (Blau and Mackie, 2016) summarized the value of the wage elasticity estimated in the main studies. Table 4.3 shows that the point estimates vary widely, and can be positive, zero, or negative.

The skill-cell approach can be expanded to address a limitation of the generic regression model in (24). A supply shock in a particular skill group affects the wage of workers in that skill group and the wage of other skill groups as well. Given the vast number of potential skill groups in the workforce, the cross-effects can be estimated only by specifying a structural model of the production technology that limits the allowable interactions. Borjas (2003) introduced the nested CES framework

Table 4.3 *Representative estimates of the wage elasticity in recent studies, as chosen by the NAS*

Study	Elasticity	Native sample
Llull (2018)	−1.7	Men
Altonji and Card (1991)	−1.7	Dropouts, black men
	−1.0	Dropouts
Borjas (2016)	−1.4	Dropouts, non-Hispanic men
	−0.5	Dropouts, non-Hispanic men
Monras (2015)	−0.7	High-school graduates or less, non-Hispanic
Borjas (2003)	−0.6	Men
Cortes (2008)	−0.6	Dropouts, Hispanic with poor English
	−0.3	Dropouts, Hispanic
	−0.1	Dropouts
Card and Peri (2016)	−0.2	Men
	−0.1	Men
Card (2001)	−0.1	Men
	+0.1	Women
Peri and Yasenov (2015)	+0.3	Dropouts, non-Cuban

Source: Blau and Mackie, 2016, table 5–2, p. 242. See the NAS report for detailed citations to the studies included in the table.

$$Q_t = [\lambda_{Kt}K_t^\delta + \lambda L_t^\delta]^{\frac{1}{\delta}}, \tag{25}$$

$$L_t = \left[\sum_s \theta_{st}L_{st}^\beta\right]^{\frac{1}{\beta}}, \text{ and} \tag{26}$$

$$L_{st} = \left[\sum_x \alpha_{sxt}L_{sxt}^\eta\right]^{\frac{1}{\eta}}, \tag{27}$$

where Q_t is output, K_t is capital, L_t denotes the number of efficiency units in the aggregate labor market, $\delta = 1-1/\sigma_{KL}$, with σ_{KL} being the elasticity of substitution between capital and labor, L_{st} gives the effective supply of workers with education s at time t, $\beta = 1-1/\sigma_S$ with σ_S being the elasticity of substitution across these education aggregates, L_{sxt} gives the number of workers in education group s and experience group x at time t, and $\eta = 1-1/\sigma_X$, with σ_X being the elasticity of substitution across experience classes.

The structural approach shows that the elasticities of substitution among different types of worker are the "fundamentals" that determine the wage impact of immigration. The (log-linear) marginal productivity conditions implied by the nested CES allow for easy estimation of these elasticities using data on wages and employment for the skill cells. Table 4.4, also drawn from the NAS report, uses the estimated elasticities to *simulate* the wage impact of the immigrants who entered between 1990 and 2010 (who are treated as a one-time shock). Even after accounting for all potential cross-effects, this supply shock reduced the wage of the least-skilled workers by 6.3 percent in the short run and by 3.1 percent in the long run.

Subsequent extensions of the framework in (25)–(27) emphasize the importance of two additional elasticities of substitution that may change the implications of the numerical simulation. Ottaviano and Peri (2012) relax the assumption in (27) that immigrants and natives who have the same educational attainment and the same labor market experience are perfect substitutes. The potential complementarity between observationally equivalent immigrants and natives would attenuate any negative wage effect. Card (2009) argues that high-school dropouts and high-school graduates are perfect substitutes, changing the definition of the low-skill workforce.

The various panels of Table 4.4 show how the alternative assumptions change the simulated wage impact. The Ottaviano-Peri (2012) estimate of

Table 4.4 *Simulated percent wage effects of 1990–2010 immigrant supply shock on native workers*

	High-school dropouts	High-school graduates	Some college	College graduates	Post-college	All natives
Percent supply shift	25.9	8.4	6.1	10.9	15.0	10.6
Basic simulation:						
Short run	−6.3	−2.8	−2.3	−3.3	−4.1	−3.2
Long run	−3.1	0.4	0.9	−0.1	−0.9	0.0
Similar immigrants and natives are complements:						
Short run	−4.9	−2.3	−2.0	−2.7	−3.3	−2.6
Long run	−1.7	0.9	1.2	0.5	−0.1	0.6
And high-school dropouts and high-school graduates are perfect substitutes:						
Short run	−2.1	−3.0	−2.0	−2.7	−3.3	−2.7
Long run	1.1	0.2	1.2	0.5	−0.1	0.5

Source: Blau and Mackie, 2016, table 5–1, pp. 236–7. The simulation results that assume that statistically similar immigrants and natives are complements assume an elasticity of substitution between the two groups equal to 20.

an elasticity of substitution of 20 between observationally equivalent immigrants and natives is too large to matter much in the simulation. The short-run impact on the wage of high-school dropouts is −4.9 percent, while the long-run impact is −1.7 percent. But the assumption that high-school dropouts and high-school graduates are perfect substitutes makes a difference. By adding the tens of millions of natives who are high-school graduates into the low-skill labor market, the impact of the entry of millions of low-skill immigrants (who often do not have a high-school diploma) is diluted because the baseline workforce grows even more. It is this assumption that produces a simulation suggesting that immigration has no adverse impact on the wage of low-skill workers.

4.5.1 Human Capital Externalities

Human capital externalities can attenuate the adverse impact of immigration on competing workers and generate very large economic gains at the same time. A number of recent studies examine specific historical events involving high-skill supply shocks to determine whether there were resulting externalities.

The work of Waldinger (2010, 2012) exemplifies the methodological approach. Immediately after seizing power in 1933, the National Socialist Party enacted the Law for the Restoration of the Professional Civil Service, which mandated the dismissal of all Jewish professors from German universities. Almost 20 percent of German mathematics professors were dismissed, including some of the most famous mathematicians of the era (such as John von Neumann, Richard Courant, and Richard von Mises).

The Jewish mathematicians had not been randomly employed across German universities, so some departments barely noticed the dismissals while other departments lost over half their faculty. If those exceptional mathematicians produced beneficial externalities for their students or colleagues, the dismissals would have had a detectable impact on the eventual productivity of the persons "left behind." Waldinger (2010) shows that the *students* left behind in the departments that suffered the heaviest losses experienced a relative decline in their productivity, suggesting that human capital externalities do matter. Waldinger (2012), however, documents that the publication rate of the *colleagues* left behind was not affected by the dismissals. The different results in the two Waldinger studies suggest that human capital externalities are not necessarily produced even when the supply shock involves exceptional workers. The outcome seems to depend on the nature of the relationship between the immigrants and the affected workers.

Borjas and Doran (2012) conduct a similar examination of another high-skill supply shock. For decades prior to 1992, there had been little intellectual contact between Soviet and Western mathematicians. As a result, the two groups specialized in very different fields. The two most popular Soviet fields were partial differential equations and ordinary differential equations. The two most popular American fields were statistics and operations research. After the collapse of the Soviet Union in 1992, several hundred Soviet mathematicians left the country and settled in the United States.

Borjas and Doran (2012) tracked the publication record of every American mathematician before and after the arrival of the Soviet émigrés to measure the impact of the supply shock on the mathematicians who had the most Soviet-like research agendas. There are two possible effects. The first is implied by the law of diminishing returns. An increase in the number of mathematicians deriving theorems in, say, partial differential equations makes the comparable American mathematicians less productive. The second is implied by human capital externalities. Exposing American mathematicians to new theorems and techniques could increase the productivity of the mathematicians working in those fields. The analysis demonstrates that there was a precipitous *decline* in the publication rate of the group whose research agenda overlapped most with the Soviets.

Finally, several studies examine the impact of the high-tech workers admitted in the H-1B visa program. The number of H-1B visas is capped and this cap has fluctuated over time. The conclusion that the H-1B program produces externalities often comes from studies that estimate spatial correlations. Because H-1B visa-holders cluster in a small number of locations (such as San Francisco), an exogenous increase in the cap would be expected to have a large impact in "H-1B dependent" cities. Kerr and Lincoln (2010) showed that an increase in the cap led to more patents originating in those cities. The increased patenting, however, came mainly from persons with Indian or Chinese surnames, suggesting that those new patents originated with the immigrants themselves, rather than from a spillover effect on native workers.

Some of the subsequent studies that estimate spatial correlations report large beneficial effects. Peri, Shih, and Sparber (2015) relate the H-1B-induced increase in the number of STEM workers to the wage of college graduates in a city and find a very strong positive effect. The magnitude, however, seems implausible; a 1 percent increase in the size of the STEM workforce raises the wage of college graduates by 8 percent (wage elasticity of +8.0). Most likely, the endogeneity plaguing spatial correlations and problems with the shift-share instrument lead the data to regurgitate the obvious fact that high-skill immigrants end up in places where the high-skill labor market is doing quite well.

Doran, Gelber, and Isen (2015) avoid endogeneity bias by examining a natural experiment created by a peculiarity of the H-1B program. Firms can apply for the visas on a first-come, first-served basis until the visas run out. On some random day during a year, the visas run out and *on that day* more firms typically apply for visas than there are visas available. The Department of Homeland Security then runs a lottery to determine which firms get the visas. It turns out that the firms that won the lottery did not patent more and that native employment in those firms fell.

In short, the evidence supporting the conjecture that high-skill immigration generates sizable human capital externalities is mixed. There are some historical events that produced such externalities, but there are also other events where the externalities are absent.

4.6 Immigrant Skills

As the augmented Solow model suggests, the impact of immigrants on economic growth depends on the human capital stock they bring into the country, and on how that stock changes as assimilation takes place (Chiswick, 1978; Borjas, 1985).

The 2016 NAS report (Blau and Mackie, 2016) uses the census cross-sections between 1970 and 2010 to track the age-adjusted wage of specific immigrant waves over the past few decades. Figure 4.6a illustrates the trends in the relative wage. The figure reveals two interesting and well-known findings. The first is the presence of sizable cohort differences in entry wages, with more recent cohorts having lower earnings potential than earlier cohorts through the year 2000. In 1970, the most recent immigrant wave earned 23.5 percent less than comparable natives at the time of entry. By 1990, the entry wage disadvantage had grown to 33.1 percent, before contracting to 27.3 percent in 2000.

Figure 4.6a also hints at a slowdown in the rate of "economic assimilation." The immigrant cohorts that arrived prior to the early 1980s experienced faster relative wage growth than the more recent arrivals. Consider, for example, the cohort that arrived in the late 1960s. The relative wage of this group improved from a disadvantage of 23.5 percent in 1970 to 2.0 percent by 2000 – a growth of about 20 percentage points over two decades. In contrast, the relative wage of the cohort that entered the country in the late 1980s improved only from an entry disadvantage of 33.1 percent to 25.2 percent by 2010.

The assimilation slowdown is also evident in data that are far less sensitive to the impact of transitory economic conditions on the relative wage of immigrants. Figure 4.6b shows the comparable trends in the fraction of immigrants who speak English very well (or only speak English). Note that 30.9 percent of the immigrants who arrived between 1975 and 1980 were proficient in English at the time of arrival, and this fraction increased to 46.2 percent by 2000. In contrast, the proficiency rate of the cohort that entered the country in the late 1980s increased by only 7 percentage points during the first twenty years. The evidence revealed in Figure 4.6, therefore, suggests that there is no inevitable assimilation process that will mechanically increase per-capita income as the immigrant population acquires skills that attenuate the initial productivity disadvantage.

It is insightful to compare the modern evidence with the historical record. Although it is widely believed that the human capital stock of the

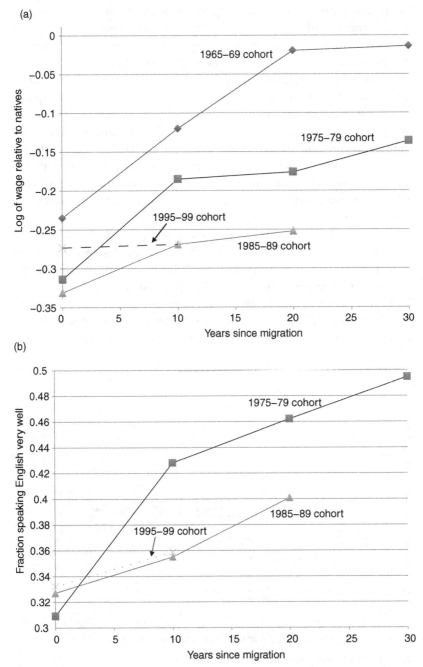

Figure 4.6 Economic assimilation of immigrants, 1970–2010
(a) Relative wage profiles
(b) English proficiency profiles
Notes: Blau and Mackie, 2016, table 3–12, p. 110, and figure 3–16, p. 115.

immigrants who arrived at the beginning of the twentieth century increased dramatically during their lifetime, recent research suggests that the widespread consensus may be wrong. The public release of the census manuscripts compiled at the time allows modern historians to track specific *persons* from census to census. This tracking lets us inspect the career paths of specific natives and immigrants. The exercise turns the widespread perception of rapid improvement on its head. As Abramitzky, Boustan, and Eriksson (2014, pp. 269–70) conclude: "The notion that European immigrants converged with natives after spending 10 to 15 years in the US is ... exaggerated, as we find that initial immigrant-native occupational gaps persisted over time." In short, the historical experience provides surprisingly little evidence of *any* relative economic improvement for the Ellis Island immigrants during their lifetime.

Finally, the available evidence suggests a positive correlation between the skills that immigrants bring into the United States and the rate of subsequent growth in earnings. Figure 4.7 illustrates the link between the wage growth experienced by a national origin group in its first ten years in the United States and the average education of the group at the time of arrival. It is evident that more-skilled groups experience faster assimilation. The evidence, therefore, supports the conjecture of complementarity in the

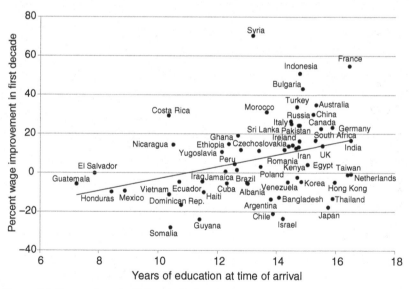

Figure 4.7 Economic assimilation and education
Source: Borjas, 2016, p. 101.

production of human capital: those immigrants who invested more in human capital prior to migration are likely to invest more in human capital after migration. Put differently, the relative economic contribution of high-skill immigrants to aggregate output increases over time.

4.7 The Fiscal Impact

Immigration generates a short-run economic gain through the immigration surplus and may generate a long-run increase if immigrants are sufficiently skilled or there are human capital externalities. The economic gains that accrue through the labor market, however, need to be contrasted with the fiscal impact of immigration. The fiscal impact can be either positive or negative, depending on how much immigrants contribute to the funding of government programs and how much it costs to provide public services to them.

The question of whether immigrants use government programs more or less often than natives is controversial and the answer is highly disputed. In fact, it is enlightening to illustrate how the *same* data can be manipulated in different ways to reach very different conclusions about the relative use of welfare programs by the immigrant population.

Since 1994, the Current Population Surveys (CPS) provide information on participation in various assistance programs for both immigrants and natives, making it possible to document the difference in welfare participation rates. For expositional convenience, suppose that being "on welfare" means receiving benefits from Medicaid, food stamps, or cash benefits. We can then use the CPS to determine whether the fraction of immigrants on welfare is higher, lower, or the same as the fraction of natives.

The two panels of Figure 4.8 show the trends between 1994 and 2018. Note, however, that the two panels yield very different results. In Figure 4.8, the fraction of immigrants on welfare is far higher than the fraction of natives, while in Figure 4.8, the participation rate is essentially the same for the two groups.

Both panels of the figure use the same data but manipulate them in different ways. In particular, the two panels use a different unit of analysis in the calculations. Figure 4.8 uses the *household* as the unit of analysis, which is the way in which welfare use is most often analyzed. An immigrant household is one where the head of the household is foreign-born, and a native household is one where the head is native-born. It is evident that households headed by an immigrant have high rates of welfare use (defined as anyone in the

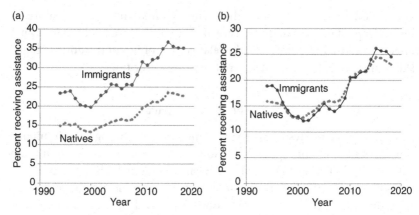

Figure 4.8 Trends in welfare participation rates, 1994–2018
(a) Households
(b) Persons
Source: Author's calculations from the Current Population Surveys, Annual Social and Economic Supplement. Welfare participation is defined in terms of use of cash benefits, food stamps, or Medicaid.

household receiving one of the three programs under analysis), and that the gap between immigrant and native households increased over time. By 2018, 35.1 percent of immigrant households were on welfare as compared to 22.6 percent of native households. In contrast, Figure 4.8 uses the *person* as the unit of analysis. In 2018, 24.5 percent of foreign-born persons and 23.1 percent of native-born persons received assistance from one of the three programs.

The reason for the difference between the two panels is easy to grasp by considering a trivial example. A young, single immigrant woman arrives in the country. After a few years, she becomes a single mother, has three children, and qualifies for Medicaid. In Figure 4.8a, the four-person grouping would be classified as an immigrant household on welfare. In Figure 4.8b, the tally would record *one immigrant person* on welfare and *three native persons* on welfare. And therein lies the numerical trick: Because the children were born in the United States, they enter on the native side of the ledger.

The 2016 NAS report contains a detailed analysis of the fiscal impact that goes far beyond the calculation of welfare participation rates (Blau and Mackie, 2016, chapters 8 and 9). The NAS report adds up both the taxes paid and the cost of the services received for *immigrants and their descendants*, so as to come up with a "bottom-line" number that summarizes the long-run fiscal impact.

This long-run perspective accounts for the fact that many current expenditures, such as schooling for immigrant children or health care, generate future returns through higher earnings when the children enter the labor market. The exercise also incorporates the possibility that immigrants might help fiscally because the native population is aging, and funds will be needed to cover current liabilities in Social Security and Medicare. The NAS used a seventy-five-year period to calculate the long-run fiscal impact.

The NAS exercise shows that the bottom line of the long-run calculation for the average immigrant depends *entirely* on the assumptions made. It is easy to generate either a very positive long-run fiscal impact or a very negative one by making different assumptions. Two distinct assumptions drive the conclusion. First, the calculation needs to allocate expenditures on public goods between immigrants and natives. Although it makes sense to assume that the cost of public goods, such as police protection or national defense, is unchanged if the country admits one more immigrant (so that the marginal cost is zero), it makes less sense to assume that the cost of public goods is unchanged if the country admits over 40 million immigrants. Similarly, any long-run scenario must make assumptions about the future path of taxes and government expenditures, and different assumptions lead to different conclusions.

Table 4.5 summarizes the results from four scenarios presented in the NAS report. The long-run fiscal impact of the average immigrant (measured as the present value of the difference between taxes and expenditures) is positive only if immigrants do not affect the cost of public goods and we also assume that future tax rates and benefit payments follow the projections made by the Congressional Budget Office (CBO). The positive long-term impact of an immigrant (a net present value (NPV) of +$58,000) becomes a loss (potentially as large as −$119,000) if one changes either of those assumptions (by assuming average cost rather than zero marginal cost pricing for public services or by assuming continuation of the fiscal policies under current law rather than the CBO projections of such policies).

Note, however, that the fiscal impact of high-skill immigration is *always* positive, while the fiscal impact of low-skill immigration is *always* negative. Although it is impossible to know which scenario (if any) best approximates the future, high-skill immigration is always a better "deal" from a fiscal perspective. The long-run fiscal benefit from an immigrant with a graduate degree is between $236,000 and $547,000, while the long-

Table 4.5 *Long-run fiscal impact of immigration*

	Future path of taxes and spending projected by the CBO (dollars)	Current path of taxes and spending continues into future (dollars)
Zero marginal cost pricing for public goods		
All workers	+58,000	−36,000
High school dropouts	−196,000	−219,000
High school graduates	−47,000	−112,000
Some college	99,000	−10,000
Bachelor's degree	280,000	123,000
Graduate education	547,000	318,000
Average cost pricing for public goods		
All workers	−5,000	−119,000
High school dropouts	−259,000	−301,000
High school graduates	−109,000	−193,000
Some college	34,000	−96,000
Bachelor's degree	216,000	39,000
Graduate education	485,000	236,000

Source: Blau and Mackie, 2016, tables 8–12, pp. 430–3. All estimates are in 2013 dollars.

run fiscal burden imposed by a high school dropout is between −$196,000 and −$301,000.

These estimates imply that a change in immigration policy that only permits the entry of high-skill workers can be an important contributor to economic growth even in the absence of human capital externalities. Consider the scenario that generates the smallest fiscal gain for the average immigrant (i.e., the scenario that assumes average cost pricing for public goods and disregards the CBO projections). The average immigrant produces a long-term loss of −$119,000. Suppose, however, that every immigrant had been a college graduate. The NPV in this scenario jumps from a burden of −$119,000 to a gain of +$39,000, or a net gain of +$158,000. Assuming a 3 percent rate of discount, the annualized gain is $4,740. There were 44.5 million immigrants in 2017. If all these immigrants had been college graduates, the country would have been $211 billion richer. The projected gain is even larger in the scenario that assumes marginal cost pricing and uses the CBO projections. The increase in the country's wealth if all immigrants had been college graduates would be $311 billion. In short, high-skill immigration can be an important determinant of economic growth simply because of its fiscal consequences.[8]

4.8 Implications

The United States offers exceptional opportunities to anyone lucky enough to live within its borders. As a result, many more people want to immigrate than the country is willing to admit. Consider, for example, the "diversity lottery" held annually since 1995. Each year, some visas are made available to persons originating in "countries with low rates of immigration to the United States." Persons living in the eligible countries can apply for a random chance at winning one of the coveted green cards. The 2018 lottery drew 23.1 million qualified applications for the 50,000 available visas.

The huge excess demand for entry visas implies that immigration policy often specifies a set of rationing rules with which to pick and choose from the many applicants. These rules may stress family ties (as is currently done for the bulk of legal immigrants) or national origin (as used to be done) or socioeconomic characteristics (as is done in other countries). Which types of immigrant should the country admit?

The case that can be made for preferring one type of immigrant over another ultimately depends on what one *assumes* about the country's policy objectives. Specifically, what should the United States seek to accomplish from immigration? Different policy goals lead to different choices about the composition of the immigrant flow. If immigration policy strives to relieve the tax burden on native-born taxpayers, it would be fiscally irresponsible to admit millions of low-skill immigrants who have a high propensity for participating in assistance programs. But if the goal is to help the millions of persons now living in poverty-stricken regions of the world, the increased cost of low-skill immigration is the price that Americans are willing to pay for their generosity.

Assume that the goal of immigration policy is to achieve a high rate of economic growth. A very strong case can be made that there would be faster economic growth, particularly as defined by the trend in per-capita income, if the United States adopted an immigration policy that limited entry to high-skill workers.

---

[8] This is a partial equilibrium exercise designed to give a sense of the magnitudes involved. The very large increase in the number of college graduates would have major labor market consequences, including a substantial drop in the relative wage of (and taxes paid by) high-skill workers.

The argument in favor of this policy contains two distinct parts. Consider first the role of the fiscal impact of immigration. There is no doubt that high-skill immigrants earn more, pay higher taxes, and require fewer government services. Put simply, high-skill immigration increases the after-tax income of natives, while the tax burden imposed by the immigration of low-skill workers reduces the net wealth of native tax-payers. And NAS estimates suggest that the fiscal benefits generated by high-skill immigration can be quite large.

The second part of the case for high-skill immigration relies on how immigrants alter the productivity of the native workforce and of native-owned firms. In the short run, the economic pie expands through the immigration surplus. Many studies suggest that there is more complementarity between high-skill labor and capital than between unskilled labor and capital. Capital-skill complementarity, therefore, suggests that the immigration surplus would be larger if the immigrant flow were composed of skilled workers.

These short-run gains, however, would dissipate as the economy adjusts to the larger workforce. In the long term, the immigrant contribution to economic growth would depend on the possibility of immigrants introducing human capital externalities that permanently increase the productivity of natives. High-skill immigrants are more likely to bring in knowledge, skills, and abilities that natives lack, and natives may be able to somehow pick up this know-how. Although the evidence on the magnitude of these externalities is mixed, the potential for the externalities to even exist is larger when the immigrant influx is composed of exceptional workers.

In short, there is little doubt that the immigrant contribution to economic growth would be far more important if the immigrant inflow was composed of high-skill workers. If a receiving country wishes to pursue an immigration policy that maximizes long-term growth, therefore, there is little uncertainty about the path that country should follow. It is far from clear, however, that immigration policy should be set solely on the basis of economic considerations.

References

Abramitzky, Ran, Leah Platt Boustan, and Katherine Eriksson, 2014. "A Nation of Immigrants: Assimilation and Economic Outcomes in the Age of Mass Migration." *Journal of Political Economy* 122 (3), 467–506.

Altonji, Joseph G., and David Card, 1991. "The Effects of Immigration on the Labor Market Outcomes of Less-Skilled Natives." In John M. Abowd and Richard B.

Freeman (eds.), *Immigration, Trade, and the Labor Market*, 201–34. University of Chicago Press, Chicago, IL.

Anastasopoulos, Jason, George J. Borjas, Gavin G. Cook, and Michael Lachanski, 2018. "Job Vacancies and Immigration: Evidence from Pre- and Post-Mariel Data." NBER Working Paper No. 24580. National Bureau of Economic Research, Cambridge, MA.

Barro, Robert J., and Xavier Sala-i-Martin, 1999. *Economic Growth*. MIT Press, Cambridge, MA.

Blau, Francine D. and Christopher Mackie (eds.), 2016. "*The Economic and Fiscal Consequences of Immigration*." National Academies Press, Washington, DC.

Borjas, George J., 1985. "Assimilation, Changes in Cohort Quality, and the Earnings of Immigrants." *Journal of Labor Economics* 3 (4), 463–89.

Borjas, George J., 1995. "The Economic Benefits from Immigration." *Journal of Economic Perspectives* 9 (2), 3–22.

Borjas, George J., 2003. "The Labor Demand Curve Is Downward Sloping: Reexamining the Impact of Immigration on the Labor Market." *Quarterly Journal of Economics* 118 (4), 1335–74.

Borjas, George J., 2014. *Immigration Economics*. Harvard University Press, Cambridge, MA.

Borjas, George J., 2016. *We Wanted Workers: Unraveling the Immigration Narrative*. W. W. Norton, New York, NY.

Borjas, George J., 2017. "The Wage Impact of the *Marielitos*: A Reappraisal." *Industrial and Labor Relations Review* 70 (5), 1077–1110.

Borjas, George J., 2019. "The Wage Impact of the *Marielitos*: The Role of Race." *Industrial and Labor Relations Review* 72 (4), 858–70.

Borjas, George J., and Kirk B. Doran, 2012. "The Collapse of the Soviet Union and the Productivity of American Mathematicians." *Quarterly Journal of Economics* 127 (3), 1143–1203.

Boubtane, Ekrame, Jean-Christophe Dumont, and Christophe Rault, 2016. "Immigration and Economic Growth in the OECD Countries 1986–2006." *Oxford Economic Papers* 68 (2), 340–60.

Card, David, 1990. "The Impact of the Mariel Boatlift on the Miami Labor Market." *Industrial and Labor Relations Review* 43 (2), 245–57.

Card, David, 2001. "Immigrant Inflows, Native Outflows, and the Local Labor Market Impacts of Higher Immigration." *Journal of Labor Economics* 19 (1), 22–64.

Card, David, 2009. "Immigration and Inequality." *American Economic Review* 99 (2), 1–21.

Card, David, and Giovanni Peri. 2016. "Immigration Economics by George J. Borjas: A Review Essay." *Journal of Economic Literature* 54 (4), 1333–49.

Chiswick, Barry R., 1978. "The Effect of Americanization on the Earnings of Foreign-Born Men." *Journal of Political Economy* 86 (5), 897–921.

Citi GPS, 2018. "Migration and the Economy: Economic Realities, Social Impacts & Political Choices." www.citibank.com/commercialbank/insights/assets/docs/2018/migration-economy.pdf.

Clemens, Michael A., and Jennifer Hunt, 2019. "The Labor Market Effects of Refugee Waves: Reconciling Conflicting Results." *Industrial and Labor Relations Review* 72 (4), 818–57.

Cortes, Patricia, 2008. "Effect of Low-Skilled Immigration on U.S. Prices: Evidence from CPI Data." *Journal of Political Economy* 116 (3), 381–422.

Dolado, Juan, Alessandra Goria, and Andrea Ichino, 1994. "Immigration, Human Capital and Growth in the Host Country: Evidence from Pooled Country Data." *Journal of Population Economics* 7 (2), 193–215.

Doran, Kirk, Alexander Gelber, and Adam Isen, 2015. "The Effects of High-Skilled Immigration Policy on Firms: Evidence from H-1B Visa Lotteries." NBER Working Paper No. 20668. National Bureau of Economic Research, Cambridge, MA.

Jaeger, David A., Joakim Ruist, and Jan Stuhler, 2018. "Shift-Share Instruments and the Impact of Immigration." NBER Working Paper No. 24285. National Bureau of Economic Research, Cambridge, MA.

Kane, Tim and Zach Rutledge, 2018. "Immigration and Economic Performance Across Fifty U.S. States from 1980–2015." Working Paper No. 18112. Hoover Institution, Stanford University, Stanford, CA.

Kerr, William R., and William F. Lincoln, 2010. "The Supply Side of Innovation: H-1B Visa Reforms and U.S. Ethnic Invention." *Journal of Labor Economics* 28 (3), 473–508.

Llull, Joan, 2018. "The Effect of Immigration on Wages: Exploiting Exogenous Variation at the National Level." *Journal of Human Resources* 53 (3), 608–22.

Mankiw, N. Gregory, David Romer, and David N. Weil, 1992. "A Contribution to the Empirics of Economic Growth." *Quarterly Journal of Economics* 107 (2), 407–37.

Monras, Joan, forthcoming. "Immigration and Wage Dynamics: Evidence from the Mexican Peso Crisis." Journal of Political Economy.

Ottaviano, Gianmarco I. P., and Giovanni Peri, 2012. "Rethinking the Effect of Immigration on Wages." *Journal of the European Economic Association* 10 (1), 152–97.

Peri, Giovanni, 2012. "The Effect of Immigration on Productivity: Evidence from U.S. States." *Review of Economics and Statistics* 94 (1), 348–58.

Peri, Giovanni, Kevin Shih, and Chad Sparber, 2015. "STEM Workers, H-1B Visas, and Productivity in US Cities." *Journal of Labor Economics* 33 (S1), S225–55.

Peri, Giovanni and Yasenov, Vasil, 2015. "The Labor Market Effects of a Refugee Wave: Synthetic Control Method Meets the Mariel Boatlift," NBER Working Paper No. 21801. National Bureau of Economic Research, Cambridge, MA.

ProPublica, 2017. "The Immigration Effect." https://projects.propublica.org/graphics/gdp.

Waldinger, Fabian, 2010. "Quality Matters: The Expulsion of Professors and the Consequences for Ph.D. Student Outcomes in Nazi Germany." *Journal of Political Economy* 118 (4), 787–831.

Waldinger, Fabian, 2012. "Peer Effects in Science: Evidence from the Dismissal of Scientists in Nazi Germany." *Review of Economic Studies* 79 (2), 838–61.

PART III

IMPLICATIONS OF TECHNOLOGY FOR GROWTH

"The $64,000 Question": Living in the Age of Technological Possibility or Showing Possibility's Age?

Glenn Hubbard

5.1 Introduction

The 1950s television quiz and game show *The $64,000 Question* was a big success. Purportedly, President Eisenhower did not want to be disturbed while the show was on. The drama and popularity of *The $64,000 Question* came from its mix of challenging questions and a large-for-the-time jackpot. Getting that final big question right could be the ticket to $64,000.

The US economy is at a "$64,000 question" crossroads: Will productivity growth and economic growth be slower going forward than in US experience over the past century or even over the postwar period, as techno-pessimists suggest? Will technological changes usher in a new era of faster productivity growth and enhanced welfare? Are "headwinds" to growth from demographic, competitive, and social trends bound to blunt potential gains trumpeted by techno-optimists in the business community and the economics profession? These big questions call to mind Nobel laureate Robert Lucas's observation that when economists think of long-term growth, it is hard to think of anything else. Compounding turns modest changes in growth into large sums – sustained acceleration in productivity growth of 1 percentage point would give a bonus cumulatively over a decade of 64 percent of today's average income, a $64,000 question indeed.

These high stakes are promoting a vigorous debate among economists over the future of technological change and productivity growth. Such debates are not new. Late-nineteenth-century US Patent Office Commissioner Charles Holland Duell observed at the turn of the twentieth century that "all previous advances in the various lines of invention will appear totally insignificant when compared with those which the present century will witness."[1] This techno-optimistic remark is belied by the techno-pessimistic quip wrongly credited to Duell, that "everything that could be invented has been invented."

The spirit of these older disagreeing views on the eve of a significant increase in productivity and living standards can help frame today's economic debates about the future of technological advance and productivity. Techno-optimists abound in the technology business community and, among economists, Erik Brynjolfsson and Andrew McAfee advance the optimistic case in thoughtful books for a general audience like *Machine, Platform, Crowd* (McAfee and Brynjolfsson, 2017) and *The Second Machine Age* (Brynjolfsson and McAfee, 2014). The economic historian Joel Mokyr (2014) has also championed an optimistic case in his scholarship on the Industrial Revolution and current technological change.

The pessimistic case has brought forth serious supporting arguments as well. Robert Gordon, in *The Rise and Fall of American Growth* (Gordon, 2016), carefully pours cold water on techno-optimism by describing problems in technological changes itself and economic "headwinds" that blunt its effectiveness in raising productivity. Other economists, including Tyler Cowen (2011) and Lawrence Summers (2013), have expressed similar skepticism about an impending revival of productivity growth, the latter channeling Alvin Hansen's (1938) description of "secular stagnation."

In this chapter, I describe the key arguments of the techno-optimists and the techno-pessimists. While Yogi Berra was right that "forecasting is difficult – especially about the future," I argue that there is little a priori reason to doubt that technological advances will continue. Instead, the focus for debate should be over the link between those advances and broad measures of productivity growth. Consistent with economic analysis of early periods of technological diffusion, the time period between general technological advances and their impact on productivity may be long; I extend these arguments to contemporary discussions of artificial intelligence (AI) and machine learning as a "general purpose technology" in particular.

US experience in productivity growth over the past few decades also suggests an influential role for public policy. While I share concerns about macroeconomic headwinds to growth and concur with macroeconomic policy counters to those headwinds and support for physical capital deepening to raise productivity, I also emphasize microeconomic policies to support intangible capital accumulation and its diffusion to general

---

[1] "Chances for the Inventor," *The Friend,* September 9, 1902, p. 28.

productivity. As the reader will no doubt see, I find economic evidence and arguments ultimately more sympathetic to the techno-optimists' case, but that progress is not simply manna from heaven.

5.2 Optimists Make Their Case

A key example of the techno-optimist case for technology-advance-led productivity enhancements and growth is *Machine, Platform, Crowd*, by Andrew McAfee and Erik Brynjolfsson (2017), both economic specialists studying technological innovation and its determinants and impacts. The authors' arguments emphasize positive microeconomic developments in AI and robotics.[2] Using as a metaphor machine learning's development of a *Go* champion beating the best human players, McAfee and Brynjolfsson (2017) put forth three trends for technological advance today. The first emphasizes increasingly more AI-capable *machines*, disrupting both productivity and business strategy. The second trend points to *platform* competition by industry-disrupting younger firms. The third trend is the emergence of the *crowd*, capturing open-source methods of incorporating both knowledge and experience in product or service design, development, and improvement.

As with previous technological waves of change surrounding electrification and the internal combustion engine, McAfee and Brynjolfsson (2017) observe that transformation's long-run effect on productivity and well-being is hard to see in real time. Part of the problem, as the authors note and I describe in greater detail in Section 5.5, is that successful industry incumbents can miss turning points given their in-place business strategies, and organizational (not just technological) changes may be required for translating technological advance into greater productivity and the diffusion of that productivity across firms.

While painting a techno-optimist future for *growth*, the McAfee-Brynjolfsson (2017) book also focuses its discussion of the future of *firms* in the spirit of Coaseian and transaction-cost-economics descriptions of the boundaries of a firm. In particular, prospects for machine-learning-enabled disruption still leave intact the need for incomplete contacts that motivate the existence of firms. The questions of *which* firms and *what*

---

[2] In addition to machine learning per se, cross-country evidence by Graetz and Michaels (2015) linking robotics to GDP growth finds a significant incremental effect in recent decades.

their boundaries should be remain important both for the link to product-ivity and for public policy, as I explain later in this chapter.

The techno-optimist view has been forcefully expressed in more schol-arly circles by economic historians such as Paul David (1991), Deirdre McCloskey (2016), and Joel Mokyr (2014). Their view centers less on the possibility of identified new technologies and more on the existence of a time period between technological advance and broad productivity gains.

Researchers at the McKinsey Global Institute (2018) also fit squarely within the techno-optimist camp. The Institute's study emphasizes tech-nology-led productivity gains through operational efficiency improve-ments and enhanced value-added. Importantly, the study also points to gains from adopting new business and organizational models and reducing barriers to entry, categories to which I return in Section 5.5.

Consistent with the techno-optimism of Brynjolfsson and McAfee, Mokyr has long grounded an optimistic case for technological advance and productivity growth in lessons of history. Mokyr (2014) has observed, for example, that the explosion of technology and productivity in the twentieth century occurred against a backdrop of "headwinds" (to antici-pate a term used by Robert Gordon (2016) in advancing his case of techno-pessimism) of war, totalitarianism, and serious talk of "secular stagnation." Noting the historical symbiotic relationship between scientific instru-ment–makers and scientists in the eighteenth and nineteenth centuries, Mokyr (2014) notes advances in computing and machine learning today that can re-advance science and technology, a point to which I return in Section 5.5. Global competitive forces and exchanges of ideas further this advance and re-advance of innovation (in computing, modern science, 3D printing, and so on) and its economic impact.

5.3 "Industrial Revolutions" to "Current Headwinds"

Robert Gordon (2016) offers a different and more pessimistic view in its assessment of future technological advance and economic growth. Gordon's book is magisterial in scope and substance, chronicling the rise and fall of US economic growth since the Civil War. In the book, this talented macroeconomic thinker about business cycles tackles the long sweep of growth. Such a treatise requires an emphasis on "why": Why was economic growth once so robust? Why, in Gordon's view, are the best days for American growth in the past?

Gordon's (2016) history of the growth experience, like the telling of the second machine age by Brynjolfsson and McAfee (2014), is a fascinating read. He also offers a framing. While techno-optimists may see positive "trends" (to borrow the term from Brynjolfsson and McAfee), those techno-optimists, in Gordon's view, either focus on microeconomic developments without connecting them to future growth in the presence of "headwinds" or take a past-is-prologue view that our past increases in prosperity augur for a more prosperous future.

Four headwinds yield Gordon's bleaker growth future: inequality that continues to grow over time, a sclerotic educational system, demographic changes, and large-scale fiscal imbalances.[3] Three immediate observations are in order. The first two headwinds are microeconomic. In particular, weaknesses in the K-12 educational system break the virtuous cycle of increased skills and productivity growth and wages that prevailed during much of the twentieth century; that broken cycle is a key contributor to the stagnating earnings of all but very skilled workers. The other two factors are more macroeconomic, reflecting stresses in hours worked and productivity from an aging society and stresses for future growth from financing large current and future levels of federal debt. Third, while Gordon is undoubtedly correct that these factors are headwinds to the American economy and society, none has implications that are immutable to changes in public policy.[4]

Gordon's (2016) headwinds and adaptation of the secular stagnation thesis carry intuitive appeal. Noting just after the publication of his book that *actual* real GDP growth slowed from 3.12 percent per annum over the 1974–2004 period to 1.56 percent in the post-2004 period, he argues that *potential* GDP growth slowed as well. The decline in potential GDP growth could be explained by a fall in potential output per hour (and productivity growth has been weak) and a fall in potential hours of work (noting

---

[3] The headwinds identified by Gordon (2016) overlap with some of the determinants of long-term growth in empirical studies, as in Barro (1991). While these studies include variables such as educational attainment, the rate of investment, and the initial level of income, other explanatory variables may belong in the "true" model.

[4] While public policy toward headwinds is generally beyond the scope of this chapter, I offer some policy suggestions later. Gordon (2016) also offers a menu of suggestions. Many economists have offered suggestions on improving education and skill development to raise wages and reduce earnings inequality. While demographic change is not easily addressed outside of changes in immigration, there are policy tools to influence labor force participation and hours worked by older workers (e.g., supported by changes in payroll taxes and Social Security benefit formulas). Finally, while fiscal restraint has been elusive in the United States, fiscal rules offer such a significant intervention; see, for example, Hubbard and Kane (2013) and Yared (2019). Later in this chapter, I describe other policy interventions that increase the likelihood of success for the techno-optimists' case as long as underlying technological change remains robust.

observed declines in both the working-age population and the labor force participation rate).

Gordon's (2016) headwinds slow productivity growth, also with a lack of future gains from new general purpose technologies. I focus on productivity growth in this chapter as well. Gordon is certainly not alone among economists in his skepticism about the underlying pace of technological change. Bloom, Jones, van Reenen, and Webb (2017), for example, examine many areas in which ideas are more difficult to find, as measured by rising costs of research inputs to yield incremental productivity-enhancing outputs. In the past, general purpose technologies have been associated with three "industrial revolutions." The first, in Gordon's (2016) telling, occurred from 1770 to 1840 (with continued impact to the turn of the twentieth century) and centered on technologies for transportation (the steam engine, steamships, and railroads), materials (the transition from wood to steel), and manufacturing (cotton spinning and weaving). These changes reduced costs of distance and assembly.

The second revolution of general purpose technologies occurred from 1870 to 1920 (with continued impact through 1970). This revolution was particularly significant, with electrification (used in lighting, elevators, machines, air conditioning, and so on), internal combustion engines (used in automobiles and air transport), communication and media (used in the telephone, phonograph, movies, radio, and television), and chemicals (used in plastics, antibiotics, and medicines). Changes in this second industrial revolution substantially improved living and work conditions.

The century before 1970 brought rapid productivity growth. The notable developments were "one-offs" in Gordon's (2016) view, including instant electricity, power tools, central heating and air conditioning, and a shift toward urbanization. In Gordon's (2016) telling, most progress in these areas was achieved by 1940. (I do not agree about this truncation of progress, as I argue in Section 5.4.)

The third industrial revolution highlighted by Gordon (2016), which has been going on since 1960, has centered on entertainment (evolution of television and media availability), information technology (personal computers, the Internet and the World Wide Web, and e-commerce), and communications (mobile telephony and smartphones). These technologies offer productivity enhancements through financial, retail, and other transaction processing, as well as through significant reductions in costs of distance and communication.

Reminiscent of the famous quip by Nobel laureate Robert Solow (1987) a generation ago that "you see productivity growth everywhere but in the productivity statistics," Gordon (2016) argues that the third industrial revolution has had only a modest boost to total factor productivity growth relative to the gains in the period from 1920 to 1970. Just as Solow's quip gave way to a period of much better performance in productivity, Gordon's question – Has most of the productivity impact of the third industrial revolution already happened? – merits further study. Rounding out the productivity pessimism, Gordon laments stasis in desktop computing, processes in retail and financial services, and higher education.

Looking forward a generation (twenty-five years), Gordon (2016) predicts a dearth of important innovations in medical efficiency, life expectancy, and 3D printing. In contrast to popular media stories by techno-optimists and technology business leaders,[5] Gordon's future sees AI providing nothing more than evolutionary changes such as driverless cars and trucks.

This techno-pessimism also stands in contrast to present popular anxiety that too-rapid productivity will replace work before new meaningful jobs can be created. As Mokyr, Vickers, and Ziebarth (2015) note, the techno-anxiety isn't new, tracing back to the Luddites and the fears expressed by Keynes (1930) about the disappearance of work.

5.4 Assessing the Optimistic and Pessimistic Arguments

The gap between the techno-pessimists like Gordon and the techno-optimists like Brynjolfsson and McAfee and many business leaders is unsettling from an economic perspective. The "Mars–Venus" character of the arguments might suggest that one side has it badly wrong, and, as I noted in the introduction (Section 1.1), the answer is consequential for our economic future and living standards. Some economists have weighed in to find chinks in the armor of the two views. One such effort argues that productivity growth is underestimated because of mismeasurement of changes in quality; see, for example, Mokyr (2014) and Feldstein (Chapter 2 of this volume). While intuitive and no doubt a factor, empirical research by Byrne, Fernald, and Reinsdorf (2016) and Syverson (2017) suggests that mismeasurement is not the principal explanatory factor for slower recent productivity growth.

---

[5] See, for example, the recounting of technology executive optimism in Brynjolfsson, Rock, and Syverson (2017).

The second argument is also familiar: An alternative skeptical examination of the optimists' camp is simply that expectations will not pan out.
While obviously difficult to refute, the many paths to productivity gains
from combinations and complements of existing technologies make such
reflective pessimism harder to embrace from an economic perspective.

This "yes versus no" debate on technological advance misses an area
potentially as important and in which economists can offer a meaningful
contribution: An economic approach to reconcile – as opposed to chip away
at – the arguments of the optimistic and pessimistic camps is that there are lags
in salutary productivity effects of existing technologies (a factor in the more
rapid productivity growth that followed Solow's earlier observation about the
failure of effects of new technologies to be found in the productivity statistics);
see, for example, Brynjolfsson et al. (2017). Factors explaining a delay between
the introduction of a new technology and its productivity impact include
a period over which the stock of the new technology is built up and a period
over which complementary investments are made to enable the potential of
the new technology to be realized. As Brynjolfsson et al. (2017) note, correlation between productivity growth over adjacent ten-year periods in postwar
US data is not statistically significantly different from zero. That is, low
productivity growth today need not be predictive of future productivity
growth. Such a pattern is not without historical precedent. David (1991), for
example, studied the long delay in carrying out electrification of manufacturing establishments, with at least half unelectrified thirty years after the introduction of alternating current. While early adopters did so to reduce costs,
broader gains and adoption required complementary organizational innovations such as individual motors to enhance flexibility.[6] And, as Syverson
(2013) finds, the acceleration in productivity growth over 1915 to 1924 in the
portable power period resembles the delayed productivity expansion from
1995 to 2004 after earlier information technology innovations.

5.5 Digging Deeper: From General Purpose Technology
to General Use

A leading general purpose technology candidate that serves as a rejoinder
to Gordon's prediction of slower productivity growth is AI. To be specific,

---

[6] In more recent experience, Bresnahan, Brynjolfsson, and Hitt (2002) have highlighted
complementarities among information technology, organizational changes, and human
capital in both investment decisions and productivity. I discuss this line of inquiry in
greater detail in Section 5.5.1.

by "general purpose technology," I follow the interpretation in Bresnahan and Trajtenberg (1995) of a technology with general uses, with improvement possibilities over time and across complementary innovations. The emphasis on complementary innovations, which may take time to occur, calls to mind such familiar examples of a general purpose technology as the steam engine, electricity, the internal combustion engine, and computers. Co-innovations and distribution throughout the economy are hallmarks of a general purpose technology and its importance for productivity growth.

Machine learning and AI fit this bill, offering possibilities of productivity enhancement across a range of industries and tasks over time. Improvements over time are easily predicted given adaptation based on data collected over time. Co-innovations in product and technology space are also easy to imagine, with machine learning gains and driverless cars, medical diagnostics, and factory automation. A particularly important element of co-innovation in this context is the ability to translate learning by sharing data experience across machines (or robots or driverless cars). Techno-optimists' view of efficiency and productivity gains from AI as a general purpose technology hardly seem far-fetched.

Yet, such arguments must face the fact – rightly emphasized by Gordon and others – that the *current* rate of productivity growth is *low* and that sluggish growth is at least not principally an issue of mismeasurement in official data. Squaring this circle requires both an observation and speculation. The observation regards the time between introduction and productivity gains for a general purpose technology. The speculation, of course, is whether this explanation warrants a rejection of Gordon's "headwinds" pessimism.

5.5.1 Observation: It Takes Time and Organizational Change

As discussed in Section 5.3, earlier general purpose technologies – including electrification and computers – took a generation before technological improvement and dissemination across activities and industries led to productivity gains.[7] The largest gains – and ones coming later – involved co-innovations and organizational changes. Historically, this process has required significant capital investments over a sustained period of time. At present, such investments are accompanied by substantial *intangible*

---

[7] In addition to technological delay, incumbent successful firms may be slow to adopt a new technology that is only incrementally faster than their current technology and knowhow (Atkeson and Kehoe, 2007).

investments. It is this intangible investment that facilitates complementarity between information technology and organizational changes, changes that can lead to substantial increases in productivity and market value in successful firms (see, for example, Brynjolfsson, Hitt, and Yang, 2002).

This time period of adaptation and realization of potential productivity improvements historically has required significant *organizational* reconfiguration in addition to developments in the underlying technology.[8] These organizational changes can be cultural (Henderson, 2006) or require new firms to replace nonadapting older firms (Arrow, 1962; Holmes, Levine, and Schmitz, 2012). The slow but mounting development and penetration of e-commerce offers a case in point (Hortacsu and Syverson, 2015).

This observation about the time and complementary investment required for AI to lead to productivity improvements is an important one. As a kind of (intangible) capital, AI requires investment, and its stock will arise from accumulated investment less depreciation. "Capital deepening" from AI will raise labor productivity. Assessing its effect on total factor productivity is more subtle. While physical capital to implement machine learning and AI will be on corporate balance sheets, "capital stocks" of complementary intangible capital may or may not be on those balance sheets. If, for example, such unmeasured AI intangible capital is growing more rapidly than output, a statistician would underestimate the growth of total factor productivity.

The observation also suggests the benefits of additional economic research on complementary investment into new technologies as a way of evaluating the merits of the techno-optimist and pessimist cases for productivity growth. Such research would study co-innovations, of course, but also changes in processes, business models, human capital, and management practices. In addition to evaluating the cases for and against more rapid productivity growth, this analysis may lead to recommendations that can shape and advance organizational changes to enhance productivity growth.

---

[8] The idea that institutional and organizational support is required for the translation of technological advance into broad productivity gains can be found at least as far back as an observation by Abraham Lincoln (1858):

The advantageous use of steam-power is, unquestionably, a modern discovery. And yet, as much as two thousand years ago the power of steam was not only observed, but an ingenious toy was actually made and put in motion by it, at Alexandria, in Egypt. What appears strange is, that neither the inventor of the toy, nor anyone else, for so long a time afterwards, should perceive that steam would move useful machinery as well as a toy.

5.5.2 Speculation: Will Productivity Growth Increase?

I observed in Section 5.2 that simple near-term "extrapolation" predictions of productivity growth are unreliable. In my view, both postwar experience and public policy lessons give support to the idea that more rapid productivity growth is feasible going forward.

Productivity increases arise from human capital, technology, and real capital investment. Cogan, Hubbard, Taylor, and Warsh (2017) present smoothed measures of nonfarm business productivity, revealing clear, cyclical trends in productivity growth. To be specific, productivity growth declined in the 1970s, rose markedly through the 1980s and 1990s, and fell again in more recent years. Cogan et al. (2017) observe that these patterns are not supportive of the pessimistic contention that the United States is in the midst of a long-term decline in productivity growth.

The authors note that productivity in the nonfarm business sector grew at only 0.5 percent per year over the 2012–16 period, a decline traceable in large part to a lack of investment in new capital equipment and software. Capital per hour of work was basically flat during this period, contributing virtually nothing to growth. By way of contrast, over the 1996–2005 period, productivity advanced 3 percent per year, with the growth rate of capital per hour of work contributing 1.2 percent per year.

Cogan et al. (2017) identify economic policies contributing to the productivity slowdown. In particular, the authors argue that high marginal tax rates, especially those on capital formation and business enterprises, costly new labor market and other regulations, and high debt-financed government spending to fund transfer programs have discouraged business investment and productivity growth. Under this view, business tax and regulatory reforms during 2017 and 2018 should increase investment and productivity growth. Indeed, Cogan et al. (2017) argue that policy changes can, in principle, raise the annual rate of economic growth to 3 percent. They note that trend nonfarm labor productivity growth of 2.3 percent per year – consistent with 2 percent labor productivity growth in terms of GDP – is well within historical experience over the postwar period.[9]

---

[9] Though not the subject of this chapter, in which I focus on productivity growth, attaining 3 percent annual GDP growth also requires that hours worked increase by 1 percent per year. Over the next decade, the civilian population aged sixteen and older is projected to increase by that amount. Because, however, the population is aging and older workers

5.6 A Policy Agenda for Reviving Productivity

The policies identified in Section 5.5 focus on business fixed investments, with implications for capital deepening and productivity growth; I return to other policies to address Gordon's (2016) headwinds later in this section. But the foregoing discussion of co-innovation and complementary organizational changes suggests consideration of a broader microeconomic agenda for public policy. Such an agenda would center on infrastructure broadly defined, development and dissemination of better management practices, and reduced barriers to competition.

Infrastructure investment is usually considered in the context of enhanced physical capital that can reduce transportation, communication, and coordination costs among firms and individuals in the economy. While useful, recent research suggests a link to productivity growth through advancing technological innovation, rather than just through capital deepening per se (Agrawal, Galasso, and Oettl, 2017). The public good features of basic research in new technologies and computing underscore a role for public research funding.

Researchers have identified a causal link between management practices and productivity; see, for example, Bloom and van Reenen (2007) and Bloom, Sadun, and van Reenen (2017). Better management practices can enhance and accelerate organizational changes that help capture productivity changes from new technologies. The development of such practices occurs in part naturally in the competitive process of organizational design. But support for university–firm partnerships can build networks and enhance dissemination of "best practices"; see, for example, National Academy of Engineering (2015).

In addition to supporting technological development and management practices that promote efficient utilization of new technologies, policies can encourage competition and the allocation of factors toward firms with greatest productivity possibilities. Ensuring that barriers to entry remain low enhances the ability of technologically disruptive younger firms to compete against established firms.

have lower labor force participation rates than prime-age workers, the labor force is not expected to increase as rapidly. To offset the effects of an aging population on the labor force, age-specific labor force participation rates must rise by 0.4 percent per year or by 4 percent over ten years. While this is a significant increase, Cogan et al. (2017) note that labor force participation fell by 4 percent over the 2006–2016 period relative to 2006 forecasts by the Bureau of Labor Statistics, which incorporated projected demographic changes and trends in labor force participation rates; they argue that it is that gap that is addressable by public policy toward work.

Likewise, policies to encourage freer flow of capital, labor, and ideas across firms enhance penetration of new technologies and productivity growth. Barriers to be questioned involve excessive use of occupational licensing and noncompete restrictions, land use zoning, and intellectual property protection. Just as low barriers to entry make possible the growth in use of new technologies, low barriers to factor movement enhance and accelerate reallocation of resources to successful productive firms.[10]

One issue for public policy is enhancing diffusion of productivity gains from technological advance. Syverson (2011) and Bartelsman, Haltiwanger, and Scarpetta (2013) find evidence of large-scale difference in firm productivity in an industry. A significant reason for total factor productivity differences among firms traces to differences in management practices; see, for example, Bloom and van Reenen (2007). "Superstar" firms (van Reenen, 2018) will have greater productivity and rising market share even in a market with price competition. Pro-entry antitrust policy will need to look beyond *current* horizontal competition to consider acquisitions that may reduce *future* competition (Cunningham, Ederer, and Ma, 2018) and an examination of the significance of who controls consumer data. Tirole (2017) has suggested steps toward a new antitrust policy toward large technology firms in these important two-sided markets.

These policies to raise productivity growth and to accelerate the benefits of new technologies both draw from economic research on complementarities among technological forces. Additional research on these complementarities and more holistic consideration of them in a public policy growth agenda will increase the likelihood of achieving the techno-optimist scenario with existing technologies and technologies to come.

While emphasizing the more microeconomic policy elements related to technological advance and its impact on productivity over time and across firms, I do not mean to suggest that addressing the more

---

[10] Policies to enhance entry must be cognizant that leading firms in this area operate in two-sided markets. While this phenomenon and its complication for measuring "price" are not new (a recent example is the antitrust inquiry into the credit card industry), the economic issues are in high relief here. In a two-sided market, competition takes place both "in the market" (among incumbents for AI inputs) and "for the market" (among both incumbents and entrants trying to win over future markets using AI). Both forms of competition are important to reduce frictions in developing AI. This pro-competitive focus may well emphasize nonprice as well as price aspects of competition; see, for example, Himel and Seamans (2017).

macroeconomic headwinds put forth by Gordon (2016) is unimportant. Indeed, each is important beyond the productivity growth context of this chapter. Strengthening skills and rewarding work are important for inclusive prosperity and social cohesion. Many mechanisms for improvements in education and skill development have been suggested by economists; elsewhere, I have focused on support for low-wage work with an expanded Earned Income Tax Credit or alternative wage subsidy (Hubbard, 2016) and a federal block grant to community colleges to support college completion and skill enhancement (Goolsbee, Hubbard, and Ganz, 2019). The unsustainable fiscal trajectory in the United States is also of general concern as it suggests future difficult choices among spending on social insurance, defense, and domestic goods, as well as possible anti-growth tax increases. Major progress likely requires action on a fiscal rule (see, for example, Hubbard and Kane, 2013).

5.7 Conclusions

The study by economists of technological change and its links to productivity continues to be important – it remains the $64,000 question for the US economy. *The $64,000 Question* was canceled in 1958 during a series of scandals in quiz shows in which contestants were tipped off with answers to questions. Alas, we do not know the answer to the question of whether future productivity growth will be slow or fast.[11] But economic analysis gives us clues with analyses of general purpose technologies, the complementary investments required for diffusion of technological change and its impact on productivity, and channels for public policies to improve that impact. And those policy interventions are useful in both the techno-pessimist and the techno-optimist scenarios. Both technological change and economic research into the link between technological change and productivity are likely to remain key questions for years to come. Distributional consequences of those productivity impacts, beyond the scope of this chapter, are likely to pose increasingly thorny questions for policy-makers as well.

---

[11] For example, Federal Reserve Chairman Powell (2018) recently urged caution and humility about forecasting long-term growth in variables like potential GDP given significant shifts over time in policy-makers' views on growth prospects. Significant uncertainty in long-term productivity growth estimates has also been highlighted by Christensen, Gillingham, and Nordhaus (2016).

References

Agrawal, Ajay, Alberto Galasso, and Alexander Oettl, 2017. "Roads and Innovation." *Review of Economics and Statistics* 99 (3), 417–34.

Arrow, Kenneth, 1962. "Economic Welfare and the Allocation of Resources for Invention." In Richard R. Nelson (ed.), *The Rate and Direction of Invention Activity*, 609–26. Princeton University Press, Princeton, NJ.

Atkeson, Andrew, and Patrick Kehoe, 2007. "Modeling the Transition to a New Economy: Lessons from Two Technological Revolutions." *American Economic Review* 97 (1) 64–88.

Barro, Robert J., 1991. "Economic Growth in a Cross-Section of Countries." *Quarterly Journal of Economics* 106 (2), 407–43.

Bartelsman, Eric, John Haltiwanger, and Stefano Scarpetta, 2013. "Cross-Country Differences in Productivity: The Role of Allocation and Selection." *American Economic Review* 103 (1), 305–34.

Bloom, Nicholas, Charles I. Jones, John van Reenen, and Michael Webb, 2017. "Are Ideas Getting Harder to Find?" NBER Working Paper No. 23782. National Bureau of Economic Research, Cambridge, MA.

Bloom, Nicholas, Raffaella Sadun, and John van Reenen, 2017. "Management As Technology." NBER Working Paper No. 22327. National Bureau of Economic Research, Cambridge, MA.

Bloom, Nicholas, and John van Reenen, 2007. "Measuring and Explaining Management Practices Across Firms." *Quarterly Journal of Economics* 122 (4), 1351–1408.

Bresnahan, Timothy F., Erik Brynjolfsson, and Lorin Hitt, 2002. "Information Technology, Workplace Organization, and the Demand for Skilled Labor: Firm-Level Evidence." *Quarterly Journal of Economics* 117 (1), 339–76.

Bresnahan, Timothy F., and Manuel Trajtenberg, 1995. "General Purpose Technologies: 'Engines of Growth'?" *Journal of Econometrics, Annals of Econometrics* 65 (1), 83–108.

Brynjolfsson, Erik, Lorin Hitt, and Shinkyu Yang, 2002. "Intangible Assets: Computers and Organizational Capital." *Brookings Papers on Economic Activity* 33 (1), 137–98.

Brynjolfsson, Erik, and Andrew McAfee, 2014. *The Second Machine Age: Work, Progress, and Prosperity in a Time of Brilliant Technologies*. W.W. Norton, New York, NY.

Brynjolfsson, Erik, Daniel Rock, and Chad Syverson, 2017. "Artificial Intelligence and the Modern Productivity Paradox: A Clash of Expectations and Statistics." NBER Working Paper No. 24001. National Bureau of Economic Research, Cambridge, MA.

Byrne, David M., John G. Fernald, and Marshall B. Reinsdorf, 2016. "Does the United States Have a Productivity Slowdown or a Measurement Problem?" *Brookings Papers on Economic Activity* 47 (1), 109–82.

Christensen, Peter, Kenneth Gillingham, and William Nordhaus, 2016. "Uncertainty in Forecasts of Long-Run Productivity Growth." Working Paper. Yale University Press, New Haven, CT.

Cogan, John F., Glenn Hubbard, John B. Taylor, and Kevin Warsh, 2017. "On the Prospects for Higher Economic Growth." Working Paper. Hoover Institution, Stanford University, Stanford, CA.

Cowen, Tyler, 2011. *The Great Stagnation: How America Ate All the Low-Hanging Fruit of Modern History, Got Sick, and Will (Eventually) Feel Better.* Penguin Group, New York, NY.

Cunningham, Colleen, Florian Ederer, and Song Ma, 2018. "Killer Acquisitions." Working Paper. Yale University Press, New Haven, CT.

David, Paul, 1991. "Computer and Dynamo: The Modern Productivity Paradox in a Not-Too-Distant Mirror." In OECD, *Technology and Productivity: The Challenge for Economic Policy,* 315–47. OECD, Paris, France.

Goolsbee, Austan, Glenn Hubbard, and Amy Ganz, 2019. "A Policy Agenda to Develop Human Capital for the Modern Economy." In Melissa S. Kearney and Amy Ganz (eds.), *Expanding Economic Opportunity for More Americans,* 16–36. Aspen Institute, Washington, DC.

Gordon, Robert J., 2016. *The Rise and Fall of American Growth: The U.S. Standard of Living Since the Civil War.* Princeton University Press, Princeton, NJ and Oxford, UK.

Graetz, Georg, and Guy Michaels, 2015. "Robots at Work." Discussion Paper No. 1335. Centre for Economic Performance, London, UK.

Hansen, Alvin H., 1938. *Full Recovery or Stagnation?* W.W. Norton, New York, NY.

Henderson, Rebecca, 2006. "The Innovator's Dilemma as a Problem of Organizational Competence." *Journal of Product Innovation Management* 23 (1), 5–11.

Himel, Samuel, and Robert Seamans, 2017. "Artificial Intelligence, Incentives to Innovate, and Competition Policy." *Antitrust Chronicle* 1 (3), 1–10.

Holmes, Thomas J., David K. Levine, and James A. Schmitz, 2012. "Monopoly and the Incentive to Innovate When Adoption Involves Switchover Disruptions." *American Economic Journal: Microeconomics* 4 (3), 1–33.

Hortacsu, Ali, and Chad Syverson, 2015. "The Ongoing Evolution of U.S. Retail: A Format Tug-of-War." *Journal of Economic Perspectives* 29 (4), 89–112.

Hubbard, Glenn, 2016. "Supporting Work, Inclusion, and Mass Prosperity." In Michael R. Strain (ed.), *The U.S. Labor Market: Questions and Challenge for Public Policy.* AEI Press, Washington, DC.

Hubbard, Glenn, and Timothy Kane, 2013. *Balance: The Economics of Great Powers from Rome to Modern America.* Simon and Schuster, New York, NY.

Keynes, John Maynard, 1930. "Economic Possibilities for Our Grandchildren." In John Maynard Keynes, *Essays in Persuasion,* 358–73. W.W. Norton, New York, NY.

Lincoln, Abraham, 1858. "Lecture on Discoveries and Inventions." Speech to the Young Men's Improvement Association of Bloomington, Illinois, April 6.

McAfee, Andrew, and Eric Brynjolfsson, 2017. *Machine, Platform, Crowd: Harnessing Our Digital Future.* W.W. Norton, New York, NY.

McCloskey, Deirdre N., 2016. *Bourgeois Equality.* University of Chicago Press, Chicago, IL.

McKinsey Global Institute, 2018. *Solving the Productivity Puzzle: The Role of Demand and the Promise of Digitization.* McKinsey & Company, New York, NY.

Mokyr, Joel, 2014. "The Next Age of Invention." *City Journal* 24 (1), 12–21.

Mokyr, Joel, Chris Vickers, and Nicolas L. Ziebarth, 2015. "The History of Technological Anxiety and the Future of Economic Growth: Is This Time Different?" *Journal of Economic Perspectives* 29 (3), 31–50.

National Academy of Engineering, 2015. *Making Value for America: Embracing the Future of Manufacturing, Technology, and Work.* National Academies Press, Washington, DC.

Powell, Jerome H, 2018. "Monetary Policy in a Changing Economy." Remarks at the Federal Reserve Bank of Kansas City Symposium on Changing Market Structure and Implications for Monetary Policy, August 23–25, Jackson Hole, WY.

Solow, Robert M, 1987. "We'd Better Watch Out." *New York Times Book Review,* July 12, 36.

Summers, Lawrence H., 2013. "Why Stagnation Might Prove to Be the New Normal." Remarks at the 14th International Monetary Fund Annual Research Conference, November 18, Washington, DC.

Syverson, Chad, 2011. "What Determines Productivity?" *Journal of Economic Literature* 49 (2), 326–65.

Syverson, Chad, 2013. "Will History Repeat Itself? Comments on 'Is the Information Technology Over?'" *International Productivity Monitor* 25 (Spring), 37–40.

Syverson, Chad, 2017. "Challenges to Mismeasurement Explanations for the U.S. Productivity Slowdown." *Journal of Economic Perspectives* 31 (2), 165–86.

Tirole, Jean, 2017. *Economics for the Common Good.* Princeton University Press. Princeton, NJ.

Van Reenen, John, 2018. "Increasing Differences between Firms: Market Power and the Macro-Economy." Remarks at the Federal Reserve Bank of Kansas City Symposium on Changing Market Structure and Implications for Monetary Policy, August 23–25, Jackson Hole, WY.

Yared, Pierre, 2019. "Rising Government Debt: Causes and Solutions for a Decades-Old Trend." *Journal of Economic Perspectives* 33 (2), 115–40.

Artificial Intelligence Technologies and Aggregate Growth Prospects

Timothy Bresnahan

6.1 Introduction

This chapter examines the commercial application of Artificial Intelligence Technologies (AITs), seeking to address questions about these technologies specifically and about twenty-first-century technical progress and its current and potential impact on economic growth. I focus on the highly valuable *applications* of AITs today, in production systems at the Internet Giants, in new user interfaces (UIs), and elsewhere. My empirical conclusion about these applications is that the lazy idea of AI – that is, of computer systems that are able to perform productive tasks previously done by humans – is irrelevant to understanding how these technologies create value. Here "irrelevant" does not mean that substitution of machine for human tasks is less important than other determinants of the value in use of AITs. It means irrelevant: task-level substitution of machine for human plays no role in these highly valuable systems.

The absence of task-level substitution is unsurprising to scholars of production based on information and communications technology (ICT), and it does not mean that there has been no factor substitution at all. The transition to ICT-based production has largely proceeded at the production system level, not the task level. Consider examples from the largest area of AIT use so far: consumer–product matching and targeting. The production systems by which Google and Facebook present targeted advertisements to individual consumers differ from those of the older advertising business. To be sure, some of the differences are in factor utilization – the new advertising industry production systems run on ICT capital. But other differences are equally important, such as in the distinction between targeted and mass-media advertising. System-level substitution, generally, is driven as much or more by output characteristics such as ad targeting as by cost minimization.

That leads to analysis of the characteristics of the AIT-using systems and the structure of incentives and opportunities to invent new AIT-based production processes. In their economically important initial applications, and in the early stages of diffusion, AIT-using systems are largely capital deepening in already capital-intensive production processes and services. As with several other recent important new ICTs, the largest applications are in mass-market marketing and distribution, focusing on consumers. Media markets, advertising markets, and the marketing functions of consumer products and services companies appear likely to get the deepest investments in AITs. In the sections that follow, I examine the complementarity of AITs with specific aspects of existing capital-intensive production processes that explain the tendency toward capital deepening. AIT capital–other capital complementarities and scale economies at the firm level are an important element. I also examine the aspects of new capital-intensive production processes, with and without AITs, that have limited their range of application to mass-market environments with low-stakes transactions.

Many observers hope that AITs will become General Purpose Technologies (GPTs).[1] That appears to be half right in the early going, but it leads us away from AITs' visible role in growth. The half that is clearly right is positive feedback loops running through improvements in AITs and their applications.[2] Positive feedback loops are associated with social scale economies and thus, potentially, with growth (Romer 1986). But thus far there is little indication that the diffusion of AIT-based systems will contribute most of its value through *broadening* the range of applications of new capital to a range of industries and functions. While we can anticipate widespread use of AITs, thus far the economically important applications lie in capital *deepening* in a narrow range of industries and functions. In that important regard, AITs are like the other big twenty-first

---

[1] Many recent economic papers on AI pose the question of whether all of it will become a GPT. See Brynjolfsson, Rock, and Syverson (2017), Taddy (2018), and Cockburn, Henderson, and Stern (2018). Most importantly, see Trajtenberg (2018), as well as Agrawal, Gans, and Goldfarb (2018), which provides an excellent overview of these issues.

[2] GPT analytics emphasize the innovational complementarities between the GPT itself and inventions of applications (Bresnahan and Trajtenberg, 1995; Rosenberg and Trajtenberg, 2004; Helpman and Trajtenberg, 1998). Bresnahan and Greenstein (1996) emphasize the role of difficult-to-invent applications in slowing the diffusion of, and easy-to-invent applications accelerating the diffusion of, ICT GPTs. Rosenberg (1997) writes about the role of post-invention uncertainty (often about the most important applications).

-century waves of ICT, such as Web 2.0 and mobile. Earlier, ICT spread out over more and more economic activity for many decades, from a few functions in large firms, to many functions, to system access by individual workers, to extensive consumer applications. Recently, that nature of the positive feedback loop driving ICT invention and ICT-application invention has moved from broadening to deepening. In our era, rapid ICT technical progress leads to some universal benefits but, importantly, also leads to ICT-capital deepening in particular firms, industries, and functions.

For many years, there has been a research area – General Artificial Intelligence – with the imprecise goal of designing computer systems that can do tasks previously requiring human intelligence.[3] Taking this research goal as a metaphor, looking at laboratory phenomena and demonstration projects and adding technological determinism is the basis of most writing about AITs. This metaphor underlies the focus on task-level substitution in the literature. General AI research goals have not been met. Instead, the statistical turn in AI research of a generation ago dramatically accelerated progress in a number of separate but related laboratory technologies. These technologies are based on the idea of statistical prediction – if in very different domains – ranging from "seeing" pictures to forecasting what book a consumer might read next. The actual AITs that exist – like all software technologies – are designed into systems. In this chapter, I look at those systems. Spoiler alert: Do not hope for a lot of sci-fi in them.

It is not too early to look at the systems that embody AITs, and the analysis is not based on speculation. AITs are now central elements of working commercial systems generating revenues in the hundreds of billions of dollars. AITs are broadly used in UI subsystems. Both the earliest production uses and the UIs have begun to diffuse away from those first applications, enough to at least examine the early diffusion path. There is another category of AIT applications, smaller at this stage, where AIT laboratory phenomena are very close to already-algorithmic production steps. Finally, I will examine other growing AIT applications

---

[3] The Oxford Living Dictionary defines Artificial Intelligence as "[t]he theory and development of computer systems able to perform tasks normally requiring human intelligence, such as visual perception, speech recognition, decision-making, and translation between languages." Technologists recognize the imprecision of this definition, which stems both from "normally" and from "such as." What is a "task normally requiring human intelligence"? Computers have been doing tasks previously done using human intelligence for over seventy years, starting with arithmetic.

such as driver assist, the rebirth of expert systems, and improved decision support.

I will have two research goals in mind. First, what has been the business and economic logic of the AIT applications? Once we learn that AIT application does not emphasize the task-level substitution of machine thinking, seeing, etc. for human labor, we come to the question of what the important forces determining AIT value creation might be. Second, does the commercialization of AIT, at this early stage, exhibit continuity or discontinuity with prior rounds of technological commercialization of ICT? Either continuity or discontinuity (along a particular dimension) will offer valuable clues to the future direction of technical progress in the application of AIT and of ICT more generally.

That leads to a discussion of where ICT application has been going in the twenty-first century, and to an attempt to understand it. An easy-to-understand thing is that there has been a remarkable series of waves – beginning with the web browser – of new technologies that serve consumers directly, enable mass markets, and support the creation of mass-marketing commercial applications. Another easy-to-understand thing is that many of those waves, including Web 2.0, mobile, cloud, and now AITs, have led to substantial capital deepening in those same areas (consumption, mass marketing, etc.). A harder-to-understand thing is why the very impressive technical progress in those areas has had limited – that is, some, but only limited – impact on applications in the rest of the economy, where ICTs went first. The conclusion, in Section 6.5, will focus on this growth question.

In forecasting the long-run factor demand implications of AITs, there is as yet no evidence that they are different from other ICTs – working at the system level to slowly change to a more capital-intensive, less labor-intensive, more human-capital-intensive form of production, but not a form of production in which the main new feature is different factor use.

6.2 Product–Consumer Matching Applications

I begin with AIT-based product–consumer matching engines at Amazon, Google, Facebook, Netflix, and other consumer-oriented Internet Giants. Based on machine learning using these firms' considerable "big data" assets, these applications have created substantial economic value for their inventors. These are not demonstration projects or experiments. They are production systems generating revenues in the hundreds of billions of dollars.

These systems are impressive business and engineering accomplishments, involving not only use of new AITs but also the invention of new and better ways to match products to consumers. I look at them together because they have a common role in their use of AIT. These engines match a specific potential buyer to a specific potential seller. At Amazon, this matching yields product recommendations for a particular customer; at Google, it ranks advertisements that a specific searcher might see.

This use of AITs is no small thing. Improvements in targeting buyer-seller matches amount to a marketing revolution in the twenty-first century.[4] The private returns to the invention driving that revolution – returns captured thus far mostly by the Internet Giants – have been enormous, significantly increasing capital's share of output. In short, the use of AITs in product recommendation engines has been a central part of one of the most valuable technical advances of the twenty-first century – and is thus a good place to start understanding how AITs create value.

6.2.1 Amazon

Amazon, both in its own store and now in its online mall, recommends products to consumers. Excellence at recommendation has been a goal of the company from the outset. One of the firm's earliest employees attributed to founder Jeff Bezos the idea that the firm's web page should display for each consumer one book, the one they are going to buy next (Brandt, 2011). Product recommendation at Amazon has been algorithmic for many years; today, the firm uses recommendation algorithms built with AIT and machine learning. Amazon also has other AIT applications and products, to which I shall return later in this section.

Amazon's recommendation system responds to users' input with lists of potential products to examine or to buy. The data used for these systems have grown over time. Amazon has long known a great deal about what products individual customers have searched for or bought and where the customer is in the search process. The span of that information has increased as Amazon's range of products has grown from books, to many products, to hosting a mall. More recently, a number of Amazon services and products, such as Amazon Prime, Kindle, and Alexa, have increased the amount of data associated with individual customers. Amazon also has much product information, including both sellers'

---

[4] See Goldfarb (2014) on the targeting revolution in marketing.

descriptions of category, etc. and data on which consumers did or did not consider or choose the product.

For many years, algorithms have made recommendations that, for example, suggest additional products based on what a consumer has chosen to search for and what they have bought in the past. More recently, machine learning and AITs drive the algorithms that Amazon uses in these areas.[5] Amazon has sufficient data to do a good job of predicting what a particular consumer will look at, buy, etc., based on machine-learning-based product–consumer matching systems. One outcome is improved recommendations from a consumer perspective (who find items they want) and from an Amazon and merchant perspective (who get matched to customers interested in their products), consistent with the strategic goals for the company.

Beyond the large volume of data (not all of it high quality – this is "big data") and those strategic goals, there are a number of features of the Amazon mall that make it particularly suitable for an application of AIT. Amazon had a preexisting recommendation system that was part of its well-functioning and *modularized* online store/mall. Making that recommendation system more targeted to the individual customer by using the AIT of machine learning would not require changing other elements extensively because of the modularization. This benefit of a modular production process has been known to economists since Simon (1962), and a deep literature has turned it into practical management doctrine (e.g., Baldwin and Clark, 2000).

The Amazon production process was already highly modularized in part because it was already algorithmic and software developers see many benefits of modular systems. Among those benefits is that modularization at Amazon and the other Internet Giants permits them to gain *scalability* in the face of growing and changing loads.[6] Having a scalable production

---

[5] The language I use draws heavily on Bezos (2017), who also notes that related AITs based on machine learning do other matching functions, such as product and deal recommendations, merchandising placements, etc. In short, a lot of what Amazon.com shows a consumer and what an Amazon app or a Kindle show a consumer is managed by AITs.

[6] Modularity helps the scalability of a system with multiple moving parts in a number of ways. Modularity permits the addition of processing power and storage as needed when loads change. Similarly, modularity permits the addition of new data streams (e.g., adding information from Gmail) or analytical elements (e.g., thwarting ill-behaved search engine optimization at Google) as systems change. Dynamically, modularity permits improvement of the system architecture such that it can do new things while not undercutting the scalability of the existing components. A business discussion of this topic can be found in Baldwin and Clark (2000), notably in the subchapter of chapter 3 on "dimensionless, scalable design rules." Hennessey and Patterson (2012, p. 260) make a similar observation

system has, in turn, let the firm gain scale economies. To understand this, we need to examine how the economic concept of "economies of scale" interacts with the computer science concept of "scalability."

"Scale economies" mean that marginal cost is lower than average cost. "Scalability" means that a system has been designed so that its workload can be increased without changes to its architecture (again following Simon, 1962). Scalability is not just scale economies – when workloads are uncertain, for example, a scalable production process has the flexibility to be changed quickly.

Amazon is a large-scale firm in the sense that it and its online mall tenants engage in a large number of transactions with a large number of consumers. The firm's online store and now its mall have an architecture that permits scalability through modularization. A number of complex systems, most centrally the product recommendation systems, are elements of this modularized online store/mall architecture. Changing to AIT recommendation systems preserved modularity and did not affect scalability. Amazon already had good estimates of the costs and benefits of algorithmic recommendations, and could reuse those in an AIT algorithmic system.

One implication for the firm's economic costs is that, with an automated selling system including an automated recommendation system, the level of sales can be increased with approximately zero contribution of human work to the marginal cost (MC) of selling.[7] The resulting low MC, together with the fixed costs of designing the selling system, including using AITs in the recommendation system, and the need for a large body of data on multiple customers, led to considerable scale economies at the firm level. The day-to-day production process that leads to an advertisement shown or a product recommendation made is carried out by capital. MC would rise dramatically if human activity were required as part of each transaction. The fixed costs (FC) of these systems, on the other hand, are large and include much human work. The architecture of the system is designed, however, by extremely smart humans, not by machines.

---

about software: "Scalability is also not free in software. To build software applications that scale requires significantly more attention to load balance, locality, potential contention for shared resources, and the serial (or partly parallel) portions of the program."

[7] Amazon has vertically integrated into several complementary businesses, such as warehousing, where human workers do contribute to MC. The large number of Amazon businesses means that there are several places where the firm applies AITs. One example is inventory prediction in the warehouses, already a statistical prediction problem before application of AITs.

What about the shift to AIT from earlier algorithms? MC falls with the transition to AIT if AIT does a better job of recommending than did the prior algorithm. The human efforts to design and specify the AITs themselves contribute to the large FC of the Internet Giants. Invention that has a large FC to lower MC will be economic only for large firms. Whether "large" means as many product recommendations as occur at Amazon or a significantly smaller number is a topic to which I will return in Section 6.5.

Finally, the product recommendations made by Amazon are just that – recommendations. The consumer ultimately decides what to buy.[8] This has important implications for the loss function associated with bad match predictions. Choosing to recommend a product the consumer does not buy may be a lost revenue opportunity for Amazon, but, typically, it has no broader negative consequences.

The implications for the economics of adding AIT to the recommendation algorithm are straightforward. The FC of switching to an AIT-based production system can be spread over a large volume of sales. AIT is based on statistical prediction, so AIT-based matching systems have the four possible outcomes listed in Table 6.1.

A core feature of AIT product recommendation systems is that they are statistical. The profitabilityof the system thus depends on its effectiveness, on the rate of true positives, and on the error costs. Increasing the rate of true positives increases profits by increasing sales.[9] At Amazon's scale, modest increases in that rate represent considerable dollar profit. Profits increase whether the rate of true positives increases at the expense of either false negatives or true negatives – a profitable sale occurs either way. The second element of payoffs is error costs, which are small in this context. The error costs associated with false negatives are no more than the lost profits to Amazon and the lost purchase opportunity to the customer. Similarly, a false positive is just a sales recommendation that was not accepted by the customer. The role of the recommendation engine

---

[8] Agrawal et al. (2018), in a "thought experiment," consider the possibility that the Amazon prediction engine might become so good that it ships products without the consumer choosing them, and point out that Amazon has clearly done some technological development that might lead toward this. While such a change would fulfill one version of the firm's founder's early vision, it would require significantly more than a statistical improvement in the prediction engine. That last step of consumer product choice after recommendation makes the current system much more forgiving of errors in prediction.

[9] Much of Amazon's costs is the costs of getting the customer to the point of receiving a recommendation. The incremental costs of making an additional sale are largely limited to costs of goods sold and of fulfillment.

Table 6.1 *AIT-based matching system results*

Results	Outcomes
True positives	Made suggestions that led to sales
False positives	Made suggestions that did not lead to sales
False negatives	Unmade suggestions that would have led to sales
True negatives	Unmade suggestions that would not have led to sales

as advisor to the user means that its output is not the final word; the user can simply turn down the recommendation. This lowers the stakes for false positives. In Sections 6.22, 6.23, and 6.5, I shall examine other AIT applications where the costs of false positives are significant. Those costs are not, however, significant for Amazon, which has a *low stakes loss function.*

The availability of enormous data, the use of AI to achieve large scale at low MC, the modular system in place before AIT was deployed, the readily available payoff function, and the low-stakes loss function for match errors will reappear as systematic features of applications at the internet giants. Together with Amazon's strategic goals and position, and the firm's terrific technical capability, these features provide much of the explanation of Amazon's successful adoption of AIT for product-matching prediction.

6.2.2 Google

Google's largest revenue product is targeted advertising. The firm's online, mobile, and voice search products match particular searching consumers to particular advertisers. Google runs an auction to decide which advertisements, in which order, each searching consumer sees. Each consumer is more likely to click on some ads than others if they are shown. Part of the complex rules of the auction makes it easier for an ad to win if that particular consumer is more likely to click on it. To implement those rules, Google uses an AIT engine to predict specific searcher–ad click rates. This function is similar to the Amazon product recommendations engine described in Section 6.2.1, though the difference between a product recommendation and an advertisement means that the details are different.

Google uses AITs in a variety of ways: to attract users (e.g., translation), to communicate with users (e.g., Google Assistant), and, critically, to rank advertisements in a way that is targeted to each user. Google Search has been extensively studied in marketing and economics, as has Google's auction-based system for selling searchers' attention to advertisers (see, e.g., Varian,

2007; Athey and Ellison, 2011). I will review it only briefly, with emphasis on the parts that draw on AIT to match consumers and advertisers.

Consumers use Google to find information, including information about products and services they might buy. Google has significant big data about many of these consumers, based on both their searching activities and on other use of Google products, such as Gmail.[10] When a consumer searches, two kinds of result are returned. The "organic" search results are Google's guess at what the consumer was looking for. There are also advertisements, that is, information that is seeking the consumer's attention. A particular advertiser's ad will be displayed, or not, depending on the outcome of an advertising auction.

For each search, Google runs an auction to sell the searcher's attention. These auctions can scale to millions of searches per second because, on Google's side, they are automated. The auctions are granular; advertisers can choose to target detailed "AdWords." The AIT forms one important element of the auctions. Google is paid by advertisers when users click on their ads, not just for showing the ad. To maximize ad revenue, Google uses a system for ranking advertisements.[11]

Google's system, loosely called "quality score," has elements that are calculated in real time for each advertisement in each auction.[12] As the relevant economic theory makes clear, a central part of Google's profit maximization problem is predicting the probability that *this* consumer will view *this* ad if it is shown in a particular slot; that probability – not just the advertisers' bids in the auction – determines Google's expected ad revenue. AIT is used in determining this advertising ranking for a particular consumer search.

---

[10] Many Google products use AIT to offer the consumer a better service so that the firm gains more user data. Gmail, for example, has a smart reply function. Searched-to pages or entered text can be machine translated and recorded.

[11] The interaction between this ranking and the incentive-compatible elements of bidding in the auction are very well explored in the relevant economics literature. The core incentive idea is simple: if the best slot for an advertisement is filled by the highest-bidding advertiser, advertisers who get clicked on only very rarely – but who make a large profit if clicked on – will bid their way to the top. This is great for them, but bad for Google and likely bad for searching consumers.

[12] The elements are the click-through rate, the "relevance" of the ad to the user's search, and the "landing page experience" if the user clicks on the ad and goes to the advertiser's website. "Quality score" refers both to a number and to the system that generates the number, which can change the number in real time without informing either advertisers or consumers. Google has excellent reasons for imprecision in its public discussion of its search products, since websites and advertisers might otherwise game it. They game it anyway, but the imprecision lessens the effectiveness of the gaming.

Predicting the probability of a click on an ad is a near-ideal use of predictive AIT with machine learning. The situation is complex. The probability is specific to a given advertisement, advertiser, searcher, search terms, device the searcher is using, and time of day, as well as to the interactions among all those factors, for example, the relevance of the advertisement to the search. Google has big data on all these items. Finally, for profitability, the ad ranking does not need to predict very well; it just has to predict well enough for Google to achieve significant revenue from the ad auctions. The prediction system that ranks ads for the auction has relied heavily on predictive AITs for some time.

Prediction – in this case prediction of the revenue that will come to Google from showing a particular advertisement to a particular consumer, or to Amazon from recommending a particular product to a particular consumer – is one of the important parts of modern AIT. In this case, "prediction" means exactly what it means in basic statistics. The "deep learning" part of the system is automated estimation of the prediction model. Automation scales well. Google's computer can create prediction models that apply to a very large number of searchers, a very large number of searches, and a very large number of advertisements/advertisers/products without human intervention at the margin. Since Google has vast data, the prediction can be based on a great many data elements associated with the searcher, the search, and the ad. It is just prediction – the deep learning algorithm is not about *why* a group of data elements are good predictors of a match, only that they *are*.

When will deep learning work? It needs a lot of data, a lot of computer power, and a quantitative measure of a good prediction (in this case, the probability of clicking on the ad and/or revenue). Deep-learning algorithms work well in predicting based on many complex data elements if the sample sizes are large. All of these conditions for success by a deep-learning algorithm are satisfied for the problem of ranking different advertisements in the Google AdWords auction. Deep learning also needs to avoid bad product–consumer matches if they are high stakes.

The role of the AIT in this case lies in matching specific potential buyers (the searchers) to specific potential sellers and their products and services (the advertisers). In this regard, the purpose of the AIT application at the heart of Google Search is quite like the product recommendation at Amazon.[13] The economics of this early highly valuable application of AIT also follows the

---

[13] AITs are used elsewhere in Google Search, notably NLP technologies in RankBrain and in voice search.

same logic as at Amazon. Google has very large scale with enormous big data for the machine-learning part of the systems, has a search profit model that requires its systems to scale at low MC, had an already modular system before the AIT was deployed, has a readily available payoff function for the learning engine to maximize, and, finally, has a low-stakes loss function as the displayed advertisements are advisory to the consumer.[14] To be profitable, AIT matching needs only to cover its (high) FC of invention by increasing the probability of a successful match a small amount.

6.2.3 Facebook

Facebook is also ad-supported and it also uses AIT to match particular advertisements to particular consumers.[15] The business logic of that subsystem is like those just seen. It is a product–consumer matching problem, finding the advertisements that will draw a response from a particular consumer in particular circumstances. Facebook already had a scalable, modularized system based on very large volumes of data (including social connections data among billions of users) before it began to use AIT. Like Google, Facebook uses AITs to make consumer-attraction features outside its core production process.[16]

Facebook is also different in ways that will help us illuminate the economics of AITs. Facebook has big data on the "social graph" among users, information that it uses to decide what information, including ads, to show to users, in contrast to Amazon's and Google's observations of consumer searches for information, products they might buy and topics they want to know about. Facebook is used by consumers as a communications medium, so there is a flow of information across the social graph influenced both by users and by Facebook. As a result of these information differences, Facebook has a different set of algorithmic tasks. Facebook chooses which advertisements to show users without an explicit product search by the user. This was long algorithmic and is now based on

---

[14] Google blocks ads on certain kinds of searches because some searchers or advertisers might find them offensive. This avoids a high-stakes loss problem.

[15] Quoting Mark Zuckerberg on Facebook's July 2017 earnings call: "Now you can put a creative message out there, and AI can help you figure out who will be most interested."

[16] Facebook has both an AI research group and an Applied Machine Learning engineering function. Their inventions include automatic picture tagging, which uses photo recognition AITs and is deployed as a user-decision-support system, other social recommendations made to users for their potential action, and machine translation. Facebook also attempts to detect problems such as suicidal users and posts that are not from real users, etc., an area I shall revisit later in this section.

AIT. Facebook now uses AIT in the long-algorithmic function of deciding what nonadvertising information to show, that is, in populating users' "news feed."

The algorithm used by Facebook to prioritize items for the news feed uses "who" information as well as "what" information. The Facebook "social graph" forms the background to the news feed, so the "who" includes the poster of information as well as the reader of it. A tricky bit – to which I shall return – is the interesting difference between *I want to see this item on my news feed* and *You want me to see this item*. All of these factors were part of Facebook's move from its "EdgeRank" algorithm to one using significantly more AIT to fill the News Feed in 2013.[17] The feasibility conditions for using machine learning – tons of data and much information about what users like (literally "like," or read, or don't hide, etc.) to give the optimizer a quantitative goal – are well satisfied here.

In a closer parallel to Google, Facebook also uses AIT to target advertisements to specific consumers. For commercial ads, where there is a low-loss function, many of the same positive conditions noted in Sections 6.2.1 and 6.2.2 apply. Facebook has scale, needs scalability (low MC through automation), has very "big data," and had, because it needed to, an already modularized production system before widespread use of AITs. Matching an ad to a user is a difficult prediction for an algorithm, but the vast amount of low-quality "big data" can make that prediction more accurate. There is a low-stakes loss function within commercial advertisements for both false negatives and false positives.

Beyond commercial advertisements and the narrow limits of reading posts from one's own friends, a few of the important limitations to the use of AI matching technologies have been revealed at Facebook. The complexity of the entire system of Facebook – readers, posters, friends, friends of friends, likes, comments, the whole social graph – makes it difficult both to decide what algorithms should do and to set rules for posters, advertisers, and so on. Problems with a policy change can ripple through the complex system and then blow up. Facebook has systematically used business model experiments to learn what constitutes a mistake, to apologize, and to repair.[18] Typically, these experiments cannot be contained within a sample of users, for users interact and overlap. This makes

---

[17] See McGee (2013) who notes that Facebook had switched to an algorithm based on machine learning.

[18] A typical apology from Facebook's Mark Zuckerberg can be seen in McCarthy (2006). There have been over a dozen significant experiment/problem/redesign/apologize cycles.

Facebook a great place to examine the limits of recommendation systems based on predictive AIT, especially the limits associated with actions associated with a higher loss function for false positives because the outcomes matter too much to consumers.

One area where Facebook has experienced limits to the use of AIT is flagging "inappropriate content."[19] Partly, this is because some "inappropriate content" involves higher stakes associated with false positives. In many cases, a user is shown a post they dislike so intently that the mere fact that it was shown to the user is seen as a significant negative by the user.[20]

This problem has been made worse by the complexity of the "social graph" and by the creation of communities that insert and push content that others see as inappropriate, where in some cases "others" is nearly everyone. These communities might meet in Facebook groups, but they might also meet elsewhere, for example, in Reddit, to plan coordinated assaults. These communities create problems using a number of strategies, including manipulating humans to like the post, creating fake humans, and so on. The combination of high-stakes loss categories of content and the organized pushing of such content has led Facebook to retreat from its AIT-based inappropriate content system and to hire tens of thousands of human content editors. Guy Rosen, Facebook Vice President of Product Management, provided the rationale for all of this human effort in a recent blog post: "[W]e have a lot of work still to do to prevent abuse. It's partly that technology like artificial intelligence, while promising, is still years away from being effective for most bad content because context is so important."[21] Rosen cites three problems for AITs. The first two are about statistical power to discriminate between problematic and regular

---

[19] Another area of algorithm use is suggesting "people you may know," which sometimes suggests people you really don't want to know or, perhaps, be reminded about. This can be a high-stakes loss function for an erroneous false positive recommendation, but it seems to be a problem that can be contained.

[20] One example is the reaction to the Cambridge Analytica scandal, where many people and governments felt that Facebook had crossed important limits. My point has nothing to do with the merits of any of those arguments politically, in terms of privacy policy, the regulation of "troll farms," or anything similar. Instead, what is relevant to the inquiry about value creation from the use of AITs is that the scandals reveal difficulties in algorithmically policing political posts because the reader can be offended by seeing one.

[21] Rosen, "Facebook Publishes Enforcement Numbers for the First Time," https://news room.fb.com/news/2018/05/enforcement-numbers/. The Facebook representatives discussing this problem, good technologists all, tend to say the problem is that AIT has not yet advanced enough. This error lies somewhere between the anthropomorphic metaphor – the future of AIT is anything people can do – and the ordinary techno-centrism of those with computer science training.

Table 6.2 *Incidence of and algorithmic effectiveness against inappropriate content on Facebook*

Form of problematic content	Incidence*	Algorithmic effectiveness**
Spam	837.0	nearly 100%
Adult nudity and sexual activity	21.0	96%
Graphic violence	3.5	86%
Hate speech	2.5	38%

* Number of items removed by Facebook in the first quarter of 2018, in millions.
** The percentage "identified by our technology before it was reported to Facebook."

content: (1) telling the difference between "someone . . . pushing hate" and someone (else) telling of their own experience to raise awareness of a problem, and (2) that Facebook lacks sufficient data (!) for machine-learning "training" for problems that are not frequent (e.g., a new example of hate speech, early in its ugly life). To understand these first two problems for AITs, consider Table 6.2, which is based on the Rosen post.

Success in AIT fighting spam (the first row) is much like success at Google in ordering advertisements. Spam messages succeed by reaching an enormous number of readers of whom a tiny fraction click. This gives the spam detector AIT plenty of sample size – nearly a billion messages a quarter – to work with. Meanwhile, spam, while annoying, is not outrageous, so the loss function for false positives is low. The AIT spam detector usually wins the race against complaining readers.

The pornography and violence lines are different. Picture recognition, like other aspects of machine vision, is at an advanced state in AIT. On the other hand, people are likely to react strongly to being shown offensive images. The loss function for failure to recognize an offensive image is high, so the race between human complaints and AIT is won rather more frequently by the human complainers when there are new pornographic or violent images. The high-loss function for errors works against AIT.

Hate speech is even lower in frequency and in AIT's rate of winning the human v. machine race. This is easy to explain as high-loss-function hate speech poses severe problems for AITs. Human complaints about hate speech multiply rapidly in a social network if the speech arrives either at its (hated) target audience or at enough people appalled by it. This leaves every new hate-speech utterance with relatively low sample size before detection, and little information to assign a negative payoff in a machine-learning algorithm until after the hate speech has done significant harm.

Thus, human complaints typically win the race with machine learning for new hate-speech utterances. This is a structural problem of the application context, not something that improvements in AIT itself can easily remedy. Not surprisingly, after some experience with AITs, Facebook decided to utilize "people power" in combatting hate speech.

"Fake news," while not cataloged in Mr. Rosen's list, is also getting a large application of people power at Facebook.[22] This is wise on Facebook's part. Predicting what is "fake news" is a daunting statistical problem, as any particular piece of "fake news" is highly welcome by some readers – not always many – and highly disliked by others.[23] The loss function has high stakes.

Mr. Rosen flags a third problem: "[W]e're up against sophisticated adversaries who continually change tactics to circumvent our controls, which means we must continuously build and adapt our efforts."[24] This is an old market regulation problem, long familiar to economists (usually in the context of public policy rather than business policy). AITs based on machine learning are about statistical prediction rather than causation, selection, or other structural considerations. A change in policy can lead to changes in market behavior that break formerly reliable statistical predictions – the ones that formed the basis for the policy.

This applies to changes in business policies that rely on statistical prediction in much the same way that it applies – familiarly – to changes in public policy. The policy change might cause changes in behavior that invalidate the prediction. Facebook discovered this the hard way. When Facebook introduces an AIT-based set of "controls" designed to block certain bad behaviors, its "sophisticated adversaries" then "change tactics" – invalidating the statistical prediction model. This is a limitation on the usefulness of AITs. It is difficult to use any statistical prediction model, including those in AITs, to detect problems when the problematic behavior will change in response to policy changes. If the stakes are high and sophisticated adversaries are deliberately seeking to impose the false-positive losses, AIT will struggle. Hate speech, trolling, and fake news

---

[22] For example, see CNET, "Can Facebook's New Hires Take on Troll Farms and Data Privacy?," April 11, 2018, www.cnet.com/news/can-facebook-mark-zuckerberg-new-hires-take-on-troll-farms-and-data-privacy-after-cambridge-analytica/.

[23] Some technologists have suggested, implausibly, that advances in AIT will enable machines to determine the truth of all news. This is one of the few AIT overreaches not driven by the anthropomorphic metaphor.

[24] Rosen, "Facebook Publishes Enforcement Numbers for the First Time," https://newsroom.fb.com/news/2018/05/enforcement-numbers/.

stories of high emotional impact fall outside this boundary. Because the problematic actors change behavior in response to a policy change, there will always be periods during which the AIT seeking to predict the bad behavior will be catching up. Because of the high-stakes loss function for errors, waiting until there is enough sample size to train an AIT-based algorithm is more costly to the firm than replacing the technology with human workers.[25]

This illustrates the difficulty of applying AI prediction technology when the stakes and thus the loss function are not low, and it is thus one of the current boundaries of application of AITs. It is also consistent with the initial large-scale production uses of AIT recommendation systems having been developed in low-stakes loss function environments, like showing an ignorable advertisement.

6.2.4 Netflix and Others

The entertainment distributor Netflix has significantly fewer products available than Amazon. Over that restricted range, Netflix faces a similar product recommendation problem. What movies or shows would this user like to consider next? The number of choices Netflix can present is limited not only by customers' attention but also by the clumsiness of the TV screen and the TV remote. The Netflix business model also depends on matching customers to content they like; it is particularly profitable to match users to content that falls outside the list of the most popular shows and movies. Finally, Netflix has impressive big data on users' past choices.

Netflix long used a matching algorithm called CineMatch to suggest movies. A 2006 contest offered outsiders a reward for improving the algorithm and supported them with a Netflix dataset, so more is known publicly about "big data" at this firm than at almost any other. The contest winners did improve the algorithm. However, Netflix uses an internally developed machine-learning algorithm. For this application, it is fair to say that AI matching technologies are better than a wide variety of human-written algorithms.

Netflix has also faced, and solved, lower-stakes versions of problems like "fake news" and hate speech, after it discovered early on that some movies

---

[25] These last two paragraphs are dedicated to every econometrician or statistician who has suffered in one of those appalling machine learning seminars in which we were told that all of the traditional concerns of econometrics and statistics – other than prediction – are outdated.

are liked by some viewers and disliked by others. (The example it discussed publicly was *Napoleon Dynamite*.)

Netflix has other AITs in use.[26] More recently – as the firm has become a more important producer as well as distributor – it has made "trailers," that is, advertisements for shows and movies. Which trailer to show a customer is an advertising choice. AI matching technology makes consumer–trailer matching recommendations, leaving Netflix with a blend of product recommendation engines (like Amazon) and advertising choice engines (like Google or Facebook).

A few smaller-scale – and more specialized – voice user interfaces (Voice UIs) have been introduced – voice search for TV programming at cable companies is an example. A number of entertainment-delivery firms use Voice UI to permit users to choose content. Both Comcast and Dish Networks, for example, offer a "voice remote." Typing with a TV remote is tedious. In contrast, the Voice UI permits the user merely to say the name of the item for which they're searching. These examples bring together the virtues of the Netflix Voice UI (limited range of vocabulary) and the virtues of the UI applications on cell phones (high value of UI improvements in environments that are difficult for typing) discussed in Section 6.3.3.[27]

6.2.5 Technical Progress Based on AITs

Some readers will be disappointed. The "deep learning" in these systems does not resemble human learning, and the use of AIT in these systems is not what people were imagining when they heard about AI – not as sci-fi as an anthropomorphized robot. Instead, these AITs are software technologies, not sci-fi. They are tools that permit the design of new productive systems. They are embedded in the capital of those productive systems. In that regard, these AITs are like earlier ICTs. They combine technical progress, tools for invention of applications, and technical progress embedded in capital.

---

[26] For example, Netflix needs to predict the bandwidth-management version of inventory stockouts and allocate accordingly. This problem is made more difficult as some content is more bandwidth sensitive than others. Machine learning technology has proved useful in this function, which has long been a statistical prediction problem.

[27] There are many other Internet firms and related prediction applications, including LinkedIn (for jobs individuals may be interested in), and Waze, Google Maps, applications searching for a best route or local vendors, Google Image Search for similar images, and TaskRabbit matching workers and tasks.

Task-level substitution plays no role in these applications of AIT. These very valuable early applications are not ones in which labor was undertaking a task and was replaced by capital. Observers focus on task-level substitution not because it occurs but because the definition of general AI includes "tasks usually done by humans." Until general AI is commercialized, which is not likely in the foreseeable future, analysis should focus on the capabilities and applications of actual AITs. While there may be some task-level substitution in the future, it is unrelated to the value proposition of AITs.

System-level substitution is an entirely different matter. System-level substitution, such as using (the supply chain that includes) Amazon instead of (the parallel, partly overlapping bricks-and-mortar supply chain that includes) bookstores, is important in ICT-based production. System-level substitution has led to a great deal of substitution of capital for labor in the ICT era. The newly designed systems that are growing tend to be more capital intensive and more human-capital intensive than the old ones they replace. The pace, locus, and scope of that substitution have multiple determinants, of which static cost saving, that is, the degree to which new kinds of capital can be substituted for labor in particular production process tasks, has not systematically been the most important. Instead, it depends on the pace at which whole new production processes and business models are invented (Amazon's store and mall were invented and have been constantly improved). System-level substitution depends on the competition between old and new firms, and on the effectiveness of old firms at inventing competitive responses (e.g., Walmart inventing e-commerce services). In short, system-level substitution entails a wide variety of opportunities and barriers to invention, involves competition, and involves the development of complementary markets and services. It is the opposite of local and simple – and of task-level substitution.

6.2.6 Matching Engines Like Earlier ICT Waves

The AIT-based matching engines discussed in this section are like many recent waves of ICT technology. Their largest uses are in (mass) marketing, they are complements to existing ICT systems and assets, and, at a system level, they increase the growth of capital-intensive production processes. As with many other early rounds of ICT, they are deployed in already modularized production processes, or they call for difficult-to-invent modularization. The technologies are scale-using and increase the degree of scale economies. These are familiar features of new rounds of ICT, particularly since the great turn toward consumption and mass markets that followed the widespread use of the Internet.

Another important sense in which the matching engines are like earlier rounds of ICT goes back much farther than the twenty-first century. Facebook, as discussed in Section 6.2.3, struggles to control the system-wide implications of new communications technology because it changes incentives. This is an old, old story inside large organizations moving to a more digital production process.[28] What is new is that lowered costs of access to ICT services through cheaper and easier-to-use devices have made the scale of the "organization" wider in society than just a firm.

6.3 UI Improvements Based on AITs

A second important area of AIT application is in UI improvements, which have contributed to the lowered cost of access to ICT services, especially for consumers.

A number of voice-based "personal digital assistants" (PDAs) have been introduced, such as Alexa (Amazon), Siri (Apple), Cortana (Microsoft), and "Google Assistant." These form new UIs on mass-market general purpose consumer devices and offer the user a voice-based connection to many of the services running on or through those devices. Other new voice interfaces, such as voice search for video or audio entertainment on set-top boxes and new versions of telephone voice response units (VRUs), work on narrower domains. AIT-based improvements in text processing are making UI improvements on other dimensions, such as more-forgiving response to typed input from users. It all adds up to a remarkable technology deployment that is another very widespread and valuable use of AITs.

VUIs tend to make casual observers think of the Turing (1950) test. If the user "can't tell" that they are talking to a machine, but rather thinks that they are talking to a human, then the machine has achieved "artificial intelligence."[29] This confusion about the Turing test, however, makes an elementary mistake about what a UI is and does. A UI is an interface – it works between two things. In this case, it works between the user and a system or service, as indicated by Al Lindsay, the manager of Amazon's

---

[28] See, e.g., Zuboff (1988) and Bresnahan and Greenstein (1996).

[29] Many people recall the Turing test as "Could you tell?" – are you conversing with a human or a machine? The Turing test was set as a game. A computer and a human in isolated rooms, communicating only by text, vie to convince a (human!) judge that they are the human. Will the computer be better at appearing to be human than the human? Turing thus gave the machine a goal, anticipating much modern machine learning.

Alexa service (quoted by Oremus, 2018): "[W]hen I think about Alexa, I think about user-interface paradigm. I think about the voice interface only as a way to interact with technology, your platform, or a service that underlies it."

New and improved UIs can have very great economic importance. They can make user access to existing applications easier, and they can enable the invention of new applications that make economic sense only with easier access. In this sense, UIs are GPTs – but this is not the sense that observers have in mind when they hope that "AI will become a GPT."

It is easiest to understand the impact of the new AIT-based UI improvements by thinking about the series of mass-market UI improvements that preceded it. New UIs can make ICT systems available to more users by requiring less training in "using computers." The PC enabled computer use by a wide range of white-collar workers, especially after the deployment of graphical user interfaces (GUIs). It was economic to have more people, at more locations, having access to more computer systems with PCs as the UI devices than with the earlier "terminals." The World Wide Web and the web browser permitted access to applications and services from multiple locations. More and more enterprise and consumer-oriented systems could be used from more places, as many enterprise systems have a "web interface." And many consumer-oriented websites were enabled by the access improvements of the PC–browser combination.

The same analysis applies to a series of UI and access-device improvements in the consumer-ICT era. Smartphones and tablets are more portable than PCs, allowing access from more places. These new devices are "always on" and have touchscreen interfaces, permitting new kinds of access. These devices often connect to cell-phone networks (significantly more easily than PCs), permitting more access. Invention of complementary network technology, the "cloud," permits access to the same services from different devices and locations. These new UI and UI device technologies have increased the value of existing applications and enabled new ones, especially for consumers. This view of what UI improvements do reflects technological and business reality. Again quoting Al Lindsay of Amazon (from the same Oremus (2018) interview about Alexa): "I think about the voice interface as a natural evolution of those technology interfaces. . . . I think adding a voice capability to something like shopping just removes friction and it makes things easier for customers." Mr. Lindsay, of course, works for Amazon, so he hopes that UI improves shopping, but the general point is that UI improvements "remove friction" to increase access to applications.

The rate of technical progress in the AITs called natural language processing (NLP) increased when they became based on statistical prediction. They are similar to the matching engines examined in Section 6.2.6 but are distinct technologies. The value creation attributable to AITs is not associated with a broad, general scientific area called "Artificial Intelligence" but instead with specific technologies sharing and taking on directions of their own.

Google has invested in NLP technology, improving its Voice UI and its connection to underlying services. For example, Google "Voice Search" is an improvement in Google's core product: Search. Voice Search for YouTube videos has similar logic. Voice Control of Gmail has a different set of capacities, which are related to Gmail's increasing ability, based on a modularly separate AIT-based writing engine, to guess what message the author wants to write.[30] Google also exposes an application programming interface (API) for apps running on Android smartphones to take advantage of the Voice UI. Apple, the other important smartphone UI firm, also exposes an API to "Siri," so that non-Apple apps can use voice commands and use spoken output. Finally, both firms have (modularly separate) AIT services that try to predict how users will use their phone or tablet. It is easiest to describe that with the anthropomorphic metaphor, for example, Siri "suggests" opening a particular app, but it is also foolish, as this is precisely the same as the Google website "suggesting" a particular ad. Using devices in environments where it is difficult to type or read, such as in cars and kitchens, raises the value of VUI, of course.

These are statistical prediction technologies, so quality increases with the sample size of the voice data stream used to "train." Speech that can be linked to context and to the user's goals is particularly demanding of scale for training. After years as a moderately important technology, Voice UIs became important after cell phones were widely distributed. Cell phones are terrific locations to gather "big data" on voice and to use a VUI. Scale and competition played a role with Apple, Google, Amazon, and others in the mix at very large scale.

---

[30] Text UIs have also been improved using AITs. Since 2015, a Google algorithm called "RankBrain" running behind the search page tries to learn what the consumer might be interested in. Has a user typed a partial search? It suggests completions. Has a user made an oddly worded version of a common query? It guesses the underlying query. At the public announcement of RankBrain, Google stated that it was the third most frequently used algorithm (Clark, 2015). These NLP technologies, characterized in the Googlesphere as the switch "from strings to things," are valuable both to the searcher and to advertisers. They help searchers find what they are truly looking for and they help communicate what that is to advertisers.

The improvements to smartphone VUIs are made more economic by the very large-scale deployment of those devices, their use by UI-sensitive demanders (consumers), and the available voice data at large scale. So, this is – once again – a class of applications of AIT in which existing complementary assets, scale, and competition among the Internet Giants play a role.

6.3.1 Amazon: Alexa and Kindle

Alexa, a Voice UIT, and new hardware clients Echo were introduced together by Amazon. Alexa software also runs on other devices, including Android and iOS smartphones and tablets.[31] Many of the popular systems accessed through the Alexa Voice UI are home-control or media-demand applications. Alexa has been a hit, turning Amazon into a home-device company with large scale, and drawing competitive responses from other Internet Giants.[32]

Amazon has now made two successful attempts to create consumer clients, Kindle and Alexa. Compared to a smartphone or a tablet, each is more of a special purpose device. The Kindle functions primarily as an e-reader.[33] Echo devices running Alexa have only a voice interface and do not include a screen or keyboard. Both Kindle and Alexa embody new UI elements suitable to their goals. For both, Amazon's success represents not only impressive technical progress in the client devices and software themselves but also an extension of Amazon's large-scale store and rapidly growing digital media business to new distribution channels. One can read a book on Kindle; many of an Amazon Prime account's features, not least music, work through Alexa. Given this large-scale distribution strategy, it is not surprising that software clients for both Kindle and Alexa run on many non-Amazon devices. Kindle and Alexa are also complements to Amazon's product-matching AIT engines as well as to its other services, algorithmic or not.

---

[31] There are Kindle clients for PCs, for Android, and for iOS devices. There are Alexa clients for Windows PCs and Android phones. Alexa clients for Apple devices are a more complicated story at the time of writing, with Alexa running in the Amazon store app on iPhones but not yet as "Alexa," for example. Apple pleads the "app approval process" as usual, though suspicion of competitive motives (Apple iTunes versus Amazon Prime music, for example) swirls in the vast Apple rumor mill.

[32] Alexa involved fundamental advances in voice NLP, such as picking one voice out from ambient conversation or other "noise." It also involved building a new application system.

[33] Like most efforts to create an Android tablet to compete with iPad, versions of Kindle that run many Android apps have not had much market impact.

Despite their differences, I put Kindle and Alexa in the same group for two reasons. The first is to emphasize the importance of scale and marketing in the widespread deployment of new UIs. Amazon is a mass-market online store and media company, and had a powerful economic motivation to build a client presence in the mobile era. Amazon, particularly through its Amazon Prime volume discount program, was also well posed to encourage consumers to adopt Alexa. The scale of existing complements and the modularity of Amazon's existing systems encourage new UI invention.

6.3.2 Scale (of Complements Already Distributed) and Continuity of Invention

Like the technical improvements in smartphone VUIs, the technical improvements behind Alexa are impressive. Alexa can pick out individual voices in a crowded room with several people talking, making the UI more valuable in kitchens, living rooms and (soon) automobiles.[34] Siri, Google Assistant, and others can learn the voices of heterogeneous speakers. These are just some of the technical achievements in voice and text UIs in our era.

Despite this high rate of technical progress, the UI improvements do not, yet, materially alter the direction of technical change. They improve the ability of ICT-based systems to support media, retail, and related applications in large-scale, consumer-facing deployments. They have broadly the same economic implications as other important ICT advances since the widespread use of the Internet. They are capital-deepening marketing technologies deployed largely in mass markets. The existing complements and the large scale of existing applications have created a powerful economic incentive to use new UI inventions in this largely narrow capital-deepening direction. Demand forces have not yet pulled AITs far beyond that range of consumer and mass-market applications, just as they did not pull earlier rounds of impressive technical progress like the smartphone far beyond it.

6.3.3 What Will the UI Improvements Enable?

Platforms – in the narrow sense of that phrase, GPTs over which applications may be built – can enable applications in a narrow and immediate sense (a new application built on the platform) or in a broader sense (the

---

[34] Amazon acquired a startup working on those capabilities as part of its building of Alexa.

platform recombined with other elements in new systems). For the new UI elements in mobile devices, there are conjectures about both senses.

Before adding AIT elements to their UIs, Android and iOS enabled a great deal of "app" complementary innovation. Access by a mass market of consumers enabled consumer and entertainment applications such as games. Access to that same mass market of consumers enabled consumer product and services firms to create marketing and customer service apps.[35] There were, of course, some apps for tablets and smartphones that formed other parts of the production process. But consumption, sales, and marketing have been the center of it. As the UIs of smartphones and tablets improve with voice capabilities, the immediate direction of application change stays squarely within that area.

Alexa "skills" are examples of VUIs enabling applications in the narrow sense. Alexa hardware devices open up opportunities for consumers and for those who would like to reach consumers. Accordingly, there is a new range of applications, programmed into the "skills" APIs, that run on Alexa machines and on the networked system behind them. These are, once again, largely applications aimed at a consumer end-user and thus fall in the range of media, entertainment, sales, and marketing.

Task-level substitution also plays no role in these UIs, which substitute AIT capital for capital to increase convenience and access. New software technology – based on NLP (AIT) – replaces old as new UIs replace earlier UIs in some uses. They also expand the use of devices to new activities. Voice UIs partially replace touchscreen UIs, WIMP (windows, icons, menus, pointers) UIs, and so on. At a task level, this is substitution, not of machine for human but of machine for machine.

One sense in which there is substitution of capital for labor through UI improvements is increased convenience for the user. Some user time can be saved, either by the UI permitting a task to be done during less-expensive time or by the UI enabling an underlying system to respond more quickly to the user. "Alexa, play Fox News" (or CNN for other tribes) saves a walk across the kitchen, for example. This sense of saving consumer time could become a related sense of saving worker time, which is one of the directions of diffusion of AIT-based UIs under active consideration today. But, thus far, time saving is not the centerpiece of even consumer UIT; instead, the centerpiece is broadening access.

---

[35] The latter category was later than the former but surprisingly large (Bresnahan, Davis, and Yin (2015)).

6.4 Broader Diffusion: Other Marketing Applications

The early successful AIT applications have created interest among firms beyond the Internet Giants in a number of different AITs. These include the prediction technologies used in the matching and targeting applications, NLP technologies including voice and text, and perception technologies such as image recognition and matching. While there are no large areas of application, the early examples and the world of ideas make it easier to fund any project that can be labeled "Artificial Intelligence,"[36] so there are many experiments.

Programmer toolkits are available for many AITs.[37] This reduces the narrow programming costs of an AIT application but not the (usually) more difficult and expensive part of a novel application, its business specification. Each application must be invented, will still have its own costs (including error costs), will fit in existing systems modularly or not, etc.

There is little application of the AITs outside the Internet Giants as of spring 2018. However, over the last two years, large firms' approaches to AIT applications have crossed from speculation and investigation to experimentation and development.[38] Surveys of firms about their applications intentions now mention specific use cases; there are applications plans, applications experiments, and ideas.[39]

The largest category of experiments is *marketing* applications. Using the AITs' underlying product–consumer matching systems and NLP, "chatbots" and the like have been applied in marketing interactions with customers; the scope is not only initial customer acquisition (advertising) but

---

[36] This is one narrow sense in which the "AI Technology Boom" resembles the Internet Bubble (and its underlying boom). Then, as now, the CTO could dominate the CFO because of the widespread interest in a technical area.

[37] Through Amazon Web Services (AWS), Amazon is an important supplier of services for applications for Web, Cloud, etc., especially those with "big data" storage and programming needs. AWS now includes a large number of AITs. Microsoft is also an important supplier of tools and services for cloud computing, now including AITs. Other established firms, such as IBM, Google, and Oracle, are supporting their customers with new toolkits in this area, as are many startups. The big consulting houses are all seeking to establish "thought leadership" in AITs. A number of deep learning software technologies have been moved to open source.

[38] Compare the sources cited in Bresnahan and Yin (2017) to more recent sources, e.g., Chui et al. (2018), Walker, Andrews, and Cearley (2018), or Schubmehl (2017).

[39] A Gartner survey of chief information officers is representative (Gartner Research, 2018b, p. 20) "Only four percent of CIOs say their organization has deployed AI, but we expect a substantial increase in deployments as one-fifth say they are experimenting with AI, or have short-term plans for AI."

also answering customer queries, supporting/encouraging repeat purchases, retaining customers for the long run, etc. Surveys show that the area many firms see as a priority for ICT-based technical progress, generally, lies within the marketing function. I will summarize these priority areas as "customer experience" (CX).[40] Surveys of firms about their AIT application plans typically show this as the largest area of planned applications growth. This is the main direction of diffusion in the present.[41]

This early diffusion has many of the features of the applications at the Internet Giants. Scale is important, as is the presence of complementary capital assets, such as big data, preexisting systems that communicate with customers, and so on. The early stages of diffusion, thus far, are not revolutionizing the way in which ICT is deployed in production, but they are improving ICT systems, and advancing them along their existing path.

While the complementarity of new AIT capital with existing capital is more important, the sales and marketing applications to which AI matching technology and AI NLP technology are now starting to diffuse have some modest prospects for substituting machines for human work. We can expect both some expansion of the range of customer support activities and some replacement of customer support people. This is *not* an outbreak of cost reduction via task-level substitution. Instead, the relevant demand-side forces are competition to improve consumer experiences and preexisting knowledge of where automated CX might work. Some of that knowledge comes from old "VRU" efforts, which were often inconvenient for the customer. The voice chatbots are a better version of VRUs. Other parts of that knowledge come from ineffective FAQs – text chatbots are a more targeted (with AIT doing the targeting) FAQ page.

6.4.1 Diffusion of Matching Engines to Advise Employees Rather than Customers

Another area of potentially important application experimentation, the second largest according to surveys, deploys AIT to advise employees.

---

[40] The areas include "customer engagement," "customer satisfaction," "customer support," "customer experience," and others. For example, Murray (2018) looks at consumer package goods manufacturers and reports that CX is the top priority for marketing technology spending. He argues that of the technology areas that might be used to improve ICT-based marketing, AIT is still emergent as a purchase driver, as just under half of firms anticipate that it will influence their "marketing technology" purchases going forward, while about three-quarters anticipate that CX will influence those purchases. Other product areas (described in reports not cited here) are similar.

[41] See, e.g., Murray (2018), Rollings (2018), and Gartner Research (2018a).

This is a bit of a portmanteau category, as it includes at-work versions of "digital assistants" like Alexa and Siri, improved help functions in enterprise software like Cortana, as well as systems described as decision support. Some aspects of this category may be less certain and farther off in the future than others.

The use of Alexa, Siri, or Google Assistant to undertake chores at work, much like their use at home, is one direction of diffusion. It has very high visibility, changes at most the job of the worker at hand rather than the organization, and provides only output chosen by the worker, thus avoiding outcomes with losses. One early focus seems to be on simple chores, for example, Alexa skills for sending an email and setting up a meeting. The factor market implications appear to be a modest increase in individual worker productivity.

Actual organizational productivity improvements following from this kind of use are harder to forecast positively. As with many earlier rounds of ICT adoption, the use of smartphone-based email has led to accidental organizational changes – email from the boss at night. Voice UI on the email device is not the solution to this – and "AI-based screening of emails" confuses a technical problem with an organizational one.

Another early focus is in enterprise software ease-of-use. Cortana's role in Windows plus Microsoft's role in enterprise software have led a number of observers to forecast growth for AIT-based Cortana in this role (Finnegan, 2018). The software predicts what the user wants to do next and suggests that more prominently. This is a use of matching technology that increases the productivity of software users and may have a low loss function.

A third area of experimentation is improvement of decision support (DS) systems using AI matching technology. Indeed, some forecast that the category of decision support will be taken over by AITs entirely. That would be a substantial increase in the role of AIT in advising human decision-making. Adding AIT to existing DS systems may let them draw on big data to make better recommendations. This area is immature, so it is not obvious what recombination with what new inventions can or will advance it beyond low-error-cost applications. At least some AIT applications can take advantage of a modular boundary already drawn between the decider and business systems. Growth beyond those low-adjustment cost areas will be more difficult.

These are areas of potential expansion in AIT use beyond the marketing function to other areas where existing systems can be improved by AIT interfaces, at the boundary between ICT systems and human users. Their labor market implications are approximately the opposite of task-level substitution: the human worker continues to do their job with better input from the AIT-based computer system.

Finally, some AIT demonstration projects have generated excitement and are spinning off useful applications. The most visible of these is the "driverless automobile" originally envisaged as a task-level substitution technology involving replacing a driver with an "autonomous" vehicle. The very important inventions from this effort are rapidly moving into use as driver-assist technologies rather than as task-level substitution. Many observers have made the – vapid – remark that a "driverless car" "proves" that "computers can do anything humans used to do." The vapidity lies in the laxity about proof and about task-level substitution, not in the engineering. Commercial application of driverless trucks awaits large-scale modularization of truck drivers' jobs, which typically involve much more than driving, especially for short-haul trucks. Market application of the "driverless" technologies as driver-assist safety features in high-end automobiles is growing rapidly.

6.4.2 Diffusion Implications

The early diffusion – today in experiments – of AITs away from the Internet Giants suggests a narrow range of very valuable applications of ICT-based production, many in the "customer experience" elements of mass-market selling efforts, most involving complementarity with existing capital assets of a particular form, and many involving scale and scalability. In short, the early stages of diffusion look much like the initial highly valuable applications. Other applications appear likely to increase individual worker productivity. In terms of scope, the early range of valuable diffusion looks like other recent waves of ICT, such as mobile devices and Web 2.0, with much capital deepening in the consumer-marketing-oriented industries. Scale economies at the firm level, at least for the high-value CX applications, appear important in the early diffusion path, just as in the initial applications.

6.4.3 Laboratory Results Close to Use

A third category of early applications is those in which laboratory results are close to commercial use. These do not reflect diffusion of production process inventions such as those described in Sections 6.2 and 6.3. They are, instead, a series of parallel tracks. Most of these do not call for modularizing organizations or production processes.

Production scheduling, inventory management, shipment scheduling, and related systems often relied on statistical prediction by algorithm before AIT. Inventory measurement has come to be automated at many factories, warehouses, and retail stores, and the problem of predicting inventory stockouts has long been statistical in many firms. Demand forecasting for capacity management at hotels, airlines, and so on – anything with capacity constraints and/or a queue – is a related area. AIT draws on machine learning to make a better statistical prediction of the same thing. Similarly, decades of automatic measurement for process control have led to algorithmic process control systems with elements of statistical prediction. In these areas, machine learning's value proposition – offering a better statistical prediction – is pushing on an open door: serving multiple rounds of control technologies, many with a statistical prediction element.

In finance, some asset market traders have prediction models of trades and price movements. These are also reliable adopters of new technologies that will let them get a slightly better or faster prediction. They need little organizational change to link to AIT prediction models.

A more complex example can be seen in credit card fraud systems. These are statistical, but for years they have faced a tradeoff between effective fraud detection and customer service. A phone call or text to a customer about a fraudulent transaction can stop the fraud. A false positive fraud warning, however, can annoy the customer. This is a problem of high stakes. Both statistical goals – predicting when a transaction is fraudulent and predicting when a message will annoy a customer – could be improved by AIT. This is one of those interesting examples where the system has been designed for decades to deal with the problem of a high-stakes-loss function for false positives (incorrect flagging of fraud). The addition of AIT that predicts better than an algorithm – better on both sides, not just in catching more fraud – need not decrease the level of losses.

Science and engineering applications, generally, have significantly smaller organizational adjustment costs than commercial applications. Further, many scientific and engineering disciplines have a strong statistical tradition. Unsurprisingly, AITs are coming into use as scientific toolkits. For example, Cockburn et al. (2018) are particularly interested in such important commercial scientific areas as drug discovery and development. They offer an interesting analysis of reorganization of the research process to take advantage of deep learning.

This might offer a different starting point to the diffusion of AIT as a GPT. Important ICTs, from the computer to the Internet, have started life as scientific and engineering tools. Leaps from "technical" to commercial domains typically require recombination and application invention and thus take decades.

AIT – including voice and image recognition – is being used for computer and network system security. This is an area in which the early applications were close to the laboratory, but considerable progress is being made in the field.

AIT-using security systems raise the return to better sensors more widely deployed. This is creating a great deal of experimentation with "biometrics," making an image of a person and matching it to a file of approved images to verify identity. The image could be a fingerprint, a photo of the iris, etc. These techniques may also diffuse to security systems that are more organizationally complex than computer systems access – for example, in air travel. Once again, we can see a path toward more general use with potentially greater and more widespread economic value creation with organizational changes.

Improvements in ICT security systems are complementary to the expansion of ICT-based production systems. ICT-based production systems, including marketing, entertainment, transacting, control, and the production of information goods, among others, are subject to security threats. Improvements in security systems permit ICT production systems to be delivered more conveniently, for example, through "cloud" or mobile channels. Improvements in ICT security systems remove an externality – fraud or theft – that holds back the broader use of ICT. Thus, security systems support the application of ICT-based production broadly and generally. The factor market implications of better security systems are those of system-level substitution of ICT-based production for older production systems as well as those of ICT-based production of new goods and services.

Photo and voice recognition applications are diffusing to other kinds of nonsecurity application as well. An early use was in flagging pornography at Google. Product search by photo makes product search generally more valuable. There are a number of examples in which pictures and sound recordings are being used in growing commercial systems. This diffusion involves some – but not a great deal of – adjustment costs. The adjustment cost boundaries that are being most tested and pushed are likely in the security examples.

6.5 Conclusion

AITs are a highly valuable group of technologies that represent a substantial increase in the *rate* of technical progress in ICT. They do not, however, represent a major change in the *direction* of technical progress in the applications of ICT.

These new waves of technology continue a twenty-first-century trend. Much of the profitable and inventive ICT in our century lies in consumer-oriented applications (retail, entertainment, mass-market product and services businesses, etc.) and devices (smartphones, tablets, etc.) creating value for new network forms (cell service, Wi-Fi)[42] and in mass-market marketing and sales applications. I do not mean to imply that this is all of the ICT applications in our era; rather, it is the subset that is creating large private returns to invention and to application, and to which technologists point when they claim that we are in an era of rapid technical change. The discussion in this chapter has repeatedly shown that the application of AITs follows these developments. What are these developments? Why did they occur? Why do AITs reinforce them rather than changing their direction?

The Internet era has seen much consumer-facing technical change. The most visible of these changes – and the longest awaited – are breakthroughs in consumer-oriented devices, cell phones, tablets, media players, e-readers, and now smart assistants. Now AIT in the form of NLP is reinforcing the trend toward devices that can be used more quickly by more people in more places.

Complementary to the new devices are online mass-market products and services, first based on the widely used Internet and the World Wide Web, and later on "Web 2.0." These enabled many mass-market services to be delivered online. Another set of complements arose because the new consumer devices were largely mobile phones and tablets. This enabled mass-market mobile web applications, and then mobile applications. Complementarities among these technologies make them mutually re-inforcing, as, for example, consumer-oriented websites became mobile websites and then mobile app-accessible services. Recombination, such as cloud technologies that link web, mobile, and e-reader access to the same content, communications services, and e-commerce, has sped the mutual reinforcement. AITs, particularly AIT matching services, are now being recombined with these existing assets into a web of mutual reinforcement. Again, there is substantial deepening of an existing trend in the early AIT era.

---

[42] See Bresnahan and Yin (2010) for a discussion of the causes of the emphasis of ICT on consumption and of the limited spread of consumer-oriented technologies beyond consumption and mass marketing applications.

That series of waves of ICT innovation, and the building web of mutual reinforcement, did not just contribute services directly to consumers. Firms who serve mass markets also took advantage of the new technologies. Many of the most valuable applications of all of the recent waves of ICT are as *marketing technologies* in consumer product and services firms, and to some degree in other mass markets. They have sales and service websites, mobile websites, and mobile apps. They advertise on new ICT-based media. A number of consumer-facing industries, notably the distribution and making of entertainment, retail, and retail finance, are going through dramatic structural changes as a result.

The consumer-facing products and services, and their relationship to mass marketing and mass markets, are familiar. Perhaps less well known, but also economically important, is the trend in ICT generally and in the applications of ICT more particularly toward an emphasis on marketing technologies. The original conceptualization of the value proposition of computers in business was "cost savings" through human work being replaced by computer work. The "cost savings" view of ICT application value creation has never disappeared, but it has been in steady decline as a portion of ICT applications for five decades. "Strategic" ICT applications – many in marketing and procurement – have been growing in its place.[43] Their growth accelerated with the PC and the widely used Internet. The factor market implications of "strategic" applications typically arise, of course, through systems-level substitution, not through task-level substitution.

In short, much of the early application of AIT in highly valuable uses, and much of the planned (versus conjectured) path of diffusion, continues the direction of technical progress that has been most rapid and sustained over the last twenty-five years: marketing, customer service, and their interaction in using customer service to create customer attention which is then monetized, whether in an advertising function or inside a standing buyer–seller relationship. AIT use restarts a cycle of improvement that has been deepening in particular areas of economic activity since the mid-1990s.

This is not the only thing that has been happening in technical progress, not even in ICT and its applications. Some of the previous rounds of new ICT in recent times have gone beyond consumption and mass marketing,

---

[43] The "cost savings" versus "strategic" language comes from Cortada (2004), reflecting an effort to quote or paraphrase businesspeople in many industries describing their goals and plans for technical progress.

including Cloud technologies, the Internet, and mobile telephony. AITs may join these earlier technologies in having a broader commercial impact in the future.

Any explanation of the great narrowing must begin with the under-served status of consumer computing and of mass markets before the widespread use of the Internet. It is now perfectly obvious that mass-market devices, communications services, online content, and e-commerce represent a substantial overlap of technological opportunity and market demand in our century. Similar applications, but not mass-market ones, were already present for e-commerce, online content, and electronic communication. Foresighted businesspeople saw the opportunity to extend these applications to mass markets.[44] As a result, much of the thinking about how to exploit the opportunity was in place before the widespread use of the Internet. The last twenty-five years or so have seen an explosion of mass-market, mass-marketing, and consumer-oriented ICT.

The extension of ICT production into mass marketing also drew on existing complements. Airline reservations systems, for example, were one of the oldest enterprise applications categories. They were complementary to direct passenger access through web interfaces and to the extension of those web interfaces to mobile devices. Existing corporate applications – the reservation system is the primary example – in consumer products and services firms were complementary to advances like the Internet and mobile devices, and together they enabled new rounds of rapid invention in consumer-facing marketing and customer services applications. That pattern of complementarity with existing capital supporting very rapid advance is, as has been discussed, a central feature of the use of AITs.

All of these factors explain why ICT deepening has been a powerful force. But why not broadening? I have identified two specific limitations of AITs – stakes and modularization.

Stakes help explain the subset of mass-market industries where AIT, like earlier rounds of ICT, has had big effects. It is more difficult to transform the marketing side of consumer-facing industries with high-stakes transactions. I am thinking here of health care, government, and many professional services. Modularity helps explain the slow rate of cost-reducing (versus "strategic," including marketing) advances. It has always been difficult to modularize many bureaucratic production processes, and this

---

[44] In many cases, these individuals did not just talk about the opportunity for mass market versions of all those services; they also launched large, mostly failed experiments before the browser (Bresnahan, 2012).

has always been part of the slow rate of improvement of productivity through the application of ICTs in business. Production processes and the related markets and supply chains are difficult to modularize, so organizational adjustment costs have been large. Other applications of ICTs have required little organizational change, for example, workers seeing information on a cell phone they could already see on a PC, and thus have proceeded more rapidly. Modern ICTs have raised the benefits of organizational change, but the cross-section distribution of the costs of organizational change has been the key determinant of the diffusion of ICTs generally. AIT seems ill-posed to change this long-standing picture.

Changing organizations and supply chains is a slow economic process, even when motivated by large opportunity. International factor cost differences and new technologies each represent a large opportunity in our time. Exploiting those opportunities has been slow, since replacing labor either with combinations of capital and human capital or with overseas labor, transportation, and communications calls for modularizing production processes and supply chains. There is progress on that front, but not the kind of instant breakthroughs suggested by technological determinists. Diffusion of AITs beyond the applications seen thus far involves either breakthrough invention in applications (with modularization and organizational change) or the addition of important new complements, unknown today, to the AITs, or both.

One hope for AITs as a GPT is that production processes and supply chains will not need to be modularized – workers will simply be replaced by machines without any change in job description. In this case, no modularization would be needed. This hope is driven by a metaphor, not by business and technological reality.

Finally, I note that there has been a steady increase in the relative success of the leading firms in a large number of industries relative to other firms in the industries. This is seen in a dramatic increase in measured firm effects, in a wide number of metrics, including wages, profits, growth, capital share, and firm size. These are typically associated with firm use of ICT. We have also seen an increase in industry concentration, positively correlated with the measured margins for the larger firms in the industry.[45] The tendency of AIT to be scale-using and to be complementary with existing capital assets at the firm level suggests that AIT use will continue these

---

[45] The resulting increase in concentration may or may not reflect a decline in competition, and the origin of firm effects in pro-consumer investments in ICT applications may or may not mean that the changes are efficient.

trends rather than change them. The capital deepening arises out of a cluster of characteristics that arise at the firm level: scale economies, complementarity of new AIT capital with existing capital assets, particularly with big data and with modularized production processes, and the ability to specify a quantitative goal for production in an environment with low stakes in the case of error. These important economic and technical elements of AIT-using systems inventions are far from task-level substitution.

References

Agrawal, Ajay, Joshua Gans, and Avi Goldfarb, 2018. *Prediction Machines: The Simple Economics of Intelligence*. Harvard Business Review Press, Boston, MA.

Athey, Susan, and Glenn Ellison, 2011. "Position Auctions with Consumer Search." *Quarterly Journal of Economics* 126 (3), 1213–70.

Baldwin, Carliss Y., and Kim B. Clark, 2000. *Design Rules*. MIT Press, Cambridge, MA.

Bezos, Jeff, 2017. "2016 Letter to Shareholders." https://blog.aboutamazon.com/company-news/2016-letter-to-shareholders.

Brandt, Richard L., 2011. *One Click: Jeff Bezos and the Rise of Amazon.com*. Penguin Group, New York, NY.

Bresnahan, Timothy F., 2012. "Generality, Recombination, and Reuse." In Josh Lerner and Scott Stern (eds.), *The Rate and Direction of Inventive Activity Revisited*, 611–56. University of Chicago Press for the NBER, Chicago, IL.

Bresnahan, Timothy F., Jason P. Davis, and Pai-Ling Yin, 2015. "Economic Value Creation in Mobile Applications." In Adam Jaffe and Benjamin Jones (eds.), *The Changing Frontier: Rethinking Science and Innovation Policy*, 233–86. National Bureau of Economic Research, Cambridge, MA.

Bresnahan, Timothy, and Shane Greenstein, 1996. "Technical Progress and Co-Invention in Computing and in the Uses of Computers." *Brookings Papers on Economic Activity: Microeconomics* 27 (3), 1–83.

Bresnahan, Timothy F., and Manuel Trajtenberg, 1995. "General Purpose Technologies: Engines of Growth?" *Journal of Econometrics* 65 (1), 83–108.

Bresnahan, Timothy, and Pai-Ling Yin, 2010. "Reallocating Innovative Resources around Growth Bottlenecks." *Industrial and Corporate Change* 19 (5), 1589–1627.

Bresnahan, Timothy, and Pai-Ling Yin, 2017. "Adoption of New Information and Communications Technologies in the Workplace Today." In Shane Greenstein, Josh Lerner, and Scott Stern (eds.), *Innovation Policy and the Economy* 17 (February), 95–124. National Bureau of Economic Research, Cambridge, MA.

Brynjolfsson, Erik, Daniel Rock, and Chad Syverson, 2017. "Artificial Intelligence and the Modern Productivity Paradox: A Clash of Expectations and Statistics." NBER Working Paper No. 24001. National Bureau of Economic Research, Cambridge, MA.

Chui, Michael, James Manyika, Mehdi Miremadi, Nicolaus Henke, Rita Chung, Pieter Nel, and Sankalp Malhotra, 2018. "Notes from the AI Frontier: Applications and Value of Deep Learning." Discussion Paper. McKinsey Global Institute, McKinsey & Company, New York, NY.

Clark, Jack, 2015. "Google Turning Its Lucrative Web Search Over to AI Machines." *Bloomberg Business*, October 26, www.bloomberg.com/news/articles/2015-10-26/ google-turning-its-lucrative-web-search-over-to-ai-machines.

Cockburn, Iain M., Rebecca Henderson, and Scott Stern, 2018. "The Impact of Artificial Intelligence on Innovation." NBER Working Paper No. 24449. National Bureau of Economic Research, Cambridge, MA.

Cortada, James, 2004. *The Digital Hand*. Volume 1. Oxford University Press, Oxford, UK.

Finnegan, Matthew, 2018. "Report: AI Assistants and Chatbots Gain Traction in the Enterprise." *Computerworld*, April 4, www.computerworld.com/article/3268075/ai-assistants-and-chatbots-gain-traction-in-business.html.

Gartner Research, 2018a. "Gartner Says Global Artificial Intelligence Business Value to Reach $1.2 Trillion in 2018: Customer Experience Represents the Majority of AI Business Value Through 2020," April 25, www.gartner.com/en/newsroom/press-releases/2018-04-25-gartner-says-global-artificial-intelligence-business-value-to-reach-1-point-2-trillion-in-2018#:~:text=Customer%20Experience%20Represents% 20the%20Majority,reach%20%243.9%20trillion%20in%202022.

Gartner Research, 2018b. "Market Guide for Conversational Platforms." Gartner Research, Stamford, CT.

Goldfarb, Avi, 2014. "What Is Different about Online Advertising?" *Review of Industrial Organization* 44 (2), 115–29.

Helpman, Elhanan, and Manuel Trajtenberg, 1998. "Diffusion of General Purpose Technologies." In Elhanan Helpman (ed.), *General Purpose Technologies and Economic Growth*, 85–120. MIT Press, Cambridge, MA.

Hennessey, John L., and David A. Patterson, 2012. *Computer Architecture: A Quantitative Approach*. Elsevier, Cambridge, MA.

McCarthy, Caroline, 2006. "Facebook's Zuckerberg: 'We Really Messed This One Up'." *CNET*, September 8, www.cnet.com/news/facebooks-zuckerberg-we-really-messed-this-one-up/.

McGee, Matt, 2013. "EdgeRank Is Dead: Facebook's News Feed Algorithm Now Has Close to 100 K Weight Factors." *MarketingLand*, August 16, https://marketing land.com/edgerank-is-dead-facebooks-news-feed-algorithm-now-has-close-to-100k-weight-factors-55908.

Murray, Gerry, 2018. "IDC's 'Next Tech' Survey of Marketing and MarTech in Consumer Packaged Goods Manufacturers." IDC, Framingham, MA, www .idc.com/getdoc.jsp?containerId=US43613518.

Oremus, Will, 2018. "When Will Alexa Know Everything? A Conversation with the Chief of Amazon's Voice Assistant on What Alexa Hears, What She Remembers, and How She's Learning." *Slate*, April 6, https://slate.com/technology/2018/04/alexa-chief-al-lindsay-isnt-worried-about-users-privacy-concerns.html.

Rollings, Mike, 2018. "Deliver Artificial Intelligence Business Value: A Gartner Trend Insight Report." Gartner Research, Stamford, CT.

Romer, Paul M, 1986. "Increasing Returns and Long-Run Growth." *Journal of Political Economy* 94 (5), 1002–37.

Rosenberg, Nathan, 1997. "Uncertainty and Technical Change." In Ralph Landau, Timothy Taylor, and Gavin Wright (eds.), *The Mosaic of Economic Growth*, 334–56. Stanford University Press, Redwood City, CA.

Rosenberg, Nathan, and Manuel Trajtenberg, 2004. "A General-Purpose Technology at Work: The Corliss Steam Engine in the Late-Nineteenth-Century United States." *Journal of Economic History* 64 (1), 61–99.

Schubmehl, David, 2017. "IDC Market Glance: Cognitive/AI Systems, Search, and Content Analytics." IDC, Framingham, MA.

Simon, Herbert, 1962. "The Architecture of Complexity." *Proceedings of the American Philosophical Society* 106 (6), 467–82.

Taddy, Matt, 2018. "The Technological Elements of Artificial Intelligence." NBER Working Paper No. 24301. National Bureau of Economic Research, Cambridge, MA.

Trajtenberg, Manuel, 2018. "AI as the Next GPT: A Political-Economy Perspective." NBER Working Paper No. 24245. National Bureau of Economic Research, Cambridge, MA.

Turing, Alan M., 1950. "Computing Machinery and Intelligence." *Mind* 59 (236), 433–60.

Varian, Hal, 2007. "Position Auctions." *International Journal of Industrial Organization* 25 (6), 1163–78.

Walker, Mike J., Whit Andrews, and David W. Cearley, 2018. "Top 10 Strategic Technology Trends for 2018: AI Foundation." Gartner Research, Stamford, CT.

Zuboff, Shoshana, 1988. *In the Age of the Smart Machine: The Future of Work and Power.* Basic Books, New York, NY.

PART IV

THE EFFECTS OF FISCAL POLICY ON GROWTH

Taxes and Economic Growth

Robert J. Barro

7.1 Introduction

As discussed in Barro and Furman (2018), there are sharp differences in views among economists and policy-makers about the macroeconomic effects of the 2017 US tax reform, commonly referred to as the Tax Cuts and Jobs Act (TCJA). Some observers think that the likely effects of the TCJA on economic growth were important; others think not.

Barro and Furman (2018) estimated the effects of the TCJA from its changes in business and individual taxation. The bottom-line forecast was an increase in the growth rate of real GDP by 1.1 percentage point per year over 2018–19, the two years following the enactment of the tax reform. Hence, if we use a baseline growth forecast of 2 percent per year in the absence of the tax reform, then projected growth for 2018–19 was approximately 3.1 percent per year. Over the longer term, say, from 2020 to 2028, the estimated growth effect was an increase of about 0.2 percentage point per year. Thus, with a baseline of 2.0 percent per year, the projected growth rate was around 2.2 percent per year.

The bulk of the predicted short-run growth response (in 2018–19) reflected the cuts in individual marginal income tax rates). These effects were temporary for the growth rate but permanent for the level of real GDP. The comparatively small predicted increase in the long-run growth rate came from the cuts in business taxes, particularly those applying to C-corporations. These responses implied a gradual positive effect on the level of real GDP extending over ten years and beyond.

The main approach in Barro and Furman (2018) for gauging effects on businesses – C-corporations and pass-through enterprises (S-corporations, partnerships, and sole proprietorships) – involved the effects of the tax reform on the user cost of various types of capital.[1] We used the projected changes in user costs within a simple, calibrated neoclassical framework to gauge the long-run impacts of the tax changes on capital–labor ratios, output per worker, and the real wage rate.

Given the projected long-run responses, we estimated shorter-run effects by using empirically estimated rates of convergence that come from the empirical literature on economic growth (Barro, 2015). Thus, for example, we projected how capital and output per worker for C-corporations and pass-through businesses would evolve over a ten-year horizon starting in 2018.

A complementary empirical analysis used data on corporate-profits tax rates for about eighty countries in the context of cross-country growth regressions. The results from this approach were similar to those derived from the analysis that calculated the long-run effects from a simple calibrated model and then derived the short-run effects from estimated convergence rates. Thus, the regression results enhance the confidence in the estimates obtained from the calibrated model.

Barro and Furman (2018) assessed the effects of the changes in individual income tax rates on GDP growth by using empirical estimates from existing reduced-form time-series regression models. According to the Tax Policy Center, the cut in the (labor-income weighted) average marginal income tax rate contained in the 2017 law was substantial at 3.2 percentage points. We lowered this estimate to 2.3 percentage points by factoring in the drastically reduced deductibility of state and local income taxes following the 2017 reform. This 2.3 percentage points tax cut is substantially below the 4.5 points reduction in the Reagan Tax Reform Act of 1986 and the 3.6 percentage points reduction in the Kennedy-Johnson Tax Reduction Act passed in 1964. However, the 2.3 percentage points reduction is similar to the 2.1 point cut in the Bush 2003 Jobs and Growth Tax Relief Reconciliation Act (for further details, see Barro and Redlick (2011)).

7.2 Effects on C-Corporations and Pass-Through Businesses

For C-corporations, the main effects of the 2017 tax reform on user costs – and, hence, on business investment – come from the cut in the tax rate, τ,

---

[1] The concept of user costs goes back at least to Keynes (1936) and has since been employed in public and corporate finance by many economists, including Hall and Jorgenson (1967), who did not use the explicit term. The current approach to user cost uses the conceptual framework of King and Fullerton (1984).

on corporate net income (profits) and the increase in the degree of expensing, λ, used to calculated this taxable income. Public-finance economists seem to agree that permanent 100 percent expensing is efficient because it matches the deductions from taxable income with the actual cash flows for buying equipment and structures and other forms of business capital. The TCJA represents a partial movement toward this "ideal" tax treatment of investment.

I focus the present discussion on the scenario in Barro and Furman (2018) where the changes in the corporate tax law as of 2018 were unanticipated and permanent. In practice, some of these changes may be temporary; in fact, some elements of the changes enacted had sunset provisions. More generally, the path of future corporate taxation depends on the decisions of future congresses and presidents.

Barro and Furman (2018) began by analyzing the impacts on the C-corporate user cost of capital for various forms of capital under the assumption that the provisions in effect in 2018 would be permanent. We then used a simple calibrated neoclassical model to derive long-run effects on capital–labor ratios, K/L, output per worker, Y/L, and the real wage rate, w. We then applied a parallel analysis to pass-through businesses and to the overall economy.

The baseline model assumes a Cobb-Douglas production function,

$$Y_t = A K_t^\alpha L_t^{1-\alpha}, \tag{1}$$

where Y is a firm's expected output, K_t is capital input, L_t is labor input, and the exponent satisfies $0 < \alpha < 1$. The parameter α corresponds to the standard concept of the capital share of gross income. The empirical application assumes five types of capital equipment: structures, residential rental property, R&D intellectual property, and other intellectual property. Each form of capital enters with an exponent that gives its share of gross income. The analysis can also readily be extended to allow for a more general constant-elasticity-of-substitution production function.

Corporate cash flow is Y_t less wages $w_t L_t$ less gross investment, $(K_t - K_{t-1} + \delta K_{t-1})$, less taxes, T_t, where δ is the true depreciation rate on capital. Taxes are a fraction τ of taxable earnings, computed as Y_t less $w_t L_t$ less the fraction λ of gross investment that is expensed. A flat-rate tax is a good approximation to US corporate-profits taxation, as the graduation in the schedule for τ applies to relatively little corporate income.

Barro and Furman (2018) assumed that businesses choose inputs to maximize the expected discounted present value of future profits. The discount rate used for the present-value calculation, r^k, is the required expected real rate of return on capital (computed after corporate taxes but before individual taxes). This discount rate, r^k, is set at a relatively high value to accord with the high observed average real rate of return on equity, which, as discussed later in this section, is approximately 8 percent per year. The analysis uses the same r^k for all components of corporate cash flow. The risk characteristics of this overall net cash flow – for example, the correlation with overall business conditions – dictate which discount rate applies.

The formula for determining the long-run capital–labor ratio, K/L, comes from equating the marginal product of capital, MPK_t, to the user cost of capital, Ω, calculated by King and Fullerton (1984), or

$$MPK_t = \Omega = \frac{(1 - \tau\lambda)}{(1 - \tau)} \cdot (r_t^k + \delta), \qquad (2)$$

where τ, λ, and δ are assumed constant. (The analysis in Barro and Furman (2018) also allows for R&D tax credits and for tax deductibility of interest payments on corporate bonds.)

Given the Cobb-Douglas production function in (1), the expression for the marginal product of capital, MPK, is

$$MPK_t = \alpha A (K_t/L_t)^{-(1-\alpha)}. \qquad (3)$$

This approach neglects adjustment costs for investment and is thus most relevant for a long-run analysis of the determination of K/L. More generally, the left side of (2) would be the marginal rate of return on investment, factoring in adjustment costs.

The key element of the analysis is the user cost, Ω, in (2). This user cost is proportional to $r_t^k + \delta$ and also depends on the characteristics of the tax system. In particular, key aspects of the tax effects that are reflected in Ω are

- $\lambda = 1$ (full expensing): τ has no effect on Ω
- $\lambda = 0$ gives the familiar formula $(1 - \tau)MPK_t = r_t^k + \delta$
- $\tau < 1$: Ω falls with λ
- $\lambda < 1$: Ω rises with τ
- $\lambda > 1$: Ω falls with τ (i.e., with more than full expensing, increasing τ has a negative effect on the user cost).

As already noted, the main calibration in Barro and Furman (2018) assumes that $r^k = 8$ percent per year. This value is the average real rate of return on equity for a group of eleven Organisation for Economic Co-operation and Development (OECD) countries, including the United

States, that have long-term data.[2] This observed r^k is roughly stable over long periods. The analysis in Barro and Furman (2018) treated r^k as given even when corporate taxes changed. This invariance property holds for real interest rates in the steady state of the standard neoclassical growth model (when the structure of individual income taxation is fixed) because of fixed rates of time preference and intertemporal substitution (Barro and Sala-i-Martin, 2004). That is, the long-run supply of capital is horizontal in this standard model.

Other models, such as the finite-horizon framework of Blanchard (1985), have an upward-sloping long-run supply of capital. In this case, a tax change that induces a long-term rise in K/L also implies an increase in the long run in r^k. However, the opposite pattern occurs if the time-preference rate falls when K/L rises; that is, if people are more patient when they are richer. The assumption of long-run constancy of r^k (which seems roughly in accord with the data) is a reasonable approximation to reality.[3]

The effective expensing rate, λ, is computed as the present value of applicable depreciation allowances and expensing, using $r^k = 8$ percent as the discount rate in the main analysis. The biggest change in expensing in the 2017 law is the introduction of full expensing for equipment. This provision applies to C-corporations and pass-through businesses. The analysis treats this change as permanent, although there are phase-outs specified in current law.

For structures, the biggest change in the 2017 law is the large cut in the C-corporate tax rate. Smaller cuts in individual tax rates apply for pass-through businesses. The analysis treats all of these changes as permanent, as in the law as written.

Table 7.1 (based on Barro and Furman, 2018, table 5) gives the C-corporate user costs for five types of capital in the baseline (pre-2018) tax system and in the system as of 2018. The C-corporate tax rate is 38 percent in the baseline and 26 percent in the new system. (These rates factor in the federal tax rate on corporate profits along with estimates of average state-level tax rates on corporate profits.) The C-corporate user cost, Ω, falls by 10 percent for equipment (because of the move to 100 percent expensing) and by 11 percent for structures and residential rental property (because of the cut in the corporate tax rate). The user cost for R&D intellectual

---

[2] The data used in this calculation reflect an update of Barro and Ursúa (2008).

[3] The analysis in Barro and Furman (2018) examined the effects of changes in the long-run r^k.

Table 7.1 *C-corporate user costs and responses to the TCJA*

	Baseline	New system
C-corporate tax rate	0.38	0.26
C-corporate user costs		
Equipment	0.19	0.17 (−10%)
Structures	0.14	0.12 (−11%)
Residential rental property	0.15	0.13 (−11%)
R&D intellectual property	0.18	0.18 (+1%)
Other intellectual property	0.30	0.29 (−3%)
Average (share-weighted)		− 8%
C-corporate capital stock and output		
K/L (share-weighted)		+13%
Y/L		+5%

Note: These results are based on Barro and Furman, 2018, table 5.

property rises slightly (because of the reduced value of the bond interest exemption due to the limitations on the deductibility of interest expense under the TCJA – the elimination of expensing for R&D does not apply in 2018) and that for other intellectual property falls by 3 percent. On average (with each type of capital weighted by its income share), the corporate user cost falls by 8 percent. The implied average increase in long-run K/L is 13 percent (using the capital–income share parameters applicable to each type of capital). This expansion of K/L implies a rise in long-run output per worker, Y/L, of 5 percent.

Table 7.2 (based on Barro and Furman, 2018, table 9) provides estimates for pass-through businesses (S-corporations, partnerships, and sole proprietorships). In this case, the baseline pass-through tax rate is estimated to be 35 percent, and the rate under the new system is 31 percent. The treatment of expensing/depreciation allowances is the same as for C-corporations. The result is that the legislation is predicted to raise the long-run average capital–labor ratio, K/L, by 8 percent, and output per worker, Y/L, by 3 percent.

Table 7.2 also provides predictions for the effect of the TCJA on the overall economy. These results (based on Barro and Furman, 2018, table 10) assume a breakdown of value added in the baseline equilibrium of 39 percent for C-corporations, 36 percent for pass-through businesses, and 25 percent for a residual sector that includes government, households (exclusive of sole proprietorships), and nonprofit institutions. The incentives for

Table 7.2 *Pass-through and overall responses to the 2017 tax reform*

	Baseline	New system
Pass-through businesses		
Pass-through tax rate	0.35	0.31
User costs (average, share-weighted)		−5%
K/L(share weighted)		+8%
Y/L		+3%
Economy-wide responses		
Y/L		+3%
Y/L, after shift toward C-corporations		+4%

Note: These results are based on Barro and Furman, 2018, tables 9 and 10.

investment in the last sector are assumed to be unaffected by the 2017 tax changes.

The result – when weighing the change in each sector's Y/L by its share of value-added – is that economy-wide output per worker, Y/L, is estimated to increase in the long run by 3 percent. In the underlying neoclassical framework, this rise in Y/L is associated with a proportionate increase in the real wage rate, w, of the same magnitude. Barro and Furman (2018) also considered an alternative scenario that allowed for shifts in business legal structure from pass-through to C-corporate in response to the changes in the tax system, which now favors the C-corporate form. This analysis also allowed for a difference in productivity levels associated with C-corporate legal structure. (This advantage is what implicitly motivates enterprises to adopt the C-corporate form, rather than a pass-through designation, despite the typical tax disadvantage to the former.) With a 10 percent level difference in productivity, the predicted effect on the long-run economy-wide Y/L increased to a gain of 4 percent.

Given these projected long-run or steady-state responses, the dynamics of the changes in real per capita GDP depend on the economy's rate of convergence toward its new steady-state position. Barro and Furman (2018) based their dynamic projections on estimated convergence rates from the growth literature (Barro, 2015). Empirical cross-country research estimates that convergence takes place at a rate of approximately 2 percent per year, a value that has been dubbed the "iron law of convergence." However, this slow rate of convergence applies economy-wide to adjustments of capital broadly defined to include human capital and, perhaps, aspects of political institutions. In contrast, the TCJA directly affected business physical capital. In this context, the rate of convergence should be faster. For example, with a physical capital share of gross income of 40 percent, the convergence rate predicted by a simple neoclassical model (as in Barro and Sala-i-Martin (2004)) is around 5 percent per year. This rate of convergence implies that the level of per capita GDP would increase by about 2 percent after ten years, which, in turn, implies that the growth rate of per capita GDP would increase over a ten-year period by 0.2 percentage points per year.

7.3 Individual Income Taxes

As mentioned in Section 7.1, the Tax Policy Center estimates that the TCJA lowered labor-income-weighted average marginal income tax rates for 2018 by 3.2 percentage points. Barro and Furman (2018) scaled down this value to 2.3 percentage points to take into account the reduced tax deductibility of state and local income taxes under the reform.

The results in Barro and Redlick (2011) and Mertens and Montiel Olea (2018) were used to translate the change in the average marginal income tax rate, AMTR, into effects on economic growth. The time-series regression results in Barro and Redlick (2011, table 2) imply that a permanent (unanticipated) cut in the AMTR of 0.01 raises the level of per capita GDP by 0.5 percent after two years. Thus, with a reduction in the AMTR of 0.023 for 2018, real GDP is projected to be up by 1.15 percent over two years, implying that the growth rate is higher by 0.6 percentage points per year for 2018–19. This effect is temporary on the GDP growth rate but permanent on the level of GDP.

The analysis in Mertens and Montiel Olea (2018) uses a structural vector auto-regression with instrumental variables (SVAR-IV). In this case, a cut in the AMTR of 0.01 is estimated to raise the level of real GDP by 1 percent after two years, that is, by twice as much as that estimated by Barro and Redlick (2011).[4] The projections in Barro and Furman (2018) averaged the Mertens and Montiel Olea (2018) results with those of Barro and Redlick (2011) to get a predicted increase in the GDP growth rate of 0.9 percentage points per year for 2018–19.

---

[4] However, in Mertens and Montiel Olea (2018), the tax rate effects on the level of GDP tend to be partly temporary because the tax changes themselves are estimated to be partly temporary. For example, the Reagan 1986 cuts in marginal income tax rates were partially reversed by future tax law changes and bracket creep. This dynamic effect was not considered by Barro and Furman (2018), who modeled the changes in the AMTR as permanent and unanticipated.

To summarize, Barro and Furman (2018) estimated that the cut in business taxes would raise the GDP growth rate by 0.2 percentage points per year over ten years, whereas the cut in the AMTR on individuals would increase the GDP growth rate by 0.9 percentage points per year over two years and have no growth effect thereafter. Combining these results implies that the TCJA enacted in 2017 would raise the GDP growth rate by 1.1 percentage points per year for 2018–19 and by 0.2 percentage points per year for 2020–8. The main two-year effect (0.9 points) comes from the cut in the marginal income tax rates for individuals, with the remainder coming from the business tax cuts, especially those applying to C-corporations. Over the next eight years, the projected increase in the GDP growth rate of 0.2 percentage points per year reflects solely the effects of the tax cuts for businesses. These results reflect the expansionary effects of the reform on long-run levels of capital and output per worker.

7.4 Effects on Federal Revenue

Barro and Furman (2018) also provided estimates of the effects of the TCJA on federal revenue. One part of the calculation involves the estimated positive effects of the tax changes on real GDP, as described in Section 7.3, for the case where the changed tax provisions were permanent, combined with the associated increases in federal revenue. The other part involves the direct revenue loss from the reduced tax rates, net of revenue gains from provisions such as the reduced federal deductibility of state and local taxes and home mortgage interest.

For the first part of the calculation, I corrected the numbers given in Barro and Furman (2018) to reflect the growth estimates described in Section 7.3. The extra annual real GDP growth rate was assumed to be 0.011 for 2018 and 2019 and then 0.002 from 2020 to 2027. Starting from a baseline GDP of $20.5 trillion in 2018, the added growth implied an overall increment to the levels of real GDP over the ten years by $5.85 trillion (in 2018 dollars). I assumed that the added real GDP each year translated into added real federal revenue in accordance with the income-weighted average marginal federal income tax rate of 0.22 that applied in 2018. The cumulated additional real federal revenue over the ten years was $1.29 trillion (in 2018 dollars). Finally, I converted each year's extra real revenue into nominal terms by assuming that 2 percent annual inflation applied for each of the ten years, which yielded cumulative additional nominal federal revenue over ten years of $1.43 trillion.

For the second part of the calculation, Barro and Furman (2018) described a number of estimates in the literature. These estimates centered on a cumulative $1.5 trillion over ten years, varying especially with whether the tax law provisions were treated as permanent or partly temporary. In any event, these estimates are similar to the estimated positive contribution to revenue from enhanced economic growth. In that sense, a net revenue contribution of the reform of approximately zero is plausible.

Note that the revenue calculations do not factor in the expansion of federal spending that occurred in 2018. Presumably, this change cannot be attributed to the 2017 tax reform, per se. However, this added spending would move the net calculation toward substantial fiscal deficit.

7.5 Effects on Business Legal Form and Productivity

Barro and Furman (2018) suggested potentially important effects from tax-induced changes in business legal form. In particular, the 2017 tax law would have motivated shifts from pass-through to C-corporate form because of the reduction in the C-corporate tax rate relative to pass-through tax rates. This section summarizes ongoing research with Brian Wheaton on the effects of taxes on choices of C-corporate versus pass-through organizational form. A central part of the project is to assess the implications of the changing choices of legal form for economy-wide productivity.

Previous research on firm choices of corporate versus pass-through status includes Mackie-Mason and Gordon (1997), Goolsbee (1998), and Prisinzano and Pearce (2018). Following Mackie-Mason and Gordon (1997), suppose that firm i has productivity $A_c(i) > 0$ in corporate (meaning C-corporate) form and $A_n(i) > 0$ in noncorporate (pass-through) form. Firm i then opts for corporate form if

$$(1 - \tau_c)A_c(i) > (1 - \tau_n)A_n(i). \tag{4}$$

The proportionate productivity advantage (positive or negative) of corporate form for firm i is

$$a(i) \equiv [A_c(i) - A_n(i)]/A_n(i). \tag{5}$$

The condition for choosing corporate form in (4) can then be expressed as

$$a(i) > (\tau_c - \tau_n)/(1 - \tau_c) \equiv \tau, \tag{6}$$

where τ is defined as the "tax wedge."

If tax rates are the same for all firms, the key factor in determining choices of legal form is the frequency distribution of the proportionate productivity advantage, $a(i)$. (The analysis can readily be extended to allow for a distribution of tax rates.) In the overall population of firms, the fraction opting to be corporate is one minus the cumulative density of $a(i)$ evaluated at the cutoff τ.

A tractable representation for the distribution of $a(i)$ is the first-order gamma, which is part of the family of exponential distributions. The specification is

$$f[a(i) + b] = \left\{ \frac{4[a(i) + b]}{(\bar{a} + b)^2} \right\} \exp\left\{ \frac{-2[a(i) + b]}{(\bar{a} + b)} \right\}. \tag{7}$$

The parameter b (set at 0.3 in the main analysis) allows for negative values of $a(i)$, that is, for the presence of some firms that have a productivity advantage in noncorporate form. The parameter $\bar{a}$ is the average value of $a(i)$. To match the observation that many firms opt for C-corporate form despite high tax wedges, $\bar{a}$ has to be large – taken to be 0.8 in the main analysis. Figure 7.1 shows the graph of the probability density for $a(i)$ with the assumed parameter values.

Figure 7.2 shows the implied relation of average output or productivity of firms as a function of the tax wedge, τ, as defined in (6).[5] Note that peak output (normalized to equal 1.0) corresponds to a zero tax wedge – that is, to neither a tax nor a subsidy on the form of legal organization. Beyond $\tau = 0$, output falls with τ.

Figure 7.3 gives the slope implied by Figure 7.2, that is, the marginal effect of τ on output or productivity (corresponding to the marginal excess burden from taxation). This marginal effect is negative for $\tau > 0$.

Figure 7.4 shows the implied share of output provided by the corporate sector as a function of the tax wedge τ. These values – which depend on the underlying parameters assumed in Figure 7.1 – can be compared to the data relating taxes to the share of economic activity originating in the corporate sector. Note that for values of τ in a realistic range – such as 0.1 to 0.6 – the model's calculated corporate output share is between 70 percent

---

[5] These calculations assume that the productivity increment, $a(i)$, is distributed independently of the baseline level of noncorporate productivity, $A_n(i)$. These results can be generalized, for example, to treat $A_c(i)$ and $A_n(i)$ as bivariate log-normal with a nonzero correlation.

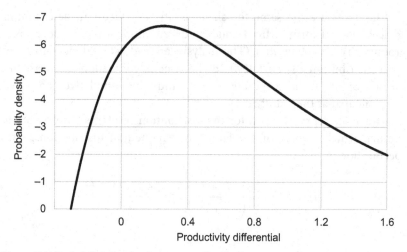

Figure 7.1 Probability density for gamma distribution
Note: The first-order gamma distribution is specified in equation (7). The variable $a(i)$ for firm i (positive or negative) is the proportionate productivity advantage of corporate over pass-through form. The parameter b (set at 0.3) is the maximum productivity advantage for pass-through form (corresponding to $a(i) = -0.3$). The parameter $\bar{a}$ (set at 0.8) is the average of $a(i)$, that is, the average productivity advantage for corporate form.

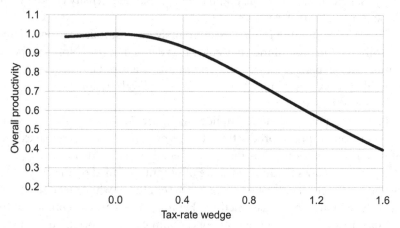

Figure 7.2 Tax rate wedge and productivity
Note: The peak productivity level is normalized to 1.0. This peak occurs at $\tau = 0$ (not $\tau = -0.3$).

and 90 percent, which accords well with the empirical data discussed later in this section.

Figure 7.5 corresponds to the slope implied by Figure 7.4. This marginal effect of τ on the corporate output share is roughly constant for realistic

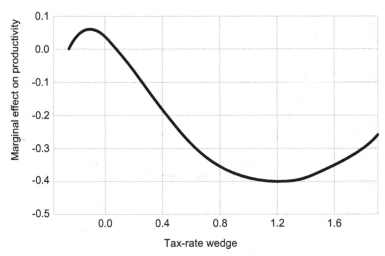

Figure 7.3 Marginal effect of tax wedge on productivity
Note: The graph shows the marginal excess burden associated with the tax wedge.

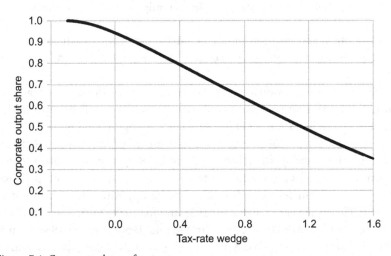

Figure 7.4 Corporate share of output
Note: The corporate share of output in the model can be compared to data on corporate shares of economic activity. In the realistic range of tax wedges, from 0.1 to 0.6, the corporate share is between 0.7 and 0.9, roughly in accord with data.

values of τ, say, between 0.1 and 0.6. In this range (and given the underlying parameters assumed in Figure 7.1), this marginal effect is approximately −0.4. The implication is that the coefficient in a regression of the corporate share of output on the tax wedge should be roughly constant –

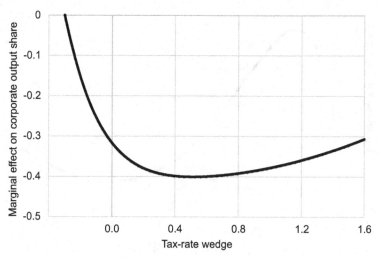

Figure 7.5 Marginal effect of tax wedge on corporate output share
Notes: This marginal effect in the model should correspond to a regression coefficient
in the relation between corporate share and the tax wedge. In the relevant range of tax
wedges, roughly 0.1 to 0.6, the marginal effect is nearly constant at approximately -0.4.

that is, a linear specification should be satisfactory – with a value near –0.4.
Results discussed later in this section are roughly consistent with this
prediction.

Figure 7.6 shows available empirical measures for the United States of
the C-corporate share of business activity. These data, available up to 2013,
come from the IRS *Statistics of Income*. The upper graph in Figure 7.6 is the
C-corporate asset share, measured out of a universe that includes
S-corporations and partnerships (but excludes sole proprietorships, for
which the IRS lacks asset data). Note that assets are a gross concept, since
they are mostly matched by liabilities on the opposite side of businesses'
ledgers. These data are available for 1953 and for 1958–2013. The C-corporate asset share is over 90 percent from the mid-1950s through 1984, then it
falls fairly steadily to 75 percent in 2013. This asset share concept was used in
the empirical analysis of Mackie-Mason and Gordon (1997).

The middle graph in Figure 7.6 is the C-corporate share of business
receipts. This concept of economic activity, available for 1958–2013, is also
a gross measure in the sense of not netting out purchases of intermediate
goods and materials from other businesses. This measure of C-corporate
share shows an increase from 75 percent in 1958 to 87 percent in 1981,
followed by a decline to 60 percent in 2013. The downward trend since the
late 1980s is similar to that shown for corporate assets.

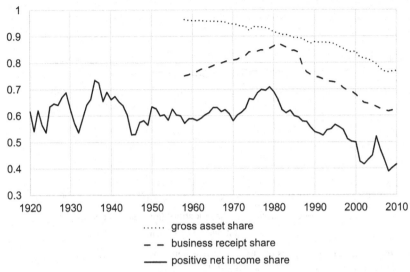

Figure 7.6 C-corporate shares of economic activity
Source: IRS *Statistics of Income.*

The lower graph in Figure 7.6 is the C-corporate share of positive net income. This measure, available for 1917–2013, is highly volatile because of the strong sensitivity of the various forms of business net income to the business cycle. The C-corporate share of overall net income is even more volatile because of the extreme sensitivity of negative net income to business conditions. The share of positive net income shown in the figure has no clear trend through the mid-1980s, but then falls from 62 percent in 1984 to 43 percent in 2013. The net income share concept was used in the empirical analyses of Mackie-Mason and Gordon (1997) and Prisinzano and Pearce (2018).

Figure 7.7 shows data from the US Commerce Department, Bureau of Economic Analysis (BEA) on the corporate share of business gross investment and capital stock. The investment data, available from 1901 to 2017, are based on a concept of corporations that combines pass-through S-corporations (originating in 1958) with C-corporations. The corporate share of gross investment shows no clear trend, especially since the mid-1970s. This share varies only between 79 percent and 84 percent from 1974 to 2017. The BEA also reports the corporate share of capital stock, based on a perpetual-inventory method. However, these data are problematic because they do not pick up, in a timely way, the effects on business ownership of stocks of capital that arise from changes in ownership – for example, when a business shifts status from C-corporation to partnership (likely, an LLC) or vice versa. In the data, these ownership changes do not

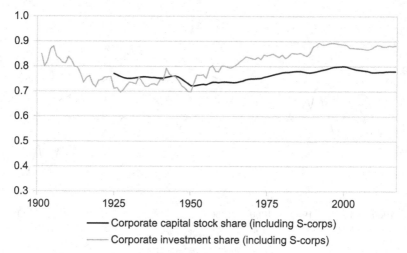

Figure 7.7 Corporate shares of business investment and capital stock
Source: Bureau of Economic Analysis (BEA).

show up contemporaneously as shifts in the ownership of capital stocks; instead, they get reflected only over time as investment outlays are associated with the new form of ownership.[6]

Figure 7.8 has two important components of the tax wedge, τ, between C-corporate and pass-through ownership. The upper graph in Figure 7.8 is the top federal tax rate on C-corporate profits. The lower graph in Figure 7.8 is the labor-income weighted average marginal tax rate in the individual federal income tax.

For measuring the C-corporate tax rate, τ_c, the main omission in Figure 7.8 is individual taxes levied on dividends and capital gains. However, because of retention of earnings, there tend to be long gaps between accrual of corporate net income and realization of dividend payouts. Also, owners of dividend-paying corporate stock tend to have relatively low or zero tax rates on dividends. Capital gains can reflect the accumulation of retained earnings within a corporation, but realizations of these gains tend to be deferred substantially by individuals, thereby implying low effective rates of taxation.

The pass-through tax rate, τ_n, corresponds to the marginal income tax rates applicable to high-income individuals who are potentially owners of

---

[6] Goolsbee (1998) states that he used these BEA data on corporate share of capital stock. However, he actually used, apparently because of confusion about the BEA table headings, the data on corporate share of gross investment. Thus, inadvertently, Goolsbee avoided the conceptual problem associated with the BEA measure of ownership of the capital stock.

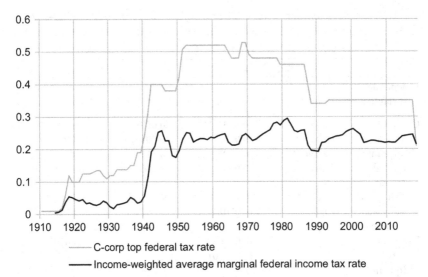

Figure 7.8 Federal C-corporate and individual tax rates
Sources: Data on the top federal rate on C-corporate profits are from IRS, *Statistics of Income Bulletin*, Fall 2003. More recent data are from IRS.gov. Data on average marginal federal income tax rates are from Barro and Redlick (2011) and the Tax Policy Center.

pass-through businesses. The labor-income-weighted average marginal individual federal tax rate in the lower graph of Figure 7.8 is an approximation to this measure.

Table 7.3 has regressions for the C-corporate share of business assets. The sample period is 1968–2013, and the dependent variable is the ten-year difference in the C-corporate asset share (see the data in the upper graph of Figure 7.6).[7] The only regressors in the first regressions are a constant (which corresponds to a trend in the C-corporate share) and the ten-year changes in the tax rate variables: the top federal tax rate on C-corporate profits and the AMTR for the federal individual income tax (Figure 7.8). A year variable is added subsequently to allow for a quadratic trend. Newey-West standard errors are calculated to allow for the serial dependence created by the overlapping ten-year differences of the dependent variable.

---

[7] Level regressions – reported by Mackie-Mason and Gordon (1997), Goolsbee (1998), and Prisinzano and Pearce (2018) – seem not to be meaningful because of the strong persistence in and possible nonstationarity of measures of the C-corporate share of economic activity. Regressions with annual first differences, carried out by Prisinzano and Pearce (2018), are likely to be dominated by measurement error. The long-difference specification is a middle ground between these two alternatives.

Table 7.3 *Regressions for C-corporate share of business gross assets, 1968–2013*

	(1)	(2)	(3)	(4)
	Specification 1		Specification 2	
Independent variable				
Constant (trend)	−0.0521*** (0.0063)	−0.0231*** (0.0057)	−0.0508*** (0.0063)	−0.0225*** (0.0048)
C-corporate top federal tax rate	−0.164*** (0.048)	−0.080** (0.038)	−0.319*** (0.106)	−0.171** (0.067)
AMTR federal individual income tax	0.220*** (0.050)	0.108** (0.050)	0.387*** (0.087)	0.205*** (0.074)
Years since 1968 (quadratic trend)	–	−0.00103*** (0.00020)	–	−0.00105*** (0.00018)
p-value for equal magnitude of tax coefficients	0.0001	0.071	0.10	0.21
R-squared	0.47	0.79	0.45	0.81
Standard error of regression	0.0155	0.0099	0.0158	0.0095

Notes: Asterisks denote significance at the 1% (***), 5% (**), and 10% (*) levels. The dependent variable is the C-corporate share of business gross assets (Figure 7.6). The C-corporate top federal tax rate, τ_c, and the AMTR for federal individual income tax, τ_n, are in Figure 7.8. Variables are ten-year differences. Standard errors, shown in parentheses, are calculated using the Newey-West method with a ten-year bandwidth. Specification 1 uses $\tau_c/(1-\tau_c)$ and $\tau_n/(1-\tau_n)$ as the tax variables. Specification 2 uses τ_c and τ_n.

In specification 1 of Table 7.3, the tax wedge is computed from (6) as $\tau = (\tau_c - \tau_n)/(1 - \tau_c)$. The two parts of the tax wedge – $\tau_c/(1 - \tau_c)$ and $\tau_n/(1 - \tau_c)$ – are entered separately into the regressions, thereby allowing for tests of equality of the magnitudes of the coefficients. Specification 2 uses the simpler tax wedge expression $\tau = \tau_c - \tau_n$.

In Table 7.3, the estimated coefficients in specification 1 (column 2) are −0.164 (standard error (s.e.)=0.048) on the variable based on the C-corporate tax rate, and 0.220 (s.e.=0.050) on the variable based on the individual AMTR. In specification 2 (column 3), the estimated coefficients are −0.32 (s.e.=0.11) on the C-corporate tax rate and 0.39 (s.e.=0.09) on the

AMTR. The fits of the two specifications are similar. Note that the signs of the estimated coefficients are correct – negative on the corporate tax rate and positive on the individual AMTR. In theory, the magnitudes of the coefficients should be equal, and empirically they are close. At a 5 percent significance level, the hypothesis of equality is rejected in the first specification (p=0.0001) and accepted in the second (p=0.10).

The coefficient magnitudes, estimated at approximately 0.2 in specification 1 and 0.35 in specification 2, should correspond to the model-based marginal effect shown in Figure 7.5. That magnitude is 0.36–0.40 in the relevant range of τ (given the parameters assumed in Figure 7.1). Therefore, the regression results are roughly consistent with the results generated from the calibrated model. However, in this context, specification 2 works better than specification 1.

The estimated trend in the C-corporate asset share in Table 7.3 is significantly negative, as reflected in the constant terms in columns 1 and 3. These findings accord with the clearly visible trend in the upper graph in Figure 7.6. The trend could pick up shifts of the economy out of sectors, including manufacturing, in which the C-corporate legal form has the highest productivity advantage. The trend could also reflect the gradually improved legal status of pass-through alternatives. For example, S-corporations with limited liability began in 1958 but are heavily restricted with respect to numbers and types of shareholder. Master limited partnerships (MLPs), which began in 1981, allow limited liability and public trading of shares for limited partners but only for enterprises operating in specified activities related to energy (though Blackstone managed to qualify as an MLP). Attractive forms of partnership with limited liability – LLCs – became widespread after their tax status (partnership treatment) was clarified by the IRS in 1988. However, explanations of the trends based on changes in the economy-wide composition of output or in legal changes for pass-throughs may not be valid because the trends in corporate shares look different with alternative measures of the corporate share of economic activity – for example, there is little trend in the corporate share of gross investment in Figure 7.7.

Columns 2 and 4 of Table 7.3 add a year variable, which allows for a quadratic trend (as in the specifications of Mackie-Mason and Gordon (1997)). This year variable is significantly negative, meaning that the negative trend in the C-corporate asset share intensified over time since 1968. This pattern can be discerned in the upper graph of Figure 7.6, but the underlying source of this quadratic trend is unclear.

Reassuringly, even with the quadratic trend, the pattern of estimated coefficients on the tax rate variables is similar to the earlier results, although the magnitudes of the estimated coefficients are smaller. The hypothesis of equal magnitude coefficients related to the C-corporate and individual tax rate variables is now accepted in each specification at the 5 percent significance level. These results suggest that the effects of tax rates may be well identified even though the source of the underlying trends has not yet been related to changes in economic and legal fundamentals.

The main estimated historical effects of tax rates on the C-corporate share of economic activity can be summarized by considering the major tax changes that have occurred since 1960. In Table 7.4, τ_c corresponds to the federal tax rate on C-corporate profits and τ_n to the average marginal tax rate from the federal individual income tax (Figure 7.8). These values imply a tax wedge of $\tau = (\tau_c - \tau_n)/(1 - \tau_c)$, from (6). The values shown for economy-wide productivity are those given by the calibrated model in Figure 7.2.

In 1960, the C-corporate tax rate, $\tau_c=0.52$, was well above the pass-through rate, $\tau_n = 0.23$, so that the tax wedge, τ, was very high, 0.60. Correspondingly, estimated productivity, based on the underlying model, was 86 percent of its potential peak, corresponding to $\tau=0$. Then, until 1986, τ_c fell to 0.46, while τ_n rose to 0.26; both changes contributed to a fall in the tax wedge, τ, which reached 0.37. The model implies a cumulative tax-induced rise in productivity by a substantial 10 percent, that is, by 0.4 percentage points per year from 1960 to 1986.

The Reagan Tax Reform Act of 1986, which was phased in between 1986 and 1988, is well known to have lowered individual marginal income tax rates. However, the fall in the corporate rate, to $\tau_c=0.34$, more than offset the fall in the noncorporate rate, τ_n, to 0.20, so that the tax wedge, τ, fell further, to 0.22. The model implies another expansion of productivity, in this case by 4 percent.

From 1988 to 2017, τ_c was virtually unchanged, but τ_n rose to 0.24, as the Reagan tax changes were substantially undone. As a result, the tax wedge, τ, fell further, to 0.16. The model implies an additional expansion of productivity, by 1 percent.

Finally, in 2018 after enactment of the TCJA, the large cut in τ_c, to 0.21, more than offset the fall in τ_n, which reached 0.22. Consequently, the tax wedge, τ, became negative, or −0.01, for the first time. However, because τ was already comparatively low, 0.16, by 2017, the further increase to productivity was only another 1 percent.

Table 7.4 *Estimated productivity effects from major historical US tax changes*

1960: τ_c = 0.52, τ_n = 0.234., τ = 0.60, productivity=0.861
1986: τ_c = 0.46, τ_n = 0.258, τ = 0.37, productivity = 0.943, up 9.5%
1988: τ_c = 0.34, τ_n = 0.195, τ = 0.22, productivity = 0.981, up 4.0%
2017: τ_c = 0.35, τ_n = 0.244, τ = 0.16, productivity = 0.990, up 0.9%
2018: τ_c = 0.21, τ_n = 0.215, τ = –0.01, productivity = 100, up 1.0%

Notes: τ_c equals the top federal corporate tax rate and τ_n equals the federal average marginal income tax rate for individuals (Figure 7.8). The tax wedge, τ, is calculated from (6). The correspondence between τ and the economy's overall productivity is reflected in Figure 7.2.

7.6 Conclusion

The TCJA enacted in the United States in 2017 cut tax rates for C-corporations, expanded expensing for business equipment, and cut marginal tax rates in the individual income tax. When the provisions in place for 2018 are treated as permanent, the calibration of a neoclassical model implies that output per worker rises in the long run by around 5 percent for C-corporations, 3 percent for pass-through businesses, and 4 percent for the overall economy. Over ten years, the estimated increase in the growth rate of per capita GDP is about 0.2 percentage points per year. The cut in individual marginal income tax rates has a larger estimated short-run effect on economic growth, 0.9 percentage points per year over 2018–19. Hence, the main short-run growth response involves the individual income tax, and the main long-run response involves business taxes.

The estimates take into account tax-induced shifting of business legal form between C-corporate and pass-through status. Since 1960, there has been a large drop in a measure of the tax wedge between the C-corporate form and the pass-through form – which has fallen from 60 percent in 1960 to 37 percent in 1986, to 22 percent in 1988, to 16 percent in 2017, and to 0 in 2018. The cumulative estimated positive effect on productivity of the elimination of this tax wedge is 16 percent. At the same time, there has been a marked negative trend in the C-corporate share of economic activity, likely reflecting shifts toward sectors that benefit less from C-corporate legal form and enhanced attractiveness of pass-through alternatives, notably partnerships in the form of LLCs.

References

Barro, Robert J., 2015. "Convergence and Modernisation." *Economic Journal* 125 (585), 911–42.

Barro, Robert J., and Jason Furman, 2018. "Macroeconomic Effects of the 2017 Tax Reform." *Brookings Papers on Economic Activity* 49 (1) Spring, 257–345.

Barro, Robert J., and Charles J. Redlick, 2011. "Macroeconomic Effects from Government Purchases and Taxes." *Quarterly Journal of Economics* 126 (1), 51–102.

Barro, Robert J., and Xavier Sala-i-Martin, 2004. *Economic Growth.* MIT Press, Cambridge, MA.

Barro, Robert J., and José F. Ursúa, 2008. "Macroeconomic Crises since 1870." *Brookings Papers on Economic Activity* 39 (1) Spring, 255–350.

Blanchard, Olivier J., 1985. "Debt, Deficits, and Finite Horizons." *Journal of Political Economy* 93 (2), 223–47.

Goolsbee, Austan, 1998. "Taxes, Organizational Form, and the Deadweight Loss of the Corporate Income Tax." *Journal of Public Economics* 69 (1), 143–52.

Hall, Robert E., and Dale W. Jorgenson, 1967. "Tax Policy and Investment Behavior." *American Economic Review* 57 (3), 391–414.

Keynes, John Maynard, 1936. *The General Theory of Employment Interest and Money.* Macmillan and Co., London, UK.

King, Mervyn A., and Don Fullerton, 1984. *The Taxation of Income from Capital: A Comparative Study of the United States, the United Kingdom, Sweden, and West Germany.* University of Chicago Press, Chicago, IL.

Mackie-Mason, Jeffrey K., and Roger H. Gordon, 1997. "How Much Do Taxes Discourage Incorporation?" *Journal of Finance* 52 (2), 477–505.

Mertens, Karel, and José L. Montiel Olea, 2018. "Marginal Tax Rates and Income: New Time Series Evidence." *Quarterly Journal of Economics* 133 (4), 1803–84.

Prisinzano, Richard, and James Pearce, 2018. "Tax-Based Switching of Business Income." PWBM Working Paper W2018-2. Penn-Wharton Budget Model, Philadelphia, PA.

Carbon Taxes: Macroeconomic and Distributional Effects

John W. Diamond and George R. Zodrow

8.1 Introduction and Overview

The Tax Cuts and Jobs Act (TCJA) enacted in 2017 did not include any environmental taxes and the prospects for such taxes in the very near future are dim. Nevertheless, many recent tax policy debates in the United States have included discussions of implementing a carbon tax – that is, a tax on fossil fuels proportional to their carbon content as a proxy for the emissions of carbon dioxide that will occur upon combustion, typically coupled with measures that would "recycle" the resulting revenues, for example, as payroll or income tax reductions or per-household lump-sum rebates, sometimes referred to as "carbon dividends." Carbon taxes have long been recommended by liberal and progressive policy-makers as a means of addressing climate change by reducing carbon emissions.[1] Recent years have also seen interest in carbon taxes from individuals on the other side of the political spectrum. In particular, a group of influential policy-makers that includes former Treasury secretaries James Baker and George Shultz and Harvard economists Greg Mankiw and the late Martin Feldstein (Baker et al., 2017; Climate Leadership Council, 2018) has formulated a "conservative case" for a carbon tax that would replace existing and future environmental regulations; the group has offered a proposal (the "Baker-Shultz Carbon Dividends Plan") under which revenues from a carbon tax, which would begin at $40 per ton and

---

[1] For example, see Larry Summers, "It's Time the US Placed a Price on Carbon," Climate Home News, www.climatechangenews.com/2015/01/05/larry-summers-its-time-the-us-placed-a-price-on-carbon/, and Joseph Stiglitz, "Summary of Carbon Tax Views," Carbon-Price.com, http://carbon-price.com/joseph-stiglitz/.

increase over time, would be rebated on an equal per capita basis. Similarly, Brill (2017) provides a "conservative dialogue" examining pro-growth methods of implementing a carbon tax policy to replace current environmental regulations and, prior to the passage of the TCJA, Holtz-Eakin et al. (2017) recommended a carbon tax as part of a corporate income tax reform package. Moreover, some observers have argued that the need to finance the large deficits associated with the newly passed TCJA – estimated to be in the order of $1.0–$1.5 trillion over the next ten years (Joint Committee on Taxation, 2017) and perhaps $2.0 trillion if individual and business tax provisions currently scheduled to expire are extended – may strengthen the case for future enactment of a carbon tax (Gleckman, 2017; Mathur and Morris, 2017).

Indeed, in 2018, Congressman Carlos Curbelo (R-FL) introduced the "Market Choice Act," which would impose a $24 per ton carbon tax in the United States that would begin in 2020 and increase at an annual real rate of 2 percent per year until 2030; the tax would replace the federal gasoline tax and also provide funds for grants to low-income households and coastal flooding mitigation projects. An earlier Democratic proposal, the "American Opportunity Carbon Fee Act of 2018," introduced by Senator Blumenauer (D-OR), would introduce a carbon tax of $50 per ton in 2019 that would also increase at an annual real rate of 2 percent per year until an emissions reduction target was reached; the proceeds would finance payroll tax offsets, additional payments to Social Security beneficiaries and others, and grants to the states for relief to low-income families and displaced workers.

Although none of these proposals have been enacted, recent surveys suggest that support for carbon taxes may be broader than commonly believed. For example, a September 2018 poll by the Climate Leadership Council found that 81 percent of the likely voters surveyed, including 65 percent of Republicans, believed that the government should take action to limit carbon emissions, and 56 percent, including 55 percent of Republicans and 58 percent of Democrats, supported the Baker-Shultz Carbon Dividends Plan, while 26 percent opposed it and 17 percent indicated that they were unsure.[2]

---

[2] Climate Leadership Council, "National Survey Results on the Baker-Shultz Carbon Dividends Plan," www.clcouncil.org/media/Baker-Shultz-Carbon-Dividends-Plan-Survey-Results.pdf. The survey also found that 71 percent of millennials supported the plan and that using carbon tax revenues to finance rebates or "carbon tax dividends" was much preferred (by a factor of at least three) to any of eight alternative revenue recycling options.

A carbon tax is an example of a "Pigouvian tax," as it is designed to offset the negative externalities of carbon dioxide emissions associated with climate change. The primary advantage of the carbon tax approach is that it results in consumer prices that reflect the total social costs of production, including the external costs associated with climate change, so that consumers and producers take such costs into account in their private decision-making. As a result, assuming that the carbon tax is set accurately to reflect the marginal social cost of carbon (SCC), the market equilibrium with carbon taxes retains the efficiency properties associated with private markets, including efficient allocations of goods across consumers, and efficient use of production inputs and equalization of marginal abatement costs across firms, assuming that the other conditions for the efficiency of private markets are satisfied. Additional "command and control" regulations on carbon emissions, such as limits on individual emission sources or mandated emission-reducing technologies, which are often administratively cumbersome, distortionary, and unnecessarily costly, are generally not required. Equally important, firms face the correct price incentives to find new and innovative ways to reduce the carbon intensity of their production processes.

The calculation of the SCC, the marginal social damages that result from greenhouse gas emissions along an "optimal" global emissions path, is both difficult and controversial – including the contentious issues of the appropriate discount rate and whether the measure of costs should include worldwide costs or simply domestic costs – with estimates varying widely. For example, Marron, Toder, and Austin (2015) report that in one set of estimates, the SCC, measured in dollars per metric ton of CO_2 equivalents, ranges from slightly below zero[3] to more than \$100, with a central tendency of roughly \$42 per ton in 2015, while the US Environmental Protection Agency (EPA) (2015) cites a range for the SCC of \$11 to \$105 per ton in 2015. In addition, most estimates suggest that the SCC increases over time because the damages associated with marginal emissions increase as the total stock of greenhouse gases in the atmosphere increases. Marron et al. (2015) note that it is difficult to measure the SCC because (among other reasons) (1) costs must be measured over many years since greenhouse gases in the atmosphere are long-lived; (2) costs depend on the highly

---

[3] Negative estimates for the SCC are unusual but can arise if the benefits of climate change, such as increased agricultural production due to greater concentrations of carbon dioxide, are sufficiently large. The FUND (Climate Framework for Uncertainty, Negotiation, and Distribution) integrated assessment model, in particular, captures such carbon dioxide fertilization effects (Anthoff and Tol, 2013).

uncertain stock of greenhouse gases at each point in time; (3) cost estimates depend on a wide variety of controversial assumptions, including the choice of discount rate,[4] the costs of adapting to climate change, and the valuation of low probability but extremely costly catastrophic events, especially in the presence of risk aversion on the part of policy-makers; and (4) estimates of the SCC in the United States vary significantly depending on whether global or only domestic costs are considered – greenhouse gases emitted in the United States impose worldwide costs,[5] but the United States bears only 7–10 percent of the global SCC.[6] This uncertainty naturally complicates choosing the efficient level of a carbon tax. Nevertheless, Baker et al. (2017) argue that "[m]ounting evidence of climate change is growing too strong to ignore," so that such a plan is desirable because "the risks associated with future warming are too big and should be hedged. At least we need an insurance policy." We do not attempt to estimate the SCC in this chapter or to address the issues that make such estimates controversial.[7] Instead, in our simulations, we analyze the macroeconomic and distributional effects of a federal carbon tax for a representative carbon tax under a variety of revenue recycling options.

Although opponents of carbon taxes raise many objections, two of the most commonly expressed concerns, which are the focus of this chapter, are that (1) the implementation of a carbon tax would seriously hamper economic growth, especially to the extent that it would act as a tax on energy-intensive production inputs, increase consumer prices, and lower real wages; and (2) the burden of a carbon tax would be regressive, that is, it

---

[4] The range of discount rates used is large. For example, the central estimate in the Stern (2007) Review is 1.4 percent while, in a review of that report, Nordhaus (2007) recommends a 4.5 percent rate. The Trump administration has recently proposed using discount rates of 3 and 7 percent (and considering only domestic costs in estimating the SCC). See Drupp, Freeman, Groom, and Nesje (2018) for a recent discussion of the issues raised by the choice of discount rate.

[5] For example, Auffhammer (2018, p. 35) stresses that because "the externality is global ... from an economic point of view, the global number is the correct estimate of the externality." However, Viard (in Brill, 2017, p. 45) argues that using a global SCC is appropriate only if the US tax is part of a "comprehensive international climate change agreement" under which all countries "impose taxes equal to the global social cost of carbon." Auffhammer also notes that the amount of resources that has thus far been devoted to measuring the economic impacts of climate change is relatively small.

[6] For additional discussion, see Newbold, Griffiths, Moore, Wolverton, and Kopits (2010), Nordhaus (2014a, 2014b), Pizer et al. (2014), Gillingham and Stock (2018), and Auffhammer (2018), and, for a critical view, see Pindyck (2017).

[7] For recent surveys, see Auffhammer (2018) and Rose, Diaz, and Blanchard (2017).

would be borne disproportionately by lower-income households, who spend a relatively large fraction of their income on carbon-intensive goods, especially gasoline, electricity, natural gas, and fuel oil.[8] These two concerns are the focus of our analysis.

Specifically, in this chapter we use the Diamond-Zodrow dynamic computable general equilibrium (CGE) model, calibrated to the tax rates in effect since the 2017 enactment of the TCJA, to analyze the effects of the implementation of a carbon tax coupled with various revenue recycling options (1) on GDP, other macroeconomic variables, and economic growth, and (2) on intragenerational and intergenerational lifetime income distributions. In particular, we assume a "representative" carbon tax of roughly $50 (in 2016 dollars) per metric ton of CO_2 equivalent that is introduced in 2020, increases for thirty years at roughly a 2 percent rate (the precise time path is specified in Interagency Working Group (IWG) on Social Cost of Greenhouse Gases, 2016), and is then held constant in real terms beginning in 2050. We consider the following five revenue recycling options:

- providing equal lump-sum-per-household rebates;
- proportionally reducing the payroll tax;
- proportionally reducing personal income taxes on labor income;
- eliminating personal income taxes on dividends and capital gains, with remaining revenues used for equal lump-sum-per-household rebates;
- reducing the national debt for a period of ten years and then using carbon tax revenues for equal lump-sum-per-household rebates.

Such an analysis requires estimates of the effects of the carbon tax on the prices of producer and consumer goods, which are a function of their carbon intensity. Because our model is relatively highly aggregated and does not consider differences in carbon intensity, we cannot perform such an analysis. Accordingly, we rely on estimates prepared by the Rhodium Group (RHG) (Larsen, Mohan, Marsters, and Herndon, 2018) as part of an earlier research project in which we participated (Diamond and Zodrow, 2018), which was conducted under the auspices of the Carbon Tax Research Initiative of Columbia University's SIPA (School of International and Public Affairs) Center for Global Energy Policy

---

[8] For example, see US Senate, H.Con.Res.119, www.congress.gov/bill/115th-congress/house-concurrent-resolution/119/text.

(CGEP).[9] As part of its analysis, RHG analyzed the price effects of the representative carbon tax described above using a highly disaggregated model of the US economy, which includes considerable detail on energy production and usage. In particular, RHG uses the National Energy Modeling System (NEMS) constructed by the US Energy Information Administration, which provides a detailed representation of the energy and carbon intensity of production in the United States across a wide variety of business sectors. The RHG version of this model, RHG-NEMS, was utilized to estimate (among many other outputs) the effects of the representative carbon tax on the prices of a group of fifteen major consumer goods (based on the National Income and Product Accounts (NIPA) classifications of personal consumption expenditures, with "Gasoline and Other Goods" and "Housing and Utilities" disaggregated into two and four subcategories, respectively, resulting in a total of nineteen consumer goods). As described in Diamond and Zodrow (2018), we use the carbon tax–induced consumer price effects calculated by RHG and convert them into the analogous price increases for the four consumer/producer goods in our model (described further in Section 8.5).[10] We then simulate the short-run and long-run macroeconomic and distributional effects of the representative carbon tax policy under the five revenue recycling options.

We begin in Section 8.2 by recognizing that most of the literature examining the growth effects of carbon taxes, including our own research, takes a rather narrow perspective by simply ignoring their environmental benefits – a perspective that greatly simplifies the analysis but also increases the likelihood that carbon taxes will result in reductions in both GDP and economic welfare. We report the results of a recent study by Goulder and Hafstead (2018) that estimates those direct benefits of reducing carbon emissions. Given that caveat, in Section 8.3 we provide a brief overview of

---

[9] SIPA CGEP, "Carbon Tax Research Initiative," https://energypolicy.columbia.edu/our-work/topics/climate-change-environment/carbon-tax-research-initiative.

[10] The RHG study estimates that the representative carbon tax would reduce carbon emissions by 35–36 percent below 2005 levels by the year 2025, and by 37–49 percent by 2050, with most of the reductions occurring due to reduced use of coal in the electric power generation sector, with coal production falling by 28–84 percent by 2030. The average price of gasoline would initially increase by 44 cents a gallon, or roughly 20 percent, while the average price of electricity would increase to 12.5 cents per kWh or by 19 percent. The projected reductions in emissions would be more than sufficient to meet the US goal under the Paris Agreement of a 26 percent reduction in emissions by 2025, but they would clearly fall considerably short of the goal of an 80 percent reduction in emissions by 2050.

some of the results in the literature that examine the macroeconomic and distributional effects of carbon taxes in models that ignore their environmental benefits. We then describe our simulation model in Section 8.4 and, in Section 8.5, provide the results of our analysis simulating the macroeconomic and distributional effects of the representative carbon tax detailed earlier in this section. Section 8.6 concludes by summarizing the results and suggesting directions for future research.

8.2 The Direct Economic Effects of Climate Change

We begin with a brief discussion of the direct economic effects of climate change – a topic that is highlighted in the recently released National Climate Assessment (2018) but ignored in many CGE analyses of the effects of a carbon tax, including our own. We focus on a recent comprehensive analysis of carbon taxes (as well as other environmental policies) by Goulder and Hafstead (2018), who construct a dynamic, perfect-foresight, infinite-horizon CGE model with thirty-five production sectors, two regions (the United States and the rest of the world), and investment adjustment costs. In their central case, they analyze a tax that is phased in uniformly over three years to a rate of \$20 per ton and then increases at a real annual rate of 4 percent until it reaches a value of \$60 per ton some thirty-one years later, with the revenues returned as lump-sum-per-household rebates in their benchmark case. Goulder and Hafstead (2018) also consider three other revenue-recycling options – payroll tax reductions, personal income tax reductions, and corporate income tax reductions.

In the Goulder and Hafstead (2018) benchmark case, CO_2 emissions decline by 17 percent after the three-year phase-in of the tax, by 30 percent fifteen years later, and by 38 percent thirty years later, which is the steady-state level of emissions reduction. Goulder and Hafstead (2018) include three factors in their estimate of the economic value of these emission reductions, in all cases using a discount rate of 3 percent to calculate the discounted present values of future benefits and costs.

The first is the climate benefits from reduced carbon emissions, for which they utilize the estimates of the SCC calculated by the IWG (2016).[11] As noted previously, there is a great deal of uncertainty surrounding these estimates, and Goulder and Hafstead (2018) utilize (among others) what they describe as the "most widely cited" IWG estimate,

[11] As discussed, the IWG calculation of the SCC includes all global costs associated with increased carbon emissions on the grounds that such emissions create a global externality.

which is an SCC in 2017 of $42.69 per metric ton of CO_2 in 2013 dollars, increasing at roughly 1–2 percent per year to an SCC of $77.52 per metric ton of CO_2 in 2050 (again in 2013 dollars).[12] As described by Newbold et al. (2010, p. 2), the damages from climate change include, among other factors, "the impacts of global warming on agricultural productivity and human health, loss of property and infrastructure to sea level rise and extreme weather events, diminished biodiversity and ecosystem services, etc." Using this estimate of the SCC coupled with their estimate of the time path of CO_2 reductions associated with the carbon tax specified in Section 8.1, Goulder and Hafstead (2018) estimate that the present discounted value (PDV) of the costs of the carbon tax in their benchmark case is 0.64 percent of GDP and that the ratio of total climate benefits to the total welfare costs associated with the carbon tax is 1.69; that is, the total PDV of climate benefits ($5,679 billion) exceeds the total PDV of the welfare costs of the tax ($3,356 billion) by nearly 70 percent. When carbon tax revenues are used to reduce payroll taxes, the PDV of costs is 0.49 percent of GDP and the ratio of benefits to costs is 1.99. The analogous figures for the personal income tax cuts are 0.45 percent of GDP with a 2.28 ratio of benefits to costs, and for the corporate income tax cuts, 0.19 percent of GDP with a 5.10 ratio of benefits to costs.

Second, using EPA data on pollutant emissions by source, Goulder and Hafstead (2018) estimate the health benefits of the reductions in pollution associated with reduced carbon emissions, primarily reduced carbon monoxide, nitrous oxides, sulfur dioxide, volatile organic compounds, ammonia, and particulate matter. The health benefits ($8,455 billion) associated with reducing only emissions of nitrous oxides, sulfur dioxide, and certain particulates (data are not available for the other pollutants) exceed the welfare costs of the carbon tax with per-household rebates by an even larger margin, with a benefit–cost ratio of 2.52. The health benefit–cost ratios for the payroll tax cuts, personal income tax cuts, and corporate income tax cuts are 2.90, 3.26, and 6.58, respectively.

Finally, drawing on the calculations of Brown and Huntington (2013), Goulder and Hafstead (2018) estimate the energy security benefit of reduced reliance on imported oil. These benefits, however, are quite small, ranging from 0.01 to 0.03 percent of the welfare costs of the carbon tax.

---

[12] Auffhammer (2018) notes that one potential problem with these estimates, cited in a recent study by the National Academies of Sciences-Engineering-Medicine (2017), is that much of the data used to calculate the SCC are outdated. For example, Moore, Baldos, Hertel, and Diaz (2017) estimate that the impact of climate change on agriculture is more than three times that estimated in earlier studies.

Aggregating these three quantities implies that the ratio of total benefits to total welfare costs of the carbon tax coupled with per-household rebates is 4.24. Moreover, the ratio of benefits to costs is significantly larger for carbon tax policies that use the revenues raised to reduce payroll taxes, personal income taxes, or corporate income taxes, primarily because the costs of the tax are mitigated by the efficiency gains associated with reducing distortionary taxes rather than using the revenues for lump-sum-per-household rebates. Indeed, for reductions in the corporate income tax (the most distortionary tax in their model), the ratio of total benefits to total welfare costs associated with the carbon tax policy is 11.78.[13] For the carbon tax with payroll tax cuts and personal income tax cuts, these benefit–cost ratios are 4.91 and 5.57, respectively.

These estimates (and many others calculated by Goulder and Hafstead (2018) and others) are subject to a great deal of uncertainty, and other studies naturally arrive at different estimates. Indeed, this uncertainty provided some of the impetus for the double dividend literature discussed in the following section, as the prospect of showing that environmental taxes would generate efficiency gains independent of uncertain environmental benefits was enticing to the proponents of such taxes. Nevertheless, the Goulder and Hafstead (2018) simulation results suggest that the climate and health benefits associated with reductions in carbon emissions are significant. Moreover, these benefits are of sufficient magnitude that they are likely to offset any welfare costs of implementing a carbon tax at a level equal to current consensus estimates of the SCC estimated in models that ignore these climate and health benefits.

Another often-cited estimate of the SCC is due to 2018 Nobel Prize winner William Nordhaus (2017), who uses his DICE (Dynamic Integrated model of Climate and the Economy) – one of the three "integrated assessment models" utilized to generate the IWG estimates – to obtain a lower estimate of the SCC of $31 per metric ton of CO_2 (in 2015, in 2010 dollars) but one that increases more rapidly at a real annual rate of 3 percent until 2050. Nordhaus (2017) estimates that climate damages are 2.1 percent of global income with an average warming of 3 degrees Celsius (5.4 degrees Fahrenheit) and 8.5 percent of global income with a warming of 6 degrees Celsius (10.8 degrees Fahrenheit). The DICE model assumes that global damages can be approximated as a quadratic function of global average temperatures.

---

[13] Note that, in this case, the total benefits accruing solely to the United States are roughly equal to the total welfare costs of the tax.

8.3 Selective Review of Previous Studies

In this section, we provide a selective review of several studies that estimate the macroeconomic and distributional effects of carbon taxes. We consider first models of the effects of a carbon tax on GDP and economic growth, and then turn to studies that examine the distribution of the burden of the tax.

8.3.1 GDP and Growth Effects

One of the main objections to a carbon tax is that it will have a negative effect on GDP and economic growth, both due to its direct impacts on the prices of consumer goods and because it imposes a differential tax on production inputs. This concern is related to some of the results in the academic literature (especially in early studies) regarding the difficulty of attaining a "double dividend" from environmental taxes. This literature investigates whether the use of carbon tax revenues to reduce existing distortionary taxes can generate a welfare improvement (the second dividend from the policy) in addition to the environmental benefits of the policy associated with reduced emissions (the policy's first dividend, which is ignored in these analyses). Under such circumstances, environmental taxes would be desirable – relative to the status quo characterized by use of only the distortionary taxes – even if their environmental benefits are small or zero, as social welfare increases when the carbon tax is substituted for an existing distortionary tax or taxes, considered independently of environmental factors. In this case, as stressed by Bovenberg (1999, p. 421), the implementation of a carbon tax can be viewed as a "'no regret' option: even if the environmental benefits are in doubt, an environmental tax reform may be desirable" due to the efficiency benefits of the tax substitution.

Unfortunately, the literature suggests that double dividends from environmental taxes are relatively difficult to obtain. The basic intuition underlying this result can be seen in a simple model with variable labor supply and a "clean" good and a "dirty" good, where the environmental tax is imposed on the latter good. The tax effectively creates a system of differential commodity taxes that, neglecting its environmental benefits, will distort consumer choices regarding both consumption patterns and labor supply (because the consumer good price increases imply that the real wage declines) and thus decrease economic efficiency. In particular, if the carbon tax replaces a relatively efficient broad-based tax – such as a tax on all wage income – then the tax substitution is likely to reduce economic welfare. Moreover, an increase in an existing environmental tax on the polluting or "dirty" good will result in reductions in the demand for that good, the tax base, and tax revenue as consumers substitute away from the taxed dirty good to the untaxed "clean" good (an effect that would not obtain with a uniform consumption tax on both goods). As a result, a higher tax on the dirty good is needed to maintain revenue neutrality. This implies consumer prices increase more than after-tax wages fall due to the reduction in the wage tax, the real wage falls, and labor supply declines (assuming a positive labor supply elasticity), further reducing the tax base and causing additional inefficiencies. Moreover, the resulting efficiency costs are likely to be significant, as relatively large existing taxes on labor income imply that the labor supply decision is already highly distorted and that efficiency costs increase disproportionately with the size of the effective tax rate. Since all environmental taxes have such tax interactions and tax base effects, one cannot assume that environmental taxes will result in a double dividend. Indeed, in an influential early paper, Bovenberg and de Mooij (1994, p. 1085) conclude "that environmental taxes typically exacerbate, rather than alleviate, pre-existing distortions – even if revenues are employed to cut pre-existing distortionary taxes."

Nevertheless, environmental taxes can be welfare enhancing, even ignoring their environmental benefits, under certain circumstances. Two related scenarios are especially prominent in the literature and highly relevant to this chapter. First, revenue recycling approaches that take the form of reductions in taxes on capital income, including both personal income taxes on dividends and capital gains and corporate income taxes, tend to be especially beneficial; the resulting increases in investment, capital accumulation, labor productivity, and wages – relative to an initial equilibrium in which saving and investment are inefficiently low due to the distortions imposed by the existing income tax structure – may improve economic efficiency sufficiently to result in net gains or a double dividend. Second, economic efficiency may also increase if the consumer price changes induced by the environmental tax act to offset (rather than exacerbate) distortions in the initial equilibrium attributable to the existing tax system.[14] We address each of these issues in our analysis.

---

[14] Other possibilities, not addressed in our analysis, occur when environmental taxes are imposed (particularly in the presence of unemployment) on goods that are complementary to untaxed leisure and thus indirectly reduce labor supply distortions, when environmental quality is a substitute for leisure, when the incidence of environmental taxes is on economic rents, and when environmental quality affects production by increasing labor productivity. Note that in the last case, a reduction in emissions could increase the

The literature on carbon taxes is quite voluminous, and many studies estimate the macroeconomic effects of implementing various carbon tax policies on GDP, relative to a baseline without such a policy. Goulder and Hafstead (2018) provide a useful overview of a sample of such studies, comparing the results of several models that analyzed numerous alternative common carbon tax policies as part of the recent comprehensive Stanford Energy Modeling Forum 32 study.[15] Goulder and Hafstead (2018) focus on the case of a carbon tax imposed in 2020 at $25 per metric ton of CO_2 (in 2010 dollars), increasing at a real annual rate of 5 percent until 2050 and then held constant in real terms. The revenue recycling options considered are lump-sum-per-household rebates, cuts in labor income taxes, and cuts in capital income taxes. They report the effects of the carbon tax on GDP initially and ten and twenty years after enactment for simulations with their model and five other models that were included in the study.

The six models considered are the following:

- The Goulder-Hafstead E3 (Energy-Environment-Economy) model is a perfect-foresight, infinite-horizon CGE model with thirty-five production sectors and two regions (the United States and the rest of the world). The model includes investment adjustment costs and a single housing services sector. Incidence is measured with respect to lifetime income.
- The Duke DIEM (Dynamic Integrated Evaluation Model) (Ross, Fawcett, and Clapp, 2009) is a perfect-foresight, infinite-horizon CGE model with seventeen production sectors, nine US regions, and eight rest-of-the-world regions). The model differentiates between existing and new capital, allowing substitution only with respect to the latter, and has a single housing services sector. Incidence is measured with respect to annual income.
- The IGEM (Intertemporal General Equilibrium Model) (Jorgenson, Goettle, Ho, and Wilcoxen, 2013, 2015, 2018) is a perfect-foresight, infinite-horizon CGE model with thirty-five production sectors.

steady state rate of growth (which is held fixed in our analysis) and thus have a direct impact on the rate of economic growth. In addition, some efficiency gains are likely to be obtained if a carbon tax replaces relatively inefficient and thus costly environmental regulations; Carroll (in Brill, 2017, p. 22) estimates that current regulations designed to reduce carbon emissions "reduce the size of the US economy by nearly 1 percent, or approximately $1,310 per household annually in the long run."

[15] For an overview of the study, see McFarland, Fawcett, Morris, Reilly, and Wilcoxen (2018).

Owner-occupied and rental housing are treated separately. It has four US regions and models the US economy in an open economy context. Incidence is measured with respect to annual income.

- The NewERA model (NERA Economic Consulting, 2013) is a perfect-foresight macro model that covers thirty years with thirteen production sectors, six US regions, and a single rest-of-the-world region. The model differentiates between existing and new capital, allowing substitution only with respect to the latter, and has a single housing services sector. Incidence is measured with respect to annual income.
- The RTI-ADAGE (RTI International, Ross, 2014) model is a perfect-foresight, infinite-horizon CGE model with ten production sectors, and nine US regions in a closed US economy. The model differentiates between existing and new capital, allowing substitution only with respect to the latter. Incidence is measured with respect to annual income.
- The ReEDS-USREP (National Renewable Energy Lab and the MIT Joint Program on the Science and Policy of Global Change) model is a limited-foresight, infinite-horizon, recursive-dynamic CGE model, with eleven production sectors, six US regions, and fifteen rest-of-the-world regions. The model differentiates between existing capital, which is partially immobile, and new capital. Incidence is measured with respect to annual income.

The simulation results from the six models are summarized in their table 5.2 (Goulder and Hafstead, 2018, p. 97), which is reproduced as Table 8.1 below.[16]

Several general conclusions are suggested by these results. First, all of the simulated effects on GDP of the carbon tax policies, neglecting any environmental benefits, are relatively moderate. The model average effects range from a loss of 0.8 percent to a gain of 0.3 percent, with the largest loss being the 1.4 percent loss in 2040 simulated by the E3 model for the lump-sum-per-household rebate, and the largest gain being the 1.0 percent gain simulated by the RTI-ADAGE model in 2040 for the capital income tax cut. Note that the largest loss of 1.4 percent in the level of GDP in 2040 corresponds to a very small reduction in the average annual growth rate of GDP of less than 0.1 percentage points (approximately 0.07 percentage points). Moreover, the previous discussion suggests that such losses are

[16] Note that although the GH E3 model, like our model, considers only the national impacts of a carbon tax, the other five models listed all examine the regional impacts of various carbon tax policies.

Table 8.1 *GDP effects of carbon tax in various models*

Model	2020			2030			2040		
	Lump sum rebate	Labor inc. tax cut	Capital inc. tax cut	Lump sum rebate	Labor inc. tax cut	Capital inc. tax cut	Lump sum rebate	Labor inc. tax cut	Capital inc. tax cut
E3	-0.2	-0.2	-0.3	-0.8	-0.7	-0.6	-1.4	-1.3	-1.1
DIEM	-0.4	-0.2	0.4	-0.4	-0.2	0.8	-0.6	-0.4	0.9
IGEM	-0.5	-0.1	0.3	-0.8	0.2	0.5	-1.1	0.2	0.5
NewERA	-0.3	-0.2	0.1	-0.5	-0.4	0.2	-0.7	-0.6	0.2
RTI-ADAGE	-0.6	-0.4	0.6	-0.8	-0.6	0.9	-1.1	-0.8	1.0
ReEDS-USREP	-0.5	-0.3	-0.4	-0.3	-0.1	0	-0.2	0.1	0.2
Model Avg.	-0.4	-0.2	0.1	-0.6	-0.3	0.3	-0.8	-0.5	0.3

Source: Goulder and Hafstead (2018, p. 97)

likely to be offset by the environmental gains from the carbon tax policy, while the gains would be supplemented by such environmental gains. These results suggest that predictions of highly negative effects of a carbon tax on GDP – and certainly on the rate of economic growth – are seriously misplaced for carbon taxes of the magnitude analyzed in these studies.

Second, the various models exhibit a significant range of results. For example, for the results in the year 2040, the degree of variability is the greatest (2.1 percentage points) for the carbon tax with revenue recycling in the form of a capital income tax cut, with somewhat smaller variability – ranging from 1.2 to 1.4 percentage points – for the other two policies. The E3 model is somewhat of an outlier, with generally less favorable results, especially in the longer run and for the capital income tax policy. Goulder and Hafstead (2018) attribute this to their more detailed modeling of the tax system, which captures larger initial tax distortions and thus implies larger efficiency costs when these distortions are worsened by the price distortions associated with the carbon tax.

Third, the general pattern of the results is that the lump-sum redistribution policy is the least favorable in terms of effects on GDP, as revenue recycling in this form does not have the added benefit of reducing other existing tax distortions. By comparison, the capital income tax policy is the most favorable, as capital income taxation is relatively distortionary in these models. Indeed, most of the models suggest a "double dividend" from the carbon tax coupled with a cut in capital income tax revenues, with the E3 model the sole exception (except for the impact effect under the ReEDS-USREP model). Revenue recycling in the form of labor income tax cuts results in intermediate effects on GDP, reflecting the fact that labor income tax distortions are less costly than capital income tax distortions, although they are, of course, still more distortionary than a lump-sum tax. In general, the models suggest that the effects of the carbon tax on GDP get larger over time, but in a few cases the opposite pattern occurs.

8.3.2 Effects on Income Distribution

The second major concern voiced by opponents of a carbon tax is that its burden will be regressive, borne disproportionately by lower-income households who spend a relatively large fraction of their income on carbon-intensive goods, especially gasoline, electricity, natural gas, and fuel oil. Diamond and Zodrow (2018) provide an extended discussion of six papers that are representative of the literature that has addressed this issue over the last ten years or so. The discussion focuses on models with many production sectors that estimate detailed differential effects on consumer goods and production inputs (that we cannot address in our much more highly aggregated four-sector model). We summarize and extend that discussion in this section.

Before turning to these studies, however, it is important to note that the incidence or distributional impact of a carbon tax – most commonly described in terms of average progressivity or regressivity – will depend on the measure of taxpaying capacity used in the analysis. The most often used concept is some measure of annual income. However, numerous studies, including Fullerton and Rogers (1993) and Bull, Hassett, and Metcalf (1994), have stressed that annual income tends to overstate the regressivity of consumption-based taxes, such as the carbon tax analyzed in this report, for two reasons, both of which are related to the fact that household consumption is more stable over time than household income.

First, household income often fluctuates considerably from year to year. Because households tend to smooth consumption (and thus consumption tax payments) over time by drawing down savings to maintain consumption in low-income years and replenishing savings in high-income years, measuring a consumption tax burden with respect to annual income will systematically overstate the regressivity of the tax.

Second, household income fluctuates systematically over the life cycle, with annual income relative to consumption low for the young and the elderly and high for those in their prime earning years. This again implies that with consumption smoothing, measuring the burden of a consumption tax with respect to annual income will overstate the regressivity of the tax.

For these reasons, the distributional effects of consumption taxes are sometimes measured with respect to income over a longer time period than a single year, and indeed often with respect to a measure of lifetime income – a natural way to measure incidence in our model, given its overlapping generations structure in which each household maximizes lifetime utility over its life cycle subject to a lifetime income constraint. The differences between studies that measure incidence with respect to annual and lifetime income, as well as alternative methods for approximating lifetime income, are highlighted in the discussion in this section.

The six studies that we examine are as follows:

- Hassett, Mathur, and Metcalf (2009) examine the effects of a tax of $15 per metric ton of CO_2 under the assumptions of full forward shifting of the tax to forty-two consumer goods and no individual or firm behavioral responses. They use both annual income and a measure of lifetime income as measures of taxpaying capacity.

- Grainger and Kolstad (2010) also examine the effects of a tax of $15 per metric ton of CO_2 under the assumptions of full forward shifting without behavioral responses, but they include an analysis of the effects of adjusting incidence estimates for family size, using equivalence scales to take into account economies of scale in providing household services. They generally use annual income as the measure of taxpaying capacity.

- Rausch, Metcalf, and Reilly (2011) also analyze the distributional impacts of carbon pricing using a general equilibrium model coupled with microsimulation data. They analyze the near-term (five to ten years) effects of a $20 per ton tax on CO_2 emissions.

- Williams, Gordon, Burtraw, Carbone, and Morgenstern (2015) link a dynamic overlapping generations model with nineteen production sectors and a microsimulation model to analyze the initial incidence of a $30 per ton of CO_2 carbon tax held constant in real terms. Their analysis includes general equilibrium changes in factor prices and they adjust their measure of taxpaying capacity, which is based on annual income, for family size.

- Cronin, Fullerton, and Sexton (2017) use the Treasury Distribution Model, which has data on 322,000 households including 22,000 nonfilers, to analyze the static incidence of a $25 per ton tax on all carbon emissions. They assume that transfers are indexed for inflation and that there is full forward shifting of carbon taxes, and they ignore changes in factor prices and behavioral responses. They generally measure incidence with respect to annual consumption as a proxy for lifetime income.

- Rosenberg, Toder, and Lu (RTL) (2018) use the Tax Policy Center Microsimulation Model to provide a detailed static analysis (no changes in factor prices and no behavioral responses) of the same carbon tax analyzed in this report. They measure incidence with respect to annual income – although they also note the advantages of measuring incidence with respect to a longer time period, including over the life cycle.

The main results of these studies (with a focus on the two most recent studies by Cronin et al. (2017) and Rosenberg et al. (2018)) can be summarized as follows.[17] First, before accounting for the revenue uses and assuming full forward shifting of carbon taxes into consumer prices,

---

[17] For additional details, see Diamond and Zodrow (2018).

carbon taxes are regressive with respect to annual income. For example, for households ranked by annual income with no indexation of transfers, Cronin et al. (2017) show that a carbon tax is regressive, with an average burden on households (adjusted for family size and economies of scale in sharing resources) equal to 1.2 percent of annual income for the bottom income decile and 0.52 percent for the highest income decile. Broadly similar results (by annual income quintile) are obtained by Rosenberg et al. (2018) for the carbon tax trajectory analyzed in this chapter. As noted already, this regressivity is due primarily to the fact that lower-income households tend to spend a disproportionately large share of their income on carbon-intensive products, especially gasoline, electricity, natural gas, and fuel oil. Grainger and Kolstad (2010) show that the regressivity of carbon taxes is exacerbated if tax burdens are adjusted for family size using equivalence scales because lower-income households tend to have fewer persons. By comparison, the regressivity of carbon taxes may be reduced or eliminated if general equilibrium effects result in reductions in the rate of return to capital that is held primarily by high-income households. For example, the Rausch et al. (2011) simulations indicate that the carbon tax is roughly proportional with respect to annual income in this case.

Second, there are compelling reasons to measure the regressivity of a carbon tax with respect to lifetime rather than annual income, and a carbon tax is less regressive when annual consumption expenditures are used as a proxy for lifetime income. For example, Cronin et al. (2017) show that with incidence measured relative to annual consumption as a proxy for lifetime income and inflation indexation of transfer payments and income tax brackets, the carbon tax is progressive, with a tax burden equal to 0.45 percent of annual consumption for the lowest consumption decile and 0.80 percent for the highest consumption decile. On the other hand, Rausch et al. (2011) find that using lifetime income does not reduce the regressivity of a carbon tax when two alternative proxies for lifetime income are used – restricting the sample to heads of households who are between the ages of forty and sixty and using the educational level of the head of household (under the assumption that lifetime income is positively correlated with educational attainment).

Third, the regressivity of carbon taxes is further reduced under the highly plausible assumptions that government transfers and tax parameters such as income tax brackets are indexed for inflation. Indeed, the analysis by Cronin et al. (2017) suggests that the combination of measuring incidence with respect to annual consumption expenditures as a proxy for lifetime income and taking into account the effects of inflation indexing converts the carbon tax into a moderately progressive tax.

Fourth, all of the studies suggest that the distributional effects of carbon tax policies are determined primarily by the approach used to distribute the revenues raised by the tax. Carbon tax proposals that recycle revenues in the form of a constant per capita rebate are quite progressive but also relatively inefficient.[18] For example, Cronin et al. (2017) find that this policy is uniformly progressive across all consumption deciles, with households in the first seven consumption deciles experiencing tax reductions; the lowest consumption decile experiences a tax reduction equal to 2.59 percent of consumption, while the richest households experience an increase in their tax burdens equal to 0.58 percent of consumption. Similarly, Rosenberg et al. (2018) find that with a per-household rebate, the lowest quintile has an increase in after-tax income of 5.4 percent, while the middle quintile experiences a gain of 0.6 percent, and the top quintile suffers a loss of 0.8 percent.

By comparison, policies that use carbon tax revenues to reduce highly distortionary taxes on capital income are relatively efficient but highly regressive. For example, Rosenberg et al. (2018) estimate that using carbon tax revenues to further reduce the corporate income tax rate from its post-2017 level of 21 percent is the most regressive of the carbon tax policies and is uniformly regressive throughout the income distribution. The lowest quintile has a decline in after-tax income of 1.7 percent, the middle quintile experiences a loss of 1.0 percent, and the top quintile has an increase in after-tax income of 0.8 percent.

Policies that reduce labor income taxation fall in between these two options as they are more efficient than the lump-sum rebate approach due to their positive effects on labor supply; they are also less regressive than the reduction in capital income taxation since labor income is less concentrated among higher-income households. For example, Rosenberg et al. (2018) show that when carbon tax revenues are used to reduce the payroll tax, the carbon tax is only mildly regressive except at the top of the income distribution, where the carbon tax becomes progressive. Specifically, the after-tax income of the lowest quintile falls but by only 0.5 percent, while the middle quintile experiences a net effect of zero, the fourth quintile has a gain of 0.4 percent, the highest quintile suffers a loss of 0.1 percent, and the top 1 percent experience a loss of 1.1 percent.

---

[18] This policy is regressive, however, if the lump sum rebate is based on initial levels of capital income rather than being distributed equally.

Fifth, Cronin et al. (2017) find that the variation in carbon tax burdens within groups (measured as annual consumption as a proxy for lifetime income) is much larger than the variation across groups that is the focus of most studies of carbon tax incidence (including this one). In particular, they find that (1) the importance of carbon tax rebates differs considerably among poorer families so that tax burdens within lower-income groups differ significantly, (2) similar heterogeneity of burden occurs for higher-income deciles including the richest group, (3) redistributions within income groups are typically increased by the revenue recycling options they consider, and (4) policies that reduce tax burden differentials across income groups tend to increase such differentials within income groups.

Finally, carbon tax policies can be designed to achieve a wide variety of distributional objectives. For example, policies can be targeted to relieve the burden of the tax for the working poor by using the revenues to expand the Earned Income Tax Credit or to provide relief to a wide spectrum of households by reducing payroll taxes and increasing Social Security benefits. Indeed, Cronin et al. (2017) show that the latter policy can make the incidence of the carbon tax reform roughly proportional with respect to annual consumption while generating tax reductions for all but the richest consumption decile.

These general conclusions, which were obtained with models that either ignore general equilibrium adjustments or include general equilibrium effects only over a short time horizon, are confirmed in a recent study by Caron et al. (2018) that analyzes the distributional effects of various carbon tax policies within the context of four of the fully specified dynamic CGE models that were used in the Stanford Energy Modeling Forum 32 project described in Section 8.3.1. The models analyzed are the DIEM, IGEM, RTI-ADAGE, and ReEDS-USREP models.

Caron et al. (2018, p. 4) observe that the EMF study "updates, confirms and quantifies" the conclusions of earlier studies. Specifically, Caron et al. (2018) conclude that the general messages of the four studies are that (1) the distributional impacts of carbon tax policies are primarily driven by the nature of revenue recycling; (2) capital income tax reductions are the most efficient but also the most regressive of the carbon tax policies, while lump-sum redistributions are the most progressive but the least efficient; and (3) a mixed policy such as using half of revenues to reduce capital income taxes and half for lump-sum rebates can eliminate regressivity or even make the carbon tax slightly progressive, while policies utilizing transfers to hold the lowest-income quintile harmless can be achieved at a cost of roughly 10 percent of revenues.

To be more specific, consider the results for the scenario in which the carbon tax starts at $25 per ton and increases at a 5 percent rate for thirty years. The models agree that the carbon tax taken in isolation is regressive – except for the IGEM model, where it is largely neutral with slight progressivity at the highest income levels. The models agree that the carbon tax with a lump-sum-per-household rebate is progressive, with the lowest quintile experiencing a small loss or a slight gain. Revenue recycling in the form of a capital tax reduction or a labor tax reduction is generally estimated to be regressive; however, the DIEM model is the exception, as both policies are progressive, although much less progressive than the lump-sum rebate. All of the models agree that recycling schemes that are more efficient are, on average, more regressive. However, the IGEM model is unique in that it indicates that revenue recycling in the form of labor income tax cuts is slightly less regressive than recycling in the form of capital income tax cuts. In addition, all of the models indicate that the lowest-income quintile would experience losses if carbon tax revenues were recycled as capital income tax cuts. However, they all also indicate that holding the bottom quintile harmless by compensating them with lump-sum transfers requires less than 10 percent of carbon tax revenues.

Finally, Goulder, Hafstead, Kim, and Long (2018) analyze the distributional effects of a carbon tax using the E3 model described in Section 8.3.1, utilizing a comprehensive measure of welfare including the value of leisure (as do we in our analysis). Their results are consistent with the earlier literature. In particular, they find that the "uses side" of incidence – attributable to changes in the prices of consumer goods – is regressive but is generally fully offset by the progressive effects of revenue recycling on the "sources side" of incidence – the changes in factor prices and transfer income attributable to revenue recycling – as well as the indexation of transfers for the inflationary effects of carbon taxes, implying that most carbon tax policies are progressive on net.

Goulder et al. (2018) also examine the effects of using some of carbon tax revenues for targeted compensation designed to avoid losses to lower- and middle-income groups. They find that the costs of targeted compensation are an order of magnitude higher when the alternative use of carbon tax revenues is to reduce the corporate income tax relative to reductions in personal income taxes and payroll taxes, and that the efficiency costs of targeted compensation rise dramatically if the compensation is extended beyond the lowest-income quintiles. In particular, they show that households in the second and third quintiles experience welfare losses under carbon tax policies that involve marginal tax rate cuts (the first quintile gains from all policies that include revenue recycling). For example, with a uniform rebate to households in the first two quintiles, set so that the households in the second quintile do not experience a welfare loss, the welfare costs of the policy increase, relative to the case of no targeted compensation, by 1.4 percent for payroll tax cuts and by 1.9 percent for personal income tax cuts, but by 22.9 percent for corporate income tax rate cuts. By comparison, with a uniform rebate to households in the first three quintiles, set so that the households in the third quintile do not experience a welfare loss, the welfare costs of the policy increase, relative to the case of no targeted compensation, by 14.6 percent for payroll tax cuts and by 28.0 percent for personal income tax cuts, but by 220.9 percent for corporate income tax rate cuts.

8.4 The Diamond-Zodrow Model

This section provides a brief description of the model used in this analysis; for more details, see Zodrow and Diamond (2013). The Diamond-Zodrow (DZ) model is a dynamic, overlapping generations, CGE model of the US economy that focuses on the macroeconomic, distributional, and transitional effects of tax reforms. To simplify the analysis, we use the closed economy version of our model[19]; for the open economy version of our model, which adds modeling of US and foreign multinationals including income shifting, see Diamond and Zodrow (2015).

Using the carbon tax–induced price increases from the RHG-NEMS model, our model is well suited to simulating in considerable detail the dynamic short-run and long-run macroeconomic effects as well as the inter-generational and intragenerational distributional effects of the implementation of a carbon tax.[20] The DZ model is a micro-based general equilibrium model in which households act to maximize utility over their lifetimes and firms act to maximize profits or firm value, with behavioral responses dictated

---

[19] The assumption of a closed economy should not be especially problematical because (1) international capital flows would be affected by changes in the after-tax return to captial, and the carbon tax reforms considered have relatively small effects on this variable; and (2) all of the carbon tax proposals currently under consideration include border adjustments for the relatively small changes in relative consumer prices that occur so that the effects on trade of any carbon tax, including those analyzed in this report, should also be relatively small.

[20] For a recent comparison of various models used to simulate the effects of tax reforms, including macroeconomic forecasting models broadly similar to the MAM/NEMS model underlying the Rhodium modeling effort and our dynamic, overlapping generations, general equilibrium model, see Auerbach and Grinberg (2017).

by parameter values taken from the literature; these responses include changes in consumption, labor supply, and bequest behavior by households, and changes in the time path of investment by firms that take into account the costs of adjusting their capital stocks. Households and firms are characterized by perfect foresight and thus do not overreact to the short-run price effects of policy changes as they typically do in models with myopic agents. By construction, the model tracks the responses to a tax policy change every year after its enactment and converges to a steady-state long-run equilibrium characterized by a constant growth rate. As a result, we can track both the short-run and the long-run responses to a tax policy change (by comparison, standard macroeconomic models are often dynamically unstable in the medium and long runs).[21]

The overlapping generations structure of the DZ model enables us to track the effects of policy reforms across generations and across income groups within each generation, rather than simply tracking the effects of reforms in terms of broad aggregate variables. Specifically, each generation includes twelve income groups, which reflect lifetime income deciles in each generation, with the first decile (the lowest lifetime income decile) split into the bottom 2 percent and the remaining 8 percent and the tenth decile split into the top 2 percent and the remaining 8 percent.

The model includes considerable detail on business taxation, including separate tax treatment of corporate and pass-through entities, separate tax treatment of owner-occupied and rental housing, and separate tax treatment of new and old capital (including explicit calculation of asset values before and after the enactment of a reform). We also model in considerable detail the progressive taxation of labor income for households at different income levels, capture differential taxation of different types of capital income (although we do not model differential capital income taxes across income groups), and model government expenditures, including government transfers and a pay-as-you-go Social Security system.

The model includes four consumer/producer sectors, characterized by profit-maximizing firms and competitive markets. The goods produced by these four sectors are: (1) a composite good C produced by the "corporate" sector, which includes all business subject to the corporate income tax; (2)

---

[21] For example, for the case of the carbon tax coupled with the payroll tax reduction discussed in Section 8.5, 40 percent of the long-run increase in GDP is achieved within ten years, nearly 60 percent is achieved within twenty years, and 93 percent occurs within fifty years, with the simulations continuing for at least 150 years until a true steady-state equilibrium (in which all of the macroeconomic variables increase precisely at the fixed growth rate) is reached.

a second composite good N produced by the "noncorporate" sector that encompasses all pass-through entities including S corporations, partnerships, LLCs, LLPs, and sole proprietorships; (3) an owner-occupied housing good H; and (4) a rental housing good R.

On the consumption side, each household has an "economic life" of fifty-five years, with forty-five post-education working years and a fixed ten-year retirement, and makes its consumption and labor supply choices to maximize lifetime welfare subject to a lifetime budget constraint that includes personal income and other taxes as well as a fixed "target" bequest. There are thus fifty-five overlapping generations at each point in time in the model, and each generation includes the twelve lifetime income groups just described.

The government purchases fixed amounts of the composite goods at market prices including the carbon tax, makes transfer payments, and pays interest on the national debt. It finances these expenditures with revenues from the corporate income tax, a progressive labor income tax, and flat-rate taxes on capital income.

All markets are assumed to be in equilibrium in all periods. The economy must begin and end in a steady-state equilibrium, with all of the key macroeconomic variables growing at the exogenous growth rate, which equals the sum of the exogenous population and productivity growth rates.

8.5 Simulated Effects of Carbon Tax in the DZ Model

We simulate the macroeconomic and distributional effects of the enactment of a carbon tax under the five different scenarios described in Section 8.1. In each case, we compare the macroeconomic and distributional effects of the policy change to the values that would have occurred in the absence of any changes – that is, under a current law long-run scenario, which includes the permanent features of the TCJA enacted in 2017, such as the corporate income tax rate cut to 21 percent, but does not include provisions like expensing and the personal income tax rate cuts that are currently scheduled to be phased out.

As described in Section 8.1, we assume that the carbon tax is imposed in 2020 at a rate of $49.40 (in 2016 dollars) per metric ton of CO_2 equivalent, increases for thirty years at a real annual rate of roughly 2 percent, and then is held constant in real terms beginning in 2050. Mapping the carbon tax–induced price increases calculated by Larsen et al. (2018) into the four goods in our model (see Diamond and Zodrow (2018) for details) yields the following increases in consumer prices: (1) 1.3–1.6 percent in the corporate (C) sector, (2) 1.5–1.7 percent in the noncorporate (N) sector, and (3) 1.7–2.7 percent in the owner-occupied housing (H) and rental housing (R) sectors. Note that the price increases in the model are largest for the two housing sectors and smallest for the corporate sector, with a price increase for the noncorporate sector that is slightly larger than the price increase for the corporate sector. This is broadly consistent with earlier studies (e.g., Grainger and Kolstad (2010) and Rausch et al. (2011)) that found relatively large price increases for utilities, which are included in the housing sector in our model.

This pattern implies that the carbon tax–induced consumer price increases act to offset existing production distortions in the model, as (1) the corporate sector, taking into account both the new 21 percent federal corporate income tax rate and individual level taxes, is slightly more heavily taxed than the noncorporate sector, taking into account the 20 percent income deduction allowed under the TCJA, and, more importantly, (2) the housing sector – at least the owner-occupied housing sector which accounts for more than 85 percent of the capital in the housing sector – is the least heavily taxed sector of all due to the various tax preferences for owner-occupied housing under the income tax, including the exemption of imputed rent, mortgage interest deductibility (which is less important under the TCJA since it roughly doubled the standard deduction, which implies that many fewer taxpayers will itemize deductions[22]), and very low effective capital gains tax rates.

At the same time, the high level of aggregation in our model (a total of four consumer/producer sectors with only two nonhousing sectors and no intermediate goods) implies that the distortionary effects on consumer choices of many of the price differentials attributable to the carbon tax tend to cancel each other out; the only tax differentials we capture are among the corporate and noncorporate sectors and the owner-occupied and rental housing sectors. For the same reason, the revenue costs of the resulting carbon tax–induced reallocations of consumer demand are muted because the tax differentials across the four sectors are smaller than the tax differentials that would arise in a more disaggregated model with numerous untaxed goods. This has the effect of muting the distortionary effects of the carbon tax on both consumption and labor supply. Finally, we also do not

---

[22] The Tax Policy Center estimates that the fraction of taxpayers who itemize will fall from 26.9 percent to 10.9 percent under the TCJA ("Impact on the Number of Itemizers of H.R.1, The Tax Cuts and Jobs Act (TCJA), by Expanded Cash Income Level, 2018"), www.taxpolicycenter.org/model-estimates/impact-itemized-deduc tions-tax-cuts-and-jobs-act-jan-2018/t18-0001-impact-number.

capture the distortionary effects on the decisions of firm managers of carbon tax–induced price differentials on production inputs, including carbon-intensive intermediate goods.

Thus, given that the carbon tax acts to offset existing relative consumer price distortions in our model rather than exacerbate them (although it still acts to reduce the real wage and thus worsen the distortion of the labor–leisure choice) and because the high level of aggregation of our model implies that we do not capture the distortionary effects of the existing tax system on some production and consumption decisions, we would expect that the overall gains in GDP simulated in our model would be larger than the gains simulated in the models described in Section 8.3, which are more highly disag-gregated but also, generally, have less detail on the tax system. This pattern, in fact, occurs in our simulation results.

Finally, note that, given the overlapping generations nature of our model, we identify gains and losses by generation and by lifetime income group rather than summing the discounted values of all of the future gains and losses caused by a carbon tax reform into a single aggregate measure of reform-induced welfare changes. In particular, the long-run gains in GDP we report are not offset by short-run losses (as they would be in a calculation of the present value of all future changes in GDP). Note also that the implementation of the carbon tax tends to impose windfall losses on the elderly at the time of enactment due to the reform-induced increases in consumer prices, which are only partially offset by the indexation of transfer payments including Social Security benefits; these losses are not at all offset by any reduc-tion in payroll taxes since these individuals are retired, but they may be offset, especially for higher-income households, by lower taxes on dividends and capital gains. Analogous but smaller losses are imposed on those who are near retirement at the time of enactment of the carbon tax. These losses cannot be shifted to future generations because our model assumes a fixed target bequest. As a result, these windfall losses give rise to a one-time revenue increase for the gov-ernment that, if utilized for reductions in payroll or income taxes, stimulates additional labor supply and saving and increases in production.[23]

---

[23] See Zodrow (2002) for a discussion of such reform-induced losses.

8.5.1 Carbon Tax Revenues Finance Uniform Per-Household Rebates

We first consider the macroeconomic effects of the carbon tax detailed in Section 8.1 when the revenues are used to finance uniform per-household rebates. The carbon tax raises revenue equal to 1.23 percent of GDP in 2020 ($259 billion in 2016 dollars[24]) and 1.48 percent of GDP in the long run.[25] These revenues finance rebates that are initially $1,751 per household and increase to $2,091 per household by 2029, to $2,945 per household by 2039, and to $5,985 per household by 2069. The simulation results are shown in Table 8.2. In contrast to the case of revenue recycling in the form of reductions

Table 8.2 *Macroeconomic effects of carbon tax with uniform per-household rebates*

Variable % change in year:	2020	2024	2029	2039	2069	LR
GDP	−0.42	−0.31	−0.36	−0.40	−0.37	−0.37
Total consumption	−0.37	−0.38	−0.45	−0.56	−0.57	−0.57
Corporate good	0.11	0.09	−0.01	−0.14	−0.19	−0.18
Noncorporate good	−0.67	−0.62	−0.69	−0.66	−0.59	−0.59
Rental housing	−0.68	−0.42	−0.30	−0.41	−0.11	0.00
Owner-occupied housing	−1.60	−1.76	−1.71	−1.94	−2.04	−2.06
Total investment	−1.01	−0.32	−0.28	−0.04	0.14	0.12
Total capital stock	0.00	−0.16	−0.26	−0.30	−0.07	−0.05
Total employment (hours worked)	−0.37	−0.34	−0.36	−0.40	−0.46	−0.47

Note: Percentage changes in variables, relative to steady state with no carbon tax.

[24] These revenues are similar but not identical to those estimated by Larsen et al. (2018), as we can duplicate their carbon tax rates exactly but can then only approximate their revenue levels within the context of our model specification.

[25] This figure represents the total revenue raised by the carbon tax. Note that static estimates of the effects of carbon taxes, such as those prepared by RTL (2018), typically include a "revenue offset" of roughly 25 percent (the specific offset RTL estimate is 26 percent), which reflects the estimated reduction in income and payroll tax revenues due to the decline in labor and capital income attributable to the imposition of the carbon tax. By comparison, such income and payroll tax revenue effects are calculated endogenously in our general equilibrium model so that no revenue offset is needed. A rough "partial equilibrium" or static calculation suggests that our model parameterization is consistent with a revenue offset of approximately the same magnitude as that estimated by RTL and others.

in other distortionary taxes, such lump-sum rebates have no incentive effects on labor supply or saving. In particular, this policy creates carbon tax–induced increases in consumer prices that lead to reductions in real wages that are not offset by any positive effects on labor supply attributable to the recycling of carbon tax revenues.

As a result, the macroeconomic effects of this policy are generally negative. In particular, declining real wages imply that aggregate labor supply declines by 0.37 percent initially, by 0.40 percent after twenty years, and by 0.47 percent in the long run. The reduction in labor supply is accompanied by a reduction in total investment that decreases initially by 1.01 percent and by 0.04 percent after twenty years but increases slightly – by 0.12 percent – in the long run. This leads to a reduction in the total capital stock of 0.16 percent five years after enactment of the reform and 0.05 percent in the long run. GDP declines initially by 0.42 percent, by 0.40 percent after twenty years, and by 0.37 percent in the long run. Similarly, aggregate consumption declines by 0.37 percent initially, by 0.56 percent after twenty years, and by 0.57 percent in the long run.

The changes in the composition of consumption reflect the price increases in owner-occupied and rental housing relative to nonhousing goods and in the price of the noncorporate good relative to the corporate good. Upon enactment, the consumption of owner-occupied housing declines by 1.60 percent, the consumption of rental housing declines by 0.68 percent,[26] the consumption of the noncorporate good declines by 0.67 percent, and the consumption of the corporate good increases by 0.11 percent. In the long run, with total consumption declining by 0.57 percent, consumption of each of the individual goods declines or is unchanged, with the largest decline by far occurring for owner-occupied housing.

The distributional effects of this reform are shown in Figure 8.1. We utilize an equivalent variation measure, defined as the percentage change in remaining lifetime resources, including the value of leisure but excluding the value of the inheritance/bequest (which is simply transmitted across generations and grows at the exogenous growth rate) that is required in the initial equilibrium for a household to achieve the same level of lifetime utility as under the newly enacted carbon tax. The figure shows the equivalent variation by age at the time of enactment of reform for all living

---

[26] The decline in rental housing is smaller than the decline in owner-occupied housing because the per-household rebates are relatively more important for lower income households, who are primarily renters.

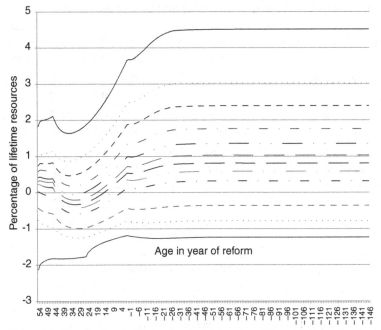

Figure 8.1 Distributional effects of carbon tax with uniform per-household rebates
Note: Present value of all future equivalent variations, relative to present value of all remaining lifetime resources.

generations as well as for future generations (those with a negative economic age at the time of enactment), for each of the twelve lifetime income groups in each generation.

Uniform per-household rebates disproportionately benefit households with relatively low lifetime incomes, so this carbon tax plan is highly progressive. For example, among those retired and near retirement at the time of enactment, the second-poorest lifetime income groups experience welfare gains of roughly 2 percent of remaining lifetime resources,[27] while the richest lifetime income groups experience losses of roughly 2 percent, with the magnitudes of the welfare changes declining uniformly for all households between these two lifetime income groups. By comparison, for younger and future generations, all lifetime income groups in the bottom eight deciles (groups 1–9) experience gains from reform, while the higher-

[27] The second-lowest lifetime income group experiences larger welfare gains than the lowest group primarily because the price of rental housing increases more due to general equilibrium effects than the price of owner-occupied housing and the lowest lifetime income group consumes significantly more rental housing than the second group.

Table 8.3 *Macroeconomic effects of carbon tax with payroll tax reductions*

Variable % change in year:	2020	2024	2029	2039	2069	LR
GDP	−0.12	0.12	0.18	0.26	0.42	0.45
Total consumption	−0.30	−0.15	−0.08	0.00	0.13	0.16
Corporate good	0.18	0.32	0.37	0.43	0.53	0.57
Noncorporate good	−0.60	−0.39	−0.31	−0.09	0.12	0.16
Rental housing	−1.17	−1.03	−0.88	−0.96	−0.93	−0.93
Owner-occupied housing	−1.41	−1.38	−1.22	−1.26	−1.16	−1.13
Total investment	0.36	1.10	1.03	1.16	1.41	1.40
Total capital stock	0.00	0.22	0.42	0.66	1.12	1.22
Total employment (hours worked)	0.11	0.12	0.12	0.15	0.18	0.18
Payroll tax rate (chg. in % points)	−2.34	−2.22	−2.34	−2.80	−3.07	−3.09

Note: Percentage changes in variables, relative to steady state with no carbon tax.

income households in the top two lifetime income deciles (groups 10–12) are net losers from reform. For example, in the long run, the second-poorest lifetime income group experiences a welfare gain of 4.5 percent of remaining lifetime resources, while the richest lifetime income group experiences a loss of roughly 1.2 percent.

The U-shaped patterns in Figure 8.1 during the transition period for generations that are not retired at the time of enactment reflect the effects of the decline in after-tax real wages. In addition, they reflect a "bequest effect," the interaction between the target bequest and slightly lower interest rates, which cause welfare to decline for those above the economic age of twenty-five at the time of enactment who have already received their inheritance and must augment it each year after reform in order to achieve their target bequest. This effect is diminished for those who are younger than twenty-five (in economic years), since the latter effect is not relevant until they receive their inheritance – they have more years to adjust to the need for reduced consumption to finance the target bequest in the presence of lower post-enactment interest rates. Note that the bequest is far more important for the top lifetime income group (the top 2 percent) than for any other group, since these households account for 65 percent of all bequests (group 11 accounts for 13 percent, group 10 for 8 percent, and the aggregate share of all of the other groups combined is below 3 percent). Thus, small changes in interest rates in the years after enactment of reform have a disproportionately large impact on the highest income group.

8.5.2 Carbon Tax Revenues Finance a Payroll Tax Reduction

The macroeconomic results for the case in which carbon tax revenues are used to finance proportionate reductions in payroll taxes are shown in Table 8.3. In this case, carbon tax revenue enables a reduction in Social Security payroll tax rates of 2.34 percentage points in 2020 and 2029, 2.80 percentage points in 2039, and 3.09 percentage points in the long run.[28] These figures include the effects of indexing Social Security benefits in the short run for the price increases associated with the carbon tax; this indexing is phased out over a thirty-year period to reflect the fact that, in the long run, Social Security benefits are indexed to wages rather than to consumer prices.

The simulation results indicate that the net effect on GDP of the carbon tax coupled with a payroll tax reduction is initially (in the year after enactment of the reform) slightly negative (−0.12 percent), but it rapidly turns slightly positive, equals 0.26 percent after twenty years, and reflects an increase of 0.45 percent in the long run.

Aggregate consumption follows roughly the same pattern as GDP, falling initially (by 0.30 percent) but eventually increasing with a long-run gain of 0.16 percent. The pattern of changes in the components of consumption follows the pattern implied by the carbon tax–induced price changes described in the introduction to this section. Specifically, the demand for rental and especially owner-occupied housing declines the most dramatically (by 1.17 and 1.41 percent, respectively, initially and by 0.93 and 1.13 percent, respectively, in the long run), the demand for the noncorporate good initially declines by 0.60 percent while increasing by 0.16 percent in the long run, and the demand for the corporate good increases (by 0.18 percent initially and by 0.57 percent in the long run).

Total employment increases gradually over time, with the increases ranging from 0.11 percent to 0.18 percent.[29] This reflects the net effect of

---

[28] Medicare payroll taxes are not reduced, and the 0.9 percent tax on high-income taxpayers enacted under the Affordable Care Act is also unchanged.

[29] Recall that our model assumes full employment, so the increase in employment or hours worked reflects additional hours worked by a fixed number of employees rather than new jobs.

the changes in after-tax real wages due to the use of carbon tax revenues solely to reduce payroll taxes and thus increase after-tax real wages and offset the effects of carbon tax–induced price increases (which apply to both working and retired households). These wage changes vary considerably across income groups. Specifically, the after-tax real wage increases for the bottom nine income groups and decreases for the top three income groups, with the net result being an increase in hours worked.

Total investment (including replacement investment) increases by 0.36 percent initially and by 1.40 percent in the long run, which reflects modest growth as well as the reallocation of production from housing, where the economic depreciation rate is very small, to the corporate and noncorporate sectors, where economic depreciation and thus replacement investment are significantly larger. The capital stock increases gradually as a result, by 0.22 percent after five years and by 1.22 percent in the long run.

The distributional effects of the carbon tax proposal across generations and across the twelve income groups are shown in Figure 8.2. These results indicate that the carbon tax with revenue recycling in the form of payroll tax reductions (1) uniformly redistributes from the old (retired and near-

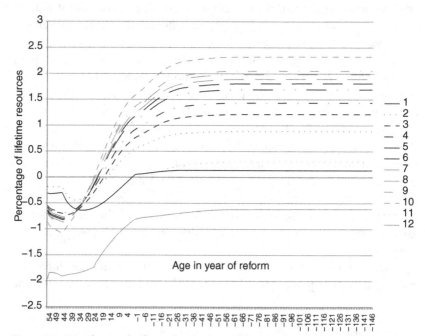

Figure 8.2 Distributional effects of carbon tax with payroll tax reductions
Note: Present value of all future equivalent variations, relative to present value of all remaining lifetime resources.

retired) to the young and future generations within each lifetime income group, (2) has a roughly proportional impact across the income distribution for retired and near-retired generations – except for a relatively low burden on households in the lowest lifetime income decile and a disproportionately large burden on households in the top lifetime income decile, and (3) for future generations alive in the long run is a moderately regressive policy across much of the income distribution, although it eventually becomes progressive as the largest percentage burden is borne by households in the top lifetime income decile (lifetime income groups 11 and 12).

At the time of enactment, all elderly retired and near-retired households lose from reform as they face higher carbon tax–induced prices for consumer goods (which are only partially offset by indexation of transfers including Social Security benefits) but receive little or no benefit from the higher after-tax wages attributable to the reduction in payroll taxes. In addition, because interest rates decline slightly with the enactment of the carbon tax reform,[30] elderly households, especially those who are relatively wealthy and have disproportionately large bequests, have to save more to finance their target bequests, which are fixed in nominal terms; they thus have less income to finance consumption during retirement. As a result, the highest three lifetime income groups (groups 10–12) experience the largest reductions in welfare among elderly households at the time of enactment. For example, the oldest retired households in the highest lifetime income group (the twelfth group, or the top 2 percent of the lifetime income distribution) suffer a loss of roughly 2 percent of remaining lifetime resources, groups 10 and 11 suffer losses of roughly 1 percent of remaining lifetime resources, and the elderly households in the bottom and middle lifetime income groups lose roughly 0.2–0.7 percent of remaining lifetime resources.

These losses tend to diminish with reductions in age at the time of enactment for generations that are in the labor force (those with an economic age of forty-four or less, or roughly sixty-five to sixty-seven years old or younger) when the carbon tax is enacted. These declining losses reflect four factors. First, households that are not retired at the time of enactment have some time to benefit from the payroll tax reduction, and this effect increases as the age at the time of enactment declines. Second, younger households benefit most from the modest increase in economic growth, including increases in real after-tax wages, an effect that also

---

[30] Interest rates decline slightly – by 13–20 basis points – after enactment of this carbon tax reform.

increases with time and indeed continues, albeit at a modest rate, for roughly a hundred years after the time of enactment. Third, the reform causes interest rates to decline slightly, which implies that households alive at the time of enactment have to increase their savings to finance their target bequests, which are fixed in nominal terms. Younger generations have more time to make this adjustment, so the negative impact on their welfare is smaller. Finally, the decline in interest rates implies that the return to existing assets declines, and the importance of this effect also decreases with declines in age at the time of enactment.

In the long run, this version of the carbon tax is moderately regressive for future generations except at the top of the income distribution. For example, the lowest lifetime income group experiences a gain of only 0.1 percent of lifetime resources. Welfare gains increase monotonically from 0.9 percent for the second lifetime income group to 2.3 percent for the tenth lifetime income group. This regressivity reflects the fact that at the margin, the payroll tax reduction results in a disproportionately large increase in after-tax wages for higher-income groups relative to lower-income groups because the reductions in the payroll tax are equal across the bottom ten income groups, though marginal income tax rates increase with income. Thus, higher- and lower-income groups suffer a proportional loss in income due to the carbon tax–induced price increases, but the higher-income groups have a larger increase in after-tax income due to the payroll tax reduction. Households in the top decile of the income distribution do not fare as well from the reform, as the gain for the eleventh lifetime income group is only 0.3 percent of lifetime resources while the twelfth lifetime income group experiences a loss equal to 0.6 percent of lifetime resources. This occurs for three reasons. First, the top lifetime income group benefits less than proportionately from the reduction in the payroll tax because much of their earnings are above the Social Security earnings cap while all of their expenditures are subject to carbon tax–induced price increases. Second, these groups finance virtually all of their consumption with funds that are not subject to indexing for carbon tax–induced price increases. Third, because we assume that the target bequest is fixed in nominal terms, these households receive an inheritance that is smaller in real terms than it would be in the absence of the tax; this effect is disproportionately more important in the top income decile (lifetime income groups 11 and 12). The net result is that all households except the highest income group (the top 2 percent, which comprises lifetime income group 12) benefit from the reform, with the middle- and upper-income groups (through the ninth decile of the lifetime income distribution) benefiting the most.

8.5.3 Carbon Tax Revenues Finance Reductions in Wage Taxes

In this simulation, carbon tax revenues finance a 28.4 percent reduction in personal income taxes on wage income earned by the top seven lifetime income groups (the groups that pay positive labor income taxes over their life cycles). Table 8.4 shows that the net effect on GDP of the carbon tax coupled with a wage income tax reduction is initially positive (0.27 percent) and then grows steadily to 0.96 after twenty years and 1.36 percent in the long run. These results are more positive than for the payroll tax, reflecting the benefit of focusing wage tax cuts on relatively high-income, high-productivity individuals, as well as the benefits of carbon tax–induced reductions in relative consumer price distortions.

Aggregate consumption follows roughly the same pattern as GDP, increasing very slightly initially (by 0.09 percent), by 0.77 percent after twenty years, and by 1.16 percent in the long run. The pattern of changes in the components of consumption is somewhat different than for the payroll tax. As in that case, consumption of the corporate good increases initially (by 0.55 percent) and in the long run (by 1.57

Table 8.4 *Macroeconomic effects of carbon tax with wage tax reductions*

Variable % change in year:	2020	2024	2029	2039	2069	LR
GDP	0.27	0.59	0.73	0.96	1.29	1.36
Total consumption	0.09	0.33	0.52	0.77	1.08	1.16
Corporate good	0.55	0.80	0.96	1.19	1.48	1.57
Noncorporate good	−0.24	0.09	0.27	0.66	1.06	1.15
Rental housing	−1.50	−1.78	−1.80	−2.16	−2.66	−2.86
Owner-occupied housing	−0.81	−0.61	−0.32	−0.12	0.27	0.37
Total investment	1.17	1.90	1.84	2.00	2.38	2.40
Total capital stock	0.00	0.44	0.83	1.29	2.03	2.23
Total employment (hours worked)	0.65	0.69	0.74	0.88	1.04	1.07
Wage tax rate (top seven LI groups)	−28.4	−28.4	−28.4	−28.4	−28.4	−28.4

Note: Percentage changes in variables, relative to steady state with no carbon tax.

percent), while consumption of the noncorporate good initially declines (by 0.24 percent) but increases in the long run (by 1.15 percent). However, rental housing declines significantly (by 1.5 percent initially and by 2.86 percent in the long run), while owner-occupied housing initially declines more moderately (by 0.81 percent) and increases modestly in the long run (by 0.37 percent). The more positive effects on owner-occupied housing are attributable to the fact that the wage tax reductions are concentrated on the top seven lifetime income groups, who consume a disproportionately large amount of such housing.

Total employment increases uniformly, from 0.65 percent initially to 1.07 percent in the long run, reflecting the net effect of the changes in after-tax real wages due to the carbon tax, which vary considerably across income groups. Specifically, increases in the after-tax real wage for the top seven lifetime income groups range from 6.28 percent for the fifth decile to 13.9 percent for the top decile.

Total investment increases by 1.17 percent initially and by 2.40 percent in the long run, which reflects growth as well as the reallocation of production from housing to the corporate and noncorporate sectors, where economic depreciation and thus replacement investment are significantly larger. The capital stock increases gradually as a result, by 0.44 percent after five years and by 2.23 percent in the long run.

The distributional effects of the carbon tax coupled with wage tax reductions are shown in Figure 8.3. These results indicate that the carbon tax with revenue recycling in the form of wage income tax reductions redistributes income from retired and low-lifetime-income households who do not benefit from the wage tax reduction to young and future generations in the middle and higher lifetime income groups who do benefit from the wage tax cut. The reform causes losses of up to 1.5 percent of remaining lifetime resources for retired and near-retired households; these losses have a progressive impact as the rich do not benefit from the indexing of transfers and receive a relatively small benefit from the indexing of Social Security. Younger and future generations benefit over time due to the growth attributable to the increase in labor supply and investment and the less-distorted consumer price structure; the four factors detailed in the discussion of the effects of the payroll tax in Section 8.5.2 are also operative. However, the transition is lengthy; for example, households in the seventh lifetime income group benefit only if they are of economic age of roughly minus twenty (approximately two years old) at

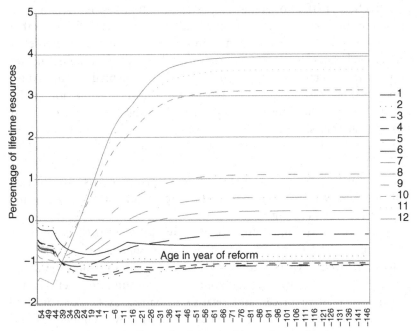

Figure 8.3 Distributional effects of carbon tax with wage tax reductions
Note: Present value of all future equivalent variations, relative to present value of all remaining lifetime resources.

the time of enactment. In the long run, lifetime income groups 7–12 benefit from the reform, but the gains are regressive, as groups 7–9 gain roughly 0–1 percent of remaining lifetime resources, while groups 10–12 gain 3–4 percent of lifetime resource since the equiproportionate wage tax cut disproportionately benefits them with a progressive rate structure.

The next two simulations are hybrid carbon tax policies, combining policies favorable to capital formation and thus to higher income households (using carbon tax revenues to eliminate personal income taxes on dividends and capital gains or to reduce the national debt) with per-household rebates that favor low-income households but are less favorable to growth.

8.5.4 Carbon Tax Revenues Finance Elimination of Dividend and Capital Gains Taxes Coupled with Household Rebates

In this simulation, some of carbon tax revenues are used to eliminate personal income taxes on dividends and capital gains, with the remaining revenues used to increase government transfers other than Social Security (as a fraction of GDP) by roughly 5 percent. As discussed in Section 8.3.1, reductions in taxes on capital income tend to be relatively efficient as they reduce tax disincentives for saving and investment and thus increase the capital stock, labor productivity, and wages; they also favor higher income households who receive a disproportionate share of capital income. At the same time, per capita household rebates favor lower-income households but do not generate any efficiency gains since they do not reduce any distortionary taxes.

The results of this simulation are shown in Table 8.5. The net effect on GDP of the policy is initially negative (by −0.41 percent) but quickly turns positive as increased investment results in a larger capital stock, yielding a gain of 1.28 percent after twenty years and 1.45 percent in the long run.

Aggregate consumption follows roughly the same pattern as GDP, declining initially (by 1.27 percent) but then increasing by 0.47 percent after twenty years and by 0.67 percent in the long run. The pattern of changes in the components of consumption reflects the changes in relative prices and relative demands, as (1) the demand for owner-occupied housing declines the most (by 2.60 percent initially and by 0.91 percent in the long run), while rental housing declines initially by 2.07 percent while increasing in the long run by

Table 8.5 *Macroeconomic effects of carbon tax with elimination of dividend and capital gains taxes coupled with per-household rebates*

Variable % change in year:	2020	2024	2029	2039	2069	LR
GDP	−0.41	0.75	1.03	1.28	1.44	1.45
Total consumption	−1.27	−0.26	0.13	0.47	0.65	0.67
Corporate good	−0.76	0.14	0.53	0.87	1.04	1.06
Noncorporate good	−1.53	−0.57	−0.16	0.34	0.63	0.65
Rental housing	−2.07	0.44	0.87	1.01	1.41	1.55
Owner-occupied housing	−2.60	−1.36	−1.01	−0.93	−0.89	−0.91
Total investment	3.24	5.45	5.16	4.94	4.92	4.89
Total capital stock	0.00	1.15	2.24	3.34	4.11	4.18
Total employment (hours worked)	−0.11	−0.10	−0.15	−0.23	−0.31	−0.32
Transfers (nonSS)/GDP	5.66	4.89	4.87	4.85	4.85	4.85

Note: Percentage changes in variables, relative to steady state with no carbon tax.

1.55 percent (reflecting the relative importance of per-household rebates to poorer households who are predominantly renters); (2) the effects on the demand for the noncorporate good are initially more muted (a decline of 1.53 percent) and eventually turn positive, with an increase of 0.65 percent in the long run; while (3) the demand for the corporate good declines initially by 0.76 percent but eventually increases by 1.06 percent in the long run.

Total investment increases due to the elimination of dividend and capital gains taxes by 3.24 percent initially and by 4.89 percent in the long run. As a result, the capital stock increases by 1.15 percent after five years and by 4.18 percent in the long run. The decline in the real wage rate due to carbon tax–induced price increases (the real wage declines by 1.1 percent initially and by 0.4 percent after ten years, then increases by 0.2 percent in the long run) as well as an increase in leisure demand due to the increase in income are sufficient to cause total employment to decline slightly, from 0.11 percent initially to 0.23 percent after ten years, and by 0.32 percent in the long run.

The distributional effects of the carbon tax coupled with the elimination of dividend and capital gains taxes and an increase in per-household rebates are shown in Figure 8.4. The impact on retired and near-retired households is progressive. For example, for retired households, the lowest lifetime income groups gain 0–2 percent of remaining lifetime resources as indexed transfers and rebates offset the carbon tax–induced price increases, while middle and high lifetime income households lose 0–12 percent of lifetime resources since they receive few indexed transfers and benefit relatively little from the rebates but suffer as the effects of the carbon tax–induced price increases and the bequest effect dominate the benefits of the elimination of dividend and capital gains taxes.[31]

The capital accumulation due to the elimination of personal income taxation of dividends and capital gains coupled with the rebates implies that all younger and future generations experience welfare gains that range 0–4 percent. The combination of these tax cuts and the indexed transfers and rebates, coupled with an increase in GDP, implies that all lifetime income groups gain from reform in the long run. Interestingly, the policy is progressive as lower lifetime

---

[31] The large 12 percent loss experienced by the wealthiest households in the last year of life is due to a first-year decrease in the interest rate of 1.4 percentage points that requires them to sacrifice consumption in order to meet the target bequest. Reductions in interest rates are much smaller in future years (ranging from an increase of 40 to a decline of 8 basis points) but still have a negative effect on all wealthy generations who received their bequest under the pre-reform tax system (those with an economic age less than twenty-five at the time of enactment).

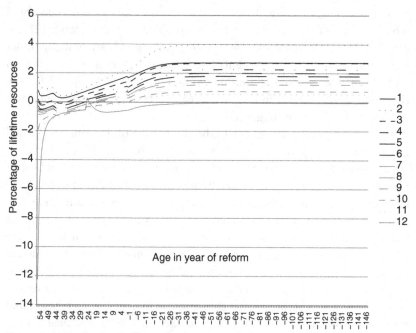

Figure 8.4 Distributional effects of carbon tax with elimination of dividend and capital gains taxes and per-household rebates
Note: Present value of all future equivalent variations, relative to present value of all remaining lifetime resources.

income groups benefit from the higher wages due to increased capital accumulation, indexed transfers, and the rebates, while the higher lifetime income groups, who benefit from higher wages and from the dividend and capital gains tax cut but do not gain from indexed transfers and benefit relatively little from rebates, experience gains of under 1 percent, with the highest income group roughly breaking even from the reform, in part due to a decline of roughly 10 basis points in the return to capital.

8.5.5 Carbon Tax Revenues Finance Reduction in Debt Followed by Per-Household Rebates

In this final simulation, we examine the effects of a carbon tax under which the revenues are first used to reduce the domestically held portion of national debt[32] for a period of ten years, and from that point forward are

---

[32] Given our assumption of a closed economy, we do not model foreign ownership of US debt.

used to finance uniform per-household rebates. This reduces the domestically held debt/GDP ratio from 44.5 percent to 31.2 percent and reduces interest rates by roughly 0.5 percentage points (50 basis points). The reduction in the level of debt and in interest payments on the debt frees up savings for investment, which results in gradual increases in the capital stock and labor productivity and creates upward pressure on wages.

The macroeconomic effects of this reform are shown in Table 8.6. This carbon tax policy has favorable effects on investment, which increases by 0.40 percent initially and by 2.91 percent in the long run, and on GDP, which initially falls by 0.43 percent but eventually increases by 0.30 percent. The capital stock increases by 0.28 percent five years after reform and by 2.65 percent in the long run. However, labor supply declines, initially by 0.30 percent and by 0.57 percent in the long run, indicating that the negative effects of the carbon tax on the real wage (with revenues beyond the first ten years of enactment used to finance uniform per-household rebates rather than reductions in payroll or wage taxes) dominate the positive effects of greater capital accumulation and greater productivity. The net effect is that total consumption declines, initially by 0.72 percent and by 0.42 percent in the long run. The changes in the composition of consumption indicate a sizable decline in owner-occupied housing (of 1.97 percent initially and 2.40 percent in the long run) as the rebates are relatively unimportant to higher-income households who disproportionately consume owner-occupied housing.[33]

The distributional effects of this policy are shown in Figure 8.5. All retired lifetime income groups experience a loss due to the carbon tax–induced increase in consumer prices and the decline in interest rates coupled with a fixed nominal bequest; the latter effect is especially important in the year of enactment for the richest income group, which experiences a reduction in welfare equal to more than 2 percent of remaining lifetime resources, while all other groups suffer losses that range from 0.2 to 1.1 percent of remaining lifetime resources. These losses are gradually mitigated as the growth benefits of a smaller national debt (including more consumption of leisure) are realized. The policy is highly progressive in the long run, as all lifetime income groups but the wealthiest group benefit from the reform, with the gains declining uniformly beginning with

---

[33] In addition, in the case of revenue recycling in the form of debt reduction, interest rates decline more significantly than in the other simulations, which has a disproportionately large impact on the wealthy, who must save more to finance their target bequest; this also causes a reduction in the demand for owner-occupied housing.

Table 8.6 *Macroeconomic effects of carbon tax with ten-year debt reduction followed by uniform per-household rebates*

Variable % change in year:	2020	2024	2029	2039	2069	LR
GDP	−0.43	−0.15	−0.04	0.07	0.29	0.30
Total consumption	−0.72	−0.65	−0.61	−0.54	−0.49	−0.42
Corporate good	−0.22	−0.16	−0.14	−0.07	−0.02	0.06
Noncorporate good	−1.01	−0.87	−0.82	−0.59	−0.43	−0.35
Rental housing	−1.33	−1.06	−0.85	−0.70	−0.04	0.33
Owner-occupied housing	−1.97	−2.04	−1.98	−2.15	−2.41	−2.40
Total investment	0.40	1.72	2.08	2.33	3.13	2.91
Total capital stock	0.00	0.28	0.73	1.37	2.58	2.65
Total employment (hours worked)	−0.30	−0.27	−0.30	−0.39	−0.56	−0.57

Note: Percentage changes in variables, relative to steady state with no carbon tax.

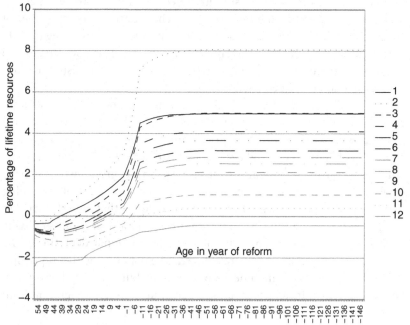

Figure 8.5 Distributional effects of carbon tax with ten-year debt reduction followed by uniform per-household rebates
Note: Present value of all future equivalent variations, relative to present value of all remaining lifetime resources.

the second lifetime income group. All households benefit from the capital accumulation due to the debt reduction, but the subsequent equal per-household rebates provide a disproportionately large benefit to lower lifetime income groups while the relatively large decline in interest rates disproportionately hurts the wealthy. For example, in the long run, the highest income group suffers a loss of 0.4 percent of lifetime resources, while the second-lowest income group experiences a gain equal to 8.1 percent of remaining lifetime resources.

8.6 Conclusion

Although the recently enacted TCJA did not include any environmental tax provisions, numerous discussions of tax policy options in the United States have considered the possibility of implementing a carbon tax, with concerns often raised about their potential negative effects on output and economic growth and on income distribution. In this analysis, we examined the macroeconomic and distributional effects of the implementation of a representative carbon tax under a variety of assumptions regarding recycling of the resulting tax revenues. We reviewed some earlier results and then simulated these effects using the DZ dynamic, overlapping generations CGE model with twelve lifetime income groups, a model that is designed to estimate the short-run and long-run macroeconomic effects and the intergenerational and intragenerational distributional effects of tax reforms in the United States.

Both the earlier literature and our simulation results confirm two general points. First, any negative effects on the level of future GDP are moderate for the magnitude and trajectory of the carbon tax modeled in this chapter, with negligible effects on the rate of economic growth. Second, any regressive effects of a carbon tax reform due to tax-induced increases in the prices of goods consumed disproportionately by the poor can readily be offset with the appropriate revenue-recycling policy. In particular, in our simulations, the net impact of policies that use carbon tax revenues to finance uniform per-household rebates, either entirely or as part of a plan that includes policies that are favorable to capital formation, such as the elimination of personal taxes on dividends and capital gains or reductions in the national debt, can be highly progressive.

The results of our simulations can be summarized as follows. The general pattern of the results is consistent with other studies. For the macroeconomic effects of the various carbon taxes analyzed, (1) the least favorable results are obtained when carbon tax revenues are used to finance per-household rebates, since such rebates do not have the advantage of reducing other distortionary taxes; (2) more favorable results are obtained when carbon tax revenues are used to finance either payroll tax cuts or wage tax cuts, thus reducing disincentives to work under the current tax structure, with the larger effects occurring with the wage tax since it is concentrated on workers in the middle- and upper-income groups who are relatively productive; (3) the most favorable macroeconomic results are obtained when carbon tax revenues are used to lower personal income taxes on dividends and capital gains as the taxation of capital income, including both corporate and individual level taxes, is relatively more distortionary than the taxation of labor income (this result obtains even though some of the carbon tax revenues in this case are used to finance per-household rebates and the overall level of taxation of capital income is reduced with the implementation of a 21 percent corporate income tax rate and other changes under the TCJA passed in 2017); and (4) relatively modest effects with increases in investment coupled with declines in labor supply and output, falling in between those for per-household rebates and payroll tax cuts, are obtained when carbon tax revenues are used to reduce the national debt for ten years and then used to finance per-household rebates.

However, our results are generally more positive than those found in the literature. Given the highly aggregated nature of our model, these results should be viewed with caution. In particular, our model does not capture some of the distortionary effects of the existing tax system on consumption decisions (e.g., across more goods than the four goods modeled in our analysis) and production decisions (e.g., across more production inputs than the two inputs modeled in our analysis, including carbon-intensive intermediate goods) that might be worsened with a carbon tax. Nevertheless, our detailed modeling of the existing tax structure does allow us to capture some interesting phenomena that are not always captured in other models. For example, the largest price increase due to the imposition of the carbon tax occurs for housing, with smaller price increases for nonhousing production especially in the corporate sector. These tax-induced price changes act to offset existing tax distortions in our model, since investment in owner-occupied housing faces the lowest effective tax rate, with the corporate sector facing a slightly higher tax rate than the noncorporate sector or the rental housing sector, in the initial equilibrium. The resulting efficiency gains act to offset the efficiency loss due to the carbon tax–induced reduction in the real wage. In addition, the overlapping generations structure of our model allows us to capture intergenerational effects, most importantly the windfall losses suffered at the time of enactment by retired and near-retired households (due to both carbon tax–induced price increases and in some cases the absence of a benefit from cuts in payroll and wage taxes), which result in lower future tax rates and higher welfare levels for young and future generations.

The distributional effects of the various carbon tax reforms are also generally similar to those obtained in other studies although, given our relatively positive macroeconomic effects, they tend to be more positive than those obtained in other studies as well. Because uniform per-household rebates disproportionately benefit households with relatively low lifetime incomes, the carbon tax plan with such rebates is highly progressive both for retired and older generations as well as for younger and future generations, although the net benefits of the policy are larger for the latter group.

By comparison, when carbon tax revenues are used to finance payroll tax reductions, the policy (1) redistributes income from the old to the young and future generations, (2) has roughly proportional impacts across the income distribution for retired and near-retired generations – except for a relatively low burden on households in the lowest lifetime income decile and a disproportionately large burden on households in the top lifetime income decile, and (3) in the long run is a moderately regressive policy across much of the income distribution for future generations, although it eventually becomes progressive at the highest lifetime income levels.

The carbon tax coupled with wage tax reductions redistributes income from retired and near-retired generations and from low lifetime income households who do not benefit from the wage tax reduction to younger and future generations in the higher lifetime income groups who do benefit from the wage tax cut. The policy is progressive for retired generations who do not benefit from the wage tax cut, but it is regressive for younger and future generations, with especially large benefits accruing to the top two lifetime income deciles, who benefit the most from the wage tax cut.

The last two simulations are hybrid carbon tax policies, combining policies favorable to capital formation and thus to higher-income households (using carbon tax revenues to eliminate personal income taxes on dividends and capital gains or to reduce the national debt) with per-household rebates that favor low-income households but are less favorable to economic growth.

When carbon tax revenues are used to finance the elimination of dividend and capital gains taxes and per-household rebates, the impact on retired and near-retired households is progressive due to the transfers. Most of the younger generations (other than the richest) and all future generations gain from the policy, and the impact of the policy is progressive as the effects of indexing transfers and the rebates offset the effect of the elimination of personal taxes on dividends and capital gains.

Finally, similar results obtain when carbon tax revenues are used to finance a reduction in the national debt for ten years and then used to finance per-household transfers. All retired lifetime income groups and many near-retired and younger groups experience a loss due to the carbon tax–induced increase in consumer prices and the decline in interest rates coupled with a fixed nominal bequest; the impact is progressive as the latter effect is disproportionately important for the higher-income groups. The policy is highly progressive for future generations, as all households benefit from the capital accumulation due to the debt reduction, but the subsequent equal per-household rebates provide a disproportionately large benefit to lower lifetime income groups while the relatively large decline in interest rates disproportionately hurts the wealthy.

These two policies suggest that hybrid approaches to carbon taxation that combine features favorable to growth with features that increase the progressivity of its impact can be designed. In addition, note that at the cost of some future growth, some carbon tax revenues could be used for rebates targeted toward reducing or eliminating the welfare losses suffered by retired, near-retired, and middle-aged generations at the time of enactment of the policy. Such an approach would presumably increase the political viability of a carbon tax. We leave the design of such approaches to future research.

Acknowledgments

This paper draws on earlier research (Diamond and Zodrow, 2018) sponsored by the Columbia University SIPA Center on Global Energy Policy. We would like to thank Noah Kaufman for his assistance with that project, John Larsen, Shashank Mohan, Peter Marsters, and Whitney Herndon of Rhodium Group for the use of their calculations of the price effects of carbon taxes (Larsen et al., 2018) utilized in this study as well as in the earlier project, Rick Evans and the participants at a conference on the "Prospects for Economic Growth in the United States" sponsored by the Center for Public Finance, Baker Institute for Public Policy, Rice University, Houston TX, December 6–7, 2018 for very helpful comments, and Meghana Gaur for excellent research assistance. The opinions expressed in this chapter are those of the authors and should not be construed as reflecting the views of the Baker Institute for Public Policy or any other entity. The study used the Diamond-Zodrow model, a dynamic computable general equilibrium model copyrighted by Tax Policy Advisers, LLC, in which the authors have an ownership interest. The terms of this arrangement have been reviewed and approved by Rice University in accordance with its conflict of interest policies.

References

Anthoff, David, and Richard Tol, 2013. "The Uncertainty about the Social Cost of Carbon: A Decomposition Analysis Using FUND." *Climatic Change* 117(3), 515–30.

Auerbach, Alan J., Itai Grinberg (convening authors), Thomas Barthold, Nicholas Bull, W. Gavin Elkins, Pamela Moomau, Rachel Moore, Benjamin Page, Brandon Pecoraro, and Kyle Pomerleau (discussing authors), 2017. "Macroeconomic Modeling of Tax Policy: A Comparison of Current Methodologies." *National Tax Journal* 70 (4), 819–36.

Auffhammer, Maximilian, 2018. "Quantifying Economic Damages from Climate Change." *Journal of Economic Perspectives* 32 (4), 33–52.

Baker, James A. III, Martin Feldstein, Ted Halstead, N. Gregory Mankiw, Henry M. Paulson Jr., George P. Shultz, Thomas Stephenson, and Rob Walton, 2017. "The Conservative Case for Carbon Dividends." Climate Leadership Council, Washington, DC, www.clcouncil.org/media/2017/03/The-Conservative-Case-for-Carbon-Dividends.pdf.

Bovenberg,A. Lans, 1999. "Green Tax Reforms and the Double Dividend: An Updated Reader's Guide." *International Tax and Public Finance* 6 (3), 421–43.

Bovenberg, A. Lans, and Ruud de Mooij, 1994. "Environmental Levies and Distortionary Taxation." *American Economic Review* 84 (4), 1085–9.

Brill, Alex M., 2017. *Carbon Tax Policies: A Conservative Dialogue on Pro-Growth Opportunities.* Alliance for Market Solutions, Washington, DC.

Brown, Stephen P. A., and Hillard C. Huntington, 2013. "Assessing the U.S. Oil Security Premium." *Energy Economics* 38 (C), 118–27.

Bull, Nicholas, Kevin A. Hassett, and Gilbert E. Metcalf, 1994. "Who Pays Broad-Based Energy Taxes? Computing Lifetime and Regional Incidence." *Energy Journal* 15 (3), 145–64.

Caron, Justin, Jefferson Cole, Richard Goettle, Chikara Onda, James McFarland, and Jared Woollacott, 2018. "Distributional Implications of a National CO_2 Tax in the U.S. Across Income Classes and Regions: A Multi-model Overview." *Climate Change Economics* 9 (1), 1–32.

Climate Leadership Council, 2018. "Exceeding Paris: How the Baker-Shultz Carbon Dividends Plan Would Significantly Exceed the U.S. Paris Commitment & Achieve 50% U.S. CO_2 Reduction by 2035." Climate Leadership Council, Washington, DC, www.clcouncil.org/media/Exceeding-Paris.pdf.

Cronin, Julie Anne, Don Fullerton, and Steven E. Sexton, 2017. "Vertical and Horizontal Redistributions from a Carbon Tax and Rebate." NBER Working Paper No. 23250. National Bureau of Economic Research, Cambridge, MA.

Diamond, John W., and George R. Zodrow, 2015. "Modeling U.S. and Foreign Multinationals in a Dynamic OLG-CGE Model." Working Paper. Rice University, Houston, TX.

Diamond, John W., and George R. Zodrow, 2018. "The Effects of Carbon Tax Policies on the US Economy and the Welfare of Households." Report. Columbia SIPA Center on Global Energy Policy, New York, NY, https://energypolicy.columbia.edu/re search/report/effects-carbon-tax-policies-us-economy-and-welfare-households.

Drupp, Moritz A., Mark C. Freeman, Ben Groom, and Frikk Nesje, 2018. "Discounting Disentangled." *American Economic Journal: Economic Policy* 10 (4), 109–34.

Fullerton, Don, and Diane L. Rogers, 1993. *Who Bears the Lifetime Tax Burden?* Brookings Institution Press, Washington, DC.

Gillingham, Kenneth, and James H. Stock, 2018. "The Cost of Reducing Greenhouse Emissions." *Journal of Economic Perspectives* 32 (4), 53–72.

Gleckman, Howard, 2017. "Did the GOP Just Open the Door to a Carbon Tax in 2025?" Urban-Brookings Tax Policy Center, www.taxpolicycenter.org/taxvox/did-gop-just-open-door-carbon-tax-2025.

Goulder, Lawrence H., and Marc Hafstead, 2018. *Confronting the Climate Challenge: U.S. Policy Options.* Columbia University Press, New York, NY.

Goulder, Lawrence H., Marc A. C. Hafstead, GyuRim Kim, and Xianling Long, 2018. "Impacts of a Carbon Tax Across U.S. Household Income Groups: What Are the Equity-Efficiency Trade-Offs?" NBER Working Paper No. 25181. National Bureau of Economic Research, Cambridge, MA.

Grainger, Corbett A., and Charles D. Kolstad, 2010. "Who Pays a Price on Carbon?" *Environmental Resource Economics* 46 (3), 359–76.

Hassett, Kevin A., Aparna Mathur, and Gilbert Metcalf, 2009. "The Incidence of a U.S. Carbon Tax: A Lifetime and Regional Analysis." *Energy Journal* 30 (2), 155–77.

Holtz-Eakin, Douglas, Gordon Gray, Kimberly VanWyhe, Anne Krueger, Aparna Mathur, Irwin Stelzer, 2017. "Tax Reform Initiative Group: Briefing Book." American Action Forum, Washington, DC, and www.americanactionforum.org/research/tax-reform-initiative-group-briefing-book/.

Interagency Working Group on Social Cost of Greenhouse Gases, 2016. *Technical Support Document: Technical Update of the Social Cost of Carbon for Regulatory Impact Analysis under Executive Order 12866.* Interagency Working Group on Social Cost of Greenhouse Gases, Washington, DC.

Joint Committee on Taxation, 2017. *Macroeconomic Analysis of the "Tax Cut and Jobs Act" as Ordered Reported by the Senate Committee on Finance on November 16, 2017 (JCX–61–17).* Joint Committee on Taxation, Washington, DC.

Jorgenson, Dale W., Richard J. Goettle, Mun S. Ho, and Peter J. Wilcoxen, 2013. *Double Dividend: Environmental Taxes and Fiscal Reform in the United States.* MIT Press, Cambridge, MA.

Jorgenson, Dale W., Richard J. Goettle, Mun S. Ho, and Peter J. Wilcoxen, 2015. "Carbon Taxes and Fiscal Reform in the United States." *National Tax Journal* 68 (1), 121–38.

Jorgenson, Dale W., Richard J. Goettle, Mun S. Ho, and Peter J. Wilcoxen, 2018. "The Welfare Consequences of Taxing Carbon." *Climate Change* 9 (1) 1840013-1–39.

Larsen, John, Shashank Mohan, Peter Marsters, and Whitney Herndon, 2018. "Energy and Environmental Implications of a Carbon Tax in the United States." Columbia SIPA Center on Global Energy Policy, New York, NY.

Marron, Donald, Eric Toder, and Lydia Austin, 2015. "Taxing Carbon: What, Why, and How." Tax Policy Center, Washington, DC.

Mathur, Aparna, and Adele Morris, 2017. "Fill the Gaps in the Tax Bill with a Carbon Tax and Expanded Benefits for Working Families." Brookings Institution Press, Washington, DC, www.brookings.edu/blog/planetpolicy/2017/12/08/fill-the-gaps-in-the-tax-bill-with-a-carbon-tax-and-expanded-benefits-for-working-families/.

McFarland, James R., Allen A. Fawcett, Adele C. Morris, John M. Reilly, and Peter J. Wilcoxen, 2018. "Overview of the EMF 32 Study on U.S. Carbon Tax Scenarios." *Climate Change Economics* 9 (1), 184002.

Moore, Frances C., Uris Baldos, Thomas Hertel, and Delavane Diaz, 2017. "New Science of Climate Change Impacts on Agriculture Implies Higher Social Cost of Carbon." *Nature Communications* 8, 1607, www.nature.com/articles/s41467-017-01792-x.

National Academies of Sciences-Engineering-Medicine, 2017. *Valuing Climate Damages: Updating Estimation of the Social Cost of Carbon Dioxide.* National Academies Press, Washington, DC.

National Climate Assessment, 2018. "Fourth National Climate Assessment, Volume II: Impacts, Risks, and Adaptation in the United States." National Climate Assessment, Washington, DC, https://nca2018.globalchange.gov/.

NERA Economic Consulting, 2013. "Economic Outcomes of a U.S. Carbon Tax." National Economic Research Associates Economic Consulting, Washington, DC.

Newbold, Stephen C., Charles Griffiths, Chris Moore, Ann Wolverton, and Elizabeth Kopits, 2010. "The 'Social Cost of Carbon' Made Simple." Working Paper No. 10–07. U.S. Environmental Protection Agency, National Center for Environmental Economics, Washington, DC, www.hypothetical-bias.net/files/the_social_cost_of_carbon_made_simple.pdf.

Nordhaus, William, 2007. "A Review of the *Stern Review on the Economics of Climate Change.*" *Journal of Economic Literature* 45 (3), 686–702.

Nordhaus, William, 2014a. "Estimates of the Social Cost of Carbon: Concepts and Results from the DICE–2013 R Model and Alternative Approaches." *Journal of the Association of Environmental and Resource Economists* 1(1/2), 273–312.

Nordhaus, William, 2014b. "Revisiting the Social Cost of Carbon." *Proceedings of the National Academy of Sciences of the United States of America* 114 (7), 1518–23.

Pindyck, Robert S., 2017. "The Use and Misuse of Models for Climate Policy." *Review of Environmental Economics and Policy* 11 (1), 100–14.

Pizer, William, Matthew Adler, Joseph Aldy, David Antoff, Maureen Cropper, Kenneth Gillingham, Michael Greenstone, Brian Murray, Richard Newell, Richard Richels, Arden Rowell, Stephanie Waldhoff, and Jonathan Weiner, 2014. "Using and Improving the Social Cost of Carbon." *Science* 346 (6214), 1189–90.

Rausch, Sebastian, Gilbert E. Metcalf, and John M. Reilly, 2011. "Distributional Impacts of Carbon Pricing: A General Equilibrium Approach with Micro-data for Households." *Energy Economics* 33 (S1), S20–33.

Rose, Steven K., Delavane B. Diaz, and Geoffrey J. Blanchard, 2017. "Understanding the Social Cost of Carbon: A Model Diagnostic and Inter-Comparison Study." *Climate Change Economics* 8 (2), 1750009.

Rosenberg, Joseph, Eric Toder, and Chenxi Lu, 2018. "Distributional Implications of a Carbon Tax." Tax Policy Center, Washington, DC, www.taxpolicycenter.org/publications/distributional-implications-carbon-tax/full.

Ross, Martin T., 2014. "Structure of the Dynamic Integrated Economy/Energy/ Emission Model." Working Paper. Nicholas Institute for Environmental Policy Solutions, Duke University, Durham, NC.

Ross, Martin T., Allen A. Fawcett, and Christa S. Clapp, 2009. "U.S. Climate Mitigation Pathways Post-2012: Transition Scenarios in ADAGE." *Energy Economics* 31 (S2), S212–22.

Stern, Nicholas, 2007. *The Economics of Climate Change: The Stern Review.* Cambridge University Press, Cambridge, UK.

U.S. Environmental Protection Agency, 2015. "Social Cost of Carbon." EPA Fact Sheet. U.S. Environmental Protection Agency, Washington, DC.

Williams, Roberton C. III, Hal Gordon, Dallas Burtraw, Jared C. Carbone, and Richard D. Morgenstern, 2015. "The Initial Incidence of a Carbon Tax Across Income Groups." *National Tax Journal* 68 (1), 195–214.

Zodrow, George R., 2002. "Transitional Issues in the Implementation of a Flat Tax or a Retail Sales Tax." In George R. Zodrow and Peter Mieszkowski (eds.), *United States Tax Reform in the 21st Century*, 245–83. Cambridge University Press, Cambridge, UK.

Zodrow, George R., and John W. Diamond, 2013. "Dynamic Overlapping Generations Computable General Equilibrium Models and the Analysis of Tax Policy." In Peter B. Dixon and Dale W. Jorgenson (eds.), *Handbook of Computable General Equilibrium Modeling*, 743–813. Elsevier Publishing, Amsterdam, Netherlands.

PART V

SPECIAL TOPICS ON ECONOMIC GROWTH

9

Banking on Prosperity

Ross Levine

9.1 Introduction

People don't like banks. There is a powerful sense that banks collect money from the many, lend most to the privileged, and get an exorbitant return in the process. If one were to poll random people on a street corner about what they think of the earnings of bankers, one would likely hear the words "undeserved," "unmerited," "unreasonable," "unwarranted," and "excessive." Such sentiments are not new. Many centuries ago, Buddhist, Christian, Islamic, and Jewish leaders condemned moneylenders. More recently, the second President of the United States, John Adams, argued at the close of the eighteenth century that "banks have done more injury to the religion, morality, tranquillity [sic], prosperity, and even wealth of the nation than they can have done or ever will do good" (Adams, 1819, p. 375). And – still more recently in the aftermath of the first global financial crisis of the twenty-first century – many writers argued that bankers do little to identify and fund the most promising entrepreneurs but rather do much to extract larger bonuses for themselves. People are clearly distrustful of banks and often angry about the role they play in society.

In this chapter, I assess the impact of the functioning of the banking system on economic prosperity. By the functioning of the banking system, I mean the degree to which banks effectively mobilize savings, allocate those savings, monitor the use of those resources by firms and individuals, provide mechanisms for the pooling and management of risks, and facilitate trade in goods, services, and securities. By economic prosperity, I do not only mean the overall amount of goods and services produced by an economy; that is, I define economic prosperity more broadly than gross domestic product (GDP). In defining prosperity, I give special consideration to the incomes of those at the lower end of the income distribution, to poverty, to the economic opportunities available to people throughout society, and to a broader array of factors shaping prosperity than real per capita GDP.

When banking systems perform these functions well, they tend to promote prosperity. For example, when banks screen borrowers effectively and identify firms with the most promising prospects, this is a first step in boosting productivity growth. When they mobilize savings from disparate households to invest in these promising projects, this represents a second crucial step in fostering growth. Furthermore, when banks monitor the use of investments and scrutinize managerial performance, this is an additional ingredient in boosting the operational efficiency of corporations and reducing waste, fraud, and the extraction of private rents by corporate insiders. But that is not all. When banking systems facilitate the diversification of risk, this encourages investment in higher-return projects that might be shunned without effective risk management vehicles. And, when banks lower transactions costs, this promotes trade and specialization, which are fundamental inputs into technological innovation and economic growth.

However, when banking systems perform these functions poorly, they hinder economic growth and curtail economic opportunities. For example, if banks simply collect funds with one hand and pass them along to cronies with the other hand, this produces a less efficient allocation of resources that slows economic growth and limits the economic horizons of many people. If banks fail to exert sound corporate governance, this makes it easier for managers to pursue projects that benefit themselves rather than the firm and the overall economy. Thus, poorly functioning banking systems can become an effective tool for restricting credit – and hence opportunity – to the already rich and powerful rather than a mechanism for financing the best projects and entrepreneurial ideas. And, when banks create new, complex financial instruments and trick unsophisticated savers into buying them, this can boost the bonuses of financial engineers and executives while distorting credit allocation and attracting talented individuals into these socially unproductive activities (e.g., Philippon and Reshef, 2011).

Evidence from around the world shows that better-functioning banking systems accelerate long-run economic growth, where "long-run economic growth" means growth over decades. Using many different research methodologies, investigators consistently find that countries with better-functioning banking systems enjoy much faster rates of long-run economic growth than economies with malfunctioning banking systems. A virtual avalanche of research shows that this result does not reflect a "chicken-and-egg" problem. It is not just that rich countries develop better banking systems. The evidence indicates that better banking systems accelerate economic growth.

The evidence also explains that banks spur growth by improving the allocation of resources, not by increasing savings. Better banking systems exert a first-order impact on the economy by getting resources to the most productive entrepreneurs and ensuring that those entrepreneurs use those resources efficiently. While better banking systems more ably mobilize savings from individuals, the evidence indicates that banks do not primarily boost economic growth by raising the savings rate. Rather, by mobilizing savings into the hands of an entity that is especially good at screening borrowers and exerting governance over borrowers, better banking systems allocate scarce resources more efficiently, with positive ramifications for economic growth.

Economic prosperity, however, involves more than increasing the size of the economic pie. Part of evaluating the impact of banks on economic prosperity involves understanding how banks shape the sizes of the slices of the economic pie. Do better-functioning banks increase GDP only by boosting the incomes of the rich? Do better-functioning banks materially boost the living standards of lower-income households? Moreover, part of evaluating the impact of banks on economic prosperity involves focusing on economic opportunities. Do better-functioning banking systems influence the degree to which the contours of an individual's economic possibilities are shaped by the individual's abilities versus the degree to which those opportunities are predetermined by the wealth and connections of the individual's family?

The evidence will surprise many: Better-functioning banks disproportionately help lower-income families and expand the economic opportunities available to economically disadvantaged individuals and groups. To see how this works, again consider how banks shape long-run growth. Better-functioning banks boost growth by funneling capital to the most promising entrepreneurs. This does not mean that better-functioning banks funnel credit to those endeavors run by the wealthiest families. Rather, it means that better-functioning banks boost growth by funneling credit to those entrepreneurs with projects that have greater risk-adjusted expected returns. By reducing the connection between wealth and access to credit, better banking systems can expand the economic opportunities for low-wealth people, improve the efficiency of resource allocation, and spur growth. It is not growth versus expanding economic opportunities; it is growth by expanding economic opportunities.

Crucially, research also uncovers two channels through which better-functioning banking systems reduce income inequality. First, banks do not reduce inequality by lowering the incomes of high-earners. Rather, better banking systems reduce income inequality by boosting the incomes of lower-income families by more than they boost the incomes of higher-income families. Second, banks exert a powerful influence on the poorest in society by spurring entrepreneurship and improving labor market conditions. This occurs as follows. Better banking systems lower the barriers to becoming an entrepreneur. This facilitates the entry of promising new firms, forcing the exit of unsuccessful incumbents and making the product market more competitive. The resultant intensification of product market competition means that workers – who account for the vast majority of people – look for work in a more dynamic competitive environment. A few large firms can no longer dictate terms to labor, and labor unions can no longer protect inefficient workers at the expense of more efficient ones. Better banks create more competitive product markets, which in turn enhance competition for workers, boosting wages and lowering unemployment. It is through this labor market channel that better-functioning banking systems boost the incomes of lower-income families and narrow income inequality. Thus, banking systems shape the economic lives of many – *even those who never receive a loan or start a business* – because almost everyone needs a job and that job search is materially shaped by the banking system.

The impact of the banking system on social welfare extends still further. Research suggests that bank regulatory reforms that spur competition among banks and improve the functioning of banking systems lower crime rates (e.g., Garmaise and Moskowitz, 2006), ease financing constraints and increase schooling (e.g., Levine and Rubinstein, 2014; Sun and Yannelis, 2016), shrink the black–white wage gap (e.g., Levine, Levkov, and Rubinstein, 2014), reduce corporate risk (e.g., Jiang, Levine, and Lin, 2017), and alleviate depression (e.g., Hu, Levine, Lin, and Tai, 2018). This work on the broader human welfare effects of finance needs additional study, but these findings further emphasize the value of regulatory reforms that improve the functioning of banks.

Banks are special. Many other policy areas deserve attention, such as inflation, fiscal expenditures, taxes, international trade, cross-border capital flows, and the regulation of nonfinancial industries. But measures of how well the banking system was functioning in 1960 predict economic performance over the next half-century, while none of these other features of economies has such predictive power. Similarly, while other components of the financial system are important – such as equity markets – the powerful connection between banks and economic prosperity holds even when controlling for these other features of financial systems. From cross-country comparisons, individual country studies, time-series studies, and microeconomic studies, research confirms and reconfirms the impact of banking systems on economic prosperity.

Another special feature of banks is that they must innovate and evolve to remain effective. Financial innovation is essential for improving the wealth of nations. As described by Adam Smith (1776), enhancing the wealth of nations requires increased specialization and the development of novel technologies. The resulting increase in complexity will typically make it more difficult to screen borrowers, identify the most promising entrepreneurs, and funnel credit effectively. Put differently, as technologies advance, it becomes harder to be an effective bank. If, in turn, banks allocate credit less efficiently, economic growth will slow. Thus, to maintain the same rate of economic progress, banks must adapt to changing conditions and enhance the quality of their services to avoid becoming ineffective and obsolete. Again, historical examples and new econometric evidence show that (1) better-functioning banking systems spur technological improvements, and (2) continual innovations within banks are necessary for sustaining technological innovation (Laeven, Levine, and Michalopoulos, 2015). There is a symbiotic connection among technological innovation, finance, and financial innovation.

Indeed, the evidence suggests that Paul Volcker, the former chairman of the Board of Governors of the Federal Reserve System, was wrong when he skeptically stated in 2009, "I wish someone would give me one shred of neutral evidence that financial innovation has led to economic growth – one shred of evidence."[1] In fact, an enormous body of research using examples from the last few thousand years discovers that financial innovations are essential for fostering the technological innovations that spur sustained improvements in living standards. Just to mention a few examples, the creation of tradable debt contracts 6,000 years ago in Samaria made it easier to lend and less costly to borrow, which boosted specialization and productivity. Ancient Rome developed a stock market

---

[1] "Paul Volcker: Think More Boldly," *Wall Street Journal*, December 14, 2009, www.wsj.com/articles/SB10001424052748704825504574586330960597134.

to ease the mobilization of savings for enormous mining projects. To finance oceanic explorations in the sixteenth to eighteenth centuries, banks and other financial market participants invented the joint stock company to facilitate risk diversification. And financial innovations were necessary ingredients for the Industrial Revolution and for the more recent economic revolutions in information technologies and biotechnologies. Given all of the evidence, it is perhaps more appropriate to turn Volcker's skeptical query around: "I wish somebody would give me a shred of evidence that the long-run link between financial innovation and growth is no longer operative."

The econometric findings on financial innovation and growth, of course, do not mean that *all* – or even most – financial innovations are socially productive. Just as some medical innovations have proven to be harmful to the public, some financial innovations are destructive. But, just as it is difficult to imagine broad-based increases in longevity and the quality of human life without medical innovation, it is difficult to imagine a continuous stream of technological innovations that boost living standards without a complementary stream of financial innovations that facilitate the funding of those technological advances.

A comprehensive discussion of bank regulatory and supervisory policies that create well-functioning banking systems would require a separate chapter – or book (e.g., Barth, Caprio, and Levine, 2006, 2012). Here, I would just like to make the following simple argument. Bank regulation is not just about preventing banking crises: We know how to do that. Creating sound banking regulations is also about cultivating banking systems that effectively mobilize savings, screen borrowers and allocate savings to the best ones, monitor borrowers and induce them to use those savings efficiently, and provide first-rate risk management services – and it is about creating a banking system that continually innovates to improve the quality of these financial services.

The remainder of this chapter is organized as follows. Section 9.2 reviews the cross-country evidence on linkages between the functioning of the financial system and both economic growth and the distribution of income. I provide information both from cross-country comparisons and from studies of the United States. Section 9.3 discusses the evidence on the connection between financial innovation and economic growth. In this section, I primarily discuss anecdotal evidence from across history, but I also review recent cross-country regressions on the financial innovation and growth nexus. Section 9.4 concludes.

9.2 Finance and Growth, Inequality, and Poverty

This section reviews evidence suggesting that the operation of the financial system exerts a powerful effect on national rates of long-run economic growth, the distribution of income, and the proportion of people living in poverty. Moreover, the evidence shows that financial institutions and markets affect the economy primarily by influencing the allocation of resources, not by altering the aggregate savings rate. Therefore, financial regulation can materially influence economic prosperity by shaping the operation of the financial system and hence the economy's capital allocation choices. Rather than reviewing the entire empirical literature on finance and growth as in Levine (1997, 2005), I discuss the literature's major findings first by evaluating studies that use cross-country comparisons and then by presenting evidence from studies that focus on the United States. An extensive body of research demonstrates that the findings I discuss hold when using an assortment of techniques to identify the causal impact of the functioning of financial systems on economic performance.

9.2.1 Banks, Growth, Inequality, and the Poor

9.2.1.1 Cross-Country Evidence

Broad cross-country evaluations of the impact of the functioning of financial systems on growth use one observation per country, where the data are typically averaged over thirty or forty years. The studies control for many other possible determinants of economic growth such as initial income, educational attainment, inflation, government spending, openness to trade, and political instability (King and Levine, 1993; Levine, 1998, 1999; Levine, Loayza, and Beck, 2000; Beck, Levine, and Loayza, 2000; Beck and Levine, 2004). These studies also examine whether the functioning of financial systems is associated with productivity growth and capital accumulation, which are two channels through which the operation of the financial system can influence growth.

To measure the functioning of financial systems, cross-country studies typically use *Private Credit*, which equals bank credit to the private sector as a share of GDP. This creates a problem since the objective is to measure the quality of the financial services available in an economy. But *Private Credit* does not directly measure the effectiveness of the financial system in mobilizing savings, allocating capital, monitoring the use of that capital, providing risk management services, and easing transactions. Rather, *Private Credit* measures the size of the financial intermediary sector. Another problem is that *Private Credit* focuses on banks and does not consider the broader array of financial institutions and markets. *Private Credit* does, however, exclude loans to the government and state-owned enterprises and therefore gauges the intermediation of private credit. Furthermore, the same results hold when using a broader measure that includes credits issues by nonbank financial institutions (not just bank credit) and when incorporating measures of stock market development.

As discovered by Levine et al. (2000), countries with better-functioning financial systems grow faster. When examining the relationship between growth and *Private Credit* over the thirty-five years between 1960 and 1995 and while controlling for many other potential growth determinants, they find a strong, statistically significant, and robust link between finance and growth. Furthermore, Beck et al. (2000) show that the functioning of financial systems increases growth primarily by enhancing the efficiency of capital allocation. The connection between the functioning of financial systems and the savings rate is weaker. Thus, it is the effect of the financial system on allocating society's resources that shapes national growth rates.

The operation of the financial system can also influence the distribution of income in a variety of ways, some of which disproportionately help the poor and others that primarily increase the incomes of the rich. First, better-functioning banks focus more on a person's ideas and abilities than on family wealth and political connections when allocating credit. Second, enhancing the quality of financial services will naturally benefit heavy users of financial services, which are primarily wealthy families and large firms. Finally, finance can also affect the distribution of income through its effects on labor markets. For example, improvements in finance that increase the demand for low-skilled workers will tend to tighten the distribution of income. And the financial system helps determine whether people live in a dynamic, growing economy or whether they must find work in a more stagnant environment.

As shown by Beck, Demirgüç-Kunt, and Levine (2006), countries with better-functioning financial systems tend to experience reductions in income inequality, as measured by the growth rate of the Gini coefficient of income inequality. Critically, this result holds when controlling for the economy's aggregate growth rate and the level of overall economic development, as well as a wide array of other country-specific characteristics. Thus, improvements in the functioning of financial systems tighten the distribution of income above and beyond any effect operating through economic growth on the level of economic development.

Moreover, financial development disproportionately boosts the incomes of those at the lower end of the distribution of income, including the incomes of the extremely poor. As shown by Beck et al. (2006), *Private Credit* boosts the income growth of the poorest quintile, even after controlling for many other country characteristics, including the rate of economic growth and the level of economic development. They push this examination further and focus on the extremely poor, that is, those living on less than two dollars per day.[2] They show that financial development is associated with a reduction in the fraction of the population living in extreme poverty. Critically, these results hold when controlling for average growth. It is not just that finance accelerates economic growth, which trickles down to the poor; finance exerts a *disproportionately* positive influence on lower-income individuals.

9.2.1.2 US Evidence

The United States provide a unique setting in which to examine further the causal impact of improvements in the quality of banking services on economic growth, the distribution of income, and the poor. From the mid-1970s to the mid-1990s, individual US states removed regulatory restrictions on opening bank branches within their boundaries. States changed their regulatory policies in different years. The reforms intensified competition and triggered improvements in banking services, reducing interest rates on loans, raising them on deposits, lowering overhead costs, spurring the development of better techniques for screening and monitoring firms, and reducing the proportion of bad loans on banks' books (Jayaratne and Strahan, 1998).

The driving forces behind the financial reforms that enhanced the quality of financial services were largely independent of state-specific changes in growth, income inequality, and labor market conditions. Kroszner and Strahan (1999) show that technological, legal, and financial innovations diminished the economic and political power of banks benefiting from geographic restrictions on banking. The invention of automatic teller machines (ATMs), in conjunction with court rulings that ATMs are not bank branches, weakened the geographical bond between customers

---

[2] Data on the fraction of the population living on less than $2/day are limited to less developed countries over the period from 1980 to 2005.

and banks. Furthermore, checkable money market mutual funds facilitated banking by mail and telephone, which weakened local bank monopolies. And improvements in credit-scoring techniques, information processing, and telecommunications reduced the informational advantages of local banks. These innovations reduced the monopoly power of local banks and therefore weakened their ability and desire to fight for the maintenance of these restrictions on competition. State by state, the authorities removed these restrictions over the last quarter of the twentieth century.

Although a slight digression, it is valuable to recognize that policymakers did not remove these regulations because of new, convincing information that they were hindering competition and the provision of high-quality financial services. There was already plenty of information about the adverse effects of the regulatory restrictions. Rather, technological innovation reduced the rents that banks earned from these protective regulatory restrictions, which weakened their desire to lobby for their continuation. Perhaps if the regulatory institutions had better represented the interests of the public, these growth-retarding policies would have been removed earlier.

To examine the connection between US state-level bank regulatory reforms that improved the functioning of state banking systems and (1) state economic growth, (2) state income inequality, and (3) state unemployment, Jayaratne and Strahan (1996) and Beck, Levine, and Levkov (2010) trace out the year-by-year effects of the removal of geographic restrictions on intrastate bank branching on the logarithm of gross state product (GSP) per capita, income inequality, and unemployment rates. Thus, they evaluate how a state's economy evolved after the state eased geographic restrictions on competition among banks. Since US states lowered these restrictions in different years, the analyses control for both state and year fixed effects, effectively controlling for all time-invariant characteristics of each state and for all factors influencing the United States in each year.

There are three major findings. The removal of geographic restrictions on intrastate banking – which improved the quality of banking services – (1) increased economic growth (Jayaratne and Strahan, 1996), (2) lowered income inequality (Beck et al., 2010), and (3) reduced unemployment (Beck et al., 2010). The impact is economically large. For example, consider income inequality. The regression estimates indicate that the impact of deregulation on inequality grows for about eight years and then the effect levels off. Ultimately, there is a drop in the Gini coefficient of income inequality of about 4 percent. Moreover, Beck et al. (2010) show that

intrastate branch deregulation reduced income inequality by disproportionately raising incomes in the lower part of the income distribution. That
is, better-functioning financial systems lowered inequality by helping the
poor, not by hurting the rich.

9.2.2 Banks, Markets, and Growth

While the evidence presented in Section 9.2.1 indicates that the functioning of banks influences economic growth and the distribution of income, it
does not consider equity and bond markets. Are securities markets simply
casinos where the rich come to place their bets or do the services provided
by financial markets also affect the allocation of capital and long-run rates
of economic growth? A considerable body of theoretical and empirical
research addresses this question.

Theory suggests that financial markets also matter for growth (Levine,
1991). For example, as securities markets become larger and more liquid, it
is easier for an investor who has acquired information to profit by quickly
trading in the market based on that information (Holmstrom and Tirole,
1993). Thus, larger, more liquid markets will increase the incentives of
investors to expend resources researching firms, enhancing the efficiency
of resource allocation and fostering growth. As another example, liquid,
well-functioning stock markets can improve corporate governance. For
example, public trading of shares in stock markets that efficiently reflect
information about firms allows owners to align the interests of managers
with those of owners by linking managerial compensation to stock prices
(Jensen and Murphy, 1990). Similarly, if takeovers are easier in well-
functioning stock markets and if managers of underperforming firms are
fired following a takeover, then better stock markets can promote better
corporate control. The threat of a takeover will also help align managerial
incentives with those of the owners.

The empirical evidence indicates that better-functioning securities markets encourage economic growth by increasing the efficiency of resource
allocation (Levine and Zervos, 1998; Beck and Levine, 2002). Measures of
stock market liquidity – how much trading occurs in the market – are
closely associated with economic growth. However, simple measures of the
size of the market, as measured by stock market capitalization, are not
robustly linked with economic performance.

Furthermore, both bank and stock market development are independently associated with growth, suggesting that the policy debate about
whether to promote a bank-based system or a market-based financial

system misses the big point. Banks *and* markets both matter for growth. This does not imply that banks and markets play the same roles in all economies, however. Indeed, as countries become more developed, new research indicates that markets become increasingly important for promoting economic activity (Demirgüç-Kunt, Feyen, and Levine, 2013). While still requiring additional work, this suggests that poor bank regulations are particularly costly in countries at low levels of economic development, while regulations impeding market development have larger adverse effect in richer countries.

9.3 Financial Innovation and Growth

Thus far, I have ignored the dynamics of the functioning of financial systems: How does financial innovation fit into the process of economic growth? Given the roles of credit default swaps, collateralized debt obligations, and other new financial instruments in the recent financial crisis, financial innovation has gotten a bad reputation. From this perspective, financial innovations are mechanisms for fooling investors, circumventing regulatory intent, and boosting the bonuses of financiers without enhancing the quality of the services provided by the financial services industry. Such a perspective is too narrow.

A broader, long-run consideration of the functioning of financial systems suggests that financial innovation is *essential* for growth, which is the focus of Laeven et al. (2015). Adam Smith (1776) argued that economic growth is a process in which production becomes increasingly specialized and technologies more complex. As firms become more complex, however, the "old" financial system becomes less effective at screening and monitoring firms. Therefore, without corresponding innovations in finance that match the increases in complexity associated with economic growth, the quality of the financial services diminishes, slowing future growth.

Several examples from history illustrate the crucial role of financial innovation in sustaining economic growth. Consider first the financial impediments to railroad expansion in the nineteenth century. The novelty and complexity of railroads made preexisting financial systems ineffective at screening and monitoring them. Although prominent local investors with close ties to those operating the railroad were the primary sources of capital for railroads during the early decades of this new technology, this reliance on local finance restricted growth.

In response, financiers innovated. Specialized financiers and investment banks emerged to mobilize capital from individuals, screen and invest in railroads, and monitor the use of those investments, often by serving on the boards of directors of railroad corporations (Carosso, 1970). Based on their expertise and reputation, these investment banks mobilized funds from wealthy investors, evaluated proposals from railroads, allocated capital, and governed the operations of railroad companies for investors. And, since the geographical size and complexity of railroads made it difficult for investors to collect, organize, and assess price, usage, breakdown, and repair information, financiers developed new accounting and financial reporting methods.

Next, consider the information technology revolution of the twentieth century, which could not have been financed with the financial system that fueled the railroad revolution of the nineteenth century. Indeed, as nascent high-tech information and communication firms struggled to emerge in the 1970s and 1980s, traditional commercial banks were reluctant to finance them because these new firms did not yet generate sufficient cash flows to cover loan payments and the scientists running the firms had little experience in operating profitable companies (Gompers and Lerner, 2001). Conventional debt and equity markets were also wary because the technologies were too complex for investors to evaluate.

Again, financiers innovated. Venture capital firms arose to screen entrepreneurs and provide technical, managerial, and financial advice to new high-technology firms. In many cases, venture capitalists had become wealthy through their own successful high-tech innovations, which provided a basis of expertise for evaluating and guiding new entrepreneurs. In terms of funding, venture capitalists typically took large, private equity stakes that established a long-term commitment to the enterprise, and they generally became active investors, taking seats on the board of directors and helping to solve managerial and financial problems.

Finally, consider the biotechnology revolution of the twenty-first century, for which the venture capital modality did not work well. Venture capitalists could not effectively screen biotech firms because of the scientific breadth of biotechnologies, which frequently require inputs from biologists, chemists, geneticists, engineers, bioroboticists, as well as experts on the myriad laws, regulations, and commercial barriers associated with successfully bringing new medical products to market. It was infeasible to house all of this expertise in banks or venture capital firms. The new technology promised growth, but the existing financial system could not fuel it.

Yet again, financiers innovated. They formed new financial partnerships with the one kind of organization with the breadth of skills to screen biotech firms: large pharmaceutical companies. Pharmaceutical companies employ, or are in regular contact with, a large assortment of scientists and engineers, have close connections with those delivering medical products to customers, and employ lawyers well versed in drug regulations. Furthermore, when an expert pharmaceutical company invests in a biotech firm, this encourages others to invest in the firm as well. Without financial innovation, improvements in diagnostic and surgical procedures, prosthetic devices, parasite-resistant crops, and other innovations linked to biotechnology would almost certainly be occurring at a far slower pace.

The coevolution of financial and economic systems has a valuable policy implication. Without denying the potentially harmful effects of some forms of financial innovation, these historical examples and new cross-country empirical findings by Laeven et al. (2015) suggest that financial innovation is necessary for fostering technological innovations and sustaining economic growth. Thus, financial regulations that stymie healthy financial innovation could slow, or even stop, economic growth.

9.4 Conclusions

Considerable evidence suggests that a well-functioning financial system is vital for fostering economic growth and expanding economic opportunities, especially for those at the lower end of the distribution of income. This evidence does not imply that the social productivity of all financial systems is everywhere and always positive. But it does suggest that sustained improvements in living standards are much less likely when financial systems function poorly. Finance is not just about crises; it also shapes long-run growth and the contours of economic possibilities available to individuals.

Although this chapter does not make policy recommendations, it does yield a powerful policy message. Since finance exerts a first-order impact on economic prosperity and since finance primarily exerts this impact by *choosing* where to allocate capital, the financial policies, regulations, and supervisory practices shaping the incentives underlying those capital allocation choices are critically important for human welfare. The design and implementation of financial policies matter. Thus, as argued by Barth et al. (2012), the institutions and governance systems that actually design and implement financial policies are *the* decisive ingredients in determining the social productivity of the financial sector.

References

Adams, John, 1819. Letter to John Taylor of Caroline, March 12, 1819. In Charles Francis Adams (ed.), 1856. *The Works of John Adams, Second President of the United States*, 375–7. Little, Brown and Company, Boston, MA.

Barth, James R., Gerard Caprio, and Ross Levine, 2006. *Rethinking Bank Regulation: Till Angels Govern*. Cambridge University Press, New York, NY.

Barth, James R., Gerard Caprio, and Ross Levine, 2012. *Guardians of Finance: Making Regulators Work for Us*. MIT Press, Cambridge, MA.

Beck, Thorsten, Asli Demirgüç-Kunt, and Ross Levine, 2006. "Bank Supervision and Corruption in Lending." *Journal of Monetary Economics* 53 (8), 2131–63.

Beck, Thorsten, and Ross Levine, 2002. "Industry Growth and Capital Allocation: Does Having a Market- or Bank-Based System Matter?" *Journal of Financial Economics* 64 (2), 147–80.

Beck, Thorsten, and Ross Levine, 2004. "Stock Markets, Banks, and Growth: Panel Evidence." *Journal of Banking and Finance* 28 (3), 423–42.

Beck, Thorsten, Ross Levine, and Alexey Levkov, 2010. "Big Bad Banks? The Winners and Losers from U.S. Branch Deregulation." *Journal of Finance* 65 (5), 1637–67.

Beck, Thorsten, Ross Levine, and Norman Loayza, 2000. "Finance and the Sources of Growth." *Journal of Financial Economics* 58 (1–2), 261–300.

Carosso, Robert J., 1970. *Investment Banking in America: A History*. Harvard University Press, Cambridge, MA.

Demirgüç-Kunt, Asli, Erik Feyen, and Ross Levine, 2013. "The Evolving Importance of Banks and Securities Markets." *World Bank Economic Review* 27 (3), 476–90.

Garmaise, Mark J., and Tobias J. Moskowitz, 2006. "Bank Mergers and Crime: The Real and Social Effects of Credit Market Competition." *Journal of Finance* 61 (2), 495–538.

Gompers, Paul A., and Josh Lerner, 2001. "The Venture Capital Revolution." *Journal of Economic Perspectives* 15 (2), 145–68.

Holmstrom, Bengt, and Jean Tirole, 1993. "Market Liquidity and Performance Measurement." *Journal of Political Economy* 101 (4), 678–709.

Hu, Qing, Ross Levine, Chen Lin, and Mingzhu Tai, 2018. "Mentally Spent: Credit Conditions and Mental Health." NBER Working Paper No. 25584. National Bureau of Economic Research, Cambridge, MA.

Jayaratne, Jith, and Philip E. Strahan, 1996. "The Finance-Growth Nexus: Evidence from Bank Branch Deregulation." *Quarterly Journal of Economics* 111 (3), 639–70.

Jayaratne, Jith, and Philip E. Strahan, 1998. "Entry Restrictions, Industry Evolution, and Dynamic Efficiency: Evidence from Commercial Banking." *Journal of Law and Economics* 41 (1), 239–73.

Jensen, Michael, and Kevin Murphy, 1990. "Performance Pay and Top Management Incentives." *Journal of Political Economy* 98 (2), 225–64.

Jiang, Liangliang, Ross Levine, and Chen Lin, 2017. "Does Competition Affect Bank Risk?" NBER Working Paper No. 23080. National Bureau of Economic Research, Cambridge, MA.

King, Robert G., and Ross Levine, 1993. "Finance and Growth: Schumpeter Might Be Right." *Quarterly Journal of Economics* 108 (3), 717–37.

Kroszner, Randall S., and Philip E. Strahan, 1999. "What Drives Deregulation? Economics and Politics of the Relaxation of Bank Branching Restrictions." *Quarterly Journal of Economics* 114 (4), 1437–67.

Laeven, Luc, Levine, Ross, and Stelios Michalopoulos, 2015. "Financial Innovation and Endogenous Growth." *Journal of Financial Intermediation* 24 (1), 1–24.

Levine, Ross, 1991. "Stock Markets, Growth, and Tax Policy." *Journal of Finance* 46 (4), 1445–65.

Levine, Ross, 1997. "Financial Development and Economic Growth: Views and Agenda." *Journal of Economic Literature* 35 (2), 688–726.

Levine, Ross, 1998. "The Legal Environment, Banks, and Long-Run Economic Growth." *Journal of Money, Credit, and Banking* 30 (3), 596–613.

Levine, Ross, 1999. "Law, Finance, and Economic Growth." *Journal of Financial Intermediation* 8 (1–2), 8–35.

Levine Ross, 2005. "Finance and Growth: Theory and Evidence." In Philippe Aghion and Steven Durlauf (eds.), *Handbook of Economic Growth*, 865–934. North-Holland Elsevier, Amsterdam, Netherlands.

Levine, Ross, Alexey Levkov, and Yona Rubinstein, 2014. "Bank Deregulation and Racial Inequality in America." *Critical Finance Review* 3 (1), 1–48.

Levine, Ross, Norman Loayza, and Thorsten Beck, 2000. "Financial Intermediation and Growth: Causality and Causes." *Journal of Monetary Economics* 46 (1), 31–77.

Levine, Ross, and Yona Rubinstein, 2014. "Liberty for More: Finance and Educational Opportunities." *Cato Papers on Public Policy* 3 (1), 55–93.

Levine, Ross, and Sara Zervos, 1998. "Stock Markets, Banks, and Economic Growth." *American Economic Review* 88 (3), 537–58.

Philippon, Thomas, and Ariell Reshef, 2011. "Wages and Human Capital in the U.S. Finance Industry: 1909–2006." NBER Working Paper No. 14644. National Bureau of Economic Research, Cambridge, MA.

Smith, Adam, 1776. *An Inquiry into the Nation and Causes of the Wealth of Nations.* W. Stahan & T. Cadell, London.

Sun, Stephen Teng, and Constantine Yannelis, 2016. "Constraints, Credit and Demand for Higher Education: Evidence from Financial Deregulation." *Review of Economics and Statistics* 98 (1), 12–24.

Economic Growth and Income Inequality: Insights from the Representative Consumer Theory of Distribution

Stephen J. Turnovsky

10.1 Background and Overview

Research into the relationship between the level of economic development, the rate of economic growth, and measures of inequality began with the seminal paper by Kuznets (1955). In that paper, Kuznets found that the level of a country's development and its degree of income inequality could be described by an inverted-U relationship. This relationship was essentially a statistical one that Kuznets explained in terms of the transitional dynamics associated with the structural transformation from an agricultural to an industrial economy. The case of the United States, for example, followed this pattern, with the share of wealth owned by the 10 percent richest households increasing from 50 percent to 75 percent between 1770 and 1870, and then declining back to 50 percent by 1970. More recently, this proposition has been challenged in light of evidence that many advanced economies – particularly the United States and the United Kingdom – have experienced increasing income inequality since the 1980s (Atkinson, 1999; Goldin and Katz, 2008).[1] This recent increase in inequality has been attributed to the rising skill premium as a result of skill-biased technological change and capital-skill complementarity; see, for example, Katz and Murphy (1992), Autor, Katz, and Krueger (1998), and Krusell et al. (2000).

The Kuznets proposition has stimulated both empirical and theoretical research analyzing the relationship between income inequality and growth

---

[1] The fact that inequality declined during the 1960s and 1970s only to increase in the 1980s has led Atkinson (1999) to suggest that the latter part of the twentieth century might be better characterized by an inverse Kuznets curve.

and/or economic development. Much of the empirical research has taken the form of running regressions of growth rates on measures of inequality, and other control variables. Among the earlier influential studies, Alesina and Rodrik (1994), Persson and Tabellini (1994), and Perotti (1996) find that inequality has an adverse effect on economic growth rate.[2] Various explanations for this have been offered. These include: (1) the political economy consequences of inequality, (2) the negative impact of inequality on education, (3) the presence of capital market imperfections and credit constraints, (4) the reduction in investment opportunities caused by inequality, and (5) the macroeconomic volatility that inequality may generate.

In contrast, other studies find a positive, or a more ambiguous, relationship; see, for example, Galor and Tsiddon (1997), Li and Zou (1998), Forbes (2000), and Barro (2000). Explanations include: (1) the relative savings propensities of rich versus poor, (2) investment indivisibilities, and (3) the enhanced mobility of high-ability workers to technologically advanced sectors. More recent studies are even more equivocal. Voichovsky (2005) suggests that economic growth has differential effects on different parts of the distribution, favoring those at the top and adversely impacting those at the lower end. Brueckner and Lederman (2018) find that the impact of inequality on economic growth depends upon the initial income level, increasing growth in low-income countries but reducing it in wealthier economies. Finally, Kraay (2016) provides a cautionary note, suggesting that several typical studies employ weak instruments and thus may not provide robust conclusions about the effect of inequality on economic growth.

Presumably because of its more tenuous nature, there are far fewer empirical studies directed at testing the Kuznets relationship. One early exception is Anand and Kanpur (1993), who both provided more formalization of the Kuznets process and derived conditions for a turning point in the inequality-development relationship for several alternative indices of inequality. At the same time, there has been increased interest in explaining the growing inequality in income and earnings, focusing more on potential specific determinants such as the nature of technological change, the growth of human capital, government policy, and globalization, rather

---

[2] These studies and others are discussed in detail by Bénabou (1996b) who provides a simple model to support the negative relationship between inequality and growth obtained in the majority of the studies that he reviews.

than on the more general notion of the level of development; see, for example, Aghion, Caroli, and García-Peñalosa (1999).

From a theoretical standpoint, the diversity of these empirical results is unsurprising. Aggregate measures, such as GDP and its growth rate, and the distribution of income across individual agents are all endogenous outcomes of a large economic system. Therefore, any relationship between them should reflect the underlying set of forces to which these measures are simultaneously responding. Some are likely to influence inequality and growth in the same direction, while others may not. In addition, these forces are likely to change over time and to vary between economies. As Ehrlich and Kim (2007) have suggested, "association" is a more appropriate of characterizing any relationship between economic growth and inequality, rather than trying to attribute a direct causal link. This suggests that the economic growth–inequality relationship can be understood only as a joint equilibrium outcome of a consistently specified general equilibrium growth model.

The presence of heterogeneity across agents is an existential element crucial to the presence of inequality and its relationship to economic growth or any other aggregate measure. There are many such sources, the most obvious including endowments, ability, and education; rates of time preference; tastes; technology; idiosyncratic shocks; etc. Under the most general circumstances, solving for growth and inequality simultaneously is intractable. The interaction between aggregate quantities and their distributions across many diverse individuals is too complex to enable us to advance beyond making a few general qualitative statements about the steady-state equilibrium relationship between per capita output and its distribution across agents (Sorger, 2000). In particular, it is infeasible to characterize the dynamic evolution of wealth or income distribution as the economy evolves over time, following some structural or policy development. To make progress in this dimension requires that some additional structure be imposed on the system.

Two general approaches can be identified in the literature. The first is the so-called "representative consumer theory of distribution" (RCTD), as it was named by Caselli and Ventura (2000), which in effect introduces heterogeneity coupled with complete markets, so that all agents have identical access to all markets. If, in addition, preferences are homogeneous, then, for certain important sources of heterogeneity, including initial endowments, the aggregation procedures due to Gorman (1959) can be utilized. In this case, the macroeconomic equilibrium and distribution have a simple recursive structure. First, summing over individuals leads to a macroeconomic equilibrium in which aggregate quantities, and the resulting factor returns, are determined independently of any distributional aspects. With all agents having equal unimpeded access to these economy-wide derived factor returns, the distributions of these aggregate quantities across individuals can then be determined.[3] In terms of the causality debate relating economic growth and inequality, this formulation assumes away any causality running from inequality to economic growth and can address only the reverse, as indeed was Kuznets's original focus.

In constructing any formal economic model, the choice of assumptions one makes involves a tradeoff between realism and tractability. While homogeneity is a strong assumption, in this case the tractability it yields suggests a high payoff, especially in light of the versatility of the questions it enables one to address. For example, invoking homogeneity enables one to address pertinent issues pertaining to fiscal policy and income distribution in a plausibly comprehensive macrodynamic framework. Moreover, the assumption of homogeneous utility is routine throughout modern growth theory, and indeed macrodynamics in general. While it includes the widely adopted constant elasticity utility function, more general formulations can be analyzed as well.

Almost all of my research studying the growth–inequality relationship employs the RCTD and embodies the recursive equilibrium structure just described. As the source of heterogeneity, this work has focused on the initial distribution of endowments of assets across individuals. Usually this has meant endowments of physical capital, although the model has been extended to include human capital and/or ability in considering skills as well as foreign assets in an international environment.[4]

The distribution of asset endowments across agents is arguably the most important source of heterogeneity and that is the main reason I have focused on that aspect. There is certainly much greater diversity among inherited wealth across individuals than can possibly exist due to differences in individuals' rates of time preference, which as a practical matter can deviate by only a percentage point or two across agents. Recently, the particular prominence of endowments and inheritance as sources of inequality has resulted from the influential work of Thomas Piketty and his

---

[3] Note that this implies that the representative consumer model can incorporate certain important sources of heterogeneity and does not require that all agents be identical, as is typically understood.

[4] Other papers using this approach include Chatterjee (1994), Maliar and Maliar (2001, 2003), and Sorger (2002), among others.

coauthors; see Piketty (2011, 2014), Piketty and Saez (2003), and Piketty and Zucman (2014).

An alternative approach to generating heterogeneity is to assume that people are initially identical, with heterogeneity being endogenized through uninsurable idiosyncratic random shocks; see Krusell and Smith (1998), Castañeda, Díaz-Giménez, and Ríos-Rull (1998), and Benhabib, Bisin, and Zhu (2015), among others. If, in addition, one assumes that agents have limited access to credit markets, the equilibrium structure is fundamentally reversed from that implied by the representative consumer theory in that the dynamics of inequality are driven by the idiosyncratic technology shocks and in turn determine the macroeconomic growth rate. These models, which are characterized by incomplete markets, are comprehensively reviewed by Heathcote, Storesletten, and Violante (2009).[5] They are more suited to addressing the impact of inequality on economic growth, although the aggregation involved generally forces them to be more stylized. In addition, by stressing the role of market imperfections, they are arguably more relevant to developing economies.

In parameterizing inequality, there are several potential measures that one might consider. Of these, the Gini coefficient is the most prevalent aggregate measure adopted in empirical work and the most widely available.[6] However, it may be collected from different sources and care needs to be taken in adjusting for this in any empirical study. In addition to the Gini coefficient, Atkinson (1970) proposes four other summary measures, of which the coefficient of variation is closest to the Gini and is the most convenient in terms of mapping the underlying theory to the corresponding empirically testable hypothesis. But variance is convenient if one wishes to decompose measures of inequality into various sources (Bourguignon, 1979).

However, these are all aggregate measures and may conceal the true impact of a structural or policy change. For example, an increase in the top end of the income distribution and a decrease in the bottom end may yield comparable increases in the Gini coefficient but may have very different societal impacts. To appreciate how different parts of the income distribution may be affected by a structural or policy change, it is helpful to focus on various quantiles. If the concern is with poverty, one might focus on the

---

[5] Their genesis can be traced back to Bewley (1977) and for that reason they are sometimes referred to as "Bewley models."
[6] Well-known comprehensive international sources of Gini coefficients include the "All the Ginis" database compiled by Branko Milanovic.

bottom 1 percent of the distribution. At the other extreme, much of the popular debate concerning the evils of inequality concentrates on the top 1 percent.

In addition to selecting the appropriate inequality measure, there is the issue of which economic variable is of concern. The most widely analyzed, both theoretically and particularly empirically, is income inequality. Here, the natural distinction arises between pre-tax and post-tax income, which, as will be shown in Section 10.4, can move very differently, depending upon tax rates and the mode of government finance. Wealth inequality is also important, and indeed turns out to be a key driving force generating income inequality. However, because of serious limitations with respect to data availability, empirical studies of wealth inequality are sparse.[7] Finally, with the increase in the skill premium over recent years, there is a growing interest in wage or earnings inequality. Typically, however, this focuses on the relative wage of skilled to unskilled labor, rather than variations across the entire wage distribution. In general, these various inequality measures need not move together, thereby giving rise to potential conflicts between them.

The objective of this chapter is to present a systematic approach to the representative consumer theory of distribution and to highlight the insights it offers into the growth–inequality relationship in a range of applications. I begin, in Section 10.2, by embedding the growth–inequality relationship in a basic Ramsey growth model, which offers the advantage of presenting its equilibrium recursive structure in the most transparent manner.

The first modification (Section 10.3) I consider is to assume that the increase in productivity, introduced to illustrate the dynamics of the basic canonical model, in fact occurs gradually, rather than being completed instantaneously, as is conventionally assumed. As I shall discuss, this introduces *path dependence* into the evolution of wealth inequality, and, consequently, income inequality. That is, the degree of long-run inequality will depend upon the nature of the specific time path generating the productivity increase. This is important for several reasons. First, it is a generic characteristic of this class of model and applies to any structural or policy change. Second, it may help explain that economies such as Mexico and Turkey, which have comparable aggregate characteristics, nevertheless have very different degrees of income inequality, as a reflection of very

---

[7] Also, to the extent that one may be concerned with more general welfare measures, welfare inequality naturally may be appropriate. Space limitations preclude further discussion of this aspect, although several of the papers summarized in subsequent sections address this aspect as well; see, e.g., Turnovsky and García-Peñalosa (2008), García-Peñalosa and Turnovsky (2011), and Chatterjee and Turnovsky (2012).

different time paths of development.[8] Third, as a practical policy matter, it implies that the speed with which policy changes are implemented will have implications for long-run inequality. This is particularly relevant in the case of foreign aid, which, typically, is granted over some specified time horizon.

The next modification (Section 10.4) is to consider the impact of fiscal policy by introducing government consumption expenditure that is financed in alternative ways. In doing so, I shall focus on the various tradeoffs that these entail. These include tradeoffs between aggregate performance and inequality, tradeoffs between different measures of inequality, and intertemporal tradeoffs. It also provides the basis for the design of an integrated fiscal policy that takes these tradeoffs into account.

As noted, there are other sources of heterogeneity, with one of the earliest and most prominent being heterogeneous rates of time preference. This was first formally studied by Becker (1980) who showed that differences in rates of time preference lead to the extreme implication of a degenerate long-run wealth distribution, with the most patient individual ultimately owning all the capital. But the extent to which this proposition holds depends, critically, upon the nature of the tax system. Indeed, the interaction between agents' rates of time preference and the progressivity of the tax rate is crucial in determining the long-run distribution of income. However, by generating an after-tax rate of return specific to each individual, the progressivity of the tax rate destroys the recursive structure of the equilibrium, thereby impairing the tractability of the transitional dynamics. But progressive tax structures are an important element of most developed economies and play a potentially important role in influencing growth–inequality tradeoffs. Some of this work is briefly reviewed in Section 10.5.

The basic model assumes just one source of endowment heterogeneity, namely the initial physical capital stock. As a further modification, introduced in Section 10.6, I introduce a second source of heterogeneity, whereby different agents are endowed with different degrees of ability. This introduces considerable flexibility into the dynamics of inequality and includes the possibility of mobility whereby, over time, an initially less affluent agent can potentially overtake another wealthier, but less able, agent in the wealth and income distributions.

---

[8] For example, Mexico and Turkey have comparable levels of per capita income (around $15,000 in 2010) but very different income distributions as measured by their Gini coefficients (around 0.52 and 0.40, respectively).

Most of my own work has been based on the traditional neoclassical growth model, focusing on the consequences of the accumulation of physical capital for growth and inequality. However, important empirical evidence suggests that, during the twentieth century, human capital replaced physical capital as the key engine of economic growth; see, for example, Goldin and Katz (1999, 2001) and Abramovitz and David (2000).

The change in the relative importance of human capital has spawned an extensive literature focusing on its role in fostering growth and its distributional consequences. This literature can be broadly characterized as emphasizing more of the "social" aspects involved, and it has identified several specific channels relating the accumulation of human capital and inequality. These include: (1) disparities in educational opportunities and attainment – for example, Becker and Tomes (1979), Bénabou (1996a), Durlauf (1996), and Fernandez and Rogerson (1996); (2) credit market constraints – for example, Galor and Zeira (1993) and Banerjee and Newman (1993); (3) health and demographic factors – for example, Becker and Barro (1988) and de la Croix and Doepke (2003); and (4) political considerations and education – for example, Saint-Paul and Verdier (1993) and Glomm and Ravikumar (1992). Most of this literature employs some form of overlapping generations model in which the transfer of human capital across generations is a key element of the growth process.

In contrast to this literature, Turnovsky and Mitra (2013) have adapted the seminal Lucas (1988) two-sector model of physical and human capital accumulation to examine distributional outcomes. This approach, summarized in Section 10.7, is a natural extension of the approach discussed in earlier sections and offers a very different perspective from the bulk of the literature in that it focuses on the technological aspects of the production structure and the relationship between skilled and unskilled workers. A key component of this approach involves the skill premium and how it responds to the skill-biased technological change and the capital-skill complementarity that has been receiving increasing attention.

The final issue I shall address (Section 10.8) concerns the role of public investment as a mechanism determining the dynamics of the growth–inequality relationship. This is an extremely important application that has generated extensive empirical research among development economists.[9] Much of this evidence is conflicting and underscores the need to address the

---

[9] World Bank and IMF economists in particular focus intensively on this issue; see, e.g., World Bank (2006), Calderón and Servén (2010, 2014), Seneviratne and Sun (2013), and Eden and Kraay (2014).

relationship within the context of a well-defined analytical model. While the representative agent framework may provide useful insights, one should also be cognizant of the fact that, insofar as much of the debate pertains to developing economies, to get a more complete picture, the growth–inequality relationship should also be examined from other viewpoints.[10]

10.2 Wealth and Income Inequality in a Canonical Ramsey Model

I begin with the simplest conventional Ramsey economy, which comprises a single representative firm and many heterogeneous households.[11]

10.2.1 Technology and Factor Payments

Aggregate output is produced by a standard neoclassical production function,

$$Y = F(K, L), \quad F_L > 0, \quad F_K > 0, \quad F_{LL} < 0, \quad F_{KK} < 0, \quad F_{LK} > 0, \quad (1)$$

where, K, L, and Y denote the per capita stock of capital, labor supply, and output. The wage rate, w, and the return to capital, r, are determined by the marginal physical products of labor and capital:

$$w(K, L) = F_L(K, L), \quad w_K = F_{LK}, \quad w_L = F_{LL}, \quad (2a)$$

$$r(K, L) = F_K(K, L), \quad r_K = F_{KK} < 0, \quad r_L = F_{KL} > 0. \quad (2b)$$

10.2.2 Consumers

At time 0, the economy is populated by N_0 individuals, represented as a continuum, each indexed by i and identical in all respects except for their initial endowments of capital. Each individual defines a "family." Population grows uniformly across all families at the exponential rate, n, so that at time t, family i has grown to e^{nt} and the total population of the economy is $N(t) \equiv N_0 e^{nt}$. Each member of a given family has the same capital stock, although the distribution of capital differs across families.

---

[10] See Turnovsky (2015), who compares the implications under the representative consumer theory with the alternative where the heterogeneity arises from idiosyncratic productive shocks and the absence of borrowing and finds that the impact of government investment on the growth–inequality relationship contrasts sharply in the two approaches, with both offering sharply contrasting perspectives.

[11] This material in this section draws heavily on Turnovsky and García-Peñalosa (2008).

From a distributional perspective, a key factor is family i's share of the total capital stock in the economy.

Individual i holds $K_i(t)$ units of capital at time t, so that the amount held by family i is $K_i(t)e^{nt}$. Aggregating over the N_0 families, the total capital stock in the economy at time t is $K^T(t) = \int_0^{N_0} K_i(t)e^{nt}\,di$, so that the average per capita stock of capital is

$$K(t) = (N_0)^{-1}e^{-nt}\int_0^{N_0} K_i(t)e^{nt}\,di = (N_0)^{-1}\int_0^{N_0} K_i(t)\,di.$$

Since the economy is growing, the share of capital owned by family i is

$$k_i(t) \equiv \frac{K_i(t)e^{nt}}{K^T(t)/N_0} = \frac{K_i(t)e^{nt}}{\frac{1}{N_0}\int_0^{N_0} K_i(t)e^{nt}\,di} = \frac{K_i(t)}{\frac{1}{N_0}\int_0^{N_0} K_i(t)\,di} = \frac{K_i(t)}{K(t)}.$$

With all agents in the different families growing at the same rate, the distribution in terms of relative family shares is $k_i(t)$. Note that relative capital has mean 1. I denote its initial distribution function by $H_0(k)$, the initial density function by $h_0(k)$, and the initial (given) standard deviation of relative capital by $\sigma_{k,0}$.

Each individual is endowed with a unit of time that can be allocated either to leisure, l_i, or to work, $1 - l_i$. I assume that the agent's utility function is specified by a constant elasticity function of consumption, C_i, and leisure, l_i, and its decision problem is to choose C_i, l_i, K_i to[12]

$$\max \int_0^\infty \frac{1}{\gamma}\left(C_i(t)\, l_i^\eta\right)^\gamma e^{-\beta t}dt, \text{ with } -\infty < \gamma < 1, \ \eta > 0, \ \gamma\eta < 1, \quad (3)$$

subject to the capital accumulation constraint

$$\dot{K}_i = [r(K, L) - n]K_i + (1 - l_i)w(K, L) - C_i. \quad (4)$$

Performing the optimization yields the agent's standard optimality conditions

$$C_i^{\gamma-1}l_i^{\eta\gamma} = \lambda_i, \quad (5a)$$

---

[12] The restrictions in (3) are imposed to ensure that the utility function has the appropriate concavity properties.

$$\eta C_i^\gamma l_i^{\eta\gamma - 1} = w(K, L)\lambda_i, \text{ and} \tag{5b}$$

$$r(K, L) = \beta - \frac{\dot{\lambda}_i}{\lambda_i}, \tag{5c}$$

together with the transversality (intertemporal solvency) condition.[13]

A key consequence of the optimality conditions (5a)–(5c) is that since all agents face the same real wage and the same return to capital, they choose the same growth rate for consumption and leisure (although levels differ). Summing over agents and denoting aggregate quantities by C, l, yields[14]

$$\frac{\dot{C}_i}{C_i} = \frac{\dot{C}}{C}; \frac{\dot{l}_i}{l_i} = \frac{\dot{l}}{l}. \tag{6}$$

In particular, $l_i(t) = v_i l(t)$, where v_i is a constant, to be determined in (14) in Section 10.2.4.

10.2.3 Aggregate Equilibrium Dynamics

Invoking the optimality conditions (5) and summing over individuals, the aggregate macroeconomic equilibrium can be summarized by the following set of equations in $K(t)$ and $l(t)$:

$$\dot{K} = AF(K, L) - \frac{AF_L(K, L)l}{\eta} - nK, \tag{7a}$$

$$\dot{l} = \frac{1}{H(l)} \left\{ AF_K(K, L) - \beta - n - (1 - \gamma)\frac{F_{KL}(K, L)}{F_L(K, L)} \right.$$
$$\left. \left[AF(K, L) - \frac{AF_L(K, L)l}{\eta} - nK \right] \right\}, \text{ and} \tag{7b}$$

$$L(t) + l(t) = 1, \tag{7c}$$

---

[13] Equation (5a) equates the marginal utility of consumption to the agent's shadow value of capital, (5b) equates the marginal utility of leisure to the forgone wage, measured in utility units, and (5c) equates the rate of return on capital to the rate of return on consumption.

[14] For convenience, I measure the aggregate variables in the economy by their averages across the individuals.

where

$$H(l) \equiv \frac{1-\gamma(1+\eta)}{l} - \frac{(1-\gamma)F_{LL}}{F_L} > 0.$$

This is just the conventional Ramsey model with endogenous labor supply. It describes the dynamic adjustment of the aggregate economy and is independent of distributional characteristics, which is the essential manifestation of the RCTD.

The steady state of this system is described by the familiar conditions[15]

$$AF_K(\widetilde{K}, \widetilde{L}) = \beta + n, \tag{8a}$$

$$AF(\widetilde{K}, \widetilde{L}) - n\widetilde{K} = \frac{AF_L(\widetilde{K}, \widetilde{L})\widetilde{l}}{\eta}, \quad \text{and} \tag{8b}$$

$$\widetilde{L} + \widetilde{l} = 1. \tag{8c}$$

Using the linear homogeneity of the production function, one can combine (8a) and (8b) to yield

$$\widetilde{l} - \frac{\eta}{1+\eta} = \frac{\beta\widetilde{K}}{AF_L}\left(\frac{\eta}{1+\eta}\right) > 0. \tag{9}$$

Inequality (9) will play a critical role in determining the distributional dynamics of the model. It asserts that for the steady state, (8), generated by the accumulation equation to be viable, the average allocation of time to leisure must exceed the critical fraction $\eta/(1+\eta)$.

Linearizing (7) around (8), the local dynamics in the neighborhood of the steady state are

$$\begin{pmatrix} \dot{K} \\ \dot{l} \end{pmatrix} = \begin{pmatrix} a_{11} & a_{12} \\ a_{21} & a_{22} \end{pmatrix} \begin{pmatrix} K - \widetilde{K} \\ l - \widetilde{l} \end{pmatrix}, \tag{10}$$

where the elements a_{ij} satisfy $a_{11}a_{22} - a_{12}a_{21} < 0$.[16] The stable adjustment paths for K and l are thus

$$K(t) = \widetilde{K} + (K_0 - \widetilde{K})e^{\mu t} \quad \text{and} \tag{11a}$$

---

[15] Equation (8a) equates the marginal product of capital to the sum of the rate of time preference plus growth rate; (8b) is goods market equilibrium.

[16] The precise definitions of the elements a_{ij} are provided by Turnovsky and García-Peñalosa (2008).

$$l(t) = \tilde{l} + \frac{a_{21}}{\mu - a_{22}}\left(K(t) - \tilde{K}\right) = \frac{\mu - a_{11}}{a_{12}}\left(K(t) - \tilde{K}\right). \tag{11b}$$

For plausible parameter values, $l(t)$ can be shown to increase with $K(t)$, and, indeed, the evolution of aggregate leisure over time is an essential determinant of the time path of wealth inequality and, hence, of income inequality. Thus, suppose the economy is subject to an expansionary structural shock ($K_0 < \tilde{K}$). This will lead to an initial jump in average leisure such that $l(0) < \tilde{l}$; thereafter, leisure will increase monotonically during the transition.

10.2.4 The Evolution of Relative Wealth

The next step is to derive the evolution of agent i's relative stock of capital, k_i. This is done by combining (4) with the corresponding aggregate equation and the optimality conditions (5a) and (5b). Following these steps, the evolution of agent i's relative capital stock is described by

$$\dot{k}_i(t) = \frac{w(K, l)}{K}\left[1 - v_i l\left(\frac{\eta + 1}{\eta}\right) - \left(1 - l\left(\frac{\eta + 1}{\eta}\right)\right)k_i\right]. \tag{12}$$

The aggregate variables, K, l evolving in accordance with (11a, 11b), will induce the dynamics in $k_i(t)$. To solve for the time path of $k_i(t)$, note that agent i's steady-state share of capital, $\tilde{k}_i$, is[17]

$$1 - v_i \tilde{l}\left(\frac{\eta + 1}{\eta}\right) - \left(1 - \tilde{l}\left(\frac{\eta + 1}{\eta}\right)\right)\tilde{k}_i = 0 \text{ for each } i \tag{13}$$

or, equivalently,

$$\tilde{l}_i - \tilde{l} = \left(\tilde{l} - \frac{\eta}{1 + \eta}\right)(\tilde{k}_i - 1) \text{ for each } i \tag{14}$$

Recalling (9), this condition implies a positive relationship between the agent's steady-state relative capital stock (wealth) and leisure. The intuition is that because wealthier agents have a lower marginal utility of wealth, they work less and enjoy more leisure.[18] This condition is a critical determinant of the distributions of wealth and income and explains why the evolution of

---

[17] Equation (13) also determines the constant v_i.
[18] This relationship is supported by empirical evidence from a range of sources; see, for example, Algan, Cheron, Hairault, and Langot (2003), Cheng and French (2000), Coronado and Perozek (2003), and Holtz-Eakin, Joulfaian, and Rosen (1993).

the aggregate quantities such as K and l is unaffected by distributional aspects. There are two key factors contributing to this: (1) the linearity of the agent's labor supply as a function of his relative capital, and (2) the fact that the sensitivity of labor supply to relative capital is common to all agents and depends upon aggregate economy-wide leisure. As a consequence, aggregate labor supply depends only on the aggregate amount of capital but not on its distribution across agents.[19]

In solving for the relative capital stock of agent i, k_i, a bounded solution is needed to rule out degenerate distributions of wealth. Linearizing (12) around the steady state $\tilde{K}$, $\tilde{l}$, $\tilde{k}_i$, Turnovsky and García-Peñalosa show that the bounded solution is

$$k_i(t) - 1 = \theta(t)(\tilde{k}_i - 1) = \frac{\theta(t)}{\theta(0)}(k_{i,0} - 1), \tag{15}$$

where

$$\theta(t) \equiv 1 + \left(\frac{1}{\beta - \mu}\right) \frac{AF_L(\tilde{K}, \tilde{L})}{\tilde{K}} \left(1 - \frac{l(t)}{\tilde{l}}\right) \tag{16}$$

and $k_{i,0}$ is given from the initial distribution of capital endowments.

Given the time path of the aggregate economy and the distribution of initial capital endowments, (15) and (16) determine the evolution of agent i's relative capital stock. The critical determinant of this evolution is the magnitude of $\theta(t)$, which varies over time but is common to all individuals. From (15), $\dot{k}_i(t)/(k_i(t) - 1) = \dot{\theta}(t)/\theta(t)$, so that the rates of accumulation for all agents relative to their respective relative wealth positions, $[k_i(t) - 1]$, are identical. From (16), this depends upon $l(t)/\tilde{l}$, which in turn depends upon the evolution of the aggregate capital stock, $K(t) - \tilde{K}$. Thus, if the economy is expanding so that $\dot{\theta}(t) < 0$, the relative wealth of agents having above-average wealth declines, while that of the relative poor increases and wealth inequality declines.

An important implication of (15) and (16) is that wealth inequality is generated only while leisure (labor supply) is in transition. This is a reflection of the fact that savings and wealth accumulation take time. If, following some structural change, leisure jumps instantaneously to its new steady state, relative capital stocks remain unchanged at their original pre-shock levels, since $\theta(t) = \theta(0) = 1$ and (15) implies $k_i(t) = k_{i,0}$. The extent to which this

---

[19] As Turnovsky and García-Peñalosa (2008) show, this characteristic holds for any utility function that is homogeneous of degree, b say, in consumption and leisure.

might occur depends upon the aggregate structural characteristics, as reflected in the elements a_{ij}, and the source of the underlying shock.

10.2.4.1 Wealth Inequality

Because of the linearity of (15), these equations can be aggregated over all individuals, thereby transforming them into corresponding expressions for the coefficient of variation of the distribution of capital, namely

$$\sigma_k(t) = \theta(t)\tilde{\sigma}_k = \frac{\theta(t)}{\theta(0)}\sigma_{k,0}. \tag{15'}$$

From (15'), at any point of time, wealth inequality is some multiple (either >1 or <1) of the initial endowment inequality. These observations imply the following:[20]

Proposition 1 (Relative wealth dynamics)
  (1) The long-run distribution of wealth converges to a nondegenerate steady-state distribution that is proportional to the initial distribution.
  (2) If the economy experiences an expansion (contraction) in its aggregate capital stock, that is, $K_0 < \tilde{K}$ ($K_0 > \tilde{K}$), then wealth inequality will decrease (increase) during transition, and the long-run distribution of wealth will be less (more) unequal than the initial distribution.

10.2.4.2 Income Inequality

To determine the degree of income inequality, consider the income of individual i, $Y_i = r(K, L)K_i + w(K, L)(1 - l_i)$, relative to the average economy-wide income level, $Y = r(K, L)K + w(K, L)(1 - l)$. Dividing the former by the latter, and recalling the factor returns, (2), the relative income of individual i, $y_i(t) \equiv Y_i(t)/Y(t)$, is

$$y_i(t) - 1 = s(t)(k_i(t) - 1) + (1 - s(t))\frac{l(t)}{1 - l(t)}(1 - v_i), \tag{17}$$

where $s(t) \equiv F_K K/Y$ denotes the capital share of output. The relative income of agent i has two components – relative capital income and relative labor

---

[20] In stating this proposition, I am assuming that $\theta(t) > 0$. This is certainly so for an expansion in the capital stock, when $\theta(t) > 1$. In the case of a contraction, $1 > \theta(t) > 0$ will almost certainly apply, except under extremely implausible circumstances.

income. Using (13), (17) can be expressed in a form analogous to (15), namely as a ratio of the agent's relative capital

$$y_i(t) - 1 = \varphi(t)(k_i(t) - 1), \tag{18}$$

where

$$\varphi(t) \equiv 1 - (1 - s(t))\left[1 + \frac{l(t)}{1 - l(t)}\left(1 - \frac{1}{\tilde{l}}\frac{\eta}{1 + \eta}\right)\frac{1}{\theta(t)}\right]. \tag{19}$$

Again, because of the linearity of (18) in $(k_i(t) - 1)$, this relationship between relative income and relative capital can be expressed in terms of their respective coefficients of variation

$$\sigma_y(t) = |\varphi(t)|\sigma_k(t), \tag{18'}$$

which in steady state becomes

$$\tilde{\sigma}_y = |\tilde{\varphi}|\tilde{\sigma}_k, \tag{18''}$$

where

$$\tilde{\varphi} = \lim_{t \to \infty} \varphi(t) = 1 - \frac{1}{1 + \eta}\left(\frac{1 - \tilde{s}}{1 - \tilde{l}}\right) = 1 - \frac{1}{1 + \eta}\frac{F_L(\tilde{K}, \tilde{L})}{F(\tilde{K}, \tilde{L})}. \tag{20}$$

The potential for $\tilde{\varphi}$ to be negative complicates the relationship between the agent's relative wealth, relative income, and the corresponding inequality measures. From (20) and (9), if either

$$\frac{\eta + \tilde{s}}{1 + \eta} > \tilde{l} > \frac{\eta}{1 + \eta}$$

or

$$\frac{2(1 + \eta) - (1 - \tilde{s})}{2(1 + \eta)} > \tilde{l} > \frac{\eta + \tilde{s}}{1 + \eta} > \frac{\eta}{1 + \eta},$$

then $1 > |\tilde{\varphi}|$, implying that income inequality is less than wealth inequality. In the first case, agents with above-average long-run wealth will also have above-average income, whereas in the second case, their reduced labor supply (increased leisure) will cause relatively wealthy individuals to have relatively low incomes. Moreover, if leisure is increased further to $\tilde{l} > [2(1 + \eta) - (1 - \tilde{s})][2(1 + \eta)]^{-1}$, income inequality will in fact exceed wealth inequality. Of these three scenarios, the first is the most plausible and emerges from the numerical simulations conducted by Turnovsky and García-Peñalosa (2008). From (20),

$$\frac{\tilde{\sigma}_y}{\tilde{\sigma}_{y,0}} = \frac{\tilde{\varphi}}{\tilde{\varphi}_0}\frac{\tilde{\sigma}_k}{\sigma_{k,0}} = \left(\frac{1 - \left(1/(1+\eta)\right)\left(F_L(\tilde{K}/\tilde{L})/F(\tilde{K}/\tilde{L})\right)}{1 - \left(1/(1+\eta)\right)\left(F_L(\tilde{K}_0/\tilde{L}_0)/F(\tilde{K}_0/\tilde{L}_0)\right)}\right)\frac{\tilde{\sigma}_k}{\sigma_{k,0}}. \quad (20')$$

Whether long-run income inequality following a structural change is greater than or less than initial income inequality depends on the long-run change in wealth inequality, $\tilde{\sigma}_k/\sigma_{k,0}$, and the change in factor returns, $\tilde{\varphi}/\tilde{\varphi}_0$. These two effects may or may not operate in the same direction.

From (17), the time path for the dynamics of relative income is

$$\frac{dy_i(t)}{dt} = s(t)\frac{dk_i(t)}{dt} + (1 - s(t))\frac{1 - v_i}{(1 - l(t))^2}\frac{dl(t)}{dt}$$

$$+ \left(k_i(t) - 1 + (v_i - 1)\frac{l(t)}{1 - l(t)}\right)\frac{ds(t)}{dt}. \quad (21)$$

This equation indicates how the evolution of the relative income of agent i depends upon two factors: the evolution of relative capital income, reflected in the first term in (21), and that of relative labor income. The latter can be expressed as a function of the evolution of aggregate leisure (i.e., labor supply) and of the relative rewards to capital and labor, as reflected by the capital share, $s(t)$.

It is useful to first examine a Cobb-Douglas production function. In this case, the capital share remains constant, and income inequality increases or decreases depending on whether the economy converges to the steady state from below or from above. Consider an economy that starts below its steady state, so that $K_0 < \tilde{K}$. Then $l(0) < \tilde{l}$ and leisure is rising, $dl/dt > 0$, while wealth inequality is decreasing. For an agent with above-average wealth, $(k_i - 1) > 0$, so that $dk_i/dt < 0$ and $v_i > 1$, implying that the first two terms in (21) are negative so that the relative income of the agent is decreasing during the transition. The opposite would apply for an agent having below-average wealth, $(k_i - 1) < 0$, and, hence, income inequality will decline during the transition to the steady state from below. For an economy that starts above the steady state, that is, for $K_0 > \tilde{K}$, then $l(0) > \tilde{l}$, and, together with the fact that wealth inequality is increasing (see Proposition 1), income inequality will be rising during the transition.

The evolution of factor shares may reinforce or offset these effects. For an economy that converges from below, a falling capital share, $ds/dt < 0$, reinforces the impact of the distribution of wealth, and income inequality will decline over time. If the capital share rises over time, $ds/dt > 0$, the two effects will be offsetting. If the latter effect dominates, the distribution of income becomes less equal over time. To summarize:

Proposition 2 (Relative income dynamics)
The evolution of income inequality for an economy that converges to its steady state from below, that is, $K_0 < \widetilde{K}$, (from above, $K_0 > \widetilde{K}$) is driven by three factors:

(1) decreasing (increasing) wealth inequality, which tends to reduce (raise) income inequality;
(2) increasing (decreasing) leisure, which tends to increase (decrease) the relative labor income of the capital-poor and, hence, reduce (raise) income inequality; and
(3) the change in the share of capital in income, which depends both on whether the economy is converging from below or above, and on the elasticity of substitution in production.

If the share of capital is constant, income inequality will decrease (increase) during the transition to the steady state from below (above).

10.3 Path-Dependence and the Dynamics of Inequality

Turnovsky and García-Peñalosa (2008) supplement their formal analysis with numerical simulations based on the specific parameterization of a constant elasticity utility function and a constant elasticity of substitution (CES) production function. Among the shocks they consider is a permanent productivity increase, which they specify as a discrete change that is completed instantaneously. While this assumption is conventional, its plausibility is questionable. In practice, most productivity increases occur over time, as economies gradually adopt known technologies. In this section, I compare the implications of the conventional specification with the alternative, where the productivity increase takes place gradually over time. This issue has been addressed recently by Atolia, Chatterjee, and Turnovsky (2012) with quite dramatic findings.

To examine this issue, Atolia et al. (2012) modify the model of Section 10.2 by assuming that the level of productivity, $A(t)$, increases gradually from its initial level, A_0, to its enhanced long-run level, $\widetilde{A}$, (both known to the firm) in accordance with

$$A(t) = \widetilde{A} + (A_0 - \widetilde{A})e^{-\kappa t}, \tag{22}$$

where κ defines the time path followed by the increase in productivity. The conventional approach, which specifies the increase as a discrete jump, is obtained by letting $\kappa \to \infty$.

The aggregate equilibrium now comprises the dynamic system (7a)–(7c), augmented to include (22). The steady-state equilibrium remains as specified by (8) and, since this is independent of κ, the long-run responses of aggregate variables to an increase in productivity are independent of the time path followed by the latter. However, their transitional responses are likely to be significantly affected, as the numerical experiments illustrate.

In the case of wealth and income inequality, however, the differences are striking in that the time path of the productivity increase affects not only their transitional time paths but also their long-run equilibrium values. In other words, inequality is subject to hysteresis, that is, long-run inequality will depend upon the nature of the time path generating the productivity increase. This can be seen when one solves the dynamic equation for the relative capital stock, which now reflects the adjustment of A as well as K and l.

Following the previous solution procedure, the bounded solution for $k_i(t)$ remains as expressed by (15) but with (16) modified to

$$\theta(t) \equiv \left[1 + \frac{\widetilde{A}F_L}{\widetilde{K}} \int_t^\infty \left(1 - \frac{l(\tau)}{\widetilde{l}} \right) e^{-\beta(\tau - t)} d\tau \right]. \tag{16'}$$

The crucial difference between this expression and the previous one lies in the form of the productivity shock $A(t)$, which is reflected in the time path of $l(\tau)$ and, hence, in $\theta(t)$. If the productivity increase is completed instantaneously, then $l(\tau) - \widetilde{l} = (l(0) - \widetilde{l})e^{\mu \tau}$ and (16') reduces to (16). In that case, only $l(t)/\widetilde{l}$ is relevant in determining current wealth inequality relative to its long-run level. But when the productivity increase occurs gradually over time, the entire time path of $A(t)$, reflected in the entire future time path of $l(\tau)/\widetilde{l}$, must be taken into account. If, during the transition, $l(\tau) < \widetilde{l}$ always so that leisure approaches its steady state from below, then $\theta(t) < 1$ and wealth inequality declines over time. But that need not always be the case.

Atolia et al. (2012) compare the aggregate and distributional consequences of a 50 percent increase in productivity, using the parameters employed by Turnovsky and García-Peñalosa (2008), summarized in Table 10.1.

Table 10.1 *Basic model and benchmark parameters*

Production function	$Y = A(\alpha K^{-\rho} + (1 - \alpha)L^{-\rho})^{-1/\rho}$
Utility function	$U = (1/\gamma)(Cl^\eta)^\gamma$
Basic parameters	$A = 1,$
	$\alpha = 0.4$
	$\rho = 1/3, 0, -0.2 \ (\varepsilon = 0.75, 1, 1.25)$
	$\beta = 0.04$
	$\gamma = -1.5$
	$n = 0.015$
Endogenous labor supply elasticity	$\eta = 1.75$

Source: Adapted from Turnovsky and García-Peñalosa (2008), p. 1417

The productivity increase takes effect in one of two alternative ways: (i) as an immediate unanticipated jump in productivity from 1 to 1.5, as specified by Turnovsky and García-Peñalosa (2008), and (ii) as a gradual increase over time at the rate of 10 percent per period (year).[21] As a result, the instant productivity starts to increase, the subsequent increases in productivity are fully anticipated along the transition path.

Figure 10.1 depicts the transition paths for the aggregate variables, K and l, corresponding to these two specifications of the productivity increase. To demonstrate robustness, paths are depicted for three values of the elasticity of substitution in production, ε. Although the long-run responses of leisure (labor supply), capital, and output are identical for both specifications of the productivity increase, their transitional paths are dramatically different. In all cases, a discrete productivity increase causes leisure to *decline* instantaneously (labor supply to increase), after which it immediately reverses and increases monotonically to its new steady-state level, which lies above or below its original pre-shock level, depending upon whether ε is greater or less than one. By contrast, a gradual productivity increase causes an immediate *increase* in leisure, which is then quickly reversed, causing leisure to overshoot its long-run equilibrium during the subsequent decline to the steady state.

Similar differences are displayed in the initial phases of the transitional path for capital. While a discrete productivity increase leads to a gradual

---

[21] In the latter case, the enhanced productivity level is achieved asymptotically. Atolia et al. (2012) note that one can easily adjust (22) so that the new equilibrium level of technology is reached in finite time.

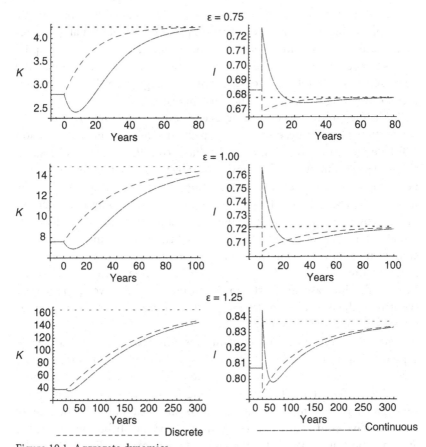

Figure 10.1 Aggregate dynamics
Source: Adapted from Atolia et al. (2012), p. 339

monotonic accumulation of capital to the new steady state, a continuous increase actually leads to a short-run *decumulation*, before capital accumulation begins. This gives the time path of the capital stock a U-shaped trajectory, the depth of which increases as ε declines. These differences in the adjustments of leisure (labor supply) and capital translate directly into differences in the dynamic adjustment of output.

The explanation for the contrasting dynamic responses of the aggregate economy for the two types of productivity change lies in the information being revealed to the agent on impact of the shock, relative to the time path of the higher productive capacity following the long-run realization of the shock. For a one-time discrete increase in A, the enhanced long-run productivity is fully realized instantaneously, and immediately raises the marginal product of both labor and capital. Consequently, labor supply immediately increases and the enhanced productivity of capital generates immediate incentives for capital accumulation, and the stock of capital begins to rise. Output increases instantaneously and can accommodate the increase in consumption associated with the higher level of permanent income resulting from the productivity increase.

But if the productivity increase occurs only gradually, the enhanced productive capacity necessary to support the increase in consumption will take effect only over time. In the short run, the long-run change in the level of productivity is fully anticipated by the agent, thereby increasing permanent income and raising aggregate current consumption. But the increase in productive capacity is immediately reflected only as an increase in its growth rate. Thus, since the instantaneous *level* of productivity remains unchanged, current output cannot rise and the increase in consumption resulting from the anticipation of higher future income is achieved through reduced investment and a decline of the capital stock. In fact, the increase in short-run consumption and lower productivity (relative to the long run) causes the agent to increase leisure, which causes output to also decline on impact.

Figure 10.2 illustrates the dynamic responses of the distributions of capital (wealth) and income to the two specifications of the productivity increase, corresponding to the three values of the elasticity of substitution, $\varepsilon = 0.75, \quad 1.00, \quad 1.25$. The most striking feature of these distributional time paths is that not only do the two specifications of productivity increase have contrasting effects on the short-run distributions of capital and income but, contrary to the aggregate economy in Figure 10.1, the long-run effects are also dramatically different. In other words, while the aggregate economy reaches identical steady states, irrespective of whether the productivity change occurs discretely or gradually, the distributions do not. This reflects the fact that the long-run distributions of wealth and income are *path dependent*, depending critically on the underlying process through which the steady-state equilibrium is attained and how this affects the time path of leisure, $l(t)$.

The path-dependence of the consequences of a structural change on distributions provides an important insight into growth–inequality dynamics, with wide-ranging ramifications. I have already noted that this implies that the model can admit a diverse set of distributional equilibria for countries having similar levels of aggregate development (per capita income), in accordance with empirical evidence. Path-' dependence is, in fact, a generic characteristic that has important

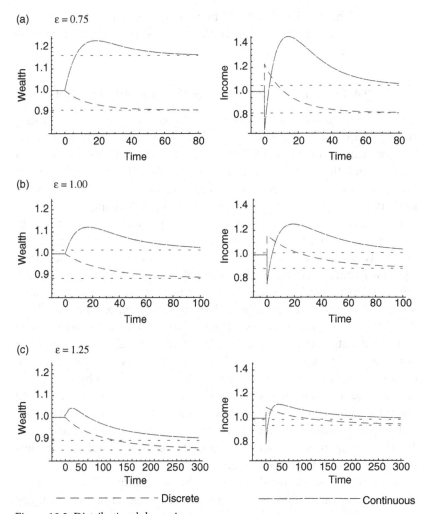

Figure 10.2 Distributional dynamics
Source: Adapted from Atolia et al. (2012), p. 340

consequences for policy. For example, it is a relevant issue in foreign aid, which, typically, is granted over time. This analysis therefore suggests that the time path over which such aid is dispensed will have long-run distributional consequences, which presumably should be taken into consideration. But path-dependence also applies to domestic policy issues as well. Raising a distortionary tax rate from, say, 20 percent to 25 percent will have long-run distributional consequences, depending upon whether the increase takes place instantaneously or is phased in over time.

10.4 Fiscal Policy and the Growth–Inequality Tradeoff

The role of fiscal policy as a source of stimulus to economic performance and growth in particular is, of course, well known. The associated distributional consequences and the tradeoffs that these may entail are less familiar, but they can be conveniently examined by a straightforward extension of the model. Three mechanisms must be considered to understand the distributional implications of a fiscal policy change.

First, as was the case for the increase in productivity considered in Sections 10.2 and 10.3, a fiscal shock will, in general, cause a change in the steady-state capital stock. During the transition to the new steady state, agents with different initial wealth levels will accumulate capital at different rates, so that wealth inequality may either increase or decrease over time. Second, changes in taxes induce labor supply responses that will have distributional implications. As before, I derive a negative relationship between agents' relative wealth (capital) and their relative allocation of time between work and leisure. Third, the dynamics of the response of income inequality (both before tax and after tax) are driven by two effects: the initial jump in leisure – which will affect relative labor incomes – and the subsequent continuous changes in the distributions of capital and factor prices that occur during the transition to the new steady state. These two responses may move in opposite directions, implying nonmonotonic responses to policy changes.

To illustrate these channels, consider the comparative effects of raising alternative tax rates to finance a given increase in government consumption spending. In addition to setting out the mechanism, I shall present numerical simulations. In all cases, the income distribution effects dominate the wealth accumulation effects, which are in general very weak and entail only minor changes in the distribution of wealth.

10.4.1 Modifications to the Basic Model

With the introduction of a utility-enhancing government consumption good, the agent's utility maximization problem is now

$$\max \int_0^\infty \frac{1}{\gamma} \left(C_i(t) l_i^\eta G^\nu \right)^\gamma e^{-\beta t} dt, \tag{23}$$

where ν measures the relative importance of public consumption in private utility. The agent's capital accumulation constraint is

$$\dot{K}_i(t) = [(1 - \tau_k) r(t) - \delta] K_i(t) + (1 - \tau_w) w(t)(1 - l_i(t))$$
$$-(1 + \tau_c) C_i(t) + T_i, \tag{24}$$

where τ_k, τ_w, τ_c, and T_i are, respectively, the tax rates on capital income, labor income, consumption, and lump-sum transfers that the agent takes as given. For simplicity, we abstract from population growth but allow capital to depreciate at a constant rate, δ. With production conditions remaining as in Section 10.3, the equilibrium structure remains essentially as in Section 10.2.

Assume that the government sets its expenditure and transfers as constant fractions of aggregate output, $G = gY(t)$, $T = \tau Y(t)$, so that g and τ specify fiscal policy along with the tax rates. Assume also that the government maintains a balanced budget, expressed as

$$\tau_k r(K, L) K + \tau_w w(K, L)(1 - l) + \tau_c C = G + T = (g + \tau) F(K, L). \tag{25}$$

Assuming that τ_w, τ_k, τ_c, and g are fixed, then as economic activity and the tax/expenditure base is changing along the transitional path, the rate of lump-sum transfers must be continuously adjusted to maintain budget balance. In order to abstract from any direct distributional effects arising from lump-sum transfers (which are arbitrary), assume $T_i(t)/T(t) = K_i(t)/K(t)$, which ensures that $\int_0^N T_i di = (T/K) \int_0^N K_i di = T$, consistent with the government budget constraint. While this assumption is restrictive in that it does not capture the major redistributive impact of direct transfers, it has the analytical advantage of allowing us to focus on the distributive impact of distortionary taxes.

Following the procedures set out in Section 10.2, the aggregate dynamics are of precisely the same form, as summarized in (7) and (8). The aggregate dynamics remain independent of the distributional characteristics, and the only difference is that the elements, a_{ij}, of the linearized transitional matrix will incorporate both the direct and the indirect effects of the distortionary tax rates (García-Peñalosa and Turnovsky, 2011). Similarly, the dynamics of the relative capital stock are determined by (15) and (16), again modified by the impact of the distortionary tax rates on $\theta(t)$.

A key aspect of income taxes is their direct redistributive effect, which differs for before-tax and after-tax income distributions. Defining the relative before-tax income of individual i as in Section 10.2, after-tax income is[22]

$$y_i^a = \frac{rK_i(1 - \tau_k) + w(1 - l_i)(1 - \tau_w)}{rK(1 - \tau_k) + w(1 - l)(1 - \tau_w)}. \tag{26}$$

The before-tax relative income of agent i remains as expressed by (19) and (20), while after-tax relative income is

$$y_i^a(t) - 1 = \psi(t)\Big(k_i(t) - 1\Big), \tag{27}$$

where

$$\psi(t) \equiv \varphi(t) + \frac{s(t)(\tau_w - \tau_k)}{s(t)(1 - \tau_k) + (1 - s(t))(1 - \tau_w)}\Big(1 - \varphi(t)\Big). \tag{28}$$

As already noted, the expression for before-tax income inequality, $\varphi(t)$, has two components, the share of capital income, $s(t)$, and relative labor income, reflected in the second term of 19, which captures the fact that less-wealthy agents supply more labor. In the case of after-tax relative income, both income tax rates, τ_k and τ_w, exert two effects on the after-tax income distribution. First, by influencing $\varphi(t)$, they influence *gross* factor returns and therefore the before-tax distribution of income. But, in addition, they have direct redistributive effects that are captured by the second term on the right-hand side of (28). Post-tax income inequality will be less than pre-tax income inequality if and only if $\tau_w < \tau_k$. In contrast, the redistributive effects of a consumption tax on post-tax inequality are only indirect and operate to the extent that $\tau_k \neq \tau_w$.

Following the procedures set out in Section 10.2, indexes of inequality can be summarized as

$$\sigma_k(t) = \theta(t)\tilde{\sigma}_k = \frac{\theta(t)}{\theta(0)}\sigma_{k,0}, \tag{15'}$$

$$\dot{\sigma}_y(t) = |\varphi(t)|\sigma_k(t), \text{ and} \tag{18'}$$

---

[22] Note that the after-tax income measure ignores the direct distributional impacts of lump-sum transfers, which are arbitrary.

$$\sigma_y^a(t) = |\psi(t)|\sigma_k(t). \tag{27'}$$

10.4.2 Steady-State Effects of Fiscal Policy: Some Analytical Characteristics

To illustrate the long-run effects of different fiscal policies on the distributions of wealth and income, I compare alternative modes of financing a specified increase in government consumption spending. The changes in tax rates required to finance the increase in government expenditure are determined by the government budget constraint (25):

$$\tau_k s + \tau_w(1 - \tilde{s}) + \tau_c C/F = g + \tau. \tag{25'}$$

To highlight the mechanism, in all cases I assume that the economy starts from an initial equilibrium in which government consumption expenditure is fully financed by lump-sum transfers, so that $g_0 + \tau_0 = 0$ in (25'), and that initial distortionary tax rates are all zero, that is, $\tau_c = \tau_w = \tau_k = 0$.

10.4.2.1 An Increase in g Is Financed by a Reduction in Transfers

Starting from $\tau_c = \tau_w = \tau_k = 0$ implies $d\tau = -dg$. It is then straightforward to show that, in this case, the increase in g proportionately raises the long-run capital stock, labor supply, and therefore output, leaving factor shares unaffected.

The increase in capital, in conjunction with condition (9), immediately implies that an increase in government expenditure reduces long-run wealth inequality, $\tilde{\sigma}_k$. As discussed in Section 10.2, pre-tax income inequality is given by $\tilde{\sigma}_y = \tilde{\varphi}\tilde{\sigma}_k$, the response of which depends upon both $\tilde{\sigma}_k$ and $\tilde{\varphi}$. Recalling the definition of $\tilde{\varphi}$ given by (19), with factor shares, $\tilde{s}$, remaining unchanged, and with the expansion in government spending increasing labor supply (reducing $\tilde{l}$), this causes an offsetting increase in $\tilde{\varphi}$. With respect to after-tax income inequality, $\tilde{\sigma}_y^a$, (28) implies that g does not have direct redistributive effects, so that its impact on $\tilde{\psi}$ operates entirely through $\tilde{\varphi}$. That is, the effect on pre-tax and post-tax income distributions is the same and they increase or decrease depending upon which effect dominates.

10.4.2.2 An Increase in g Is Financed by a Tax Increase

In the case of distortionary tax financing, assume that the corresponding tax rate is set such that it fully finances the long-run change in government expenditure. Thus, again starting from $\tau_c = \tau_w = \tau_k = 0$, the corresponding required changes in the three tax rates are, respectively,

$$d\tau_c = (\widetilde{F}/\widetilde{C})dg, \quad d\tau_w = [1/(1-\tilde{s})]dg, \quad d\tau_k = (1/\tilde{s}^{\cdot})dg. \qquad (29)$$

This requires that, during the transition, residual financing using lump-sum taxes must also be employed to ensure that the budget remains balanced at all times.

In all three cases, the expansionary effect of the increased government expenditure is offset by the contractionary effect of the higher distortionary tax rate. In the case of consumption tax financing, starting from $\tau_c = \tau_w = \tau_k = 0$, the two effects are exactly offsetting, so the net aggregate and distributional effects are zero.

When the expansion is financed by a tax on wage income, the distortionary tax effect dominates the direct expenditure effect. As a result, aggregate capital, labor, and output all fall proportionately. An increase in g financed by a tax on capital income raises the long-run marginal physical product of capital, implying that it reduces the capital–labor ratio. Although capital declines unambiguously, labor will decline only if the elasticity of substitution in production, ε, is sufficiently large.[23] While output also declines, the net effect on the factor shares depends upon the sign of $(\varepsilon - 1)$.

In contrast to financing by reducing transfers, an increase in either τ_w or τ_k decreases the long-run capital stock, resulting in an increase in wealth inequality. With a wage income tax, $\widetilde{\varphi}$ also declines, thus offsetting the wealth effect. In effect, a higher tax on labor makes the fiscal system less progressive, the reason being that labor income is less unequally distributed than capital income. As a result, the impact of the policy on $\widetilde{\psi}$ combines the direct effect that tends to reduce post-tax inequality and the indirect effect stemming from the change in ϕ, so that post-tax inequality may increase or decrease.

The impact of τ_k on $\widetilde{\phi}$ is more complex since it involves three effects. First, during the transition to the new steady state with a lower capital stock, the distribution of wealth will become more dispersed. Second, ϕ falls or increases depending on whether the new steady state generates a lower $\widetilde{l}$. Third, the reduction in the capital–labor ratio implies a change in the capital

---

[23] For example, $\varepsilon > \tilde{s}$ is a weak condition that ensures employment declines.

share, $\tilde{s}$, the impact of which depends on whether ε is greater or less than one. In the case of the Cobb-Douglas production function, this effect is zero, and since $\partial \tilde{L}/\partial \tau_k < 0$, then $\tilde{\varphi}$ also falls; in this case, the direct redistributive effect of the capital income tax reinforces the pre-tax income inequality effect and post-tax income inequality falls relative to wealth inequality.

10.4.3 Numerical Simulations

To obtain further insights into the dynamics of wealth and income distribution, I report some numerical simulations. These are based on the functional forms and parameter values summarized in Table 10.2.

These are marginally different from those in Table 10.1, a reflection of differences in specification due to the introduction of the government sector; these are justified in more detail by García-Peñalosa and Turnovsky (2011). The main issue is the choice of tax rates. We use the effective tax rates on consumption, labor, and capital constructed by McDaniel (2007), following the methodology proposed by Mendoza, Razin, and Tesar (1994). The rates listed above are the US averages for the decade 1991–2000. A key feature is that, for the US economy, $\tau_k > \tau_w$, a characteristic that has held uniformly since 1953. Finally, setting the

Table 10.2 *Fiscal model and benchmark parameters*

Production function	$Y = AK^{\alpha}L^{1-\alpha}$
Utility function	$U = (1/\gamma)(C l^{\eta} G^{\nu})^{\gamma}$
Basic parameters	$A = 1.5$
	$\alpha = 0.36$
	$\beta = 0.04$
	$\gamma = -1.5$
	$n = 0.015$
	$\eta = 1.5$
	$\nu = 0.3$
	$\delta = 0.06$
Fiscal parameters	$\tau_k = 0.276$
	$\tau_w = 0.224$
	$\tau_c = 0.08$
	$g = 0.15$

Source: Adapted from García-Peñalosa and Turnovsky (2011), p. 1562

government consumption expenditure rate at $g = 0.15$ approximates the US experience in the 1990s.[24]

Row 1 of Table 10.3 reports the benchmark equilibrium for the chosen benchmark parameters, which yields a reasonable approximation to the US economy in terms of the basic ratios and other relevant economy-wide measures. Since $\tau_k > \tau_w$ in the benchmark economy, the fiscal system entails direct redistribution and the initial equilibrium implies standard deviations of pre-tax and post-tax income distributions of $\tilde{\sigma}_{y,0} = 0.165 > \tilde{\sigma}^a_{y,0} = 0.144$.[25]

Rows 2–4 of Table 10.3 report the effects of an increase in government expenditure from its base level of 15 percent of output by 5 percentage points to 20 percent of output, financed by a reduction in transfers (i.e., a lump-sum tax), an increase in the wage income tax, and an increase in the capital income tax, respectively. Lump-sum tax financing entails an increase in output, as government expenditure encourages private consumption, leading to an increase in labor supply and capital stock, while the distortions created by capital or wage income taxes result in reduced output and less capital. These results are qualitatively identical to the theoretical results discussed in Section 10.4.2.

The distributional effects of the three modes of financing contrast sharply. In all cases, the long-run changes in wealth inequality are small, reflecting the fact that most of the adjustment in L occurs instantaneously. As a result, the changes in income distribution are dominated by the relative income effects, $\tilde{\varphi}$ and $\tilde{\psi}$. Thus, while lump-sum taxation results in a small reduction in wealth inequality, it leads to substantial increases in pre-tax and post-tax income inequality of around 25 percent and 29 percent, respectively. These effects on inequality are particularly large; although the lump-sum tax (by construction) has no direct distributive effect, the increase in government expenditure results in a sharp increase in labor supply, which in turn makes the distribution of income more dispersed. For labor tax finance, the contractionary effect of the tax dominates the expenditure effect, which results in lower labor supply that reduces pre-tax inequality by over 14 percent. At the same time, the redistributive effect makes the tax structure more regressive. This effect dominates, and post-tax income inequality rises. The opposite occurs with a capital income tax.

---

[24] García-Peñalosa and Turnovsky (2011) also choose tax rates more representative of a "European" economy. The key difference is that $\tau_w > \tau_k$, which has an important bearing on the relative size of pre-tax and post-tax income inequality.

[25] Note that we normalize the initial given distribution of capital by $\sigma_{k,0} = 1$.

Table 10.3 *Increase in government expenditure (US economy) (increase in g by 5 percentage points from 0.15 to 0.20)*

	$\tilde{L}$	$\tilde{K}$	$\tilde{Y}$	σ_k	σ_y	$\sigma_{y,a}$
Base $\tau_k = 0.276$, $\tau_w = 0.224$, $\tau_c = 0.08$, $\tau = 0.148$	0.307	2.580	0.990	1.000	0.165	0.144
Lump-sum tax finance $\tau = 0.094$	0.323 (+5.27 %)	2.716 (+5.27 %)	1.042 (+5.27 %)	0.995 (−0.50 %)	0.206 (+24.8 %)	0.186 (+29.1 %)
Wage income tax finance $\tau_w = 0.308$	0.298 (−2.82 %)	2.509 (−2.82 %)	0.962 (−2.82 %)	1.0021 (+0.21 %)	0.141 (−14.3 %)	0.156 (+7.90 %)
Capital income tax finance $\tau_k = 0.419$	0.312 (+1.63 %)	2.509 (−27.8 %)	0.962 (−9.90 %)	1.0395 (+3.95 %)	0.188 (+14.0 %)	0.102 (−29.5 %)

Source: Adapted from García-Peñalosa and Turnovsky (2011), p. 1564

The increase in labor supply, together with the more than proportionate reduction in the capital stock, reduce wages, leading to a more dispersed distribution of pre-tax income. This is nevertheless dominated by the increased progressivity of the tax system resulting from the redistribution, leading to a reduction in after-tax inequality of 29.5 percent.

Figure 10.3 plots the time paths of the economy in response to the policy changes. The left-side panels illustrate the aggregate magnitudes, capital, labor, and income, while the right-side panels represent the distributions of wealth, pre-tax income, and post-tax income. For both the aggregate quantities and the distribution measures, the quantities are measured relative to their initial pre-shock, steady-state values.[26] Note that while the aggregate capital stock and its distribution evolve continuously from their initial values, labor supply, output, and both measures of income distribution undergo initial increases, arising from the initial increase in leisure. In fact, the bulk of the adjustment in labor supply occurs through its initial increase, leading to little change in wealth inequality, although the change is more pronounced in the case of capital income tax financing.

As an example, consider the impact of an increase in g financed by a wage income tax. Three effects are in operation. The first is due to the fact that the economy converges to a smaller capital stock, leading to an increase in wealth inequality, although, as just noted, this effect is small. The second is the effect on income distribution through the change in work hours. The reduction in labor supply implies that the distribution of labor incomes becomes more dispersed, and since there is negative correlation between individual capital and labor supply, this tends to reduce income inequality. Because of the initial increase in leisure, this occurs immediately and in the simulations is always sufficiently strong to offset the impact of a more unequal distribution of capital and pre-tax income inequality increases. Lastly, because wage income is more equally distributed than capital income, the direct effect of the tax is to increase post-tax inequality. Since the increase in the tax rate is large (τ_w goes from 22.4 percent to 30.8 percent), this effect is strong and results in a more unequal distribution of post-tax income than before the policy change.

Three further aspects stand out from this figure. The first is the sharply contrasting effects of τ_w and τ_k on the pre-tax and post-tax income distributions. Financing an increase in g with a wage tax results in a more equal distribution of pre-tax income but more unequal distributions

---

[26] The paths corresponding to the different quantities are shown in the third panel of Figure 10.3.

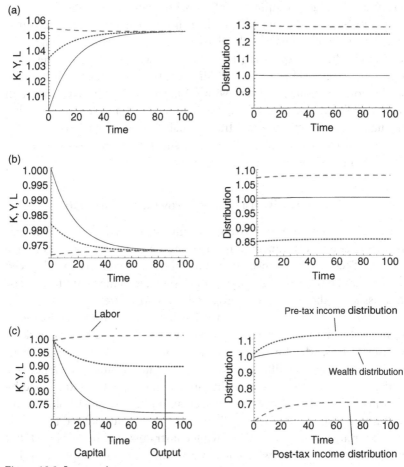

Figure 10.3 Increase in *g*
Source: Adapted from García-Peñalosa and Turnovsky (2011), p. 1566

of post-tax income. The opposite holds when the capital income tax is used. The second concerns the tradeoffs that exist between increases in output and reductions in inequality. Whereas lump-sum tax financing of the increase in expenditure raises long-run output by over 5 percent, it increases both inequality measures by well over 20 percent, while welfare inequality actually declines by over 15 percent. In contrast, capital income tax financing reduces post-tax inequality by 29.5 percent but reduces output by 9.9 percent. Wage income tax financing is a rather unattractive policy as it reduces output by 2.8 percent and raises post-tax income inequality by over 7 percent. Third, the primary change in income inequality occurs instantaneously, with relatively little adjustment over time. This reflects (1) the corresponding time path for labor supply, as a result of which there is little change in wealth inequality, and (2) the Cobb-Douglas production function, consistent with (28). The smaller initial increase in labor supply in the case of capital income tax financing implies that inequality is subject to more transitional dynamics. Nevertheless, the response of the distribution of wealth is small compared to the effect of changes in both labor supplies and factor prices.

10.5 Progressive Tax Rates, Growth, and Inequality

Most of the literature addressing the impact of taxes on growth and inequality adopts the conventional assumption of flat tax rates, as I have done in Section 10.4. Since, in reality, most tax systems in advanced economies exhibit some degree of progressivity, it is important to reassess these issues in the context of a progressive tax structure.

An important issue with progressive taxes is their interaction with agents' rate of time preference. Awareness of this issue dates back to Ramsey (1928), who formulated a model of stationary equilibrium with heterogeneous agents differentiated by their rates of time preference. He conjectured that in long-run equilibrium, all the capital would be held by the most patient household and the remaining (poor) households would consume at a subsistence level.[27] This idea was later formalized by Becker (1980) for an economy with borrowing constraints, and by Bewley (1982) in a model without borrowing constraints, where the consumption level of the impatient households is at zero.

In contrast, Sarte (1997), using a stationary Ramsey model, and Li and Sarte (2004), using an endogenous growth model with inelastic labor, showed that if the tax structure is progressive, the long-run distributions of capital and income will be nondegenerate. A progressive income tax breaks the link between the most patient household's preference rate and the return on capital, since each agent faces their own individual after-tax return. Hence, a unique nondegenerate distribution of income, in which households are ranked by their discount factors, is obtained. The most patient households are still the rich ones, but they do not own all the

---

[27] This idea actually predates Ramsey. See Becker (2006) for a detailed literature review including these early studies.

capital. Li and Sarte (2004) also show that the degree of progressivity yields a negative relationship between the growth rate and income inequality when labor supply is fixed.

To see the mechanism at work, we specify agent i's average tax rate by[28]

$$\tau_i \equiv \zeta(Y_i/Y)^\phi, \tag{30a}$$

where Y_i denotes individual i's gross income and Y is the economy-wide average level of income. If $\phi > 0$, this tax rate is an increasing function of the agent's relative income, $y_i \equiv Y_i/Y$, and increases at an increasing or decreasing rate according to whether ϕ is greater or less than one. The marginal tax rate for such a tax schedule is thus

$$\tau_i^m \equiv \frac{\partial(\tau_i Y_i)}{\partial Y_i} = (1+\phi)\zeta\left(\frac{Y_i}{Y}\right)^\phi = (1+\phi)\zeta(y_i)^\phi = (1+\phi)\tau_i, \tag{30b}$$

where ϕ represents the degree of progressivity and ζ determines the level of the tax schedule.[29] For $\phi = 0$, $\tau_i = \zeta$ for all individuals; in this case, the tax rate is flat and independent of the agent's relative income.

Li and Sarte (2004) assume that each agent has their own rate of time preference, β_i, but a common intertemporal elasticity of substitution, $(1-\gamma)^{-1}$. Assuming inelastic labor supply, the before-tax rate of return on capital, $\bar{r}$, is fixed. They show that, in steady state, the economy is on the balanced growth path in which all agents accumulate capital at the same constant rate

$$\tilde{\psi} = \frac{[1 - \tau_i^m(\tilde{y}_i)]\bar{r} - \beta_i}{1 - \gamma}. \tag{31}$$

With all agents experiencing a common long-run growth rate, (31) highlights the tradeoff between the agent's rate of time preference and long-run relative income. This equation implies:

(1) If the tax rate is progressive and all agents share a common rate of time preference, then for all I, that is, the steady-state distribution of income collapses to zero.

---

[28] This specification is a variant of that originally introduced by Guo and Lansing (1998). It imposes restrictions on the parameters ζ, ϕ to ensure that $0 \le \tau_i, \tau_i^m < 1$.

[29] Thus, ζ is the tax rate imposed on the economy-wide average level of income.

(2) If the tax rate is progressive, then for any pair of individuals i and j, if, then; that is, the more patient individual will have a higher income (both before tax and after tax).

(3) If the tax rate is uniform ($\phi = 0$) so that all agents face the same tax rate, then (1) cannot hold; the most patient individual will enjoy the highest growth rate and ultimately own all the capital.

Koyuncu and Turnovsky (2016) extend this approach in several directions. First, they focus on the more general case where labor is supplied elastically. This generalization is important since the adjustment of labor has been shown elsewhere to play a crucial role in determining the impact of structural changes on both growth and inequality, even in the absence of taxes. But it becomes an even more crucial part of this process in the presence of a progressive tax structure, with a potentially significant impact on work incentives. Moreover, the fact that an increase in the progressivity of the tax structure has an adverse effect on labor supply is well established empirically.[30] Second, Koyuncu and Turnovsky (2016) consider the entire dynamic adjustment path, highlighting how its response to structural changes is highly dependent upon the flexibility of labor supply, particularly in the short run. Lastly, their results highlight the divergent effects on the time paths of labor supply of different groups in response to policy shocks. This heterogeneity can provide useful insights to policy-makers who seek to use the tax structure to target the work effort of specific groups. This potentially important policy instrument is obscured if labor supply is fixed.

However, the introduction of a progressive tax structure introduces a major complication in that aggregate quantities and their distributions across individuals become simultaneously determined. Consequently, one can no longer employ the Gorman (1959) aggregation procedure – otherwise possible under uniform taxes – in which case a general analysis of transitional dynamics becomes intractable. The source of this problem is apparent from the individual's capital accumulation constraint, (4), which now becomes

$$\dot{K_i} = (1 - \zeta(Y_i/Y)^\phi)[rK_i + wK(1 - l_i)] - C_i. \tag{32}$$

---

[30] For example, Hausman (1981) using US data and Blomquist (1983) and Blomquist, Eklöf, and Newey (2001) using Swedish data find that higher progressivity reduces hours of work in their studies.

As long as $\phi > 0$, this relationship is nonlinear in individual quantities, complicating the aggregation process.

Koyuncu and Turnovsky (2016) are, however, able to characterize the steady state and, in particular, to establish that the ranking of wealth and income across agents obtained under inelastic labor supply extends to the case where labor is supplied endogenously. To explore further the dynamics of the inequality–growth relationship, they limit the number of agents with different rates of time preference to just two, which they label as "Poor" and "Rich." In this case, they can approximate the transitional dynamics explicitly and further characterize some of the steady-state responses. One of the potentially important insights for policy purposes is that their analysis highlights how both the base tax rate and its progressivity may play a role in determining the tradeoffs between before-tax and after-tax income as well as the equilibrium growth rate.

10.6 Heterogeneous Skills

A natural generalization of the benchmark model is to assume that agents are endowed with two sources of heterogeneity, namely their initial endowments of capital, $K_{i,0}$, and their (given) relative skill levels, a_i. Relative capital (wealth) is distributed across agents, as before – $k_i(t) \equiv K_i(t)/K(t)$ with mean 1, and with initial (given) dispersion $\sigma_{k,0}$. But now, in addition, relative skills across agents are also distributed with mean 1 and constant dispersion σ_a, with the previous model corresponding to $a_i \equiv 1$. The distributions of the endowments across agents, $k_{i,0}$, a_i, may or may not be correlated. But the extent to which they are certainly has distributional consequences.

Assuming that firms pay capital and labor according to their marginal physical products, then the return to capital remains as before but agents now receive differential wages according to their ability:

$$w_i(t) = w_i(K, L) = F_{L_i}(K, L) = a_i F_L(K, L). \tag{33}$$

The average wage rate is $w(t) \equiv w(K, L) = F_L(K, L)$ and the distribution of relative wage rates, $w_i(t)/w(t)$, is given, and reflects the given (unchanging) distribution of skill levels across agents. The macroeconomic equilibrium remains essentially as in Sections 10.2–10.4, with the locally stable aggregate adjustment paths continuing to apply.

Returning to the model of Section 10.2, the critical difference is in the dynamics of the relative capital stock, which are now

$$k_i(t) - 1 = \theta(t)(\tilde{k}_i - 1) + [1 - \theta(t)](a_i - 1) = \frac{\theta(t)}{\theta(0)}(k_{i,0} - 1)$$
$$+ \frac{\theta(0) - \theta(t)}{\theta(0)}(a_i - 1), \tag{34}$$

where, as before, $\theta(t)$, $\theta(0)$ are given by (16). From (34), the agent's relative capital at any point in time is a weighted average of the initial capital stock, $k_{i,0}$, and ability level, a_i.[31] The weights of the two endowments change over time. As the economy converges to a new steady state, factor prices change, altering the relative contributions of wealth and skill endowments to the individual's income, and hence to savings. In an expanding economy, $l(0) < \tilde{l}$, and $\theta(0) > \theta(t) > 0$, $\dot{\theta}(t) = \mu\theta(t) < 0$, and the relative weight shifts from the endowment of capital toward skills.

With the relative weights changing, (34) illustrates the potential for agents to change relative wealth positions. For example, individuals who begin with above-average capital ($k_{i,0} > 1$) but are endowed with below-average skills ($a_i < 1$) may end up with below-average capital, and vice versa. Two offsetting forces drive the accumulation of capital. First, those with large initial wealth accumulate capital more slowly (during an expansion), which tends to deteriorate their relative position. On the other hand, those with more ability have higher incomes and, hence, accumulate more capital, which tends to improve their relative position. This contrasts with the previous model where $a_i \equiv 1$.

Similar comments apply to the dynamics of relative income. Agent i's relative income is

$$y_i(t) - 1 = \varphi(t)[k_i(t) - 1] + (1 - \varphi(t))[a_i - 1], \tag{35}$$

where $\varphi(t)$, which represents the weight in current relative income due to *current* relative capital, remains defined by (19).

To examine the potential for wealth and income mobility, compare two individuals i, j, and express their wealth gap at time t as

$$k_i(t) - k_j(t) = \frac{\theta(t)}{\theta(0)}\Delta k + \left(1 - \frac{\theta(t)}{\theta(0)}\right)\Delta a, \tag{36}$$

where $\Delta a \equiv a_i - a_j$ and $\Delta k \equiv k_{i,0} - k_{j,0}$. Two offsetting forces influence this gap, the differences in initial capital and the differences in ability. In a

---

[31] This reduces to the canonical model of Section 10.2 if $a_i = 1$ and skills are uniform across agents.

growing economy, $\theta(0) > \theta(t)$, $\dot{\theta}(t) < 0$, implying that the term multiplying the capital gap is less than one and declining over time. Using (36), García-Peñalosa and Turnovsky (2015) derive propositions indicating conditions under which it is possible (or impossible) for an initially poorer and less-wealthy individual to overtake some other initially richer agent, in terms of both wealth and income.

The linearity of the expressions for relative wealth and relative income permits us to transform them into measures of aggregate wealth and income inequality, analogous to (15') and (18'). García-Peñalosa and Turnovsky (2015) consider an economy that is accumulating capital as a result of an expansionary external shock. In general, this can be associated with an increase or decrease in wealth inequality, depending upon the relative dispersions of the initial endowments of capital and skills and their correlation. Moreover, wealth inequality can emerge from differences in skill endowments alone, bringing the analysis closer to the incomplete markets model and its emphasis on idiosyncratic shocks.

10.7 Human Capital

Stimulated by the seminal work of Becker (1964) and Schultz (1963), economists have devoted increasing attention to the role of education, knowledge, and, more generally, human capital as a critical source of economic growth. This focus is supported by empirical evidence provided by Goldin and Katz (1999, 2001), Abramovitz and David (2000), and others who found that, during the twentieth century in the United States, the contribution of human capital accumulation to the overall growth rate almost doubled, while the contribution of physical capital declined correspondingly. Furthermore, this process has tended to accelerate during the last two decades of the century (Jorgensen, Ho, and Stiroh, 2005). In conjunction with the increased role of human capital, in many advanced economies, the period since the 1980s has been one of increased income inequality.

This recent increase in inequality has been explained in terms of the rising skill premium, expressed as an increase in the relative wage of skilled to unskilled workers, that has been emerging as a result of skill-biased technological change and capital-skill complementarity; see, for example, Katz and Murphy (1992), Autor et al. (1998), and Krusell et al. (2000). As a result, the role of human capital has received increasing attention, as a key source of both economic growth and rising income inequality.[32] The primary explanation of this involves the acceleration of technological progress that requires more education and skills; see, for example, Galor and Weil (2000), Galor and Moav (2004), and Goldin and Katz (1999).[33]

In a recent paper, Turnovsky and Mitra (2013) examine the effects of technological change on both the growth rate and the distributions of wealth and income, focusing particularly on the interaction between human capital and physical capital accumulation in this process. To do this, they adapt the seminal Lucas (1988) two-sector growth model to include both human capital and unskilled (raw) labor, as well as physical capital, as productive factors.

Turnovsky and Mitra (2013) assume that aggregate human capital generates an externality enabling the economy to sustain ongoing growth – a characteristic of the original Lucas model. They also assume that physical capital is specific to the production of final output, in which case the human capital production sector becomes the fundamental engine of growth, consistent with much recent empirical evidence. The model focuses on technological structure, highlighting the role of sectoral production characteristics – which need not be uniform across the economy – as potentially important determinants of long-run growth and associated inequality.

The model contrasts the impacts on the growth–inequality relationship of a productivity increase in the final output sector and a productivity increase in the human capital–producing sector. They compare the conventional assumption that a productivity increase occurs as a discrete one-time change with the alternative view that the same overall increase accumulates gradually over time. While they can provide a general analytical characterization of the long-run equilibrium, the model is sufficiently complex that the dynamics must be studied numerically. Extensive simulations bring out the stark contrasts between the effects of productivity increases according to the sector in which they occur and the time paths over which they are implemented. Overall, the conclusions are robust and the principal findings can be summarized as follows.

First, a productivity increase in the final output sector has only a transitory effect on the growth rate. It has no long-run impact on the relative

---

[32] The changing importance of physical and human capital and their interaction in the overall growth process is studied in detail by Galor and Moav (2004) and more recently by Galor (2011).

[33] Similarly, Ehrlich (2008) suggests that the reason the United States overtook the UK and other European countries as an economic superpower was largely because of its relatively faster accumulation of human capital.

usage of skilled to unskilled labor that is a key determinant of the long-run growth rate. Instead, it raises the long-run ratios of physical capital and output to human capital, leading to a corresponding increase in consumption. In contrast, a productivity increase in the human capital sector will lead to a change in the relative use of skilled and unskilled workers and a positive permanent effect on the growth rate.

Second, the long-run responses of all *aggregate* quantities, such as the rates of return of the two types of capital, the equilibrium growth rate, and the sectoral allocations, are independent of the time paths followed by the productivity increase (in either sector). There are, however, sharp contrasts in their respective transitional paths, according to whether the productivity increases occur fully instantaneously or are implemented gradually over time. This difference arises because the allocation of labor, which drives the adjustments, responds both to the relative price of human to physical capital and to the productivity increases themselves. With full instantaneous productivity increases, both effects operate immediately. But when the productivity increase proceeds gradually, the relative price effect dominates in the early stages. This is because the productivity enhancement takes time to build and becomes effective only later in the transition. Consequently, the adjustments of all aggregates initially proceed in one direction if the productivity increase is completed instantaneously, and in the opposite direction if it occurs gradually, although in all instances they converge to the same long-run equilibrium. This is true irrespective of the sector in which the productivity increase occurs.

Turnovsky and Mitra (2013) consider three inequality measures: wealth inequality, income inequality, and welfare inequality. In contrast to the aggregates, a productivity increase in the final output sector does have permanent distributional consequences, and they obtain the following conclusions in addition to the first two just noted.

Third, in general, the responses of all three inequality measures depend upon the underlying source of inequality in the economy, that is, whether it is due to unequal initial endowments of physical capital, human capital, or some combination. The range of these qualitative responses suggests that the implications of the model in terms of the sign of the growth–inequality relationship can be easily reconciled with the diverse empirical evidence.

Fourth, the dynamics of wealth inequality consist of an initial increase followed by a gradual transition. The direction of the initial increase stems from the initial change in the relative price of human capital and depends upon both the source of the initial inequality and the sectoral location of the productivity increase. The direction of the transitional path depends upon whether consumption adjusts faster or slower than wages. For a productivity increase occurring in the final output sector, consumption does indeed adjust faster and wealth inequality declines, while the opposite is true for a productivity increase in the human capital sector.

Fifth, long-run wealth inequality may either rise or fall with either form of productivity increase, depending upon the initial underlying source of the inequality and the speed with which the productivity increase occurs. Productivity increases that are spread out over time exacerbate these effects, so that, in contrast to the aggregate measures, long-run wealth inequality depends upon the time path followed by the productivity increase.

Finally, income inequality reflects the evolution of both wealth inequality and the share of income originating from wealth. In the long run, the simulations suggest that the former effect dominates so that the long-run response of income inequality reflects that of wealth inequality. This contrasts with results obtained using one-sector models where the opposite tends to be the case. The difference is largely accounted for by the initial increase in wealth inequality arising from the price response.

I should also note that, although Turnovsky and Mitra (2013) express the levels of technology as Hicks-neutral in the two sectors, the fact that they employ Cobb-Douglas production functions makes it straightforward to re-interpret the aggregate productivity changes in terms of underlying factor augmentation, and thereby to address the role of skill-biased technological change and the resulting impact on the skill premium.

Space limitations preclude setting out the model in detail. However, I do want to draw attention to the representation of the skill premium, which is typically defined as the ratio of skilled labor to that of unskilled labor. The Turnovsky-Mitra model introduces unskilled labor, which earns wage rate $W(t)$, and human capital, $H(t)$, the rate of return on which, expressed in terms of final output, is $r_H(t)$. They assume that in equilibrium, human capital reflects the present value of the differential between the skilled and the unskilled wage rate, discounted at the rate of return on human capital. They then impute a wage rate of skilled labor, $W^S(t)$, from the equilibrium relationship

$$H(t) = \int_t^\infty [W^S(\tau) - W(\tau)]e^{-\int_t^\tau r_H(s)ds}\, d\tau. \tag{37}$$

Taking the time derivative of this expression, we obtain the following expression for the skill premium $W^S(t)/W(t)$:

$$\frac{W^S(t)}{W(t)} = 1 + \frac{r_H(t) - \dot{H}(t)/H(t)}{W(t)/H(t)}. \tag{38}$$

Substituting for the equilibrium value of the terms on the right-hand side of this equation, one can show that the skill premium increases with the relative intensity of unskilled labor and the relative value of human capital. It declines with the share of human capital allocated to the human capital sector because this increases the growth rate of human capital, thereby reducing its relative scarcity. Turnovsky and Mitra (2013) then discuss how these various elements are affected by a skill-biased productivity increase directed to human capital.

The usual measure of the skill premium, derived for a one-sector economy, is an increasing function of the "capital-skill complementarity effect," which arises from the assumption that the elasticity of substitution between capital and unskilled labor exceeds that between capital and skilled labor (Krusell et al., 2000; He, 2012). In this two-sector analysis, with Cobb-Douglas production functions, this mechanism is absent. Instead, it is replaced by the return to human capital, which reflects the substitutability between unskilled and skilled labor within sectors and the mobility of human capital across sectors.

10.8 Public Investment, Growth, and Inequality: Some Observations

Public investment in infrastructure as a source of economic growth has been widely debated in both developing and advanced economies. Several emerging-market countries, for example India, China, and Brazil, have undertaken extensive public investment, which has no doubt contributed to their recent high growth rates. In contrast, several European countries have reduced public spending as an austerity measure in response to the financial crisis of 2008. Contemporaneously with these diverse policies, we have witnessed rising income inequality, both in emerging markets and in most OECD (Organisation for Economic Co-operation and Development) countries. An important question that arises in this context concerns the effect of pro-growth infrastructure investment policies on the dynamics of inequality.

Interest in the connection among public investment, output, and growth dates back to the seminal work of Arrow and Kurz (1970), who addressed the issue using a one-sector neoclassical growth model. Beginning with Barro (1990), an extensive literature has evolved addressing the issue in an endogenous growth framework. Barro's original model introduced productive government spending as a flow, but most subsequent contributions have introduced it in the form of public capital, which, along with private capital, can be accumulated and depreciates gradually; see, for example, Futagami, Morita, and Shibata (1993) and Glomm and Ravikumar (1994) for early contributions and, more recently, Agénor (2011) for an extensive survey of this theoretical literature. There is also an extensive empirical literature that focuses on estimating the elasticity of private output with respect to public capital. The consensus is that public infrastructure contributes positively and significantly to output. Bom and Ligthart (2014) provide an exhaustive review of the empirical literature and place the elasticity of output with respect to public capital at between 0.10 and 0.20.

It is clear that by interacting with labor and private capital in the production process, public investment has a direct impact on relative factor returns and is critical in the evolution of wealth and income distributions. Moreover, because of its diverse nature, public investment is likely to have significant redistributive consequences. Public investment in the form of affordable housing that is geared toward the less-affluent members of the economy is likely to reduce inequality, whereas public investment directed to high-level communication is more likely to favor the more affluent having access to these facilities and is thus likely to exacerbate inequality.

The empirical evidence on the relationship between infrastructure investment and inequality is less definitive and more anecdotal. Calderón and Servén (2004, 2010), Fan and Zhang (2004), Ferranti, Perry, Ferreira, and Walton (2004), and Lopez (2004) find that public investment has both promoted growth and helped mitigate inequality. In addition, Brakman, Garretsen, and van Marrewijk (2002) find that government spending on infrastructure has increased regional disparities within Europe. On the other hand, Artadi and Sala-i-Martin (2003) suggest that excessive public investment has contributed to rising income inequality in Africa. Furthermore, in India, Banerjee and Somanathan (2007) report that access to critical infrastructure services and public goods is positively correlated with social status. The World Bank (2006) finds that the quality and the performance of state-provided infrastructure services are worst in India's poorest states.

This diversity of empirical findings emphasizes the need for a well-specified analytical framework within which the interaction among infrastructure spending, economic growth, and inequality can be systematically addressed. In this section, we briefly summarize the insights and conclusions obtained by Chatterjee and Turnovsky (2012) in their work based on the RCTD framework.

In setting out the impact of public investment on the representative consumer approach to distribution, Chatterjee and Turnovsky (2012) focus on two issues pertaining to public spending and its financing: (1) the mechanism whereby government spending on public infrastructure and accompanying taxation policies affects the distributions of wealth, pre-tax income, and post-tax income, in the short run, during transition, and in the long run, and (2) the dynamics of the growth–inequality relationship along the transitional path.[34]

As in the benchmark economy, the underlying source of heterogeneity stems from agents' differential initial endowments of private capital. In addition, there is public capital that is nonrival and nonexcludable and that, like private capital, is accumulated gradually. Public capital interacts with the aggregate stock of private capital to generate composite externalities ("infrastructure") for both labor productivity in production and the labor–leisure allocation in utility. The government has a range of fiscal instruments available to finance its investment, namely distortionary taxes on capital income, labor income, and consumption, and a nondistortionary lump-sum tax (equivalent to government debt). The accumulation of public capital and the spillovers it generates serves both as an engine of sustained growth and as a driver of relative returns to capital and labor, with consequences for the evolution of wealth and income inequality.[35] In equilibrium, both the economy's growth rate and inequality are endogenously determined. However, with both capital goods accumulating gradually, the aggregate dynamics, which drive both wealth and income inequality, depend upon the evolution of the ratio of the two capital stocks, as well as that of labor (leisure).

Chatterjee and Turnovsky (2012) compare the effects of increases in government investment on public capital financed by the use of various fiscal instruments, and find the following four results.

First, government spending on public capital leads to a persistent increase in wealth inequality over time, regardless of how it is financed. Wealth inequality is more sensitive to government investment than to

---

[34] They also consider the tradeoffs between average welfare and its dispersion.

[35] Indeed, recent empirical evidence points to the importance of the return to capital as one of the determinants of inequality; see Atkinson (2003) and the recent empirical evidence for the OECD provided by Checchi and García-Peñalosa (2010).

government consumption because it is driven in part by the ratio of public to private capital, which evolves slowly.

Second, the time paths of both pre- and post-tax income inequality are highly sensitive to the financing policy adopted, and in many cases are characterized by sharp intertemporal tradeoffs. For example, while government investment financed by a lump-sum or consumption tax leads to a short-run *decline* in income inequality, this is completely reversed over time, leading to an *increase* in the long-run dispersion of income across agents. This is because the short-run response of income inequality is dominated by the initial response of the labor–leisure choice and its impact on factor returns, while over time it is more influenced by the evolution of both wealth and labor income inequality. They also find that more than two-thirds of the long-run increase in income inequality can be attributed to an increase in labor income inequality, consistent with the recent empirical findings of Atkinson, Piketty, and Saez (2011).

Third, public expenditure financed by capital or labor income taxes yields sharp differences between pre-tax and post-tax income inequality, both in the short run and over time. Regardless of the financing method, both measures of income inequality increase over time.

Fourth, the Chatterjee-Turnovsky (2012) results also provide insights into the growth–income inequality relationship, an issue that has been a source of lively debate. They show that this relationship depends critically on (1) how externalities impinge on allocation decisions, (2) the financing policies for government spending, and (3) the time period of consideration – that is, the short run, a transition path, or the long run. These results underscore the ambiguity in the growth–inequality relationship that is characteristic of recent empirical studies cited in Section 10.1.

To check the robustness of their conclusions, Chatterjee and Turnovsky (2012) conduct an extensive sensitivity analysis of some of the economy's structural parameters. They focus on (1) the structure of the composite public–private externality in the utility and production functions, (2) the intratemporal elasticity of substitution between private capital and effective labor in the production function, and (3) the intratemporal elasticity of substitution between consumption and effective leisure in the utility function. Overall, their benchmark results remain robust to variations in these parameters.

10.9 Conclusions

The relationship between aggregate economic growth and its distribution is arguably one of the most important in economics. It is receiving increasing attention in both academic and policy circles as a result of the general increase in inequality that has occurred during recent years in both developed and developing economies. The relationship is also a complex one, both analytically and substantively. Analytically, the complexity arises from the fact that, in general, both macroeconomic aggregates and the distribution of those aggregates across agents are jointly determined and, in general, solving for them simultaneously poses an intractable problem. Substantively, the complexity arises from the multidimensionality of the forces impinging on this relationship. The dynamics of growth and distribution are driven by many diverse factors spanning economic, sociological, demographic, political, and structural origins.

In order to make progress, one needs to impose more structure; consequently, in this chapter, I have employed the RCTD, modifying and extending the basic framework in various directions, thereby illustrating its versatility. Its tractability enables one to address the tradeoffs that exist between aggregate performance and its distribution, as well as alternative relevant measures of inequality, both at a point in time as well as intertemporally. This, in turn, provides a tractable framework for structuring policy directed at reducing the adverse effects of these tradeoffs.

One prevailing characteristic of this approach is that the time path of any structural change has implications for long-run wealth and income inequality. This also has important policy implications. It suggests that the speed with which any policy is implemented will have permanent effects on the degree of inequality and may be one explanation as to why countries having generally similar aggregate characteristics nevertheless have significantly different degrees of inequality. Other more specific policy implications can be inferred from the examples involving fiscal policy discussed in Sections 10.4 and 10.8.

To conclude, I should acknowledge several caveats. First, while I have reviewed several applications of the representative consumer approach, there are other important potential applications that have not been addressed. Of these, the most prominent is the impact of globalization on economic performance and inequality. The empirical evidence on this issue is mixed, suggesting that the impact of globalization depends upon the form that it takes, for example whether it involves financial liberalization or trade liberalization. Turnovsky and Rojas-Vallejos (2018) apply the representative consumer framework to show the sharply contrasting effects of reduced consumption tariffs and investment tariffs on inequality.

Second, in employing the infinitely lived representative agent paradigm, the analysis has abstracted from one further important source of heterogeneity, namely the reality that different individuals are at different stages of their respective life cycles. This, too, has important distributional consequences. Standard life-cycle models imply that different agents at different stages of their life cycles will have accumulated different amounts of wealth. As a result, as Atkinson (1971) suggested, there is an inherent wealth inequality in societies as a consequence of the age structures of their population. This also suggests that an important next step would be to extend the type of model developed in this chapter to incorporate the heterogeneity associated with a plausible demographic structure.

Finally, the underlying assumptions of the RCTD imply that the aggregate economy is independent of its distribution across the constituent agents. This makes it inappropriate for analyzing the impact of inequality on growth, as conducted in the studies reported by Bénabou (1996b). Also, two key features of the model – the homogeneity of the underlying preferences and the assumption that all agents have equal access to all factor markets – make it more relevant for developed economies and less so for developing economies. In that case, adopting alternative assumptions such as the absence of borrowing or lending, with agents being subject to idiosyncratic productivity shocks, may be more appropriate.

Getachew and Turnovsky (2015) employ such a framework to examine the role of public investment. Under the specific assumptions of log-normality and a CES production function, they obtain a closed form solution but one that is very different in nature from that discussed by Chatterjee and Turnovsky (2012). In this case, the equilibrium dynamics are driven by the volatility of the productivity shocks, while the role of initial endowments gradually disappears over time. The degree of inequality, as determined by the evolution of the productivity shocks, then determines the growth rate, precisely reversing the causality from that of the "representative consumer" model. This framework also implies an unambiguously negative relationship between inequality and growth. Moreover, the impact of government investment on inequality (both wealth and income) depends upon the degree of factor substitutability embodied in the production function, which plays a minor role in the Chatterjee-Turnovsky model.

The overriding conclusion of the analysis is that the growth–inequality relationship is a complex one. This is evident from the conflicting empirical evidence, but it is also supported by the more formal analysis discussed in this paper. Whether this relationship is positive or negative depends critically upon the analytical framework employed. But even having adopted a particular framework, it may depend upon the underlying financing policies, the time period under consideration, the characteristics of the technology, as well as the specific structural change and the time frame over which the change is occurring. The main contribution of this analysis is to emphasize that in order to understand the nature of the relationship between inequality and growth, one needs to embed it within a consistently specified general equilibrium growth model, recognizing that different frameworks offer different perspectives.

Acknowledgments

Much of the research reported here has been conducted jointly with various coauthors over many years. I am particularly grateful to Cecilia García-Peñalosa, with whom I began my work in this area. Since beginning our collaboration, we have completed many papers, several of which are incorporated in this chapter. I have also worked on different aspects of the growth–inequality relationship with others, and, in this regard, I want to acknowledge Manoj Atolia, Santanu Chatterjee, and Murat Koyuncu. Much of my research on this topic has been supported by the Castor Professorship and more recently by the Van Voorhis Professorship at the University of Washington; that, too, is gratefully acknowledged.

References

Abramovitz, Moses, and Paul A. David, 2000. "American Macroeconomic Growth in the Era of Knowledge-Based Progress: The Long-Run Perspective." In Stanley L. Engerman and Robert E. Gallman (eds.), *The Cambridge Economic History of the United States*. Cambridge University Press, New York, NY.

Agénor, Pierre-Richard, 2011. *Public Capital, Growth and Welfare: Analytical Foundations for Public Policy*. Princeton University Press, Princeton, NJ.

Aghion, Phillippe, Eve Caroli, and Cecilia García-Peñalosa, 1999. "Inequality and Economic Growth: The Perspective of the New Growth Theories." *Journal of Economic Literature* 37 (4), 1615–60.

Alesina, Alberto, and Dani Rodrik, 1994. "Distributive Politics and Economic Growth." *Quarterly Journal of Economics* 109 (4), 465–90.

Algan, Yann, Arnaud Cheron, Jean-Olivier Hairault, and Francois Langot, 2003. "Wealth Effect on Labor Market Transitions." *Review of Economic Dynamics* 6 (1), 156–78.

Anand, Sudhir, and Sanjiv M. Ravi Kanbur, 1993. "The Kuznets Process and the Inequality-Development Relationship." *Journal of Development Economics* 40 (1), 25–52.

Arrow, Kenneth J., and Mordecai Kurz, 1970. *Public Investment, the Rate of Return and Optimal Fiscal Policy*. Johns Hopkins University Press, Baltimore, MD.

Artadi, Elsa V., and Xavier Sala-i-Martin, 2003. "The Economic Tragedy of the XXth Century: Growth in Africa." NBER Working Paper 9865. National Bureau of Economic Research, Cambridge, MA.

Atkinson, Anthony B., 1970. "On the Measurement of Inequality." *Journal of Economic Theory* 2 (3), 244–63.

Atkinson, Anthony B., 1971. "The Distribution of Wealth and the Individual Life Cycle." *Oxford Economic Papers* 23 (2), 239–54.

Atkinson, Anthony B., 1999. "The Distribution of Income in the UK and OECD Countries in the Twentieth Century." *Oxford Review of Economic Policy* 15 (4), 56–75.

Atkinson, Anthony B., 2003. "Income Inequality in OECD Countries: Data and Explanations." *CESifo Economic Studies* 49 (4), 479–513.

Atkinson, Anthony B., Thomas Piketty, and Emmanuel Saez, 2011. "Top Incomes in the Long Run of History." *Journal of Economic Literature* 49 (1), 3–71.

Atolia, Manoj, Santanu Chatterjee, and Stephen J. Turnovsky, 2012. "Growth and Inequality: Dependence on the Time Path of Productivity Increases (and Other Structural Changes)." *Journal of Economic Dynamics and Control* 36 (3), 331–48.

Autor, David H., Lawrence F. Katz, and Alan B. Krueger, 1998. "Computing Inequality: Have Computers Changed the Labor Market?" *Quarterly Journal of Economics* 113 (4), 1169–213.

Banerjee, Abhijit V., and Andrew Newman, 1993. "Occupational Choice and the Process of Development." *Journal of Political Economy* 101 (2), 274–98.

Banerjee, Abhijit V., and Rohini Somanathan, 2007. "The Political Economy of Public Goods: Some Evidence from India." *Journal of Development Economics* 82 (2), 287–314.

Barro, Robert J., 1990 "Government Spending in a Simple Model of Endogenous Growth." *Journal of Political Economy* 98 (5), S103–25.

Barro, Robert J., 2000. "Inequality and Growth in a Panel of Countries." *Journal of Economic Growth* 5 (1), 5–32.

Becker, Gary S., 1964. *Human Capital.* Columbia University Press, New York, NY.

Becker, Gary S., and Robert J. Barro, 1988. "A Reformulation of the Economic Theory of Fertility." *Quarterly Journal of Economics* 103 (1), 1–25.

Becker, Gary S., and Nigel Tomes, 1979. "An Equilibrium Theory of the Distribution of Income and Intergenerational Mobility." *Journal of Political Economy* 87 (6), 1153–89.

Becker, Robert A., 1980. "On the Long-Run Steady State in a Simple Dynamic Model of Equilibrium with Heterogeneous Households." *Quarterly Journal of Economics* 95 (2), 375–82.

Becker, Robert A., 2006. "Equilibrium Dynamics with Many Agents." In Rose-Anne, Dana, Cuong Le Van, Tapan Mitra, and Kazuo Nishimura (eds.), *Handbook of Optimal Growth*, 385–442. Springer, Heidelberg, Germany.

Bénabou, Roland, 1996a. "Equity and Efficiency in Human Capital Investment: The Local Connection." *Review of Economic Studies* 63 (2), 237–64.

Bénabou, Roland, 1996b. "Inequality and Growth." In Ben S. Bernanke and Julio J. Rotemberg (eds.), *Macroeconomic Annual 1996.* National Bureau of Economic Research, MIT Press, Cambridge, MA.

Benhabib, Jess, Alberto Bisin, and Shenghao Zhu, 2015. "The Wealth Distribution in Bewley Economies with Capital Income Risk." *Journal of Economic Theory* 159 (PA), 489–515.

Bewley, Truman F., 1977. "The Permanent Income Hypothesis: A Theoretical Formulation." *Journal of Economic Theory* 16 (2), 252–92.

Bewley, Truman F., 1982. "An Integration of Equilibrium Theory and Turnpike Theory." *Journal of Mathematical Economics* 10 (2–3), 233–67.

Blomquist, Sören, 1983. "The Effect of Income Taxation on the Labor Supply of Married Men in Sweden." *Journal of Public Economics* 22 (2), 169–97.

Blomquist, Sören, Matias Eklöf, and Whitney Newey, 2001. "Tax Reform Evaluation Using Non-parametric Methods: Sweden 1980–1991." *Journal of Public Economics* 79 (3), 543–68.

Bom, Pedro, and Jenny Ligthart, 2014. "What Have We Learned from Three Decades of Research on the Productivity of Public Capital?" *Journal of Economic Surveys* 28 (5), 889–916.

Bourguignon, François, 1979. "Decomposable Income Inequality Measures." *Econometrica* 47 (4), 901–20.

Brakman, Steven, Harry Garretsen, and Charles van Marrewijk, 2002. "Locational Competition and Agglomeration: The Role of Government Spending." CESifo Working Paper 775. CESifo, Munich, Germany.

Brueckner, Markus, and Daniel Lederman, 2018. "Inequality and Economic Growth: The Role of Initial Income." *Journal of Economic Growth* 23 (3), 341–66.

Calderón, César, and Luis Servén, 2004. "The Effects of Infrastructure Development on Growth and Income Distribution." Policy Research Paper No. 3400. World Bank, Washington, DC.

Calderón, César, and Luis Servén, 2010. "Infrastructure and Economic Development in Sub-Saharan Africa." *Journal of African Economies* 19 (S1), 13–87.

Calderón, César, and Luis Servén, 2014. "Infrastructure, Growth, and Inequality: An Overview." Policy Research Paper No. 7034. World Bank, Washington, DC.

Caselli, Francesco, and Jaume Ventura, 2000. "A Representative Consumer Theory of Distribution." *American Economic Review* 90 (4), 909–26.

Castañeda, Ana, Javier Díaz-Giménez, and José-Víctor Ríos-Rull, 1998. "Exploring the Income Distribution Business Cycle Dynamics." *Journal of Monetary Economics* 42 (1), 93–130.

Chatterjee, Satyajit, 1994. "Transitional Dynamics and the Distribution of Wealth in a Neoclassical Growth Model." *Journal of Public Economics* 54 (1), 97–119.

Chatterjee, Santanu, and Stephen J. Turnovsky, 2012. "Infrastructure and Inequality." *European Economic Review* 56 (8), 1730–45.

Checchi, Daniele, and Cecilia García-Peñalosa, 2010. "Labour Market Institutions and the Personal Distribution of Income in the OECD." *Economica* 77 (307), 413–50.

Cheng, Ing-Haw, and Eric French, 2000. "The Effect of the Run-Up in the Stock Market on Labor Supply." *Federal Reserve Bank of Chicago Economic Perspectives* 24 (4), 48–65.

Coronado, Julia Lynn, and Maria Perozek, 2003. "Wealth Effects and the Consumption of Leisure: Retirement Decisions During the Stock Market Boom of the 1990s." Finance and Economics Discussion Series, 2003–20. Board of Governors of the Federal Reserve System, Washington, DC.

De la Croix, David, and Matthias Doepke, 2003. "Inequality and Growth: Why Differential Fertility Matters." *American Economic Review* 93 (4), 1091–1193.

Durlauf, Steven N., 1996. "A Theory of Persistent Income Inequality." *Journal of Economic Growth* 1 (1), 75–94.

Eden, Maya, and Aart Kraay, 2014. "'Crowding In' and the Returns to Government Investment in Low-Income Countries." Policy Research Working Paper Series 6781. World Bank, Washington, DC.

Ehrlich, Isaac, 2008. "The Mystery of Human Capital and Engine of Growth, or Why the US Became the Economic Superpower in the 20th Century." In Barry Smith, David M. Mark, and Isaac Ehrlich (eds.), *The Mystery of Human Capital and the Construction of Social Reality*, 113–58. Open Court, Chicago, IL.

Ehrlich, Isaac, and Jinyoung Kim, 2007. "The Evolution of Income and Fertility Inequalities over the Course of Economic Development: A Human Capital Perspective." *Journal of Human Capital* 1 (1), 137–74.

Fan, Shenggen, and Xiaobo Zhang, 2004. "Infrastructure and Regional Economic Development in Rural China." *China Economic Review* 15 (2), 203–14.

Fernandez, Raquel, and Richard Rogerson, 1996. "Income Distribution, Communities, and the Quality of Public Education." *Quarterly Journal of Economics* 111 (1), 135–64.

Ferranti, David, Guillermo Perry, Francisco Ferreira, and Michael Walton, 2004. *Inequality in Latin America: Breaking with History?* World Bank, Washington, DC.

Forbes, Kristen J., 2000. "A Reassessment of the Relationship between Inequality and Growth." *American Economic Review* 90 (4), 869–87.

Futagami, Koichi, Yuichi Morita, and Akihisa Shibata, 1993. "Dynamic Analysis of an Endogenous Growth Model with Public Capital." *Scandinavian Journal of Economics* 95 (4), 607–25.

Galor, Oded, 2011. *Unified Growth Theory*. Princeton University Press, Princeton, NJ.

Galor, Oded, and Omer Moav, 2004. "From Physical to Human Capital Accumulation: Inequality and the Process of Development." *Review of Economic Studies* 71 (4), 1001–26.

Galor, Oded, and Daniel Tsiddon, 1997. "Technological Progress, Mobility, and Economic Growth." *American Economic Review* 87 (3), 363–82.

Galor, Oded, and David N. Weil, 2000. "Population, Technology, and Growth: From Malthusian Stagnation to the Demographic Transition and Beyond." *American Economic Review* 90 (4), 806–28.

Galor, Oded, and Joseph Zeira, 1993. "Income Distribution and Macroeconomics." *Review of Economic Studies* 60 (1), 35–52.

García-Peñalosa, Cecilia, and Stephen J. Turnovsky, 2011. "Taxation and Income Distribution Dynamics in a Neoclassical Growth Model." *Journal of Money, Credit, and Banking* 43 (8), 1543–77.

García-Peñalosa, Cecilia, and Stephen J. Turnovsky, 2015. "Income Inequality, Mobility, and the Accumulation of Capital." *Macroeconomic Dynamics* 19 (6), 1332–57.

Getachew, Yoseph Y., and Stephen J. Turnovsky, 2015. "Productive Government Spending and Its Consequences for the Growth-Inequality Tradeoff." *Research in Economics* 69 (4), 621–40.

Glomm, Gerhard, and B. Ravikumar, 1992. "Public versus Private Investment in Human Capital: Endogenous Growth and Income Inequality." *Journal of Political Economy* 100 (4), 818–34.

Glomm, Gerhard, and B. Ravikumar, 1994. "Public Investment in Infrastructure in a Simple Growth Model." *Journal of Economic Dynamics and Control* 18 (6), 1173–87.

Goldin, Claudia, and Lawrence F. Katz, 1999. "The Returns to Skill across the Twentieth Century United States." NBER Working Paper No. 7126. National Bureau of Economic Research, Cambridge, MA.

Goldin, Claudia, and Lawrence F. Katz, 2001. "The Legacy of U.S. Educational Leadership: Notes on Distribution and Economic Growth in the 20th Century." *American Economic Review Papers and Proceedings* 91 (2), 18–23.

Goldin, Claudia, and Lawrence F. Katz, 2008. *The Race between Education and Technology.* Harvard University Press, Cambridge, MA.

Gorman, William M., 1959. "Separable Utility and Aggregation." *Econometrica* 27 (3), 469–81.

Guo, Jang-Ting, and Kevin J. Lansing, 1998. "Indeterminacy and Stabilization Policy." *Journal of Economic Theory* 82 (2), 481–90.

Hausman, Jerry A., 1981. "Labor Supply." In Henry J. Aaron and Joseph A. Pechman (eds.), *How Taxes Affect Economic Behavior,* 27–71. Brookings Institution, Washington, DC.

He, Hui, 2012. "What Drives the Skill Premium: Technological Change or Demographic Variation?" *European Economic Review* 56 (8), 1546–72.

Heathcote, Jonathan, Kjetil Storesletten, and Giovanni L. Violante, 2009. "Quantitative Macroeconomics with Heterogeneous Households." *Annual Review of Economics* 1 (1), 319–54.

Holtz-Eakin, Douglas, David Joulfaian, and Harvey S. Rosen, 1993. "The Carnegie Conjecture: Some Empirical Evidence." *Quarterly Journal of Economics* 108 (2), 413–35.

Jorgensen, Dale W., Mun S. Ho, and Kevin J. Stiroh, 2005. "Projecting Productivity Growth: Lessons from the US Growth Resurgence." In William H. Dutton, Brian Kahin, Ramon O'Callaghan, and Andrew W. Wyckoff (eds.), *The Economic and Social Implications of Information Technology.* MIT Press, Cambridge, MA.

Katz, Lawrence F., and Kevin M. Murphy, 1992. "Changes in Relative Wages, 1963–1987: Supply and Demand Factors." *Quarterly Journal of Economics* 107 (1), 35–78.

Koyuncu, Murat, and Stephen J. Turnovsky, 2016. "The Dynamics of Growth and Income Inequality under Progressive Taxation." *Journal of Public Economic Theory* 18 (6), 560–88.

Kraay, Aart, 2016. "Weak Instruments in Growth Regressions." Policy Research Working Paper 7494. World Bank, Washington, DC.

Krusell, Per, Lee E. Ohanian, José-Víctor Rios-Rull, and Giovanni L. Violante, 2000. "Capital-Skill Complementarity and Inequality: A Macroeconomic Analysis." *Econometrica* 68 (5), 1029–53.

Krusell, Per, and Anthony A. Smith, 1998. "Income and Wealth Heterogeneity in the Macroeconomy." *Journal of Political Economy* 106 (5), 867–96.

Kuznets, Simon, 1955. "Economic Growth and Income Inequality." *American Economic Review* 45 (1), 1–28.

Li, Hongyi, and Heng-Fu Zou, 1998. "Income Inequality Is Not Harmful to Growth: Theory and Evidence." *Review of Development Economics* 2 (3), 318–34.

Li, Wenli, and Pierre-Daniel G. Sarte, 2004. "Progressive Taxation and Long-Run Growth." *American Economic Review* 94 (5), 1705–16.

Lopez, Humberto, 2004. "Macroeconomics and Inequality." Research Workshop: Macroeconomic Challenges in Low Income Countries. International Monetary Fund, Washington, DC.

Lucas, Robert E., 1988. "On the Mechanics of Economic Development." *Journal of Monetary Economics* 22 (1), 3–42.

Maliar, Lilia, and Serguei Maliar, 2001. "Heterogeneity in Capital and Skills in a Neoclassical Stochastic Growth Model." *Journal of Economic Dynamics and Control* 25 (9), 1367–97.

Maliar, Lilia, and Serguei Maliar, 2003. "The Representative Consumer in the Neoclassical Growth Model with Idiosyncratic Shocks." *Review of Economic Dynamics* 6 (2), 362–80.

McDaniel, Cara, 2007. "Average Tax Rates on Consumption, Investment, Labor and Capital in the OECD 1953–2003." Working Paper. Arizona State University, Tempe, AZ.

Mendoza, Enrique G., Assaf Razin, and Linda Tesar, 1994. "Effective Tax Rates in Macroeconomics: Cross Country Estimates of Tax Rates on Factor Incomes and Consumption." *Journal of Monetary Economics* 34 (3), 297–323.

Perotti, Roberto, 1996. "Growth, Income Distribution, and Democracy: What the Data Say." *Journal of Economic Growth* 1 (2), 149–87.

Persson, Torsten, and Guido Tabellini, 1994. "Is Inequality Harmful for Growth?" *American Economic Review* 84 (3), 600–21.

Piketty, Thomas, 2011. "On the Long-Run Evolution of Inheritance: France 1820–2050." *Quarterly Journal of Economics* 126 (3), 1071–1131.

Piketty, Thomas, 2014. *Capital in the Twenty-First Century*. Harvard University Press, Cambridge, MA.

Piketty, Thomas, and Emmanuel Saez, 2003. "Income Inequality in the United States, 1913–1998." *Quarterly Journal of Economics* 118 (1), 1–39.

Piketty, Thomas, and Gabriel Zucman, 2014, "Capital Is Back: Wealth-Income Ratios in Rich Countries 1700–2010." *Quarterly Journal of Economics* 129 (3), 1255–1310.

Ramsey, Frank P., 1928. "A Mathematical Theory of Saving." *Economic Journal* 38 (152), 543–59.

Saint-Paul, Gilles, and Thierry Verdier, 1993. "Education, Democracy, and Growth." *Journal of Development Economics* 42 (2), 399–407.

Sarte, Pierre-Daniel G., 1997. "Progressive Taxation and Income Inequality in Dynamic Competitive Equilibrium." *Journal of Public Economics* 66 (1), 145–71.

Schultz, Theodore W., 1963. *The Economic Value of Education*. Columbia University Press, New York, NY.

Seneviratne, Dulani, and Yan Sun, 2013. "Infrastructure and Income Distribution in ASEAN-5: What Are the Links?" IMF Working Paper 13/41. International Monetary Fund, Washington, DC.

Sorger, Gerhard, 2000. "Income and Wealth Distribution in a Simple Growth Model." *Journal of Economic Theory* 16 (1), 23–42.

Sorger, Gerhard, 2002. "On the Long-Run Distribution of Capital in the Ramsey Model." *Journal of Economic Theory* 105 (1), 226–43.

Turnovsky, Stephen J., 2015. "Economic Growth and Inequality: The Role of Public Investment." *Journal of Economic Dynamics and Control* 61 (December), 204–21.

Turnovsky, Stephen J., and Cecilia García-Peñalosa, 2008. "Distributional Dynamics in a Neoclassical Growth Model: The Role of Elastic Labor Supply." *Journal of Economic Dynamics and Control* 32 (5), 1399–1431.

Turnovsky, Stephen J., and Aditi Mitra, 2013. "The Interaction between Human and Physical Capital Accumulation and the Growth-Inequality Tradeoff." *Journal of Human Capital* 7 (1), 26–75.

Turnovsky, Stephen J., and Jorge Rojas-Vallejos, 2018. "The Distributional Consequences of Trade Liberalization: Consumption Tariff versus Investment Tariff Reduction." *Journal of Development Economics* 134 (September), 392–415.

Voichovsky, Sarah, 2005. "Does the Profile of Income Inequality Matter for Economic Growth?" *Journal of Economic Growth* 10 (3), 273–96.

World Bank, 2006. "Inclusive Growth and Service Delivery: Building on India's Success." World Bank Development Policy Review Report No. 34580-IN. World Bank, Washington, DC.

PART VI

A CONCLUDING PERSPECTIVE

A Perspective on the Prospects for Economic Growth in the United States

John W. Diamond and George R. Zodrow

11.1 Introduction

The chapters in this volume provide insightful and provocative discussions of many of the issues related to whether the United States is likely to continue on the robust growth path of earlier years or whether economic growth is likely to decelerate or even enter an extended period of "secular stagnation." In this concluding chapter, we tie together some of the threads that appear in these chapters, extend the analyses in several directions, and discuss some policy implications. We organize our discussion around three themes: technology and productivity growth; labor markets and economic growth, including the importance of human capital accumulation and the role of immigration; and fiscal policy, including both expenditure and tax reform.

11.2 Advances in Technology and Economic Growth

Perhaps the most striking feature of the discussion in this volume on the prospects for future economic growth in the United States is the huge chasm between the views of the "techno-optimists" and those of the "techno-pessimists," described in Chapter 5. A prominent member of the latter camp is Gordon (2016), who argues that recent technological advances, such as the artificial intelligence technologies (AIT) and information communication technologies (ICT) described in detail in Chapter 6, are not as transformative as earlier revolutionary general purpose technologies, such as the steam engine, electricity, and the internal combustion engine, as well as the technologies associated with improved manufacturing processes, the development of new materials, and earlier advances in communications and media, chemicals, and computers. The slowdown in productivity growth experienced over the past fifty years is consistent with this view, and Gordon views as temporary the short-term increase in productivity during the decade that began in the mid-1990s and is generally attributed to increased adoption of computer technology; the subsequent decline in productivity is arguably consistent with this view. Similarly, Cohen (2011) argues that the "low-hanging fruit" of factors that led to rapid economic growth in the past, such as cheap arable land, fundamental technological breakthroughs, and the provision of secondary and tertiary education to sizable cohorts of uneducated children, have largely been exhausted.

In marked contrast, the "techno-optimists," such as McAfee and Brynjolfsson (2017), argue that recent and future productivity and growth-enhancing developments in AIT, robotics, and digitally connected sensors will, after a lag of undetermined length, spark a new era of technology-induced increases in productivity that will lead to significantly faster economic growth. Underlying this argument is the view that these advancements will be general purpose technologies that will lead to further complementary investment, innovation, and application, which together will ultimately deliver large increases in productivity growth, with the associated increases in income acting as a further driver of growth. Indeed, this view has led to concerns that such increases in productivity will eventually be so dramatic and will occur so rapidly that they will significantly increase unemployment over time, leading to often-discussed concerns about the "future of work" and prospects for significant and persistent unemployment. For example, Frey and Osborne (2017) provide one measure of the magnitude of potential job displacement, as they estimate that 47 percent of jobs are susceptible to computerization, and Summers (2016) predicts that one-third of prime-age males will be unemployed by mid-century. Acemoglu and Restrepo (forthcoming) estimate that an increase of 1 robot per 1000 workers in a local area reduces the employment-to-population ratio on average by 0.37 percent, which implies that on average a robot displaces 6.2 workers. And a recent McKinsey Global Institute (2017) report suggests that by 2030 there will be 75 million to 375 million workers, or 3 to 14 percent of the global workforce, that will have to switch occupational categories due to automation, while many others will have to adapt their skills as their occupations require significant interaction with highly capable machines. Nevertheless, a general equilibrium analysis included in the McKinsey study estimates that advanced economies will maintain full employment by 2030, although at the expense of transitional unemployment and wage adjustments. With respect to such changes in wages, a recent IMF study (Berg, Buffie, and Zanna, 2018) estimates that although AIT and robotics will eventually result in wage increases, their initial impact is negative and the transition to higher wages can take generations.

The evidence thus far can be broadly interpreted in two ways. On the one hand, the largely tepid growth in productivity despite significant technological advances over most of the last fifty years is consistent with the techno-pessimist story. On the other hand, Hubbard's argument (in Chapter 5) that significant amounts of time may be required before technological advances are translated into productivity gains but that such gains could eventually be significant strikes us as quite plausible. Moreover, the fact that recent significant technological advances have not been rapidly translated into large productivity gains suggests that problems with increasing unemployment will develop slowly. This, in turn, increases the likelihood that, over time, technological advances will, as they have with technological advances in the past, lead not only to productivity growth and increases in aggregate wealth and living standards but also to increases in employment attributable to the creation of many complementary and new jobs, many of which will be robot-assisted and some of which may not yet even be envisioned – results that will mitigate employment concerns, especially if the transition is lengthy and gradual. Moreover, declines in the size of the labor force due to aging of the population (and perhaps to reduced immigration) should also help limit the problems associated with technology-induced job losses.

Nevertheless, there is no question that the potential for more disruptive job losses with large negative effects on the affected households and regions exists. Recent productivity gains and job losses in manufacturing attributable to rapid improvements in robotics technology may be illustrative. For example, Hicks and Devaraj (2015) estimate that nearly 90 percent of the loss of nearly 6 million manufacturing jobs from 2000 to 2010 in the United States is attributable not to trade, as is often asserted, but to greater automation. They note that at the 2000 level of productivity, the 2010 level of manufacturing production would have required 20.9 million workers; instead, it was produced with only 12.1 million workers. If advances in AIT, robotics, and digital sensors were eventually to have similar effects on other industries, the implications for employment could be quite negative.

However, Osborne and Frey (2019) have recently emphasized that their estimates should not be interpreted as implying an "employment apocalypse." Instead, they stress that the potential for automation reducing certain types of employment is huge, but it is far from clear how long such a process will take. They also note that this phenomenon is not new, as similar assessments would in all likelihood have been accurate prior to earlier periods characterized by critical technological innovations.

Our view is that this debate about the implications of technological advances for economic growth suggests two broad directions for public policy. The first is to adopt policies to promote productivity growth by facilitating increased innovation, including in AIT, robotics, and digital sensors. Expanded government support for research and development (R&D), especially basic research, is appropriate. In particular, the fact that real federal R&D spending declined in each of the seven years between 2009 and 2016, resulting in a total decline of 17.2 percent (Congressional Research Service, 2019), is extremely troubling, as are recent proposals to further cut such spending. In addition, the provision in the recently enacted Tax Cuts and Jobs Act (TCJA) that will require five-year amortization of R&D expenses – rather than the long-standing treatment of immediate expensing – seems singularly misguided (the maintenance of the incremental R&D credit is appropriate, given the positive externalities associated with such investment).

The second is to anticipate losses of jobs due to further technological advances and significantly augment existing policies for retraining, ongoing education, increasing mobility, and income support during the transition between jobs – consistent with the often-expressed theoretical arguments that changes that improve aggregate welfare but cause individual losses should be accompanied by compensation for those losses. The United States currently provides such assistance for trade-related job losses under the Trade Adjustment Assistance (TAA) program. However, as stressed by the recent winners of the Nobel Prize in Economics, Esther Duflo and Abhijit Banerjee (2019), the TAA program – while successful in increasing the relative incomes of those who participate – is "minuscule" in comparison to the losses suffered, with the regions most negatively affected by trade experiencing a reduction in income of $549 per capita that has been accompanied by TAA assistance of $0.23 per capita. An expanded and better-designed program (see Goger (2019) for a recent critique), which, as suggested by the Organisation for Economic Co-operation and Development (OECD) (2016), would apply more generally to job displacement including that associated with technological advances, could at least partially address concerns about potential job losses due to advances in AIT and robotics. Indeed, Osterman (2019) stresses the importance of retraining workers in a rapidly evolving modern economy, and recommends policies that would provide information about changing skill requirements, and allocating funds to lifelong learning and training programs and to workforce development. Similarly, a recent IMF study (Peralta-Alva and Roitman, 2018) stresses that the labor market effects of technological advances will require sizable investments in human capital, including the retooling of low-skilled workers, policies to facilitate adjustment to employment disruptions, and policies that provide income support. Litan (2016) suggests that one such approach is the provision of wage insurance, under which displaced workers would be compensated for some of their wage loss in accepting a new job; such wage insurance payments could be limited to a finite time period on the order of two years and capped at, say, $10,000–$20,000 per individual.

11.3 Labor and Economic Growth

Increasing labor productivity is clearly of critical importance to maintaining economic growth. As shown in Chapters 3 and 4 by Cunha and Borjas, respectively, critical determinants of labor productivity are the accumulation of human capital, especially at early ages, and the level and nature of immigration.

Cunha presents a compelling argument that the key to improving the skills of the labor force, especially at the lower end of the income distribution, is "to promote college readiness among children who grow up in low-income households and to improve the matches between college-ready, low-income students and colleges" (Chapter 3, p. 52), and that college readiness requires investments in children at a very early age, coupled with parental education. Cunha details a wide variety of programs designed to achieve these goals. A critical implication of his analysis is that resources in the United States should be focused on both education designed to enhance cognitive skills and the development of socioemotional skills at early (preschool) ages for low-income children – rather than the enactment of expensive non-means-tested proposals for tuition-free college at two-year colleges and all public universities. In addition, significant increases in the numbers of low-income, high-ability students who apply to and are accepted at selective institutions are essential, so that such students can benefit not only from a better education but also from being surrounded by higher-quality peers.[1] Cunha notes that Hoxby and Turner (2013) have

---

[1] In a similar vein, Bell, Chetty, Jaravel, Petkova, and van Reenen (2018) stress that exposure to innovation during childhood has a significant positive effect on the likelihood that an

demonstrated that this can be achieved by providing college-ready low-income students with better guidance regarding opportunities at more selective institutions, especially information about the application process and available financial aid. Indeed, recent expansions of financial aid programs designed to facilitate attendance at elite institutions by low-income students are a positive development in this regard – while mis-guided policy measures such as the university endowment tax included in the recently enacted TCJA only limit the ability of the affected institutions to engage in such worthwhile programs.[2] Finally, more attention should be paid to alternative forms of developing skills that are in high demand, including apprenticeships, bootcamps, workforce training, as well as other programs outside of a traditional classroom setting that will help adults to retool or upgrade their skills in order to transition to new jobs when their jobs are rendered obsolete due to technological advances (discussed in Section 11.2).

As described by Borjas in Chapter 4, another way to expand the labor force is through immigration. Borjas notes that immigration is clearly associated with higher production, citing one estimate which indicates that economic growth in the United States would have been 15 percentage points lower between 1990 and 2014 without immigration, with foreign-born workers accounting for 16.6 percent of the labor force by 2016. He goes on to focus on the effects of immigration on per-capita GDP and the "immigration surplus," the gain to the preexisting population from immigration. The absolute level of growth is often the key variable for many current policy discussions, and economic growth attributable to immigration is seldom discounted. Nevertheless, the effects of comprehensive immigration reform on per-capita GDP and the incomes of native workers as well as the fiscal impact of immigrants are important considerations that should be considered in crafting policy alternatives. In addition, as noted by Borjas, goals other than increasing economic growth may also be important considerations in designing immigration policy.

---

individual will become an inventor, and that the lack of such exposure has led to many "lost Einsteins."

[2] In some admittedly unabashed promotion of our own institution, we note that Rice University has recently instituted the Rice Investment program, under which admitted students from families with: (1) incomes below $65,000 receive a grant that covers full tuition, fees, and room and board; (2) incomes between $65,000 and $130,000 receive a grant that covers full tuition; and (3) incomes between $130,000 and $200,000 receive a grant that covers half tuition.

We generally agree with the primary conclusion that Borjas reaches – namely that if the goal of US immigration policy is to increase economic growth, then the policy should be to admit high-skill immigrants, especially if such immigrants have positive external effects on the productivity of native workers. Although this basic conclusion seems indisputable, we offer two caveats or extensions.

First, the skill level of immigrants is immutable in the Borjas model. However, Abramitzky, Boustan, Jácome, and Pérez (2019) show that children of immigrants have higher rates of upward income mobility than children of native-born Americans. This is attributable primarily to geographic mobility in the form of a willingness to locate in more economically dynamic areas and also to the fact that the actual skill levels of their parents are not accurately reflected by their incomes – both factors which suggest that a policy focusing on admitting high-skill immigrants may exclude some individuals who would ultimately be highly productive members of society. Interestingly, Abramitzky and Boustan (2016) observe that "migrant selection" in recent years has been more positive than in the past – that is, migrants are on average more skilled than those who elect not to migrate from their country of origin.

Second, with respect to the externalities generated by immigrants, some anecdotal immigrant success stories suggest that they may be quite large in some cases. For example, the Center for American Entrepreneurship (CAE) (2017) calculates that 43 percent of Fortune 500 companies in 2017 were founded or cofounded by an immigrant or the child of an immigrant, with an immigrant share of 57 percent for the top thirty-five companies in that group. In the aggregate, these 500 companies accounted for $5.3 trillion in global revenues, employed 12.8 million workers worldwide, and were located in thirty-three different US states. In addition, immigrants founded almost a quarter of new businesses, one-third of venture-capital-backed companies, and half of Silicon Valley tech startups. CAE makes a compelling argument that cutbacks in immigration at a time of great concern about future economic growth prospects are highly counterproductive; in addition, they argue that many of these founders of Fortune 500 companies would not be in the United States had immigration been limited to those who were clearly high-skill at the time of immigration. In a broadly similar vein, Kerr and Kerr (2016) estimate that, in 2008, roughly 27 percent of entrepreneurs in their sample of eleven US states were immigrants, and that businesses started by immigrants perform better than businesses started by natives in terms of employment growth over three- and six-year periods, although they are similar or slightly worse in terms of payroll growth.

11.4 Fiscal Policy and Economic Growth

Three chapters in this volume address issues related to tax and expenditure policy and growth. In Chapter 2, Feldstein makes a persuasive case for raising revenues by reducing tax expenditures and enacting a carbon tax as well as reducing entitlement spending to control deficits and reduce the negative effects of a large national debt. In Chapter 7, Barro concludes that the reductions in the cost of capital due to the enactment of the TCJA in 2017, if treated as permanent, would have a modest positive long run effect on per-capita GDP, and that the TCJA roughly equalized the tax treatment of C-corporations and pass-through business entities, which also improved the efficiency of resource allocation. Finally, in our Chapter 8, we argue that implementing a carbon tax, even neglecting its considerable benefits in terms of reducing carbon emissions and other pollutants, would either have small negative effects on economic growth or actually increase growth, and would not necessarily have a regressive impact on the distribution of income, depending on how the revenues from the tax are used.

As stressed by Feldstein (Chapter 2) (and Gordon, 2016), an important issue confronting the United States is the unsustainable nature of current fiscal policy, although the present environment of extremely low interest rates and inflation has reduced the urgency of addressing this issue in comparison to previous years. Nevertheless, in the absence of meaningful reform, current policies will lead to growing budget deficits, long-run increases in the debt–GDP ratio, and eventually to higher interest rates, reductions in economic growth, and a less competitive US economy. The Congressional Budget Office's (CBO) (2019) long-term budget outlook shows that, in 2019, spending is 20.7 percent of GDP and revenue is 16.5 percent of GDP, which implies a deficit of 4.2 percent of GDP. By 2049, CBO projects, based on current policies, that spending will increase to 28.2 percent of GDP while revenue will increase to 19.5 percent of GDP, which implies a deficit equal to 8.7 percent of GDP and a debt–GDP ratio of 144 percent in 2049. The rapid growth in the deficit and debt over the next three decades is caused primarily by projected increases in spending on Social Security, Medicare and other healthcare programs, and increased interest payments on the government debt. The projected increase in Social Security and healthcare expenditures is related to demographic changes as the baby boom generation ages, as life expectancy increases, and as health-care costs per beneficiary grow faster than GDP.

Closing this fiscal gap (the difference between spending and revenues) will require either a reduction in spending or an increase in revenues. While GDP growth alone cannot close the fiscal gap, increasing GDP growth will reduce the amount by which spending must be cut or revenues increased to close the gap, and thus should be a primary concern in addressing the unsustainability of current fiscal policy.

In the United States, several groups have published ambitious plans for fiscal reforms that are designed to address the debt issue through various combinations of expenditure reductions and revenue-increasing tax reforms. These plans typically require sizable reductions in expenditures, which could be accomplished only by major entitlement reform.

These plans also propose an increase in revenues. Note that individual income tax revenue as a share of GDP is projected to increase significantly even before any policy changes are adopted to address the unsustainable nature of the US budget. CBO projects that individual income taxes will increase from 8.2 percent of GDP in 2019 to 10.4 percent of GDP in 2049. The growth in revenues is a result of the expiration of the individual tax cuts enacted under TCJA and individuals being pushed into higher tax brackets over time as nominal income grows faster than the tax bracket income cutoffs. Unfortunately, these built-in tax increases are negligible relative to the projected increases in spending. Whether revenue as a share of GDP remains at the projected level or is increased as part of a "grand bargain" addressing the nation's fiscal issues, it is imperative that the United States reform its tax system to reduce economic distortions and maximize economic growth. Otherwise, the combination of rising taxes as a share of GDP and a relatively distortionary tax system could significantly hamper economic growth, especially since the efficiency costs of economic distortions generally increase more than proportionately with the rate of tax.

A natural question is the direction of future tax reforms, especially for the taxation of business income, under the presumption that a more efficient tax system is relatively more conducive to growth. We suggest several business tax reforms as follows.

We agree with Feldstein that the elimination of many tax expenditures would be desirable; moreover, the increase in the standard deduction under the TCJA and the accompanying reduction in the number of lower-income and especially middle-income taxpayers who itemize deductions imply that such reforms would be highly progressive and thus represent a way to both increase economic efficiency and reduce after-tax income inequality. Similarly, we agree with Feldstein on the desirability of a carbon tax with revenue recycling, although we are more inclined to use at least some of the revenues to reduce distortionary taxes rather than to finance equal per-capita rebates or "carbon dividends" as recommended in the plan supported by Feldstein, James Baker, George Schultz and others (Climate Leadership Council, 2018).

Beyond that, we would complete the movement to a (largely R-based) cash-flow tax at the business level that was partially enacted under TCJA. That would require making expensing permanent and extending it to all investment including structures – while simultaneously eliminating all deductions for interest expense, which would eliminate the current tax bias favoring debt finance, eliminate one of the vehicles commonly used for income shifting, and eliminate the negative marginal effective tax rates that arise for debt-financed investment in equipment under current law. To reduce the extent to which expensing for investment in structures results in negative cash flows, we would require "present value expensing" under which deductions for such investment would be spread out over ten to twenty years but would be increased annually by the risk-free rate of interest. Moreover, these changes should be accompanied by complete elimination of all remaining special provisions deferring capital gains taxes for like-kind exchanges.

The question of the appropriate corporate income tax rate is a difficult one. TCJA dropped the top corporate income tax rate from 35 percent to 21 percent.[3] Since the marginal effective tax rate under the cash-flow tax would be zero, the statutory rate applies primarily to economic rents, which have been increasing in importance in recent years. Taxing such rents at a somewhat higher statutory rate could be nondistortionary – but only if they are not internationally mobile and not subject to income shifting.[4] Our view is that, with full expensing, the corporate rate could be raised somewhat – to around 25 percent – but that concerns about both the mobility of the firm-specific capital that generates economic rents and income shifting should

---

[3] We note in passing that, given the large rate reduction under TCJA as well as the highly accelerated deductions for depreciation that were allowed under prior law, the inclusion of a "windfall recapture tax" that would have taxed some of the income accruing to investments made prior to the implementation of reform under pre-reform rates would have been desirable; see Zodrow (1988) for a discussion of such a tax in the context of the rate reductions that were enacted under the Tax Reform Act of 1986.

[4] See McKeehan and Zodrow (2017) for a recent analysis of the "balancing act" involved in setting the statutory corporate tax rate in the face of various competing economic forces.

preclude further increases. Such an increase in the corporate rate would allow elimination of the complex and often arbitrary special deduction for pass-through business entities, while still maintaining roughly uniform treatment of investment across C-corporations subject to the corporate income tax and pass-through entities that are taxed only at the individual level.

With respect to international taxation, we are sympathetic to the general approach used in the TCJA of moving to a nominally territorial system, coupled with provisions like the Global Intangible Low-Taxed Income (GILTI) tax and the Base Erosion and Anti-Abuse (BEAT) minimum tax to limit income shifting. We note that although the move to a territorial system was promoted on "international competitiveness" grounds, the current system may not be that much of an improvement over the previous one, which was characterized by deferral of tax until repatriation, cross-crediting of foreign tax credits, and significant income shifting, and as a result raised relatively little revenue on foreign-source income.

A problematic aspect of the GILTI tax is that it allows tax credits from high-tax countries to fully offset the tax otherwise due on income from low-tax countries, thus severely limiting its effectiveness in reducing income shifting. Although grouping countries for purposes of calculating international tax liability is in general desirable in a globalized economy with complex supply chains across many countries, this argument does not extend to income earned in tax havens. One potential solution would be to create a separate basket for tax haven income that would be subject to GILTI tax without any credits for taxes paid in countries that are not designated as tax havens.

In addition, the calculation of a minimum tax under the BEAT provisions without allowing tax credits, including foreign tax credits, strikes us as far too harsh. Finally, we would eliminate the complex and arguably non-WTO-compliant export subsidy for foreign-derived intangible income (FDII), partially because it creates an incentive for US firms to invest in physical assets abroad in order to increase their base for purposes of calculating FDII (Clausing, 2019a, 2019b).

In summary, continued robust economic growth in the United States will, among many other things, require policies that encourage rapid technological innovation and increases in productivity, encourage increases in the stock of human capital, promote investment while reducing debt, encourage trade and competition, and maximize economic efficiency, including minimizing the distortions caused by the tax system. The chapters in this volume provide an insightful and provocative roadmap for achieving these critical milestones.

References

Abramitzky, Ran, and Leah Platt Boustan, 2016. "Immigration in American Economic History." NBER Working Paper No. 21882. National Bureau of Economic Research, Cambridge, MA.

Abramitzky, Ran, Leah Platt Boustan, Elisa Jácome, and Santiago Pérez, 2019. "Intergenerational Mobility of Immigrants in the U.S. over Two Centuries." NBER Working Paper No. 26408. National Bureau of Economic Research, Cambridge, MA.

Acemoglu, Daron, and Pascual Restrepo, forthcoming. "Robots and Jobs: Evidence from U.S. Labor Markets." *Journal of Political Economy*.

Bell, Alex, Raj Chetty, Xavier Jaravel, Neviana Petkova, and John van Reenen, 2018. "Who Becomes an Inventor in America? The Importance of Exposure to Innovation." *Quarterly Journal of Economics* 134 (2), 647–713.

Berg, Andrew, Edward F. Buffie, and Luis-Felipe Zanna, 2018. "Should We Fear the Robot Revolution? (The Correct Answer Is Yes)." IMF Working Paper WP/18/116. International Monetary Fund, Washington, DC.

Center for American Entrepreneurship, 2017. Immigrant Founders of the 2017 Fortune 500. Center for American Entrepreneurship, Washington, DC.

Clausing, Kimberly, 2109a. "Fixing the Five Flaws of the Tax Cuts and Jobs Act." Reed College, Portland, OR.

Clausing, Kimberly, 2019b. *Open: The Progressive Case for Free Trade, Immigration, and Global Capital.* Harvard University Press, Cambridge, MA.

Climate Leadership Council, 2018. "Exceeding Paris: How the Baker-Shultz Carbon Dividends Plan Would Significantly Exceed the U.S. Paris Commitment." Climate Leadership Council, Washington, DC, www.clcouncil.org/media/Exceeding-Paris.pdf.

Cohen, Tyler, 2011. *The Great Stagnation: How America Ate All the Low-Hanging Fruit of Modern History, Got Sick, and Will (Eventually) Feel Better.* Penguin Group, New York, NY.

Congressional Budget Office, 2019. *The 2019 Long-Term Budget Outlook.* Congressional Budget Office, Washington, DC.

Congressional Research Service, 2019. "U.S. Research and Development Funding and Performance: Fact Sheet." Congressional Research Service, Washington, DC.

Duflo, Esther, and Abhijit Banerjee, 2019. "Economic Incentives Don't Always Do What We Want Them To." *New York Times*, October 26, www.nytimes.com/2019/10/26/opinion/sunday/duflo-banerjee-economic-incentives.html.

Frey, Carl Benedikt, and Michael A. Osborne, 2017. "The Future of Employment: How Susceptible Are Jobs to Computerization?" *Technological Forecasting and Social Change* 114 (January), 254–80.

Goger, Annelies, 2019. "Displaced Workers Need More Than What Economists Are Suggesting." Brookings Institution, Washington, DC.

Gordon, Robert J., 2016. *The Rise and Fall of American Growth: The U.S. Standard of Living Since the Civil War.* Princeton University Press, Princeton, NJ and Oxford, UK.

Hicks, Michael J., and Srikant Devaraj, 2015. "The Myth and the Reality of Manufacturing in America." Center for Business and Economic Research, Ball State University, Muncie, IN.

Hoxby, Caroline, and Sarah Turner, 2013. "Expanding College Opportunities for High-Achieving, Low-Income Students." Working Paper. Stanford University, Stanford, CA.

Kerr, Sari Pekkala, and William R. Kerr, 2016. "Immigrant Entrepreneurship." NBER Working Paper No. 22385. National Bureau of Economic Research, Cambridge, MA.

Litan, Robert, 2016. "Wage Insurance: A Potentially Bipartisan Way to Help the Middle Class." Brookings Institution, Washington, DC.

McAfee, Andrew, and Eric Brynjolfsson, 2017. *Machine, Platform, Crowd: Harnessing Our Digital Future*. W.W. Norton, New York, NY.

McKeehan, Margaret, and George R. Zodrow, 2017. "Balancing Act: Weighing the Factors Affecting the Taxation of Capital Income in a Small Open Economy." *International Tax and Public Finance* 24 (1), 1–35.

McKinsey Global Institute, 2017. "Jobs Lost, Jobs Gained: Workforce Transitions in a Time of Automation." McKinsey & Company, New York, NY.

Organisation for Economic Co-operation and Development (OECD), 2016. *Back to Work: United States: Improving the Re-employment Prospects of Displaced Workers.* OECD Publishing, Paris.

Osborne, Michael, and Carl Frey, 2018. "Automation and the Future of Work: Understanding the Numbers." Oxford Martin School, University of Oxford, Oxford, UK, www.oxfordmartin.ox.ac.uk/blog/automation-and-the-future-of-work-understanding-the-numbers/.

Osterman, Paul, 2019. "Employment and Training for Mature Adults: The Current System and Moving Forward." MIT Sloan School of Management, Cambridge, MA.

Peralta-Alva, Adrian, and Agustin Roitman, 2018. "Technology and the Future of Work." IMF Working Paper WP/18/207. International Monetary Fund, Washington, DC.

Summers, Lawrence, 2016. "A Disaster Is Looming for American Men." *Washington Post*, September 29.

Zodrow, George R., 1988. "The Windfall Recapture Tax: Issues of Theory and Design." *Public Finance Quarterly* 16 (4), 387–424.

Index